CALIFORNIA
CRIMINAL LAW CONCEPTS

2008 Edition

Derald D. Hunt, B.V.E., M.S.
Associate Dean, Director Emeritus
Criminal Justice Education
Coast Community College District
Orange County, California

Devallis Rutledge, J.D.
Attorney at Law

PEARSON
Custom Publishing

Cover photograph courtesy of Philip James Corwin/Corbis Images. The back cover image courtesy of Corbis Images.

Printed in the United States of America

10 9 8 7 6 5 4 3 2 1

ISBN 0-536-54013-6

2007340097

MC/SB

Please visit our web site at *www.pearsoncustom.com*

PEARSON Custom Publishing

PEARSON CUSTOM PUBLISHING
501 Boylston Street, Suite 900, Boston, MA 02116
A Pearson Education Company

PREFACE

TO THE STUDENT

How to Make the Best Use of *California Criminal Law Concepts*. If you will use the **"Seven Step Plan"** which follows, you will learn more in less time and with less effort. Also, your retention of this new knowledge will be greatly increased!

***Step 1:* Read the "Terminology Defined" list.** You will find this list at the end of each chapter, along with a matching-type Terminology Quiz. These terms will help you to better understand the meaning of what you are reading. You are encouraged to take the Terminology Quiz after reading the chapter and/or reviewing the list.

***Step 2:* Read the True-False and Essay-Discussion Items.** These are found at the end of each chapter. If you do this *before* you read the chapter, it will help you to recognize the answers to these items when you later study the text.

***Step 3:* Make a preliminary survey.** Get an idea of what the material in each chapter is about—what the key concepts are—before you read. Do this by noting text section headings and subheadings.

***Step 4:* Read for understanding.** Formulate mental questions as you read. Look for answers to the end-of-chapter True-False and Essay-Discussion items as you read.

***Step 5:* Test yourself.** Be sure you can answer the True-False and Essay-Discussion questions before you leave each chapter.

***Step 6:* Take notes.** Highlight or underline key points in your text. Use your notebook and the margins of your text to note what you have read. Write brief answers to the end-of-chapter test items.

***Step 7:* Review.** Analyze the major points of the chapter and review any sections you do not understand. Make notes on questions you can ask at the next class meeting.

ADDITIONAL TEXT RESOURCES

World Wide Web Sites. The authors have provided you with access to hundreds of useful criminal justice WWW sites. For example: **www.leginfo.ca.gov/ calaw.html** will take you to an Internet site where you can read/print any section of the Penal Code, Vehicle Code or any other of California's 29 codes.

Go to the FBI's home page at **www.fbi.gov/** to see the "FBI's Most Wanted" (fugitives and terrorists), Uniform Crime Reports, plus scores of other items of vital interest. At: **www.albany.edu/sourcebook** you will find over 100 sources of criminal justice statistics. One of the best sites on the web is Dr. Frank Schmalleger's: **www.talkjustice.com/**. Click on "The Cybrary" to access a 12,000 link library of other criminal justice sites. Go to **www.findlaw.com/** for state and federal case law, the Constitution and "Bill of Rights" plus many other legal topics and web sites.

Use the accompanying *Link Library* booklet to access hundreds of web links for specific criminal justice terms discussed in this Revised Edition of *California Criminal Law Concepts*. Pearson Custom Publishing's *Link Library* puts a world of academic research at your fingertips, and allows you to expand your knowledge in the particular area of interest you choose.

TO THE INSTRUCTOR

This revised edition of ***California Criminal Law Concepts*** includes the following features designed to enhance both the teaching and learning experience with this text:

New Law and Court Decisions. This **Revised Edition** of ***California Criminal Law Concepts*** includes over 500 Penal Code and other criminal laws. Also included are the most recent criminal law updates and the most recent appellate court decisions applicable to 2008 California criminal law.

Meets Current Standardized Core Curriculum. This edition of your text meets the objectives and scope of the revised *Concepts of Criminal Law* course as developed jointly by the California Association of Administration of Justice Educators (CAAJE) and the Community College Chancellor's Office.

Crime Elements Chart. Appendix A provides a comprehensive chart covering the elements of the most frequently referred to sections of the Penal Code, listed in alphabetical order by name of offense.

Penal Code Index. For easy reference, **Appendix B** provides an extensive list of code sections in alphabetical order by name of offense. Also, **Appendix C** lists important and frequently used Penal Code sections in numerical order by section number.

Basic Legal Research. Appendix D offers your students easy-to-understand instructions on how to find case law and how to write a basic legal brief. A sample brief, showing proper format, is also included to assist your students.

Compendium of Landmark Cases (With Key Holdings). Appendix F provides a list of landmark court decisions.

Terms and Definitions. A list of legal and technical terms and their definitions applicable to the text is found at the end of each chapter. This list and the accompanying quiz, helps students to "learn the language" of the discipline.

Matching-Type Terminology Quiz. This quiz, based on the end-of-chapter Terminology List, is also found at the end of each chapter. Students are encouraged to answer this quiz in each chapter of their text during home-study or in class.

True-False Quiz for Each Chapter. This test covers key points relative to each chapter. It is easily scored on a "Scantron" or other electronically scored answer sheet. These items provide you with excellent weekly (or periodic) feedback for diagnostic and review purposes.

Essay-Discussion Items. These items serve a dual purpose. They provide material for stimulating class discussion. They are also useful as the basis for a more comprehensive essay test such as a midterm or final examination. Education Code, Title V, now requires students to do writing and critical thinking as part of their course work. The essay-discussion items will help your students to accomplish this objective.

A Personal Note to Instructors: The author welcomes instructor contact at any time. Please send your e-mail to: **devallis@devallis.com**

ADDITIONAL INSTRUCTOR AND STUDENT SUPPLEMENTS

An updated **Instructor's Guide** has been prepared with the 2008 Edition of the text. The new Instructor's Guide continues to offer multiple-choice test questions and answers to end of chapter materials. An electronic version of the complete guide (in Word) will also be packaged with each printed manual, for easy preparation and modification of test questions within the manual. In addition, a complete set of Powerpoint slides is included on the disk. This guide may be obtained by Instructors only, by contacting **Pearson Custom Publishing** at *pcp@pearsoncustom.com* or, 1.800.428.4466. The ISBN for the Instructor's Guide is: 0-536-54016-0.

Author Richard S. Michelson, has also updated the **Student Powernotes to accompany California Criminal Law Concepts.** The new workbook guide includes outlines of the same Powerpoints available in the Instructor's Guide, to use as a helpful note taking device. The ISBN for this item is: 0-536-54015-2.

TEXTBOOK PACKAGES

A discounted package including the textbook, student workbook, and Free Link Library will be offered to those instructors wishing to order both supplemental items for students. The Package ISBN for ordering purposes is: 0-536-53458-6.

Each textbook automatically comes packaged with our Free Link Library. That ISBN for ordering purposes is: 0-536-076782-2.

CONTENTS

CHAPTER 1

SCOPE AND SOURCE OF CRIMINAL LAW

1.1 INTRODUCTION

The basic purpose of criminal law is to establish limits on certain human behavior or activity considered harmful to society. It is *not* about oppressing people or preventing them from enjoying life. Laws are the "tools" we use to build and maintain an orderly society.

If each of us lived in a state of isolation from all other human beings, there would be little, if any, need for criminal law—or any law at all—for that matter. Obviously, we do not exist as hermits. In fact, we live in a very complex society requiring daily interaction with many other people.

In such a society, each person must know what he or she can and cannot legally do regarding our frequent contacts and dealings with others. In order to avoid societal chaos, we must have rules to govern our activities. This is why, for example, we have rules regarding the operation of vehicles on our crowded streets and highways.

Even in a complex society such as ours, if everyone did the "right" thing in relation to all other members of society, we would need few criminal laws. Unfortunately, there will always be individuals who attempt to oppress the helpless, who steal the possessions of others, or in one way or another violate the life, liberty, or property of others by force, fear or fraud.

Limitations and Controls. The law tends to provide limitations and controls. It is obvious that professionals already in the system must understand the law. Students preparing for modern-day law enforcement, corrections, or security employment, must also be well grounded in the fundamentals of criminal law. This foundation provides the framework within which each must function.

Historically, our first criminal laws came into being as a result of society's struggle to control those persons whose antisocial activity was destructive of a desirable environment in which people wanted to live. Safety, stability, and integrity are necessary for the healthy growth and benefit of the community as a whole.

We may think of crime as a violation of the *basic controls* of society, and we may think of criminal law as necessary to deter misconduct and otherwise deal with those individuals who would disrupt society. Criminal law is an instrument of social control. Without laws, criminal or civil, we would have no protection from the predatory whims of others.

In order to gain the protection of society's laws, the law-abiding members must be willing to give up a small part of their freedom to do just as they wish at all times. This is especially true when one individual's activities interfere with the rights of others. With the above in mind, we may define crime as *social conduct considered harmful to individuals and to our institutions* and therefore made punishable by law.

For a veritable gold mine of answers to frequently asked questions (FAQ) about criminal law, criminal procedure, search and seizure, laws of arrest and more, go to: **http://www.nolo.com.** In the upper right corner of your computer screen, select "Search Entire Site." Then type in "criminal law" and hit enter.

1.2 ORIGIN AND DEVELOPMENT OF CRIMINAL LAW

Most of our early criminal law was based on custom or other recognized patterns of human behavior which appeared to be beneficial to the group as a whole. Even today, laws pertaining to incestuous marriages (between closely related blood relatives) can be traced to early tribal taboos. Other crimes relating to theft, murder, child molesting, etc., have a similar basis.

Criminal law is almost as ancient in one form or another as is humankind on earth. No doubt even early cavemen eventually established some sort of basic rules as to who would eat first, who had to tend the fire, who was to stand guard, etc. No doubt, those who didn't conform to the "law" were punished in some way by the rest of the group. Their survival was based on being able to depend on one another to follow the rules. Obviously, these rules or "laws" were not written, but were undoubtedly well understood by each member of the group.

As family groups eventually joined one another to form tribes, new rules or laws were developed to avoid conflict and to assure the peaceful functioning of the group. Children were no doubt taught local customs and taboos by parents and other members of the tribe. As society developed and began to place its thoughts in writing, there emerged the concept of statutory (written) law. This was to have a profound effect on the entire civilized world.

Development of Written Law. The first "written" law was in the form of cuneiform symbols chiselled into rock tablets or impressed on wet clay tablets which were then baked hard.

Code of Hammurabi. One of the most famous examples of early written law is the *Code of Hammurabi.* This large stone tablet, now preserved in the Louvre Museum in Paris, was believed by scholars to have been written in 1780 B.C., by King Hammurabi of Babylonia during his reign (1795–1750 B.C.).

We can trace many of our legal concepts and procedures back to the Code of Hammurabi. These include: making perjury a crime, written contracts, juries, judges and the "swearing in" of witnesses.

See Web Site: **www.fordham.edu/halsall/ancient/hamcode.html** for more information about the Code of Hammurabi.

Other Influences and Developments. While the bulk of our modern law is based on English jurisprudence (body of law), we have also inherited traces of Roman law (Latin medical-legal terms) as well as French and Spanish legal concepts.

As civilization developed, we find concepts such as trial by jury emerging in early England during the 12th century. We also begin to see the emergence of representative government—that is, the election or appointment of representatives who were granted authority to pass laws. These "legislatures" adopted new laws as society and modes of conduct changed. And so it is today. Our California State Legislature and Congress pass new laws and rescind old ones as the need for change is perceived. We also find our courts placing new interpretations on old laws.

The Norman (French) Period. In 1066, William the Conqueror, a French military leader, conquered

One of the forerunners of modern law, the Code of Hammurabi was inscribed on stone tablets 4000 years ago. *Courtesy of CORBIS*

the British Isles and declared himself king. William found various individual courts in existence which were dominated by the sheriff.

Prior to 1066, no action had been taken by the various kings of Britain to reduce the laws to writing. Rather, they allowed the sheriff to enforce the various tribal or village rules as he saw fit to keep order. Criminal courts, as such, were as yet unknown. William, however, demonstrated a genius for organization. He gradually took measures to reduce the arbitrary power of the sheriff. For example, he commanded the sheriff to act, henceforth, *only* in the king's name. William thus established some degree of uniformity. Additionally, he placed all courts under royal control and issued a proclamation inviting the common people of the country to seek justice in his courts. This had never been permitted before.

In time, English courts became more centralized and uniform in their administration of the law. Within one hundred years following William's conquest, the known common law crimes were being more or less equally enforced throughout the country. The various acts which constituted crimes, were enforced by the courts based on reason and human experience of the past. Certain acts, therefore, constituted crimes by "common understanding" or by "public consent."

The Westminster Period. Gradually, during the Westminster period in England (1285-1500), procedures became more formal. As such, the known or general custom of the kingdom became more rigid. For example, to establish that a certain practice was "custom" and therefore "law," lawyers found it useful to give examples and illustrations from their own experience. They also cited facts from other trials that they could personally recall. These illustrations of what had been done before were not binding on the court, but were forerunners of what we know as *"stare decisis"* or "precedent" today. (See Section 1.5).

With the passing of time and creation of the English Parliament, new crimes were added to the "list." Thus, we see both the legislature (Parliament) and the courts adding to the body of common law.

The Common Law. As defined by Blackstone, "common law" consists of doctrines that are not set down in any written statute or ordinance, but rather, depend upon long-time usage for their authority.

Common law is obviously much more ancient than statute law. It can be described as the total of doctrines, decisions, precedents, reasonings and practices comprising the legal heritage of Anglo-American law and the source of our legal thinking.

The common law, in the sense in which it is used here, can be described as that body of law which gets its authority, not from express enactments of the legislature, like statute law, but from the fact that it has existed from time immemorial.

The Adoption of Common Law in America. With the exception of Louisiana, the United States can trace the foundations of its criminal law to early English common law. However, even Louisiana, which had a French and Spanish heritage, adopted the common law of England by passage of a statute in 1805.

As the first settlers from England arrived, they formed agreements among themselves called "compacts." In these compacts, they adopted much of the common law of England for their governance. Following the Declaration of Independence, many states either adopted the common law outright, or passed criminal statutes, which in fact, incorporated into written law most of the basic principles of the old common law.

Common Law Crimes. There are no common law (unwritten) crimes in this state. On the contrary, for an act or omission to constitute a crime in California, it must be in violation of (1) a written statute which (2) must provide a penalty for its violation. The laws which are passed by authorized bodies of local, state and federal governments make up our statutory law.

There are no common law offenses against the United States government (*United States v. Britton*, 108 U.S. 199). To constitute a crime, a written law must exist declaring any act or omission a criminal offense. The statute must also provide a punishment for its violation. In California, the law is wholly statutory and there are no common law crimes (*People v. Harris*, 191 Cal. App. 2d 754).

It is expressly provided by statute in California that no act or omission is criminal or punishable, except as prescribed or authorized by code or statute (PC 6).

1.3 SOURCES OF CRIMINAL LAW

Our criminal law in this country comes from the following three primary sources:

1. United States and State Constitutions.
2. Statutes (laws) passed by Congress, state legislatures and local governments.
3. Prevailing decisions (case law) of the appellate courts in criminal cases.

Federal and State Constitution as Sources of Criminal Law. The United States Constitution is the supreme law of the land (U.S. Constitution, Article VI).

We recognize the United States Constitution as well as the constitution of our own state as the fundamental written "law of the land." These two documents provide the framework for our criminal justice system in that they: (1) define and limit the powers of government and (2) provide for establishment and maintenance of our court system.

Bill of Rights. The first ten amendments to the United States Constitution were adopted in 1787, at the same time as was the Constitution. They are known as the *Bill of Rights*. Many of these amendments are very important to criminal law, such as free speech (First Amendment), trial by jury and right to an attorney (Sixth Amendment). The greatest impact, however, comes from the Fourth Amendment (searches, seizures, warrants) and the Fifth Amendment (self-incrimination).

The California Constitution. Our state Constitution begins with a Declaration of Rights, which reflects the same concerns as the Bill of Rights. For example, the right to freedom from unreasonable searches and seizures is found in Article 1, Section 13. The right against self-incrimination is contained in Article 1, Section 15.

During the late 1970s and early 1980s, the California Supreme Court based many of its decisions on this state's Constitution. Suspects were given more rights under the California Constitution than they are entitled to under federal law. These "independent state grounds," caused many cases to be lost, even though they could have been prosecuted under federal standards. The people of this state moved to stop this trend when they enacted Proposition 8, known as "The Victims' Bill of Rights," which amended the California Constitution in 1982. This topic is discussed in your text under Section 2.10.

United States Congress and State Legislature as Sources of Criminal Law. In addition to the United States and California Constitutions, much of our criminal law comes from statutes which appear in the various codes, such as the Penal Code, Vehicle Code, Welfare and Institutions Code, etc. Of California's approximately twenty-nine different codes, only five or six are used with any degree of frequency by police officers.

From our early beginnings in this country, our courts have consistently ruled that both congress and the state legislature have the inherent power to pass laws defining, prohibiting, and punishing criminal conduct. The only restriction is that they may not pass any laws that conflict with, and thus violate, constitutional restrictions and limitations.

The United States Congress and our own California State Legislature are the two most pro-

The Constitution of the United States, as amended, is the "supreme law of the land."
Photograph by Joseph Sohm, ChromoSohm, Inc./Courtesy of CORBIS

lific sources of our criminal law. They are both in a position to respond to changing needs of society. When a criminal law becomes outdated, it can be repealed and thus eliminated. When new technology or new societal needs are identified, new laws may be passed, or previously existing laws may be amended and updated.

Decisions of the Courts. Our appellate courts constitute another major source of our criminal law. Once a law is passed by the legislature, or directly by the people using the initiative petition (e.g., Proposition 8), it may need interpretation. The law may not be clear to everyone. Different words or terms may mean different things to different people. Obviously, if we are to have a "government of laws," some entity must have the authority to define the statute as to the legislature's meaning and intent.

This is the role of the court and can be recognized as an extension of the old English common law. The result of this procedure is known as case law or precedent and is based on the legal principle of *stare decisis*, which is discussed below in Section 1.5.

1.4 THE PURPOSE AND NATURE OF CRIMINAL LAW

Crimes are prohibited and punished on the grounds of public policy to prevent injury to the public. Injury to the public may include destruction or interference with government, human life, private property, or other valued institutions or interests. Such considerations as desire for vengeance or compensation for injury may also be involved.

Punishment is often said to be the purpose of the criminal law. This is true only up to a point. The real purpose of criminal law is to define socially intolerable conduct, and to hold conduct within limits which are reasonably acceptable from the social point of view (*Sire v. United States*, 241 Fed. Rptr. 2d 640).

Perhaps it may be said that whatever purpose is served by punishment, one purpose is that of compelling persons to cease or refrain from committing crime and forcing or persuading them to conform to established rules of conduct designed for the protection of government, life, and property.

Selections from the U.S. Constitution

Preamble
We the People of the United States, in Order to form a more perfect Union, establish Justice, insure domestic Tranquillity, provide for the common defense, promote the general Welfare, and secure the Blessings of Liberty to ourselves and our Posterity, do ordain and establish this Constitution for the United States of America.

First Amendment—Religion and Expression
Congress shall make no law respecting an establishment of religion, or prohibiting the free exercise thereof; or abridging the freedom of speech, or of the press; or the right of the people peaceably to assemble, and to petition the Government for a redress of grievances.

Fourth Amendment—Search and Seizure
The right of the people to be secure in their persons, houses, papers, and effects, against unreasonable searches and seizures, shall not be violated, and no Warrants shall issue, but upon probable cause, supported by Oath or affirmation, and particularly describing the place to be searched, and the persons or things to be seized.

Fifth Amendment—Rights of Persons
No person shall be held to answer for a capital, or otherwise infamous crime, unless on a presentment or indictment of a Grand Jury, except in cases arising in the land or naval forces, or in the Militia, when in actual service in time of War or public danger; nor shall any person be subject for the same offense to be twice put in jeopardy of life or limb; nor shall be compelled in any criminal case to be a witness against himself, nor be deprived of life, liberty, or property, without due process of law; nor shall private property be taken for public use, without just compensation.

Sixth Amendment—Rights of Accused in Criminal Prosecutions
In all criminal prosecutions, the accused shall enjoy the right to a speedy and public trial, by an impartial jury of the State and district wherein the crime shall have been committed, which district shall have been previously ascertained by law, and to be informed of the nature and cause of the accusation; to be confronted with the witnesses against him; to have compulsory process for obtaining witnesses in his favor, and to have the Assistance of Counsel for his defense.

Eighth Amendment—Further Guarantees in Criminal Cases
Excessive bail shall not be required, nor excessive fines imposed, nor cruel and unusual punishments inflicted.

Fourteenth Amendment—Rights Guaranteed Privileges and Immunities of Citizenship, Due Process and Equal Protection
Section. 1. All persons born or naturalized in the United States and subject to the jurisdiction thereof, are citizens of the United States and of the State wherein they reside. No State shall make or enforce any law which shall abridge the privileges or immunities of citizens of the United States; nor shall any State deprive any person of life, liberty, or property, without due process of law; nor deny to any person within its jurisdiction the equal protection of the laws.

Definition of Crime—PC 15. A crime is a public offense against the state (*People v. Weber*, 84 Cal. App. 2d 126). Penal Code Section 15, defines a crime or public offense as "... an act committed or omitted in violation of a law forbidding or commanding it, and to which is annexed, upon conviction, either of the following punishments:

1. Death
2. Imprisonment
3. Fine
4. Removal from office
5. Disqualification to hold and enjoy any office of honor, trust or profit in this state."

The terms "crime" and "public offense" mean the same thing and include felonies, misdemeanors and infractions (*People v. Hamilton*, 191 Cal. App. 3d Supp 13).

The word "crime," in its more extended sense, includes every violation of any public law. A general course of conduct, practice, habit, mode of life, or status which is prejudicial to public welfare may be prohibited by law, and punishment therefor may be provided by the state. Every course of conduct or practice or habit or mode of life or status falling within that class of wrongs is covered by the term "crime" (*People v. Babb*, 103 Cal. App. 2d 326).

All public offenses or crimes in California are statutory, and the court cannot have recourse to common law to determine prohibited acts (*Ex parte Harder*, 9 Cal. App. 2d 153). That a criminal action is being prosecuted by the People, and not in the interest of any person injured, is a fundamental principle of criminal law (*People v. Clark*, 117 Cal. App. 2d 134).

Go to Web Site: **www.lawyers.com** and scroll down and click on **Criminal Law** for brief articles about criminal law basics.

1.5 CONCEPTS OF *STARE DECISIS*

Stare decisis (pronounced: star-ray dee-sigh-sis) means "adhering to precedent." It also means that previously decided cases are to have a great impact and influence on the decisions in current cases. The purpose of this doctrine, which originated during the eighteenth century in England, is to provide consistency and orderliness. The laws by which people are governed should be relatively fixed, definite, and known. The term "precedent," is more commonly used today.

Precedent. It is important to understand that a court often makes its decision based on previous court decisions called "precedent." Courts, especially intermediate appellate courts, try to rule consistently with past decisions in order to maintain an orderly system so that people will know what conduct is permissible and what is not.

Departure From Precedent. For various reasons, courts do not always follow precedent. Sometimes one appellate court will simply disagree with another. Sometimes a given court will change its collective mind and disregard its own earlier opinion. The following two cases provide brief examples of where the court has reversed itself.

- Husband and wife may now be found guilty of conspiracy (*People v. Pierce*, 61 Cal. 2d 879). Previously husband and wife were considered one person in marriage and could not be guilty of conspiring (*People v. Miller*, 82 Cal. 107, decided in 1889).
- In the crime of unlawful sexual intercourse (PC 261.5), ignorance as to the victim's age was previously no defense. The court has since reversed its position. Now a good faith belief (based on reasonable cause) that the victim was 18 years of age or more is a valid defense to the crime (*People v. Hernandez*, 61 Cal. 2d 529).

Most commonly, "new law" is made, not so much by departing from precedent, but because new facts are involved. Every case has something about it that is different from any situation which has gone before. It is the application of the Constitution or statutes to these different factual situations which typically results in new law.

1.6 CLASSIFICATION OF LAWS

Substantive vs. Adjective Law. Criminal law may be classified into two broad categories. It is either *substantive* (laws defining crimes) or *adjective* (rules of procedure for administering the law).

Substantive criminal laws may define activity or behavior that is either *prohibited* (e.g., theft, assault) or *required* (e.g., supporting a child, registering a car). It is obviously a crime to do that which is prohibited by law. It is also a crime to *fail* to do that which the law *requires* one to do.

Substantive law can be further defined as: "that part of the law which the courts are established to enforce," as opposed to the rules (adjective or procedural law) by which substantive law is administered.

Adjective or Procedural Law. Peace officers need some understanding of adjective or procedural law because it includes such things as the rules of submitting evidence in court and arraignment of those charged with a crime. Adjective or procedural law is also concerned with carrying out court orders, redress (compensation) for injuries, and classification of crimes, and punishment. There are two other more familiar divisions of law—criminal and civil—which are of particular concern to law enforcement personnel.

Criminal vs. Civil Law. Criminal law, as the term implies, concerns itself with defining those specific acts and omissions (failure to act) which constitute a crime in our society. The most common crimes are described and defined in the California Penal Code. However, many other crimes are also found in about forty various other California Code books.

These other codes include the Vehicle Code (VC), Education Code (EC), Welfare and Institutions (W&I) Code, Health and Safety (H&S) Code, Fish and Game (F&G) Code, Harbors and Navigation (H&N) Code and the Business and Professions (B&P) Code, to name just a few.

The penalty for committing a crime, which is doing that which a criminal code section prohibits, or not doing that which a criminal code requires one to do, is usually a fine or a jail or prison term. Section 1.4 of your text lists all possible penalties for a crime.

The various California Codes, court interpretations, and the state and federal constitutional provisions affecting law enforcement, define the duties, responsibilities and authority of peace officers. It is also from these sources that peace officers and others in our justice system derive their legal authority and responsibility.

Civil law has to do mostly with describing or establishing rules for various legal (mostly business) relationships, contracts and other agreements. Civil laws describing the contents of a contract or the terms of a promissory note (loan), are typical examples. Some of our "codified" civil law is found in California Code books such as: Code of Civil Procedure, Business and Professions Code, and the Welfare and Institutions Code, to name a few. Most civil law, however, is found in published court cases. Violations of civil law (called a "tort") are enforced differently than are violations of criminal law.

There are several other differences between civil and criminal law. They apply primarily to civil law and have to do with: the rules of evidence, the exclusionary rule, the number of jury votes required for a verdict, and the degree and amount of proof required, to name a few. See Section 1.13 for an explanation of the key differences between criminal law (crimes) and civil law (torts).

1.7 STATUTE OF LIMITATION

Penal Code Chapter 2, "Time of Commencing Criminal Actions," covers the so-called statute of limitation. These statutes (PC 799-805.5), place a limit on the amount of time which may legally pass between the time the crime was either committed or discovered and prosecution is started (*People v. Chapman*, 47 Cal. App. 3d 597).

By way of introduction, it is necessary to consider the statute of limitation on certain offenses in order to know how long after the commission or discovery of a public offense a suspect can still be prosecuted. In some cases the time starts running from the time the crime is *discovered*. In other instances, the statute of limitation starts running when the crime is *committed*. There is a difference as to the statute of limitation between felonies and misdemeanors. There is also a difference in the statute of limitation between certain felonies and between certain misdemeanors.

Commencement of Prosecution. If prosecution is not started within the time provided by the statute of limitation, it is a defense to prosecution. Prosecution for a crime is commenced, thus stopping the statute of limitation, when any one of the following five events occurs:

1. A Grand Jury indictment is returned.
2. An "information" (criminal charge) is filed in superior court.
3. A complaint charging a public offense is filed in an inferior (municipal) court.
4. A case is certified for trial to the superior court from an inferior (municipal) court.
5. An arrest warrant, or bench warrant, is issued naming or adequately describing the defendant.

Misdemeanors: One-Year Limitation. Prosecution for a misdemeanor (any offense punishable other than by death or imprisonment in state prison) must be commenced within one year after its commission (PC 802(a)). One of the five events (see Commencement of Prosecution, above) must take place within one year, or the suspect cannot be legally prosecuted. *Note:* if the suspect has been out of the State during any part of this one year, such time does not count against the running of the statute of limitation (PC 803(d)).

Misdemeanors: Two-year Limitation. Prosecution for a misdemeanor violation of Business and Professions Code section 729 (sexual exploitation of a patient) may be commenced within two years after commission of the offense (PC 802(c)).

Misdemeanors: Three-Year Limitation. Prosecution for a misdemeanor violation of PC 647.6 (child molesting) committed with or upon a minor under the age of 14, must be commenced within three years of its commission (PC 802(b)).

Computation of Time if Defendant is Out of State. What effect does it have on the statute of limitation if the defendant is out of state at the time, or leaves shortly after, the offense is committed? No time, up to a maximum of three years, during which time the defendant is out of the state, is counted as part of the statute of limitation (PC 803(d)). It is possible, of course, for a defendant to commit a crime, such as fraud or forgery, etc., and not be in this state at the time the crime is completed. It is, also, not unusual for a suspect to flee the state immediately after committing a crime.

PC 803(d) provides, in effect, that the statute of limitation does not start for up to the first three years that a defendant is not within this state. After that three-year period, the statute starts to run. Of course, if the suspect remains in the state from the time the crime is committed, the statute starts to run immediately.

For those felonies which have a three year statute of limitation, if the suspect remains out of the state for more than six years, without a commencing of prosecution, he or she cannot be prosecuted. In the case of most misdemeanors, the statute would have run out after four years. This is calculated by adding the three years on the out-of-state provision of PC 803(d), and one year on the misdemeanor statute itself.

No Statute of Limitation. Prosecution for an offense punishable by death or by imprisonment in the state prison for life or for life without possibility of parole, or for the embezzlement of public money may be commenced at any time (PC 799).

Three Year Limit—Felonies in General. Prosecution for any felony, punishable by imprisonment in state prison, except those for which there is no statute of limitation, or for those listed below, shall be commenced within three years after *commission* of the offense (PC 801), except felony thefts and frauds by public officials, which carry a four-year limit (PC 801.5), and failure to register as a sex offender, which has a 10-year limit (PC 801.1).

Three Year Limit Following Discovery. Prosecution for each of the following crimes must be commenced within three years after it is *discovered* (PC 803).

1. Conflict of interest, Government Code 1090, 27443
2. Deceptive government agency ID, Business & Professions Code 22430
3. False affidavit, PC 118a
4. False documentary evidence, PC 132
5. False/forged birth certificates, PC 529a; Health & Safety Code 10690
6. Felony Medi-Cal fraud, Welfare & Institutions Code 14107
7. Felony welfare fraud, W&I Code 11483
8. Grand theft, PC 487
9. Insurance Fraud, Insurance Code 556
10. Perjury, PC 118
11. Preparing false evidence, PC 134
12. Presenting false claims, PC 72
13. Sale/falsification medical degree/certificate, B&P Code 580-584
14. Stock sale fraud, Corporations Code 25540, 25541
15. Theft or embezzlement from an elder or dependent adult.

Six Year Limit Following Commission. Prosecution for any offense punishable by imprisonment in the state prison for eight years or more (except for death or life imprisonment) shall be commenced within six years after *commission* of the offense (PC 800).

However, as to those felonies listed in PC 290(a)(2)(A)—including kidnap and many forcible sex crimes—the statute of limitations is 10 years from date of commission, or 1 year from the date the suspect's identity is "conclusively established" by DNA testing, whichever is later. The one-year period only applies if biological evidence collected from the crime is analyzed for DNA type within 2 years of the crime (PC 803(h)).

Ten Year Limit Following Commission. A prosecution for production of child pornography in violation of section 311.4(b) may be commenced within 10 years after date of offense.

Sex Offenses Against Children. Specified sexual offenses against children may be prosecuted within the applicable limitation period (three or six years) if reported before that period has expired, or within one year after the victim who was under 18 years of age reports the crime (PC 803(f)), or within one year after a person under 21 reports having been victimized before age 18 (PC 803(h)). "Substantial sexual conduct" (vaginal or rectal penetration or oral copulation) alleged to have been committed against a minor victim may be prosecuted within one year of being reported by a victim of any age. This extension applies only if the normal statute of limitations has expired, and there is independent corroborative evidence of the crime (PC 803(g)).

1.8 CASE CITATIONS AND APPEALS

When a superior court case is "taken up on appeal," the appeal is usually heard first by the California District Court of Appeal. The person making the appeal is known as the appellant and is, in essence, asking the appellate court to consider a question of fact or law with respect to the adjudication (hearing) of his or her case in the trial court.

The appellant will usually be the defendant in a criminal action, however, the prosecution may also appeal in certain cases (PC 1238). In such instances, the prosecution is known as the appellant, and the adverse party is the respondent.

Written Appellate Court Opinions. When either of the two appellate courts (State Supreme Court or District Court of Appeal) makes a decision, a written opinion is filed, explaining the reasoning of that court. Some of these opinions are later published if they contain some novel element. They appear in the California Appellate Reports, abbreviated "Cal. App." or "C.A." A typical example of a case citation reflecting a published opinion by the District Court of Appeal would be: *People v. Weaver*, 44 Cal. App. 4th 154. This citation refers to volume 44, California Appellate Reports, fourth series, page 154.

If the decision of an appellate court is further appealed, it is heard by the seven justices of the California Supreme Court. The written decisions reflected by this court are published in California Reports, abbreviated "Cal." or simply the letter "C." An example of a case citation of a published opinion of the California Supreme Court would be: *People v. Lucas*, 12 Cal. 4th 415. This designation refers to volume 12, California Reports, fourth series, page 415. (See Appendix D, for details on Basic Legal Research).

The two preliminary reports of cases decided by the appellate courts are subsequently published

The California Supreme Court issues opinions known as the "California Reports." The justices are, from left, Kathryn M. Werdegar, Joyce L. Kennard, Chief Justice Ronald M. George, Marvin R. Baxter, Ming Chin, and Carlos R. Moreno. *Photograph by Nick Ut, courtesy of AP/Wide World Photos*

in bound volumes. However, since it generally takes a year to publish the case reports in volume form, advance copies are published within a few weeks of being filed. The *Advance California Reports* are abbreviated "A.C." The *Advance California Appellate Reports*, are abbreviated "A.C.A." The advance reports are not completely reliable in that they are often changed in part or cases may be completely stricken from final publication in bound volumes.

Case decisions from both state and federal courts are usually available on-line within a day or two of their issuance. Commercial research outlets, such as Lexis and Westlaw, can be accessed on a fee basis. Sponsored (free) research can be conducted at various sites, such as findlaw.com and law.com.

1.9 ATTORNEY GENERAL OPINIONS

The California State Attorney General is the lawyer for the State. By law, he must give his written opinion, when requested, to the:

1. State Senate or Assembly
2. Governor
3. Secretary of State
4. Controller
5. Treasurer
6. State Lands Commission
7. Superintendent of Public Instruction
8. Any district attorney in the state.

Opinions of the Attorney General are expressions by him of his conclusions on legal questions which are presented to him by those persons whom he represents. Government Code section 12519 provides that the Attorney General shall render these opinions to the various state officials and agencies listed above. He does so on any questions of law relating to their respective offices when requested.

Section 13 of the California State Constitution designates the Attorney General the "chief law officer of the State." Government Code sections 12550 and 12560 give him ". . . direct supervision over the district attorneys of the various counties of the State and over the sheriffs of the several counties of the State."

There are generally two types of opinions rendered by the Attorney General:

1. Formal Opinion: A formal opinion is rendered when it is determined that the question presented is of general statewide interest. These opinions are printed in a series of publications called Opinions of the Attorney General of California.

2. Informal Opinion: An informal opinion is given on issues primarily of local interest. It is in the form of a letter sent to the official or organization presenting the problem. These opinions do not appear in published form. However, copies are maintained in the office of the Attorney General. Informal opinions are usually not available to the general public. Copies, however, may generally be obtained by interested persons by written request.

Authority of Attorney General's Opinions. The opinions of the Attorney General do not have the same authority as do opinions of the court. As the courts themselves have stated: ". . . although not of controlling authority, the Attorney General's opinions are, in view of his relation to the general government and the nature of his duties, regarded as having a "quasi-judicial" character and are entitled to great respect." (*Santa Clara County v. Sunnyvale City Council*, 168 Cal. App. 2d 89).

1.10 POLICE POWER OF THE STATE

The term "Police Power," does not appear in the United States Constitution. However, its significance is evident from the authority that the United States Constitution reserves to the states. The Police Power of the state, refers to a much broader area than just law enforcement. The legislatures of the different states, including California, have the inherent legal power to prohibit and punish any act, provided they do not violate the restrictions of the Federal and State Constitutions.

Areas of Police Power. Under this power, the state can legislate in the following five fields:

1. Public health
2. Public safety
3. Morals
4. General welfare
5. Economic prosperity

"No state can make any law or enforce any law which shall abridge the privileges or immunities of citizens of the United States, nor can any state deprive any person of life, liberty, or property without due process of law, or deny to any person within its jurisdiction the equal protection of the law." (*United States Constitution*, Amendment 14, paragraph 1.)

After the state legislature expressly prohibits an act and makes it a crime, there is no longer any test of public policy to be applied. The legislature has presumably enacted the law for the public good.

The courts cannot look further into its propriety other than to determine whether the legislature had the power to pass it. As previously stated, the constitutional limitations upon the power of Congress have no application to state legislatures so far as criminal law is concerned.

Even the Fourteenth Amendment, which ensures to all citizens the rights guaranteed to them in the First Amendment, does not nullify the police power of the states. Moreover, the federal government itself cannot exercise the exclusive authority given to it by the states without taking into consideration this important power.

Police power is defined in Article XI, Section VII, of the California Constitution. It states: "Any county, city, town or township may make and enforce within its limits all such local police, sanitary, and other regulations as are not in conflict with general laws." The following are some examples of the police power of the state:

- Requiring pupils to be vaccinated in schools.
- Required registration of sexual psychopaths.
- Prohibiting ex-convicts and drug addicts from possessing concealable firearms.

Police power is as broad as the legislative power of the state, with two exceptions:

1. The laws must be confined to local regulations and
2. The local laws are subject to general laws. Such laws shall not be unreasonable, arbitrary, or capricious, and they must provide equal protection to all citizens.

1.11 THE CONCEPT OF PREEMPTION

The concept of preemption is based on the premise that state law is superior to local ordinances and takes precedence over them when both are concerned with the same subject matter.

Preemption is controlled by Article XI, Section 7, of the California Constitution, which states "A county or city may make and enforce within its limits all local, police, sanitary, and other ordinances and regulations not in conflict with general laws."

The basic premise is that a municipality may not legislate in regard to matters occupied by the state law if any one of the following applies:

1. The subject matter is one of state concern and the general law occupies the entire field.
2. The local legislation is in conflict with a state law.
3. The subject matter is of such statewide concern that it can no longer be deemed to be merely a municipal affair.

Thus, a municipality may exercise its legislative power to enact local ordinances, provided such ordinances are not in conflict with the state law or the state has not fully occupied the field of law defined in the local ordinances. As stated in the case of *Morehart v. County of Santa Barbara,* 7 Cal. 4th 725: "Local legislation in conflict with general law is void. Conflict exists if the ordinance duplicates, contradicts, or enters an area fully occupied by general law, either expressly or by legislative implication."

In the past, local ordinances were held to be valid when they described criminal acts in greater detail than did state laws written on the same subject. More recent court decisions, however, indicate that the courts now feel that when the state legislature intends to occupy an entire field of subject matter, local ordinances concerning the same subject are invalid (*Los Angeles v. Alhambra*, 27 Cal. 3d 184). This is now the case when two laws are the same and the local ordinance is merely intended to supplement the state law.

An example of the foregoing philosophy would be where the state has enacted only one statute covering the area of public intoxication (PC 647f). The courts have held this field to be totally occupied by state law. The courts have ruled that local ordinances which go beyond the state law and which enumerate more specific circumstances of intoxication are invalid.

On the other hand, limited local ordinances have been upheld against preemption challenges on the subjects of gambling, loitering, licensing of establishments featuring nudity, public land use, weapons control, and advertising sign restrictions.

1.12 *EX POST FACTO* LAWS

The Constitution of the United States expressly prohibits Congress or any state from passing an *ex post facto* (after the fact) law (U.S. Constitution, Article 1, Sections 9 and 10). The California Constitution has a similar provision (Article 1, Section 16). An *ex post facto* law is one passed after the commission of an act and which changes the legal consequences of the act to the wrongdoer's prejudice. The *ex post facto* prohibition covers:

Every law which makes an act criminal, which was committed before its passage, and which was innocent when done.

- A law which makes a crime more serious than when it was committed.
- A law which inflicts a greater punishment for a crime than when it was committed.
- A law which changes the rules of evidence so that less or different testimony is sufficient to convict than was required when the act was committed.

The legislature cannot increase the punishment nor may an accused's defense be taken away. However, a statute is not within the prohibition if it makes the act a less serious crime than when committed and makes the punishment less severe. It is not *ex post facto* if it merely changes the method of procedure, unless it thereby deprives the accused of a substantial right which is vital for his or her protection.

Repeal of Statutes. The outright repeal or the repeal by amendment of a criminal statute after the commission of a crime (but before trial and conviction), does not bar a prosecution for such an offense unless the intent to bar further prosecutions is expressly declared in the repealing act (Government Code 9608).

1.13 DISTINCTION BETWEEN CRIMES AND TORTS

A crime can be described as a "public wrong," while a tort is a "private wrong." A civil wrong, such as failure to comply with the terms of a legal contract, or negligently causing another to suffer financial loss, is called a "tort."

A civil complaint against someone who commits a tort is filed in small claims court, municipal court, or superior court. In such cases, a judge, jury, court commissioner or court referee decides whether the plaintiff (the one who files suit) or the defendant was at fault.

The penalty for committing a tort is civil damages. If the case is decided in favor of the plaintiff, damages, and sometimes attorney's fees, may be awarded to the plaintiff which the defendant must pay.

The law considers a crime, even though committed against another individual, as an offense against the state (all the people). A tort or civil wrong is usually included in practically every criminal wrong. For example, in an assault the offender may be subject to punishment at the hand of the state for committing a crime. He or she may also be liable for financial damages in a civil suit (tort action) filed by the victim.

The two proceedings are distinct, however, and have different objectives. The criminal law seeks to punish, while the civil action is designed to obtain redress (payment or reimbursement) for injury. Neither proceeding is a bar to the other.

It should be noted that a *nolo contendere* (no contest) plea by a defendant in criminal court to misdemeanor charges cannot be used against a defendant as an admission of wrong doing in any civil suit based upon the same act upon which the criminal prosecution is based. A *nolo contendere* plea by a defendant has the same effect in criminal court as a guilty plea.

Intent. Another distinction between a crime and a tort is the element of *intent*. (See text Sections 3.5 and 3.6 regarding Act and Intent.) To render one criminally liable for an act, a person must have a criminal intent as provided by PC 20.

A different theory underlies the law of torts. For example, a very young child, not being able (by law) to entertain criminal intent, is legally incapable of committing a crime. The child may still be liable for damages, however, as a result of a wrongful act. In the case of *Ellis v. D'Angelo*, (116 Cal. App. 2d 310), the court held that a minor is liable for all his or her own torts in the same manner as if he or she were an adult. In this case, the parents and their nine year old child were held liable for damages caused when the child attacked a baby-sitter and inflicted serious injury.

Crime vs. Tort. As previously stated a wrongful act may give rise to two separate actions—one criminal, the other civil. The criminal action would be brought by the People of the State of California vs. the Defendant. The civil (tort) action would be brought by the victim (plaintiff) in civil court against the wrongdoer (defendant). If the plaintiff wins the suit, recovery in the civil action would likely be in the form of money damages which the court would require the defendant to pay the plaintiff. Recovery might also include punitive (penalty) damages, if allowable (Civil Code, 1714).

Thus, if a person steals an automobile, the wrongdoer may be prosecuted in a criminal court for a violation of Section 10851 of the Vehicle Code (auto theft). The victim may also sue the wrongdoer in civil court for damages in a tort action. Similarly, if a person illegally strikes another, the injured party may sign a complaint and have the wrongdoer prosecuted for battery in a criminal court. The victim may also sue in the civil court for money damages in tort action.

1.14 DEFINITION OF TERMS

Crimes *Mala in Se* and *Mala Prohibita.* For the purpose of this text, it is sufficient to say that crimes *mala in se* are those serious crimes which are wrong from their very nature. This would obviously include murder, robbery, rape, etc. These crimes are inherently so serious in their effects on individuals and on society that they invoke almost unanimous condemnation of those who commit these acts.

Crimes considered to be *mala prohibita* are wrong merely because they are prohibited by statute. These are characteristically those offenses which are enacted under the police power of the government and for control of the conduct of citizens. Examples are: most traffic laws, animal leash laws, alcoholic beverage control laws and food labeling laws.

Moral Turpitude. Most readers will have heard of crimes involving "moral turpitude." It is a term which the courts have had some difficulty in applying. One definition holds that moral turpitude "involves an act of baseness, vileness, or depravity in the social duties which a man owes to his fellow man or to society which is contrary to the accepted and customary rule of right and duty between man and man." Moral turpitude, then, relates to that which may be deemed "shamefully immoral" and suggests a lack of honesty, modesty, integrity, and good morals on the part of a criminal perpetrator.

Crimen Falsi. The term "*crimen falsi,*" is used to describe any class of crime that involves falsification. Examples of such crimes would be forgery, perjury or subornation of perjury, counterfeiting, alteration of instruments, and other frauds. The term originated from Roman civil law.

Infamous Crimes. Infamous crimes are generally those which are inconsistent with the common principles of honesty and humanity. At common law, infamous crimes were treason, any felony, and all fraudulent offenses including those of a *crimen falsi* nature. More recently, the term is associated with an act of vileness or moral depravity, such as in the infamous crime against nature (sodomy, buggery, or bestiality) as defined in PC 286 and PC 286.5.

1.15 VENUE AND JURISDICTION

Venue. Venue has to do with the physical or geographical location of the court in which a case is to be filed or tried. Venue should not be confused with jurisdiction which has to do with the court's legal authority (over the crime and over the person) to act in a specific case.

Routinely, cases are tried in the county and judicial district in which the crime was committed (PC 777). Such is only logical because the county in which the crime occurred is most likely where the victim, witnesses, and investigating officers are all located.

Sometimes a defendant may legally request and receive a "change of venue." Requests for a change of venue must be based on valid grounds such as:

- pretrial publicity precludes a fair trial,
- the defendant is such a well-known or prominent citizen (or notorious and intensely hated) that a fair trial cannot be had in the court where the case would normally be tried, or
- the feelings of the community are such that a fair and impartial jury cannot be selected from the area.

Changes of venue are not granted lightly. The burden of proof is on the party (usually the defendant) requesting the change. Proper venue for various types of crimes is defined under PC 777 through PC 786.

Jurisdiction. Jurisdiction has to do with the court's legal authority over the defendant (jurisdiction of the person) and the crime (jurisdiction of the subject matter) he or she is accused of committing. The Juvenile Court, for example, has initial jurisdiction over crimes committed by juveniles. Federal courts have jurisdiction over crimes in violation of the United States Code and other federal statutes.

Jurisdiction also has to do with where the crime was committed. For a court to have legal authority over the defendant, he or she must have committed the crime within the court's geographical borders and it must involve a crime which the court has authority to try. Generally, a court has jurisdiction if any part of a crime was committed or occurred within its geographical boundaries. The question of where to try such crimes as conspiracy, for example, where the planning took place in one jurisdiction, preparation in another, and actual accomplishment in a third jurisdiction, is therefore no major problem.

The defendant(s) may legally be tried in any of the above three jurisdictions. As a practical matter, the case would most likely be tried where the crime was "completed." Completed, in this case, could mean:

- from where the money was stolen,
- from where the victim was kidnapped, or
- where the victim was killed, if the body was found elsewhere.

A crime that was planned in one jurisdiction and carried out in another may be prosecuted in either. *Left photo courtesy of ML Sinibaldi/Corbis Images. Right photo courtesy of Craig Aurness/Corbis Images.*

STUDENT REVIEW

TERMINOLOGY DEFINED—CHAPTER 1

Each of the following terms is important for a clear understanding of the text. After reviewing the Terminology List, below, you are urged to take the Terminology Quiz at the end of this chapter.

1. Abridge: circumvent, avoid.
2. Adjective law: procedural law.
3. Appellate court: a court of appeals or Supreme Court.
4. Canon law: church law.
5. Capricious: without good (legal) reason.
6. Common law: resulting from custom and court decisions.
7. Contemporary: modern or current.
8. *Corpus delicti*: body of a crime.
9. *Crimen falsi*: crime involving falsification.
10. Custom: behavior which has become traditional with time.
11. Doctrines: rules.
12. *Ex post facto*: after the fact.
13. Incestuous: marriage or sexual relations between close blood relatives.
14. Infamous crime: violating common principles of humanity.
15. Inherent: within, basic to, built-in.
16. Jurisdiction: court's legal authority to act.
17. Jurisprudence: field of law.
18. *Mala in se*: wrong by its very nature.
19. *Mala prohibita*: wrong because prohibited by law.
20. Moral turpitude: relating to ethics, honesty, morality.
21. Nullify: to dilute or abolish.
22. Precedent: binding court decisions.
23. Public policy: best for majority, custom.
24. Sovereign: power to act, king.
25. *Stare decisis*: rigidly adhere to precedent.
26. Statutes: written laws.
27. Substantive law: laws defining crimes and their punishments.
28. Taboos: based on tribal prohibitions and customs.
29. Tort: private or civil wrong.
30. Venue: geographical location of court hearing a case.

TRUE-FALSE QUIZ—CHAPTER 1

After reading this chapter you should be able to correctly answer the following items.

___ 1. It is primarily because people live together as a society that there is a need for laws.
___ 2. Common law refers to those laws passed by the legislature which are commonly known by most people.
___ 3. California has only six common law crimes.
___ 4. An act is not a crime unless it is punishable by death, imprisonment, or fine, in this state.
___ 5. Decisions of the courts in criminal cases is a source of our criminal law.
___ 6. By adopting the Declaration of Independence, the people of America thereby rejected almost all of the English common law concepts.
___ 7. Our courts have held that the State Legislature has no inherent power to pass laws defining or prohibiting criminal conduct.

___ 8. It is ultimately up to the courts to interpret criminal laws passed by legislative bodies.
___ 9. Courts do not always strictly adhere to the concept of *stare decisis*.
___10. Adjective law is the term applied to statutes defining various crimes and their punishments.
___11. Substantive law is the term which describes laws defining criminal procedure and the rules by which the law is administered.
___12. The statute of limitation, governs the amount of maximum time for which a person can be imprisoned for a crime.
___13. When a case is appealed from the superior court, it is usually heard next in the District Court of Appeal.
___14. In a criminal case, only the defendant has a right to appeal.
___15. Being the chief law officer of the state, the Attorney General's opinions carry the same weight as do those of a court.
___16. "Police power" of the state refers to its right to pass laws regulating the police.
___17. The doctrine of preemption has its source in the California Constitution.
___18. A city ordinance is legal if it describes a crime also covered by state law.
___19. Passing a law making an act a crime after the act was committed is prohibited by the Constitution.
___20. A tort may be briefly defined as a "public wrong."
___21. The law prohibits suing someone for personal damages if he or she has already been convicted of a crime for the same act.
___22. The term, *mala in se*, means prohibited by law.
___23. The term, *crimen falsi*, would be applicable to such crimes as forgery and perjury.
___24. Jurisdiction has to do with the court's legal authority over the defendant and the crime of which he or she is accused.
___25. To request a change of venue means to ask to have the case tried in a court in another geographical location.

ESSAY-DISCUSSION ITEMS—CHAPTER 1

After reading this chapter you should be able to correctly answer the following items.

1. What are the five possible penalties which may be imposed on one convicted of a crime in California?
2. What is the basic difference between a crime and a tort?
3. What is the difference between a *mala in se* and a *mala prohibita* crime?
4. Define and give an example of a crime considered *crimen falsi*.
5. What are the four general sources of criminal law?
6. What is "common law" and what is its impact in criminal cases?
7. Define and give an example of "police power" of the state.
8. What is an *ex post facto* law and what is its legal effect?
9. How does substantive law differ from adjective law?
10. What is the statute of limitation for (a) misdemeanors, (b) residence burglary, and (c) murder?
11. Whom does the Attorney General represent and what is the legal authority of his decisions?
12. What occurred during the Westminster Period (1285-1500) in English courts which has an effect on today's courts?
13. How were the concepts of English common law first adopted in America?
14. What are the two most prolific sources of criminal law today?
15. What is meant by venue and jurisdiction as they apply to the court?

TERMINOLOGY QUIZ—CHAPTER 1

Match terms and definitions by writing the number preceding the correct term between the appropriate brackets. Answers may be written on a separate sheet for submission to the instructor at the instructor's direction.

Terms

1. Abridge
2. Adjective law
3. Appellate court
4. Canon law
5. Capricious
6. Common law
7. Contemporary
8. *Corpus delicti*
9. *Crimen falsi*
10. Custom
11. Doctrines
12. *Ex post facto*
13. Incestuous
14. Infamous crime
15. Inherent
16. Jurisdiction
17. Jurisprudence
18. *Mala in se*
19. *Mala prohibita*
20. Moral turpitude
21. Nullify
22. Precedent
23. Public policy
24. Sovereign
25. *Stare decisis*
26. Statutes
27. Substantive law
28. Taboos
29. Tort
30. Venue

Definitions

[ ] Court's legal authority to act
[ ] Circumvent, avoid
[ ] Written law
[ ] Tribal prohibitions
[ ] Behavior traditional with time
[ ] Resulting from custom and court decisions
[ ] Modern or current
[ ] Binding court decisions
[ ] Church law
[ ] Court of appeals
[ ] Rules
[ ] Wrong because of laws against it
[ ] Crimes and punishments
[ ] Wrong by very nature of act
[ ] Procedural law
[ ] Relating to ethics, honesty, morality
[ ] Rigidly adhering to precedent
[ ] Violating common principles of humanity
[ ] Body of a crime
[ ] Geographical location of court hearing
[ ] Without good legal reason
[ ] Crime involving falsification
[ ] Private or civil wrong
[ ] After the fact
[ ] King, power to act

CHAPTER 2

CLASSIFICATION OF CRIMES AND PENALTIES

2.1 LANGUAGE OF CRIMINAL STATUTES

Criminal statutes may not, by interpretation, be extended beyond their plain meaning unless common sense or the obvious purpose of the legislature so requires. In the interpretation of the statutes, or the construction of the words in such statutes, the defendant is entitled to the benefit of every reasonable doubt, just as he is as to questions of fact involved (*People v. Davis*, 29 Cal. 3d 814).

Often a word, whether coming from a foreign language or coined to meet a particular need, has been used as an English word to such an extent that its meaning has become commonly understood. In such instances it becomes a part of the English language with the meaning attached to it by such use. Such is true even if the word is not in the English dictionary (*In re Steven S.*, 25 Cal. App. 4th 598).

2.2 VAGUE AND INDEFINITE STATUTES

Criminal statutes which are vague and uncertain will result in a violation of the due process clause of the Fourteenth Amendment to the United States Constitution (*Connolly v. General Construction Company*, 269 U.S. 385).

A criminal statute which is so vague, indefinite, and uncertain that definition of a crime or standard of conduct cannot be ascertained therefrom, is unconstitutional and void (*In re Timothy R.*, 29 Cal. App. 3d 593).

Words such as "immoral," or "loiter," if used in a crime, would have to be clearly defined in terms of specific acts or actions to be constitutional. Otherwise, such laws would be declared void as too vague and indefinite.

No one can be punished for a mere *intent* to violate the law or mere *intent* to do an act prohibited by law. It takes some kind of actual overt act (or omission) which is specifically prohibited (or required) by law.

2.3 CONSTRUCTION OF PENAL STATUTES

The California legal system is, in part, based on the English common law system. However, California jurisprudence (law) is less tied to tradition and is more "people-oriented" than is the old common law. Common law is bound by the *letter* of the law. The California legal system is directed more toward the *spirit* of the law. The California Legislature expressed its intent specifically in 1872 by enacting Penal Code section 4, which reads:

"The rule of common law, that penal statutes are to be strictly construed, has no application to this Code. All its provisions are to be construed according to a fair import of their terms with a view to effect its objects and to promote justice."

Thus, when a reasonable question arises as to the meaning or intent of a given law, the courts will look at not only the literal meaning of the words used, but also the spirit in which the law was written and the legislative intent behind it.

Once the intention of the legislature is determined, it will be given effect, even though it may not be consistent with the strict letter of the statute (*In re Kali D.*, 37 Cal. App. 4th 381). Similarly, when construing a statute and seeking to determine the Legislature's intent, interpretation must be given which avoids any absurdity—especially one which goes outside of the offenses sought to be prohibited (*People v. King*, 5 Cal. App. 4th 59).

When language which can reasonably be interpreted in two different ways is used in a penal statute, ordinarily that interpretation or construction which is more favorable to the defendant will be adopted (*In re Christian S.*, 7 Cal. 4th 768). The provisions of the Penal Code must be interpreted according to the reasonable meaning of the terminology used. The courts cannot go so far as to create an offense by enlarging a statute, by inserting or deleting words, or by giving the terms used in the law an unusual meaning (*People v. Davis*, 7 Cal. 4th 797).

2.4 CONFLICT BETWEEN STATUTES

Where two state laws punish exactly the same act or omission as crimes, and they are obviously in conflict, the last one passed into law will control (*People v. Jones*, 19 Cal. App. 3d 437).

The term "conflict between statutes" should not be confused with the concept of preemption, described in Section 1.11. The concept of preemption means that state laws take priority over city and county ordinances. Conflict between statutes refers to conflicting state laws.

2.5 PENAL CODE TERMS DEFINED

Words Defined—PC 7. Words used in the Penal Code in the present tense include the future as well as the present; words used in the masculine gender include the feminine and neuter; the singular number includes the plural, and the plural the singular.

The word "person" includes a corporation as well as a natural person; the word "county" includes "city and county;" writing includes printing and typewriting; oath includes affirmation or declaration; and every mode of oral statement, under oath or affirmation, is embraced by the term "testify," and every written statement is included in the term "depose;" signature or subscription includes mark, when the person cannot write, his name being written near it, by a person who writes his own name as a witness; provided that when a signature is made by mark it must, in order that the same may be acknowledged or serve as the signature of any sworn statement, be witnessed by two persons who must subscribe their own names as witnesses thereto.

Section 7, of the Penal Code, declares the following words to have the meanings indicated below, unless otherwise apparent from the context:

1. The word "willfully," when applied to the intent with which an act is done or omitted, implies simply a purpose or willingness to commit the act, or make the omission referred to. It does not require any intent to violate law, or to injure another, or to acquire any advantage.
2. The words "neglect," "negligence," "negligent," and "negligently" import (imply) a want of such attention to the nature or probable consequences of the act or omission as a prudent person ordinarily bestows in acting in his own concern.
3. The word "corruptly" imports a wrongful design to acquire or cause some pecuniary (financial) or other advantage to the person guilty of the act or omission referred to, or to some other person.
4. The words "malice" and "maliciously" import a wish to vex, annoy, or injure another person, or an intent to do a wrongful act, established either by proof or presumption of law.
5. The word "knowingly" imports only a knowledge that the facts exist which bring the act or omission within the provisions of this code. It does not require any knowledge of the unlawfulness of such act or omission.
6. The word "bribe" signifies anything of value or advantage, present or prospective, or any promise or undertaking to give any, asked, given, or accepted, with a corrupt intent to influence, unlawfully, the person to whom it is given, in his action, vote, or opinion, in any public or official capacity.
7. The word "vessel," when used with reference to shipping, includes ships of all kinds, steamboats, canalboats, barges, and every structure adapted to be navigated from place to place for the transportation of merchandise or persons.
8. The words "peace officer" signify any one of the officers mentioned in Chapter 4.5 (commencing with Section 830) of Title 3 of Part 2.
9. The word "magistrate" (judge) signifies any one of the officers mentioned in Section 808.
10. The word "property" includes both real and personal property.
11. The words "real property" are coextensive (having same limits) with lands, tenements, and hereditaments.
12. The words "personal property" include money, goods, chattels, things in action, and evidences of debt.
13. The word "month" means a calendar month, unless otherwise expressed; the word "daytime" means the period between sunrise and sunset, and the word "nighttime" means the period between sunset and sunrise.

14. The word "will" includes codicil (addition to will).
15. The word "writ" signifies an order or precept in writing, issued in the name of the people, or of a court or judicial officer, and the word "process," a writ or summons issued in the course of judicial proceedings.
16. Words and phrases must be construed according to the context and the approved usage of the language; but technical words and phrases, and such others as may have acquired a peculiar and appropriate meaning in law, must be construed according to such peculiar and appropriate meaning.
17. Words giving joint authority to three or more public officers or other persons are construed as giving such authority to a majority of them, unless it is otherwise expressed in the act giving the authority.
18. When the seal of a court or public officer is required by law to be affixed to any paper, the word "seal" includes an impression of such seal upon the paper alone, or upon any substance attached to the paper capable of receiving a visible impression. The seal of a private person may be made in like manner, or by the scroll of a pen, or by writing the word "seal" against his or her name.
19. The word "state," when applied to the different parts of the United States, includes the District of Columbia and the territories, and the words "United States" may include the district and territories.
20. The word "section," whenever hereinafter employed, refers to a section of this code, unless some other code or statute is expressly mentioned.
21. To "book" signifies the recordation of an arrest in official police records and the taking by the police of fingerprints and photographs of the person arrested, or any of these acts following an arrest.

For an excellent source to check on legal terms, see Web Site: **http://dictionary.lp.findlaw.com.** Click on each item of interest which appears for details.

2.6 FELONIES, MISDEMEANORS, AND INFRACTIONS DEFINED

Kinds of Crimes—PC 16. Crimes in California are divided into three categories:

1. **Felony:** (PC 17). "A felony is a crime punishable with death or by imprisonment in the state prison."
2. **Misdemeanor:** (PC 17). "Every other crime or public offense is a misdemeanor except those offenses that are classified as infractions."
3. **Infraction:** (PC 19.6). "An infraction is not punishable by imprisonment. A person charged with an infraction shall not be entitled to a trial by jury . . . [or] to have the public defender or other counsel appointed at public expense to represent him or her unless he or she is arrested and not released on his or her written promise to appear, [or] his or her own recognizance, or a deposit of bail."

Felony "Wobblers." Some crimes provide for an alternative sentence i.e., they are punishable either as a felony by imprisonment in the state prison or as a misdemeanor by fine or by imprisonment in county jail. Such crimes are commonly called "wobblers." Sometimes a wobbler, filed as a felony, will be reduced to a misdemeanor by the judge at the preliminary hearing. Sometimes the prosecutor will file a wobbler as a misdemeanor from the beginning. Unless filed as a misdemeanor or reduced to such at the preliminary hearing, wobblers are otherwise felonies for all purposes (including arrest) up to the time of actual sentencing or granting of probation by the court.

A wobbler becomes a misdemeanor when filed as such by the prosecutor or is reduced to a misdemeanor by the preliminary hearing judge. For example, a person may commit an offense such as burglary in the second degree (PC 459) which is a felony, but which prescribes an alternate sentence of county jail or state prison. If the defendant is sentenced to state prison, he or she stands convicted of a felony due to the punishment imposed. If, however, the defendant is sentenced to county jail, he or she stands convicted of a misdemeanor. This is true even though at the time of the commission of the offense the crime was a felony. If not filed as, or reduced to, a misdemeanor, the offense is a felony up to the time the sentence. (*People v. Lassiter*, 202 Cal. App. 3d 352).

Effect of Suspended Sentence. Sometimes the court suspends imposition of sentence and does not pronounce judgment. Instead it places the defendant on probation. If the offense is punishable as a

Prisoners sentenced for misdemeanors serve time in the county jail, while those sentenced for felonies go to state prison. *Courtesy of Hulton Getty/Liason Agency*

felony, the defendant retains the status of a person convicted of a felony until the record is expunged pursuant to PC 1203.4 (*People v. Banks*, 53 Cal. 2d 370). See "Expungement Procedures," Penal Code Section 1203.45.

On the other hand, where imposition of sentence is suspended on conviction of a crime punishable by imprisonment in either state prison or the county jail, the court may declare the crime to be a misdemeanor at the time probation is granted, or thereafter on application of the defendant or the probation officer (see PC 17, below).

Effect on Arrest. Any crime which provides for an alternate misdemeanor-felony sentence, is and remains a felony for all purposes, including arrest, up to the time of actual sentencing by the court. This is providing it was not filed initially as a misdemeanor by the prosecutor or was not reduced to a misdemeanor by the preliminary hearing magistrate. Alternate penalty felonies (wobblers), therefore, may generally be treated the same as all other felonies for arrest purposes by a peace officer.

Classification of Crimes—PC 17.

a. A felony is a crime which is punishable with death or by imprisonment in the state prison. Every other crime or public offense is a misdemeanor except those offenses that are classified as infractions.
b. When a crime is punishable, in the discretion of the court, by imprisonment in the state prison or by fine or imprisonment in the county jail, it is a misdemeanor for all purposes under the following circumstances:
   1. After a judgment imposing a punishment other than imprisonment in the state prison.
   2. When the court upon committing the defendant to the California Youth Authority (CYA), designates the offense to be a misdemeanor.
   3. When the court grants probation to a defendant without imposition of sentence and at the time of granting of probation, or on application of the defendant or probation officer thereafter, the court declares the offense is a misdemeanor.
   4. When the prosecuting attorney files in a court having jurisdiction over misdemeanor offenses, a complaint specifying that the offense is a misdemeanor, unless the defendant at the time of his or her arraignment or plea objects to the offense being made a misdemeanor, in which event the complaint shall be amended to charge the felony and the case shall proceed on the felony complaint.
   5. When, at or before the preliminary examination or prior to filing an order pursuant to Section 872 (held to answer following preliminary hearing), the magistrate determines that the offense is a misdemeanor, in which event the case shall proceed as if the defendant had been arraigned on a misdemeanor complaint.
c. When a defendant is committed to the Youth Authority for a crime punishable in the discretion of the court, by imprisonment in state prison, or by fine or imprisonment in the county jail, the offense shall, upon the discharge of the defendant from the Youth Authority, thereafter be deemed a misdemeanor for all purposes.
d. A violation of any code section listed in Section 19.8 is an infraction subject to the procedures described in Section 19.6 and 19.7, when:
   1. The prosecutor files a complaint charging the offense as an infraction unless the defendant, at the time he or she is arraigned, after

being informed of his or her rights, elects to have the case proceed as a misdemeanor, or;

2. The court, with the consent of the defendant, determines that the offense is an infraction, in which event the case shall proceed as if the defendant had been arraigned on an infraction complaint.

Infraction: Trial by Court—Limitations—PC 19.6. "An infraction is not punishable by imprisonment. A person charged with an infraction shall not be entitled to a trial by jury. A person charged with an infraction shall not be entitled to have a public defender or other counsel appointed at public expense to represent him or her unless he or she is arrested and not released on his or her written promise to appear, his or her own recognizance, or a deposit of bail."

Provisions of Law Relating to Infractions—PC 19.7. "Except as otherwise provided by law, all provisions of law relating to misdemeanors shall apply to infractions, including, but not limited to, powers of peace officers, jurisdiction of courts, periods for commencing action and for bringing a case to trial [statute of limitations] and burden of proof."

Infractions: Classification of Offenses—PC 19.8. You will note that in PC 17(d)(1) above, if the prosecutor files a complaint charging an infraction instead of a misdemeanor, and the defendant does not object, certain offenses, listed below in PC 19.8, will proceed as infractions. The same is true if the court determines that an offense may proceed as an infraction.

These offenses are: Health and Safety 11375(b)(2), possession of specified drugs; PC 193.8, allowing intoxicated minor to drive; PC 330, gambling; PC 415, fighting; PC 485, keeping lost property; PC 555, unlawful entry on posted property; PC 652, tattooing a minor; PC 853.7, failure to appear; PC 602m, unlawfully driving on private property; VC 12500, unlicensed driver; VC 14601.1, driving with revoked license; VC 23109(c), exhibition of speed; VC 27150.1, selling nonregulation mufflers; VC 40508, violating promise to appear; VC 42005, failure to attend traffic school, Government Code section 27204, and sections 21672, 25658, 25658.5, 25661 and 25662 of the Business and Professions Code.

Except for Vehicle Code Section 14601.1, based on failure to appear, or the violations listed in VC 13202.5, a conviction for any offense made an infraction, under PC 17(d), is not grounds for the suspension, revocation, or denial of any license, or for the revocation of probation or parole of the person convicted.

Penalty for Infractions—PC 19.8. Except where a lesser maximum fine is expressly provided for the violation of any of the above sections, any such violation which is an infraction is punishable by a fine not exceeding $250.

DNA Database Specimens—PC 296. Persons convicted of enumerated crimes are required to provide two specimens of blood, a saliva sample, right thumbprints and full palm prints of both hands, for inclusion in state databases. The specified crimes include registrable sex offenses, murder, voluntary manslaughter, felony spousal abuse, aggravated sexual assault of a child, felony assaults and batteries, kidnap, mayhem, torture, first-degree burglary, robbery, arson, carjacking and terrorist activity, as indicated. Officers are authorized to use reasonable force to collect specimens from those who refuse to provide them (PC 298.1(b)(1)).

2.7 PUNISHMENT FOR OFFENSES NOT OTHERWISE PRESCRIBED

PC 19.4 states that: "When an act or omission is declared by a statute to be a public offense, and no penalty for the offense is prescribed in any statute, the act or omission is punishable as a misdemeanor."

Similarly, the courts have held that where the law provides that a particular crime is punishable by a specified period of imprisonment, but is silent as to the place of imprisonment and the offense is not declared to be either a misdemeanor or a felony, the place of imprisonment is a jail and the offense is a misdemeanor (*In re Humphrey*, 64 Cal. App. 572).

Punishment for Felonies When Not Otherwise Prescribed—PC 18. "Except in cases where a different punishment is prescribed by any law of this state, every offense declared to be a felony, or to be punishable by imprisonment in a state prison, is punishable by imprisonment in any of the state prisons for 16 months, or two or three years; provided, however, every offense which is prescribed by any law of the state to be a felony punishable by imprisonment in any of the state prisons or by a fine, but without an alternate sentence to a county jail, may be punishable by imprisonment in the county jail not exceeding one year or by a fine or by both."

Maximum Term for Misdemeanor Offense—PC 19. "Except where a different punishment is prescribed for a misdemeanor it is punishable by imprisonment in the county jail not exceeding six months or by a fine of $1,000, or by both." Except for consecutive sentences, no person shall be committed for a period in excess of one year for a misdemeanor (PC 19.2).

Consecutive Sentences for Misdemeanors—PC 19.2. Where a defendant is convicted of two or more misdemeanors, either in the same or in separate prosecutions, the court may commit the defendant to the county jail under each of such convictions, and an order directing that such terms of imprisonment shall run consecutively (one following the other) is valid (*People v. Flanagan*, 7 Cal. App. 2d 214).

2.8 INITIATIVE MEASURES

California voters occasionally pass ballot measures to amend criminal laws and procedures as in 1982 (Proposition 8) and in 1990 (Proposition 115). Such measures may often reflect a popular sentiment that legislative and judicial actions (or inactions) are out of touch with the public will. Both of these measures were aimed at restricting the rights of the accused and extending the abilities of the state to prosecute—thus bringing California more in line with the federal rules and the majority of other states. The more important aspects of Propositions 8 and 115 are discussed below and in Section 2.9.

Truth in Evidence. The Truth in Evidence part of Proposition 8, is now Article 1, Section 28, subdivision (d) of the California Constitution. It states that: "Relevant [applicable] evidence shall not be excluded in any criminal proceeding." The primary purpose of this enactment was to abolish the doctrine of "independent state grounds" as a basis for excluding evidence, and to get California's exclusionary rules back into conformity with federal rules. In two subsequent landmark cases, *In re Lance W.*, 37 Cal. 3d 873 and *People v. May*, 44 Cal. 3d 309, the California Supreme Court ruled that this purpose has largely been achieved.

Before the *Lance W.* ruling, evidence obtained in violation of the California Constitution was excluded from trial. Since *Lance W.*, because the Truth in Evidence provision of Proposition 8 made all relevant evidence admissible, such evidence is no longer suppressed—providing it does not violate the United States Constitution. In other words, "independent state grounds" no longer exists as a basis for excluding evidence.

The more recent *May* case ruling related to statements, *Miranda* rules, defendant's right to an attorney, etc. The court held in this case that if police conduct did not violate the federal Constitution, the evidence is admissible in court.

Evidence may be inadmissible under exclusionary rules promulgated by the U.S. Supreme Court to protect constitutional rights under the Fourth Amendment (searches and seizures), Fifth Amendment (compelled self-incrimination), Sixth Amendment (confrontation and right to counsel), and Fourteenth Amendment (due process).

The constitutional validity of Proposition 8 was upheld on all counts by the California Supreme Court on September 2, 1982 (*Brasnahan v. Brown*, 32 Cal. 3d 236) and by the Appellate court in 1983 (*McClanahan v. Superior Court* 139 Cal. App. 3d 31).

2.9 MAJOR PROPOSITION 8 AND 115 CHANGES

Rules of Evidence. Relevant evidence shall not be excluded in any criminal proceeding including pretrial and post-conviction motions and hearings or in any trial or hearing of a juvenile for a criminal offense, whether heard in juvenile or adult court.

This is the "Truth in Evidence" issue discussed above. It is obvious from the wording of the Constitutional Amendment that relevant evidence may no longer be excluded from a trial merely because of some technicality or honest mistake of fact that does not violate the federal constitution. This new rule of evidence was upheld by the Supreme Court in *In re Lance W.*, 37 Cal. 3d 873.

Bail Provisions. A person may be released on bail by sufficient sureties (bond, cash or property), except for capital crimes (death penalty) when the presumption of guilt is great. Excessive bail may not be required. In setting, reducing, or denying bail, the judge or magistrate shall take into consid-

The victims of serious felonies have the right to be heard at sentencing. *Photograph by Wernher Krutein, courtesy of Photovault.*

eration: (1) the protection of the public, (2) the seriousness of the offense charged, (3) the previous criminal record of the defendant, and (4) the probability of his or her appearing at the trial or hearing of the case.

Public safety shall be the primary consideration in setting bail. Previously, public safety was not a factor which had to legally be considered in setting bail (California Constitution, Article 1, Section 28e).

A person may be released on his or her own recognizance (without bail) in the court's discretion, subject to the same factors considered in setting bail. However, no person charged with the commission of any "serious felony" (see PC 1192.7) shall be released on his or her own recognizance.

Before a person arrested for a serious felony may be released on bail, a hearing is held before a magistrate. The prosecuting attorney shall be given notice and reasonable opportunity to be heard on the matter. When a judge or magistrate grants or denies bail or release on a person's own recognizance, the reasons for that decision shall be stated in the record and included in the court's minutes.

Use of Prior Convictions. Any prior felony conviction of any person in any criminal proceeding, whether adult or juvenile, shall subsequently be used without limitation for purposes of impeachment or enhancement in any criminal proceeding (California Constitution, Art. 1, Sec. 28).

The purpose of this amendment to the California Constitution was to overrule the decision of the California Supreme Court in *People v. Beagle*, (6 Cal. 3d 441). In the Beagle case the Supreme Court held that a trial court has discretion to exclude impeachment evidence of a defendant with a prior felony conviction in a criminal case. In a subsequent decision (*People v. Castro*, 38 Cal. 3d 301), the Supreme Court ruled that a defendant's prior conviction can be used to impeach his or her testimony only if the prior crimes involved "moral turpitude" (dishonesty, depravity).

Prior Conviction as Element of Offense. When a prior felony conviction is an element of any felony offense, it shall be proven to the trier of fact (judge or jury) in open court (Article 1, Section 28f).

The obvious purpose of this provision was to override the California Supreme Court in *People v. Hall*, (28 Cal. 3d 143). In *Hall*, the Supreme Court ruled that a defendant could prevent the prosecution from proving in open court to the trier of fact that the defendant in PC 12021 cases (ex-felon in possession of a concealable firearm) and in PC 666 cases (petty theft with a prior) had been convicted on a prior felony by offering to stipulate to this fact.

This amendment mandates the trier of fact be advised of the prior conviction where the prior is an *element* of the charged offense, but not where it is a *sentencing factor* (*People v. Bouzas*, 53 C3d 467). This provision is not applicable (or necessary) when a plea of guilty is entered, as in such situations there is no trier of fact.

Diminished Capacity Abolished—PC 25(a). "The defense of diminished capacity is hereby abolished. In a criminal action, as well as any juvenile court proceeding, evidence concerning an accused person's intoxication, trauma, mental illness, disease, or defect shall not be admissible to show or negate capacity to form the particular purpose, intent, motive, malice aforethought, knowledge, or other mental state required for the commission of the crime charged."

"Notwithstanding the foregoing, evidence of diminished capacity or of a mental disorder may be considered by the court only at the time of sentencing or other disposition or commitment [PC 25 (c)]."

Insanity Defense—PC 25(b). "In any criminal proceeding, including any juvenile court proceeding, in which a plea of not guilty by reason of insanity is entered, this defense shall be found by the trier of fact only when the accused person proves by a preponderance [greater weight] of evidence that he or she was incapable of [1] knowing or understanding the nature and quality of his or her act and of [2] distinguishing right from wrong at the time of the commission of the offense."

Penal Code 25(b), essentially restores the traditional "M'Naghten Rule" as to insanity, which was overturned by the California Supreme Court in *People v. Drew*, 22 Cal. 3d 333. (See your text Section 4.4, "Insanity as a Defense," for additional details).

Serious Felony Prior Conviction Enhancement. PC 667(a) provides that "any person convicted of a serious felony [see below] who previously has been convicted of a serious felony in this state, or of any offense committed in another jurisdiction which includes all of the elements of any serious felony, shall receive, in addition to the sentence imposed by the court for the present offense, a five year enhancement for each such prior conviction on charges brought and tried separately. The terms of the present offense and each enhancement shall run consecutively [one following the other]."

"This section shall not be applied when the punishment imposed under other provisions of law would result in a longer term of imprisonment." *Note*: There is no requirement of prior incarceration (imprisonment) or commitment for this section to apply (PC 667(b)). As used in PC 667, "serious felony" means a felony listed in PC 1192.7(c).

Serious Felony Defined. As used in PC 1192.7(c), "serious felony" means any of the following:

1. murder or voluntary manslaughter;
2. mayhem;
3. rape;
4. sodomy by force, violence, duress, menace, or threat of great bodily harm;
5. oral copulation by force, violence, duress, menace, or threat of great bodily harm;
6. lewd acts on a child under the age of 14 years;
7. any felony punishable by death or imprisonment in the state prison for life;
8. any other felony in which the defendant inflicts great bodily injury on any person, other than an accomplice, or any felony in which the defendant personally uses a firearm;
9. attempted murder;
10. assault with intent to commit rape, mayhem, sodomy, oral copulation, or robbery;
11. assault with a deadly weapon or instrument on a peace officer;
12. assault by a life prisoner on a non-inmate;
13. assault with a deadly weapon by an inmate;
14. arson;
15. exploding a destructive device or any explosive with intent to injure;
16. exploding a destructive device or any explosive causing great bodily injury/or mayhem;
17. exploding a destructive device or any explosive with intent to murder;
18. burglary of the first degree;
19. robbery;
20. kidnapping;
21. holding a hostage by an inmate of a state prison;
22. false imprisonment;
23. attempt to commit a felony punishable by death or imprisonment in the state prison for life;
24. any felony in which the defendant personally used a dangerous or deadly weapon;
25. selling, furnishing, administering or providing heroin, cocaine or phencyclidine (PCP) to a minor;
26. violation of PC 289(a) (penetration of genital or anal opening) accomplished against the victim's will by force, violence, or fear of bodily injury;
27. grand theft involving a firearm;
28. carjacking;
29. pattern of sexual abuse of minor under 14;
30. assault with acid or caustic substance;
31. ADW on a firefighter;
32. rape or forcible penetration in concert;
33. using a firearm during felonies specified in PC12022.53;
34. attempts of any of these crimes, except assault.

Crime Victim Rights—PC 1191.1. The victim of any crime, or his or her parents or guardian, if the victim is a minor, or the next of kin of the victim if the victim has died, has the right to attend all sentencing proceedings under this chapter and shall be given adequate notice by the probation officer of all sentencing proceedings concerning the person who committed the crime.

The victim, or his or her parents or guardian, if the victim is a minor, or next of kin has the right to appear, personally or by counsel, at the sentencing proceeding and to reasonably express his or her views concerning (1) the crime, (2) the person responsible, and (3) the need for restitution. The court, in imposing sentence, shall consider the statements of victims and next of kin and shall state on the record its conclusions concerning whether the defendant would pose a threat to public safety.

Crime Victim Defined. The definition of "victim" is found in the restitution provision of California State Constitution, Article 1, Section 28(b). This section defines victims as: ". . . all persons who suffer losses as a result of criminal activity."

This includes all persons suffering personal injury or property loss or damage. In the case of the death of the victim, the next of kin provision would apply to the person closest to the victim. Notification of all relatives of the victim would not be required.

Plea Bargaining—PC 1192.7. "Plea bargaining in any case in which the indictment or information charges any serious felony [see PC 1192.7(c), below], any felony in which it is alleged that a firearm was personally used by the defendant, or any offense of driving while under the influence of alcohol, drugs, narcotics, or any other intoxicating substance, or any combination thereof, is prohibited, unless there is insufficient evidence to prove the people's case, or testimony of a material witness cannot be obtained, or a reduction or dismissal would not result in a substantial change in sentence."

Major Proposition 115 Highlights. Extending what was begun with Proposition 8, Proposition 115 made a number of procedural changes aimed at reducing delays and inequities in the processing of criminal cases. These changes include:

- limiting voir dire (jury selection questioning) to the trial judge (most voir dire was previously done by the attorneys) except as supplemented by the attorneys when permitted by the judge;
- permitting qualified officers to testify to hearsay at preliminary hearings;
- specifying that a defendant indicted by the Grand Jury need not also receive a preliminary hearing;
- requiring the joinder of multiple defendants in a single trial, thus making it more difficult for the parties to obtain continuances; and
- granting limited discovery rights (access to evidence) to the prosecution. Previously, the prosecution had no discovery rights to defense evidence.

2.10 PRIOR CONVICTION—PENALTY ENHANCEMENT

Both the electorate and the Legislature have made many important changes in penalty enhancements, particularly as to "serious felonies," "violent felonies," and prior convictions. The most important are discussed below.

Petty Theft With Prior—PC 666. "Every person who, having been convicted of petit theft, grand theft, auto theft under Section 10851 of the Vehicle Code, burglary, robbery, or a felony violation of Section 496 and *having served a term therefor* in any penal institution or having been imprisoned therein as a condition of probation for such offense, is subsequently convicted of petit theft, then the person convicted of such subsequent offense is punishable by imprisonment in the county jail not exceeding one year or in the state prison."

Armed and Use. Sentences for specified felonies are increased by consecutive terms, ranging from one year to life in prison, where one or more principals were armed with, used, or discharged firearms with resulting injuries. In some cases, even an unloaded and inoperable firearm can support sentence "enhancement," and greater sentences are also prescribed in gang cases.

Prior Serious Felony Conviction. Any person convicted of a serious felony, as defined in PC 1192.7(c), in this state or another jurisdiction, shall receive an additional and consecutive sentence of five years in prison for each prior conviction (PC 667(a)(1)). *Note:* There is no requirement of prior imprisonment for this increased penalty to apply (PC 667(a)(2)).

If a person is convicted of any felony and it is pled and proven that she/he has been previously convicted of any "violent felony" (listed in 667.5(c)), or of any "serious felony" (listed in 1192.7(c)), punishment for the new conviction is twice the specified sentence.

Where two or more violent or serious prior felony convictions are pled and proven, the defendant must receive a life term with a minimum sentence of treble the normal sentence, or 25 years, whichever is greater. This is the so-called "three strikes, you're out" law, enacted by initiative. PC 667(e); 1192.7.

Despite the language of the statutes, the California Supreme Court held that under the broad powers of a court to dismiss cases "in the interest of justice" pursuant to PC 1385, sentencing courts have the authority to dismiss "strikes" and sentence an offender to a lower sentence. *People v. Superior Court* (*Romero*), 13 Cal. 4th 497.

Prior Felony Conviction Outside of California—PC 668. "Every person who has been convicted in any other state government, country, or jurisdiction of an offense for which, if committed within this state, such person could have been punished under the laws of this state by imprisonment in a state prison, is punishable for any subsequent [later] offense committed within this state in the manner prescribed by law and to the same extent as if such prior conviction had taken place in a court in this state."

A conviction of a felony in another state at a time when the act involved would have been a felony in California is a prior felony conviction in this state, provided the defendant served one year or more in prison for the offense in the other jurisdiction (PC 667.5(f)).

Prior Federal Convictions. California will consider most prior federal felony convictions for the purposes of increasing the severity of an offense, as long as such federal offense would be a felony under California law (*People v. Mc Vickers*, 29 Cal. 2d 264).

Violent Felonies. PC 667.5 provides that a consecutive and additional three year prison term shall be imposed by the court for each prior prison term served for a violent felony within 10 preceding years, upon conviction of a subsequent violent felony as listed below:

1. Murder or voluntary manslaughter.
2. Mayhem.
3. Rape as defined in PC 261(2).
4. Sodomy by force, fear, duress, etc.
5. Oral copulation by force, fear, duress etc.
6. Lewd acts on a child under age 14 as defined in PC 288.
7. Any felony punishable by death or life imprisonment.
8. Any other felony in which the defendant has inflicted great bodily injury on any person other than an accomplice which has been charged and proved as provided for in PC 12022.7 (PC 667.5), or used a firearm.
9. Robbery.
10. Arson.
11. Forcible penetration with a foreign object.
12. Attempted murder.
13. Explosion with intent to murder.
14. Kidnap.
15. Continuous sexual abuse of a child.
16. Carjacking.
17. First degree robbery by three or more persons.
18. Forcible rape, spousal rape or sodomy.

Habitual Sexual Offender—PC 667.61. On a second or subsequent conviction for certain specified sexual offenses, including forcible rape, sodomy and oral copulation, the habitual sexual offender is subject to imprisonment for life, and must serve at least 85 percent of a 25-to-life term before parole.

Additional Imprisonment For Use of Firearm. A punishment of three to ten years is added to the sentence of any person who personally uses a firearm in the commission or attempt to commit any felony including PC 245 (ADW) unless use of a firearm was an element of the offense of which such person was convicted (PC 12022.5).

Additional Term for Inflicting Bodily Harm In Committing Felony. PC 12022.7 provides that any person who inflicts great bodily injury on any person other than an accomplice, is subject to an additional three years in prison. As used in this section, "great bodily injury" means a significant or substantial physical injury. *Note:* this section does not apply to murder, manslaughter, PC 451 (arson) or PC 452 (unlawfully causing a fire).

Limit on Granting Probation. Generally probation may not be granted to persons convicted of possession of dangerous or deadly weapons at the time of their arrest or during perpetration of most serious crimes such as arson, robbery, burglary, etc.

Also, probation is not granted to persons who used or attempted to use a deadly weapon on another person or who willfully inflicted great bodily injury or torture on another during the perpetration of their crime. Exceptions may be made in unusual cases where the interest of justice would be served (PC 1203).

2.11 PRIOR CONVICTIONS—C.Y.A. COMMITMENT

California Youth Authority commitments can be used as prior convictions in all felony filings of the accusatory pleading providing that the C.Y.A. commitment was for a felony without the alternative of a county jail sentence. That is, if a juvenile was convicted in adult court of a straight felony and was thereafter committed to the Youth Authority, that commitment is a proper prior felony conviction regardless of the commitment date.

When a crime is punishable, in the discretion of the court, by imprisonment in the state prison or by fine or imprisonment in the county jail, it is a *misdemeanor* for all purposes under the following circumstances:

1. When the court, upon committing the defendant to the California Youth Authority, designates the offense to be a misdemeanor (PC 17(b)(2)).
2. When a defendant is committed to the Youth Authority for a crime punishable, in the discretion of the court, by imprisonment in the state prison or by fine or imprisonment in the county jail, the offense shall, upon the discharge of the defendant from the Youth Authority, thereafter be deemed a misdemeanor for all purposes (PC 17(b)(5)).

When Not Eligible For C.Y.A. No person convicted of:

1. Murder,
2. Rape, or
3. Any other serious felony, as defined in PC 1192.7, committed when he or she was 18 years of age or older, shall be committed to the Youth Authority (Welfare and Institutions Code 1732.5).

This section was added by virtue of Proposition 8. The intent of the initiative measure is clear. Any person, 18 years or older at the time of the commission of any of the crimes listed in PC 1192.7, is not eligible for commitment to the California Youth Authority.

2.12 LESSER INCLUDED OFFENSES

In California there are several offenses, the commission of which necessarily includes other lesser offenses. However, before a lesser offense may be said to constitute a necessary part of the greater offense, all of the legal elements of the lesser offense must be included in the elements of the greater offense (*People v. Greer*, 30 Cal. 2d 589). For example, every battery, which is a misdemeanor, includes an assault, but battery is the greater of the two offenses (*People v. McDaniels*, 137 Cal. 192).

Penal Code Section 1159, states that: "The jury, or the judge if a jury trial is waived, may find the defendant guilty of any offense, the commission of which is necessarily included in that with which he is charged, or of an attempt to commit the offense."

Examples of Lesser Included Offenses.

1. **Simple Assault:** The crime of simple assault is necessarily included in the crimes of battery, mayhem, assault with a deadly weapon, spouse beating, rape, robbery, and sodomy with force.
2. **Petty Theft:** Petty theft is necessarily included in the crimes of grand theft and robbery.

Examples of Lesser Offenses *Not* Included. The crime of robbery does not include the offense of receiving stolen property nor is the offense of child molesting necessarily included in the crime of oral copulation.

The crime of assault with a deadly weapon does not include battery or exhibiting a deadly weapon in an angry and threatening manner. Similarly, a charge of burglary does not include theft, attempted theft, or receiving stolen property. *Note*: a person can be guilty of burglary without stealing or attempting to steal anything.

"Lesser Related" Offenses. In *People v. Geiger* 35 Cal. 3d 510, the California Supreme Court created the concept of "lesser related" offenses, allowing defendants to ask a jury to convict them of a lesser crime that was *not* necessarily included in the charged crime. This doctrine was contrary to U.S. Supreme Court precedent, however, and *Geiger* was subsequently overruled by the California Supreme Court in *People v. Birks*, 19 Cal. 4th 108. Now, a defendant may only be convicted of the charged crimes, or lesser included crimes.

2.13 WHEN JEOPARDY ATTACHES

Jeopardy Principle. The basic principle in the law of former jeopardy is that a person who has committed a criminal act shall be subject to but one prosecution for that act. When that prosecution has resulted in a final judgment of conviction or the defendant has been acquitted, the defendant cannot be prosecuted again for the same crime.

Even if there is no formal verdict or finding that the defendant is not guilty, if jeopardy has attached (when the jury is sworn in a jury trial, or when the first witness is sworn in a court trial), no subsequent prosecution of such defendant can be had for such act. Furthermore, a conviction by plea of guilty is a valid conviction which will bar a second prosecution (*People v. Goldstein*, 32 Cal. 432).

Example: A burglar cannot usually be convicted of both receiving stolen property (his or her burglarized goods) and burglary. Two cases, (*People v. Jaramillo*, 16 Cal. 3d 752 and *People v. Hansard*, 245 Cal. App. 2d 691), clearly held that a burglar cannot also be convicted of possession of or receiving the stolen goods, unless it's a completely separate transaction. An example of such a separate transaction would be if the burglar buys back the stolen goods from a fence a few days after he or she first sold the fence the burglary loot.

In essence, the jeopardy rule prevents a second prosecution for either the identical offense involved in the first trial or for another offense based upon the act constituting the offense charged in the first trial. Furthermore, the defendant cannot be prosecuted a second time for an attempt to commit such offense, nor for any offense necessarily included therein, nor for a crime in which such offense is necessarily included (PC 1023).

If a defendant should be convicted of a lesser included offense and a greater offense subsequently results as an outgrowth of the lesser offense, the conviction of the lesser offense does *not* prevent a prosecution for the greater subsequent offense.

For example, let's assume a person is convicted of assault with a deadly weapon, which is a lesser included offense to murder. The victim later dies. The defendant could now be tried for the murder, since at the time of the conviction for the assault, a homicide had not occurred and could not be charged against the defendant (PC 194).

A conviction of a lower *degree* of a crime is an acquittal of the higher degree of that crime. For example, a person charged with first degree murder who is convicted of second degree murder cannot, upon a reversal on appeal, be prosecuted for first degree murder (*Green v. United States*, 335 U.S. 184).

As previously pointed out, both the United States Constitution and the California Constitution state in part that: ". . . no person shall be subject, for the same offense, to be twice placed in jeopardy." A similar provision is reflected in PC 687, which reads: "No person can be subjected to a second prosecution for a public offense for which he or she has once been prosecuted and convicted or acquitted."

Double Jeopardy and Double Punishment. In *US v. Dixon*, 125 LEd 2d 556, the Supreme Court held that the double jeopardy clause does not apply to successive prosecutions if each of the crimes tried separately includes at least one element that is not included in the other. Under this ruling, attachment of jeopardy on a lesser *included* offense would bar a subsequent prosecution for a greater offense committed at the same time; however, jeopardy on a lesser *related* offense would not prevent a later prosecution for a different crime.

For example, double jeopardy principles would not prevent a prosecution for robbery, after attachment of jeopardy for an ADW committed upon the robbery victim. The crime of robbery includes at least one element (taking property) that is not an element of ADW; likewise, ADW includes at least one element (assault) that is not an element of robbery. Under *Dixon*, separate prosecutions would not violate double jeopardy under the Constitution.

However, In *Kellett v. Superior Court*, 63 Cal. 2d 822, the California Supreme Court ruled that the statutory provisions of Penal Code section 654 will sometimes preclude a subsequent prosecution for a related offense that is not necessarily barred by double jeopardy. That section includes a provision that where an indivisible course of criminal conduct may make a defendant subject to punishment under more than one statute, "an acquittal or conviction and sentence under either one bars a prosecution for the same act or omission under any other." The court interpreted this provision to mean that having been sentenced to 90 days for exhibiting a firearm (PC 417), Kellett could not be prosecuted for felon in possession (PC 12021).

Kellett and PC 654 dictate that wherever possible, all related offenses from a single criminal episode be charged in a single accusatory pleading, and be simultaneously prosecuted.

STUDENT REVIEW

TERMINOLOGY DEFINED—CHAPTER 2

After reviewing the Terminology List, below, you are urged to take the Terminology Quiz at the end of this chapter.

1. Acquit: find not guilty.
2. Booking: recording an arrest, photographing, and fingerprinting.
3. Bribe: anything of value given to illegally influence another.
4. Consecutive sentences: one following after the other.
5. Due process: a legal hearing of some type.
6. Felony: a crime punishable by death or state prison.
7. Former jeopardy: previously placed on trial for the same crime, can't be retried.
8. Import: to imply, to signify something.
9. Infraction: an offense not punishable by imprisonment.
10. Justices: judges of appellate courts.
11. Knowingly: conscious of the act done.
12. Magistrate: any trial court or appellate judge.
13. Malice: a wish to injure, vex or annoy.
14. Misdemeanors: all crimes other than felonies and infractions.
15. Negligence: failing to use due care as required by law.
16. Ordinance: a city or county law.
17. Preponderance: majority of evidence, the most.
18. Real property: land, real estate.
19. Unwritten law: common law.
20. Willfully: willingness to do an act, intentional.

TRUE-FALSE QUIZ—CHAPTER 2

After reading this chapter you should be able to correctly answer the following items.

___ 1. No act is a crime unless there is a valid statute declaring it a crime and providing a penalty for its violation.
___ 2. The "unwritten law" is a legal defense to certain crimes involving spousal relationships.
___ 3. Even in the absence of any act or omission, one can still be punished for criminal intent.
___ 4. Foreign words, even those of common usage, may not be included in penal code statutes.
___ 5. Vague and indefinite laws are in violation of the 14th Amendment of the U.S. Constitution.
___ 6. When two laws punish exactly the same act as a crime, and they are in conflict, the latest in time will control.
___ 7. According to Penal Code, Section 4, criminal statutes must be very strictly construed to be legal.
___ 8. The word "willfully," when applied to the intent with which an act is done, requires a specific intent to violate the law.
___ 9. The word "malice" means an intent to do a wrongful act.
___10. Crime is classified into four levels of seriousness by the California Penal Code.
___11. A felony is a crime punishable by death or imprisonment in the state prison.
___12. The maximum punishment for misdemeanors is also applicable to infractions in California.
___13. If one commits a burglary and is sentenced to the county jail, he or she stands convicted of a misdemeanor.

____14. A “wobbler,” unless filed as a misdemeanor or reduced at the preliminary, remains a felony for all purposes until the actual sentencing.
____15. An infraction is not punishable by imprisonment.
____16. A person charged with an infraction is not entitled to a jury trial.
____17. Except as otherwise provided by law, all provisions of law relating to misdemeanors apply to infractions.
____18. When an act or omission is declared by statute to be a public offense, and no penalty is prescribed in any statute, the offense is punishable as a felony.
____19. Except where a different punishment is prescribed by law for a felony, the minimum penalty is one year in state prison, or by fine or both.
____20. Where a defendant is convicted of two or more misdemeanors, either in the same or separate prosecutions, consecutive sentences are valid.
____21. The penalty for petty theft with a prior petty theft conviction is the same as for petty theft with a prior felony conviction.
____22. The “Victim’s Bill of Rights,” provides that evidence which conforms to the U.S. Constitution, may not be excluded even if it does not meet the California Constitution.
____23. The general rule excluding hearsay evidence was not affected by the passage of Proposition 8.
____24. A jury may find a defendant guilty of any offense, the elements of which are included in the offense with which he or she is actually charged.
____25. If a defendant is found not guilty of a murder charge, then later admits his or her guilt, he or she may be retried for the crime.

ESSAY-DISCUSSION ITEMS—CHAPTER 2

After reading this chapter you should be able to correctly answer the following items.

1. In order for an act or omission to be a crime, what two things must exist relative to statute law?
2. Briefly discuss the language requirements in our criminal statutes and the legal effect of vague or indefinite statutes.
3. When two laws punish exactly the same act or omission as crimes and they are in conflict, which one controls or takes precedent?
4. Briefly define the words (a) “corruptly,” (b) “night-time,” and (c) “process,” as used in the Penal Code and as explained in the text.
5. What is the legal difference between a felony and a misdemeanor?
6. What are the two major differences between a misdemeanor and an infraction?
7. Of what classification of crime does a person stand convicted, upon being sentenced to the county jail for burglary?
8. What is the punishment for petty theft with a prior conviction of petty theft?
9. List five of the ten changes brought about by passage of Proposition 8, “Victim’s Bill of Rights,” as given in your text.
10. What is meant by “lesser and included offense?”

TERMINOLOGY QUIZ—CHAPTER 2

Match terms and definitions by writing the number preceding the correct term between the appropriate brackets. Answers may be written on a separate sheet for submission to the instructor at the instructor's direction.

Terms

1. Acquit
2. Booking
3. Bribe
4. Consecutive sentence
5. Due process
6. Felony
7. Former jeopardy
8. Import
9. Infraction
10. Justices
11. Knowingly
12. Magistrate
13. Malice
14. Misdemeanor
15. Negligence
16. Ordinance
17. Preponderance
18. Real property
19. Unwritten law
20. Willfully

Definitions

[ ] Willingness to do an act, intentional
[ ] Judges of appellate courts
[ ] A crime not punishable by imprisonment
[ ] Found not guilty
[ ] Conscious of the act done
[ ] To imply, to signify something
[ ] Any trial court judge
[ ] Recording an arrest, fingerprinting
[ ] Anything of value to illegally influence
[ ] A wish to injure, vex or annoy
[ ] One following after the other
[ ] A legal hearing of some type
[ ] Common law
[ ] A city or county law
[ ] A crime punishable by death or state prison

CHAPTER 3

THE ELEMENTS OF CRIME AND CORPUS DELICTI

3.1 *CORPUS DELICTI*

Corpus delicti means "the total body of the crime." It includes the act or omission and the existence of a criminal agency. It has to do with the rules of evidence which govern proof of the commission of crimes, particularly as concern the "act" element thereof and the commission of the act by human agency. The *corpus delicti*, or "substance of the crime," is applicable to any crime and relates particularly to the "act" element of criminality, i.e., that a certain prohibited act has been committed or result accomplished and that it was committed or accomplished by a criminal human agency.

Crime Elements. As a practical matter, the Penal Code definition of a crime clearly states those essential elements necessary to the commission of that particular crime. The "elements" of a crime can be determined from a careful reading of the statute. For example, in the crime of burglary (PC 459), reference is made to (1) anyone who enters, (2) a certain kind of structure, (3) with intent to commit grand or petty theft or (4) any felony therein. In this case, the certain essential elements to the commission of this crime are reflected by analysis of the code section. The elements of specific crimes will be explained in detail in later chapters.

In addition to the statutory elements, some crimes also contain judicially-implied elements. These "extra" elements will not be found in the statute, but only in case law, and in the published jury instructions known as CALJIC (for "California Jury Instructions Criminal"). For example, the statutory definition of robbery contains only four elements: 1) taking property possessed by another, 2) from the person or presence of the victim, 3) against the victim's will, 4) by means of force or fear (see discussion in Chapter 15).

CALJIC 9.40, however adds two additional elements: 5) the property taken must be of some value, and 6) the taking must be with specific intent to permanently deprive the victim of the property. This jury instruction reflects case law which held that robbery could not be proven without these additional facts. See *People v. Ford*, 60 Cal. 2d 772, and *People v. Coleman*, 8 Cal. App. 3d 722.

Although reference to the code section defining an offense will usually be sufficient to identify all the essential elements, this will not always be the case, so the CALJIC definition should also be consulted.

Would you like to take a look at the lighter side of the law? Go to "Dumb Laws" at **www.dumblaws.com.** You can choose specific states by clicking on "Choose a Page" on your computer screen. This fun site also includes dumb bumper stickers, dumb criminals, dumb warnings, etc.

Proof of *Corpus Delicti.* The prosecution must establish the *corpus delicti* of a crime, and failure to do so is a bar to further prosecution. The amount of proof, however, need not go beyond *prima facie* (on its face, on first view) proof, and the prosecution is said to have a *prima facie* case when evidence in its favor is sufficiently strong for the defendant to be held to answer for it. Because the *corpus* is simply proof of injury, harm or loss caused by criminal agency, the term *corpus delicti* is not synonymous with *elements of the crime.* For example, the *corpus delicti* of all homicides is the same—death by criminal agency—but the *elements* of first degree murder, second degree murder, voluntary manslaughter and involuntary manslaughter are all different.

"There is no requirement of independent evidence of every physical act constituting an element of an offense, so long as there is some slight or prima facie showing of injury, loss or harm by a criminal

A suspect's confession is powerful evidence of guilt, but there must also be independent proof of the *corpus delicti* of the crime. *Courtesy of TLW Stock & Assignment Photography*

agency. The independent proof may be circumstantial and need not be beyond a reasonable doubt, but is sufficient if it permits an inference of criminal conduct, even if a noncriminal explanation is also plausible." (*People v. Alvarez, 27 Cal.4th 1161*)

Many cases have found sufficient evidence of a *corpus*, even though there was no independent proof of any of the elements of the crimes. Examples: *People v. Jennings*, 53 Cal. 3d 334 (sufficient *corpus* of rape where a young woman's body was found unclothed in a remote location—though none of these facts is an element of rape); *People v. Alcala*, 36 Cal. 3d 604 (*corpus* of kidnaping by force or fear, where 12-year-old girl's body was found in a forest after she vanished from a beach—facts that raise a prima facie inference of harm by criminal agency, though they hardly establish every element of kidnap). The concept of "*corpus delicti*" is not the same thing as "elements of the crime".

Circumstantial Evidence. The *corpus delicti* of a crime may be proven solely by circumstantial evidence. Thus, as previously stated, the essential elements of the crime of murder may be established without producing the body of the victim. Similarly, a genuine, unaltered photograph depicting defendants involved in a sex act was held admissible and sufficient to prove the *corpus delicti* of the crime denounced by PC 288 (*People v. Doggett*, 83 Cal. App. 2d 405).

Identity of Perpetrator. The identity of the perpetrator of a criminal offense is not a necessary and essential part of the *corpus delicti*, nor is such necessary to establishing proof of the *corpus delicti*. Thus, in order to prove the *corpus delicti* of burglary, it is necessary to prove that an entry of a structure was made and that it was done with the specific intent of committing a theft or a felony. However, it is not necessary that the identity or name of the person who entered be known to the police.

Confession or Admission of Perpetrator. The law does not permit establishing the *corpus delicti* of a crime based solely on the confession or admission of the accused (*People v. Mehaffey*, 32 Cal. 2d 535). Such proof must be established independently of any statement made by a defendant. If this were not the case, countless individuals could be prosecuted for crimes which they in fact did not commit based merely on their confessions or admissions.

However, if a suspect voluntarily confesses to a crime, the information provided can be used to investigate the matter. Say, for example, that someone legally confesses to a murder and tells where the body is buried. The police may use this information to investigate. If they find the body or otherwise can prove the *corpus delicti*, the subject can be charged with whatever crime can be proved. The suspect's voluntary confession can be used to prove who committed the crime, but not that the crime, in fact, was committed.

Suppose, however, a suspect admits several burglaries, the location of which he cannot recall and the crimes were never reported. The suspect cannot be charged with the crimes unless the *corpus delicti* of each crime can be established independently of the suspect's admissions.

3.2 THE CRIMINAL ACT

Penal Code, Section 20, states that in order to constitute a crime, there must be a unity of act and intent, or criminal negligence. The joint operation of an act and general criminal intent is essential to constitute any crime (*People v. Sanchez*, 35 Cal. 2d 522).

An act is simply defined as "an effect produced through conscious exertion of will." The act varies with each crime, of course, and for that reason it is difficult to define. In some cases it may be a physical or muscular movement, while in others it may be an omission (failure) to act. The act may involve passive participation in crime or activity outside of this state which results in a crime within the state. It could be a series of acts, proximate results, or just the mere doing of something, i.e., the result of some human agency.

For example, in homicide cases the act is the killing of a human being; in larceny it is the taking and carrying away of personal property of another; in arson it is the burning of real or personal property; in rape it is the having of forced sexual intercourse. In each of these cases the act is muscular or physical in character; however, it need not always be, as in the case of omission to act or passively participating in a crime.

Omission to Act. A mere omission to act may be sufficient to complete a crime. Such omissions are generally characteristic of those crimes which involve the failure to perform a duty imposed by law. In many such crimes there is a lack of physical movement on the part of the perpetrator. Examples are: failure to provide a minor child with necessities (PC 270), causing a child to suffer (PC 273a), or contributing to the delinquency of a minor by omitting the performance of a legally imposed duty.

Under certain circumstances, a factual situation may be sufficient to give rise to a legal duty to act for the benefit of another. For example, one who undertakes to render aid to another may not be legally bound to do so, but having commenced such an undertaking, he cannot later abandon such a purpose if the person being aided will suffer further harm as the result of partial performance. Ordinarily, however, the criminal law will recognize a negative act (omission to act) only if the one who has failed to take affirmative action was under a *legal duty*, to do what was not done.

The law holds that there is no distinction between a person acting wrongfully and failing to act where there is a legal duty to act. The latter is just as much manifestation of will as acting positively when there is a duty not to act.

Passive Participation. In some classes of crime, criminal liability may result from passive participation in a criminal act wherein little physical or muscular activity takes place. For example, one who submits to an illegal drug injection is a passive participant in such an act.

The Court held in *People v. Chapman*, 28 NW 896, (Michigan), that the defendant-husband of the victim was not a mere passive onlooker, but a passive participant when he, desiring to obtain a divorce, agreed with one "R" that the latter should persuade the defendant's wife to commit adultery which subsequently resulted in the crime of forcible rape.

Acts Outside the State. An act may take place outside of this state which will result in a crime within the state. PC 497 provides that "Every person who, in another state or country, steals or embezzles the property of another, or receives such property knowing it to have been stolen or embezzled, and brings the same into this state, may be convicted and punished in the same manner as if such larceny, or embezzlement, or receiving, had been committed in this state."

PC 778 reads: "When the commission of a public offense, commenced without the state, is consummated [completed] within its boundaries by a defendant, himself outside the state, through the intervention of an innocent or guilty agent or any other means proceeding directly from said defendant, he is liable to punishment therefor in this state in any competent court within the jurisdictional territory of which the offense is consummated."

On the other hand, an act may take place within this state which is not criminal in nature, but which results in a crime without the state. PC 778a states that: "Whenever a person, with intent to commit a crime, does any act within this state in execution or part execution of such intent, which culminates [results] in the commission of a crime, either within or without this state, the person is punishable for that crime in this state in the same manner as if the same had been committed entirely within this state."

Thus, where defendant sent a box of poisoned candy from San Francisco to a person in Delaware, with intent to cause her death, which it did, the court held that the case could be prosecuted in California for the crime of murder (*People v. Botkin*, 132 Cal. 232).

Also, a person who flees into California in order to avoid prosecution elsewhere for certain sex offenses commits a misdemeanor upon entry into the state (PC 289.5).

Offense From Without State Punishable Within. "Every person, who, being out of this state, causes, aids, advises, or encourages any person to commit a crime within this state, and is afterwards found within this state, is punishable in the same manner as if he had been within this state when he caused, aided, advised or encouraged the commission of such crime [PC 778b]."

Jurisdiction—Offenses Committed Partly in One Jurisdiction and Partly in Another. When a public offense is committed in part in one jurisdictional territory and in part in another, or the acts or effects constituting the offense occur in two or more jurisdictions, the jurisdiction of such offense is in any competent court within *either* jurisdiction (PC 781).

This section applies in cases such as kidnapping, child molesting, or even murder, where the victim is taken from one place to another. It is also applicable in cases where it is difficult to determine when and where the crime began and ended or where there are repeated assaults that occur in more than one city, county, or other jurisdictional area.

Offenses Committed on Boundary of Two or More Jurisdictions. When a public offense is committed on the boundary of two or more jurisdictional territories, or within 500 yards thereof, the jurisdiction of such offense is in any competent court within either jurisdiction (PC 782). As in the instance above, this section is applicable where it is difficult to determine exactly where a crime was committed relative to city, county, or state lines.

Offenses Committed in Multiple Jurisdictions. Multiple rapes or other specified sex crimes against the same victim are prosecutable in any jurisdiction where a violation occurred (PC 784.7). Special circumstance murders and related crimes may be prosecuted in any county having jurisdiction over any charged murder [PC 790(b)].

Act of Possession. A person may be guilty of a crime where his or her act has no immediate effect upon the person or property of another. For example, mere possession of contraband material such as narcotics without prescription, certain firearms, or burglary tools would constitute a violation of the laws prohibiting such materials.

One Act Affecting Several Victims. Though there be but one act or action and one intent but more than one victim of the crime, there are instances in which there are as many crimes committed as there are persons victimized. For example, if one were to shoot and kill a person, and the fatal bullet continued through the first person, inflicting mortal wounds upon a second person, there is but one act resulting in two homicides (*People v. Majors*, 65 Cal. 138).

Similarly, where "A" shoots at "B" but misses and hits "C," there is but one act. However, "A" is guilty of an assault upon "B" and the murder of "C" based on the doctrine of "transferred intent."

Several Acts Resulting in One Offense. There are some offenses which, by their very nature, require that the wrongdoer become involved in several physical acts in order to perpetrate a crime. For example, one may embezzle from his or her employer on several occasions for one common purpose, motive, or design, which may result in one act of grand theft rather than several acts of petty theft (*People v. Willard*, 92 Cal. 482).

3.3 MULTIPLE OFFENSES—PUNISHMENT

Punishment for two offenses arising from the same act is prohibited by the Constitution of the United States and again by the California Constitution, Article 1, Section 13. Also, Penal Code, Section 654, states that "whenever an act or omission could be punished under more than one statute, it is to be punished under the provision imposing the greatest punishment, but may not be punished more than once."

Dual Convictions—Multiple Punishment. While PC 654 prohibits multiple punishment for a single act or omission which may violate more than one statute, it was modified *In re Hayes*, 70 Cal. 2d, 604.

In the *Hayes* case, the defendant was convicted of (1) driving with a suspended license and (2) driving while intoxicated based on the operation of an automobile on one occasion. The Supreme Court ruled that PC 654 prohibits multiple punishment for a single "act or omission which is made punishable" by different statutes, that is, a single *criminal* act or omission. The court said that since the mere act of driving is not made punishable by any statute, it is not the type of act or omission referred to in section 654. The acts made punishable were (1) driving while intoxicated and (2) driving with a suspended license, two separate and distinct *criminal* acts.

Both criminal acts were committed simultaneously and share in common the neutral noncriminal act of driving. This does not render the petitioner's punishment for both crimes in conflict with Penal Code section 654. In effect, the Supreme Court ruled that PC 654 prohibits multiple punishment for a single *criminal* act or omission.

Penal Code, Section 654 precludes multiple punishment, not only where one act is involved, but also in cases where there is a course of conduct which violates more than one statute and comprises an indivisible transaction. For example, where a burglary, robbery, and assault were all incident to and a means of obtaining the victim's possessions, it was immaterial that the burglary was complete before the robbery and the assault. Judgment in such instances must be reversed insofar as it imposes multiple punishment. The court held in this case that all offenses committed by the defendant were "incident to one objective." As was pointed out in *People v. McFarland* (58 Cal. 2d 748), the fact that the burglary was complete in each case before the robbery and the assault is immaterial.

Penal Code, Section 654, prohibits double punishment and not double conviction (see section entitled "Former Jeopardy"). Thus, where a trial court has erroneously imposed double punishment, the Appellate Court eliminated the effect of the judgment only as to the penalty imposed for the lesser offense and permitted the punishment for the most serious offense to stand (*People v. McFarland*, above).

3.4 PROXIMATE CAUSE

Proximate Cause Defined. *Cochran's Law Dictionary*, Police Edition, defines proximate cause as: "that which produces an event and without which the event could not have occurred."

Some causal relationship (proximate cause) must exist between the defendant's act or the act of another in his behalf, and the prohibited result which constitutes the crime. This causal relationship is said to exist when a defendant's act was the proximate cause of the injury inflicted. To be proximate, the defendant's act need be only a contributing cause, as in the case of concurrent acts of two persons acting with a common design.

Generally speaking, it may be said that the defendant in a criminal case is not liable for remote and indirect consequences of his or her acts. He or she is, however, liable for the direct and proximate consequences of his or her acts. Thus, a defendant is criminally liable, assuming the required intent is present, if his act or omission was the proximate cause of the death of the victim in a homicide case. The defendant would also be liable if the injury, which ultimately causes death, was a natural and probable consequence of the defendant's act.

The results intended by the perpetrator are proximate if they, in fact, take place, regardless of

Every member of a gang is criminally liable for the crimes they jointly agree to commit.
Courtesy of CORBIS

time or place. This fact is illustrated in the previously mentioned case where the defendant in California sent a box of poisoned candy to a person in Delaware, who ate the candy and died.

Proximate Cause—Attributed Liability. California courts have recognized three different theories for attributing liability for a homicide that incidentally results during the commission of other criminal activity (such as robbery, burglary, kidnap, etc). These theories are:

1. the felony murder rule,
2. the vicarious liability doctrine, and
3. proximate cause/provocative act liability.

Felony Murder Rule. Under the felony murder rule, all persons aiding and abetting the commission of any felony listed in PC 189 (1st degree murder) are guilty of first degree murder when any one of them kills in furtherance of the common design (*People v. Washington*, 62 Cal. 2d 777, 781-782). The felony murder rule does *not* apply to situations in which the intended felony victim kills a suspect in self-defense, or where a suspect is killed by responding police. It applies *only* if one of the suspects kill in furtherance of the criminal conspiracy.

Vicarious Liability Doctrine. The vicarious liability doctrine holds that where two or more suspects have agreed to kill as part of their plan to carry out their crimes, each of the perpetrators is guilty of murder when any one of them kills (*People v. Antick*, 15 Cal. 3d 79). For example, if a carload of gang members agreed to do a drive-by shooting to kill rival gang members, all of the suspects would be liable for the resulting murder, even though only one of them did the actual killing.

Provocative Act Theory. Under the proximate cause provocative act theory, surviving accomplices can be convicted of murder where the intended victim or police kill one of the accomplices in response to a *provocative act* committed by one of the *surviving* accomplices (*People v. Caldwell*, 36 Cal. 3d 210 and *People v. Gilbert*, 63 Cal. 2d 690). However, if the suspect who committed the provocative act (such as starting a gunfight) is killed by the third party and none of the other suspects committed any such provocative acts themselves, they cannot be convicted of murder for their co-conspirator's death (*In re Joe R.*, 27 Cal. 3d 496).

3.5 CRIMINAL INTENT—HOW MANIFESTED

"In every crime or public offense there must exist a union, or joint operation of act and intent or criminal negligence [PC 20]." Criminal intent is the second of the two elements (first element is the act) necessary to the commission of every offense. Intent is a mental element of the perpetrator, often referred to as *mens rea* or the "guilty mind" of the individual who fosters a criminal intent.

Not all crimes require the same intent. Some crimes, by their very nature, require a particular designated state of mind, such as burglary, larceny (theft), assault, etc. For example, to commit burglary, one must have entered a structure with the *specific intent* to steal or to commit a felony. Entry of a structure without such intent would be insufficient to constitute burglary.

A second example is seen in the crime of theft. Here there must generally exist a specific intent on the part of the perpetrator to *permanently* deprive the owner of his property. Thus, a temporary taking with intent to return the property is not theft. The taking of property in jest or as a practical joke would not constitute theft. Similarly, temporarily depriving one of a motor vehicle (joy riding) is difficult to prove as theft, since the state of mind of the perpetrator is usually not to *permanently* deprive the person of the vehicle.

Intent Defined. Intent may be generally defined as "a design, resolve or determination of the mind" (*Bovier's Law Dictionary*). It is also defined as "the act or fact of intending or purposing; intent, purpose which is formed in the mind;" and similarly, "design, resolve; determination of the mind" (*Cochran's Law Dictionary*, Police Ed.).

Evidence of Intent. PC Section 21(a), states that: "intent or intention is manifested by the circumstances connected with the offense." In view of this section, it is important to note that all persons are presumed capable of committing crime except those listed in Penal Code, Section 26, (persons capable of committing crimes). Further, Penal Code Section 1026, states that during the "guilt phase" of a trial, the defendant ". . . shall be conclusively presumed to have been sane at the time the offense is alleged to have been committed." If he is found guilty, his claim of insanity would then be litigated in the "sanity phase" of the trial.

An unlawful act is presumed to have been done with intent to violate the law. Also, the intent to commit a crime can be inferred from established facts and circumstances (*People v. Ramirez*, 101 Cal. App. 2d 50). Intent to commit a crime may be proven by evidence of surrounding circumstances and inferences drawn from proven facts (*People v. Ross*, 105 Cal. App. 2d 235). In other words, the facts of the case usually "speak for themselves." If a suspect runs up behind a woman in a parking lot, grabs her purse and tries to yank it away, his or her "intent" at that moment is reasonably obvious.

3.6 TYPES OF INTENT

There are generally three types of intent which may be manifested by the perpetrator of a crime and which will accompany the criminal act. They are:

1. general intent,
2. specific intent and
3. constructive or transferred intent.

1. General Intent Defined. General intent is the type of intent which is inferred from the mere doing of an act, or failure to act, when prohibited or commanded by law. General intent may even exist in the presence of a belief that the act is right and lawful.

When a person acts without justification or excuse and commits an act which is prohibited as a crime, his intention to commit the act constitutes criminal intent. In such a case, the existence of the criminal intent is presumed from the commission of the act itself.

The intent which is necessary to the commission of a crime does not necessarily involve an intention to do a known criminal act. Thus, where an act is prohibited by law, the criminal intent necessary to violate that law is nothing more than an intention to do the act, regardless whether the wrongdoer knows that it is criminal. A general criminal intent is sufficient in all cases in which a specific or other particular intent or mental element is not required by the law defining the crime.

Some crimes, by their very nature, are perpetrated by the intentional doing of an act. In these cases, there is no necessity of proving the actual intent to commit the crime. General intent statutes enacted under the police power of the state are good examples of this rule of law (*People v. Heal*, 40 Cal. App. 2d 115). Violations of restaurant sanitation laws are an example of "police power" laws.

The law presumes that persons intend the necessary and direct consequences of their acts. Thus, if "X" beats "Y" with a hammer and kills him, "X" is presumed to have intended to kill "Y." The intentional doing of an act expressly prohibited by statute constitutes the offense denounced by the law regardless of good motive or ignorance of criminal character (*People v. Reznick*, 75 Cal. App. 2d 832). In addition, a person is presumed to intend to do things which he does, and especially so when they are done in the commission of a crime, excepting where the intent must be proved as a necessary element, such as in specific intent cases (*People v. Head*, 9 Cal. App. 2d 647). But where the act becomes criminal only when performed with a particular (specific) intent, such intent must be alleged and proven (*People v. Pineda*, 41 Cal. App. 2d 100).

2. Specific Intent Defined. When a crime consists not merely in doing the act, but in doing it with a specific intent, the existence of that intent is an essential element of the crime. The existence of criminal intent is not presumed from the commission of the act, but the specific intent must be proven as an independent factor.

Depending on the particular wording of a criminal statute, a crime may be so defined as to require a designated state of mind necessary when committing an act. Usually such crimes are written in such a manner as to indicate the specific intent necessary by the inclusion of descriptive words such as "for the purpose of obtaining ransom," "with intent to defraud," etc.

Additionally, most crimes, with the exception of the theft statute, will include the phrase "with intent" to signify the necessity of proving specific intent as an independent factor. Thus, in the crime of burglary, entering a structure with specific intent to commit theft or any felony, is a necessary element to the crime.

Certain penal statutes provide for the "assault with intent to commit a crime" (e.g. sodomy, rape, robbery, mayhem, etc.), or the "attempt to commit a crime." In both cases, proving specific intent would be necessary in an assault to commit or an attempt to commit such crimes. Thus, in the crime of assault with intent to commit rape (PC 220), evidence must show that the assault was committed with the intent (specifically) to rape the victim. Similarly, an attempt to commit a crime requires the existence of a specific intent to commit the crime attempted (*People v. Gallardo*, 41 Cal. 2d 57).

3. Transferred (Constructive) Intent. Transferred intent, also referred to as constructive intent, involves crediting liability to the perpetrator for the *unintended* consequences of his acts. Thus, where a person, engaged in an unlawful act, commits another unlawful act, unintended by him, the intent to commit the first act is carried over to the act actually committed. This is called "transferred" or "constructive" intent. Thus, it is not essential to the commission of a crime, that the wrongdoer needs to commit the very act intended by him. Where several persons cooperate to rape another, and while accomplishing this purpose the victim is killed, all are guilty of homicide. This is true even though the killing is done unintentionally and without malice.

Where one intends to assault or kill a certain person, and by mistake or inadvertence assaults or kills another, it is nevertheless a crime. The intent is transferred from the party who was the intended victim to the other party (*People v. Neal*, 97 Cal. App. 2d 668). Although the doctrine of transferred intent does not apply to the crime of attempted murder, evidence of concurrent intent to kill is sufficient to support attempted murder convictions of everyone in the "kill zone" (*People v. Bland, 28 Cal.4th 313*). In a manner of speaking, the law treats as intentional all consequences of a criminal act due to that form of negligence which is distinguished as recklessness.

3.7 HOW INTENT IS PROVED

Criminal intent (general, specific and transferred) may be proven by circumstantial evidence and may be inferred from the manner in which the unlawful act was committed (*People v. Hunt*, 59 Cal. 430). Intent (all three types) may also be proved by direct evidence, such as by words spoken by the defendant or by the circumstances surrounding the crime. The accused may have told someone of his or her intentions before committing the crime. Also, the suspect may have made a statement such as "this is a stick-up" during the commission of the crime. Words spoken by the accused during an assault may very well reveal his intent, i.e., rape, mayhem, sodomy, etc. For the purpose of proving intent, the conduct of the defendant before, during, and after the offense is admissible to prove intent (*People v. Welsh*, 63 Cal. 167).

3.8 INTENT IN NEGLIGENCE CASES

In crimes which consist of negligence to observe proper care in performing an act, or in culpable (wrongful) failure to perform a duty, criminal intent consists in the state of mind which necessarily accompanies the negligent act or culpable omission. To constitute criminal negligence, one must enter into an act with some appreciable measure of wantonness or flagrant or reckless disregard of the safety of others or willful indifference (*People v. Drigas*, 111 Cal. App. 42).

In some crimes the criminal act or omission to act consists of a mere neglect to observe proper caution in the performance of an otherwise lawful act, or failure to perform a legally imposed duty. Traffic violations and child neglect cases are graphic examples. In these cases criminal intent is proved by the obvious lack of due care, caution, or circumspection which, in essence, amounts to criminal negligence. It will be noted that this concept of intent closely resembles that of general intent referred to in the preceding paragraphs.

Criminal Negligence. Criminal negligence consists in reckless or indifferent omission to do what a reasonable and prudent person would do or not do under the same or similar circumstances. Criminal negligence is something beyond "ordinary" negligence. It amount to "gross" or a "culpable" (wrongful) departure from the required standard of care. Criminal negligence is conduct so aggravated or reckless that it shows indifference to the consequences and a disregard for human life (*People v. Peabody*, 46 Cal. App. 43).

There are generally five factors to consider in order to find intent from criminal negligence:

1. Defendant must have a legal duty (or contractual relationship) toward a person, group, or society in general.
2. Defendant must know, or reasonably should know that he has a legal duty and that there is a present existing danger.
3. There must be an apparent ability upon the part of the defendant to perform the legally imposed duty.
4. It must be shown that the defendant failed to perform the duty which is legally imposed.
5. It must appear that the defendant's negligent act or omission was the cause of the injury sustained.

Example: An operator of a motor vehicle who drove in excess of fifty miles per hour in a residential area and killed a pedestrian whom he did not see was guilty of "gross negligence" and of man-

A previous conviction for DUI can be used to prove implied malice in a subsequent second-degree murder prosecution from a later DUI resulting in death. *Courtesy of PhotoDisc/Getty Images*

slaughter (*People v. Flores*, 83 Cal. App. 2d 11). In this case Flores had a legal duty to drive within the speed limit. A lack of "due caution and circumspection," referred to in PC 192 (manslaughter) places a criminal responsibility on a defendant who acts without due caution and circumspection and is equivalent to "criminal negligence" (*People v. Hurley*, 13 Cal. App. 2d 208).

Malice. The term "malice" has been used synonymously with general intent and is usually regarded as indicating a mental condition more intent on harm or injury than is involved in general intent to commit a crime. Malice means a wrongful act done intentionally without justification or excuse. It involves a disposition to injure another, a willful disregard of the rights or safety of others. Malice is most often used in connection with particular crimes such as murder, malicious mischief, extortion, malicious prosecution, assault with caustic chemicals, and other similar crimes.

Malice—Express and Implied. Malice is *express* when there is manifested a deliberate intention unlawfully to take away the life of a fellow creature. Malice is *implied* when no considerable provocation appears, or when the circumstances attending the killing show an abandoned and malignant heart.

When it is shown that the killing resulted from the intentional doing of an act with express or implied malice, as defined above, no other mental state need be shown to establish the mental state of "malice aforethought."

Malice in Vehicular Murder. If a person drives with such wantonness and conscious disregard for life as to support a finding of *implied malice*, or if he drives under facts which show *express malice*, he can be charged with murder (*In re Watson*, 30 Cal. 3d 290).

Malice v. Criminal Negligence. Malice requires something more than criminal negligence. It requires a greater kind of social harm than is involved in criminal negligence and yet does not require an actual intent to cause the resulting harm. In one case the courts stated that "malice may be said to exist [in a legal sense], whenever there has been a wrongful or intentional killing of another without lawful excuse or mitigating circumstances [*People v. Taylor*, 36 Cal. 255]."

The state of mind required for malice, while less than an actual intent to cause the wrongful act, includes a vicious or callous disregard of the likelihood of some harm resulting from what is being done. It is this viciousness or callousness which distinguishes malice from criminal negligence. Where a defendant, having provoked and instigated a fist fight, subsequently draws and uses a knife on his adversary, such evidence will show malice with an intent to kill (*People v. Hoover*, 107 Cal. App. 635).

3.9 MOTIVE AND INTENT DISTINGUISHED

Motive is never indispensable to a crime or criminal prosecution, nor is it an essential element of a crime. Motive is the desire or inducement which incites or stimulates a person to do an act, as contrasted with intent, which is the purpose or resolve to do an act. A bad motive will not necessarily make an act a crime, nor will a good motive prevent an act from being a crime.

For example, one may administer a lethal drug to a terminal cancer patient to hasten death and to relieve pain and suffering. While the motive in the eyes of some persons may be good, the act itself is no less criminal homicide. Similarly, a parent who neglects to provide medical aid for a dependent child, in violation of a criminal statute, cannot thereafter excuse himself or herself on the ground that he or she was actuated in such refusal by religious motives.

The law does not seek to punish a bad motive, but only the criminal acts that result from such a motive. Thus, unless one's illicit motive actually results in a criminal act, there is no crime.

Motive and Intent. While motive is not a necessary element of a crime, it may help to prove the intent necessary to the consummation of a crime. For example, in murder, the emotional urge of the perpetrator may not only aid in his identification, but may assist greatly in establishing the purpose or intent of his act. Or, in the crime of embezzlement, one's reason or moving cause (motive) for stealing from his employer, such as an overdue gambling debt, will help in proving the specific intent (fraudulent appropriation) necessary to the commission of the crime of embezzlement.

Motive and ***Corpus Delicti***. As stated previously, motive is not part of the *corpus delicti* of any crime and need not be proved (*People v. Larrios*, 220 Cal. 236). Evidence of motive, however, is quite often valuable in removing doubt in the jury's collective mind. Motive may either be shown by direct testimony or it may be inferred from the facts surrounding the act. Motive, in such cases, becomes a circumstance to be considered by the court or jury. By the same token, absence of motive may be a circumstance in favor of the accused and can be given such weight as the jury deems proper. Evidence of motive is admissible and may be used:

1. To show the intent with which the act was committed (*People v. Miller*, 121 Cal. 343).
2. To rebut a claim of self-defense (*People v. Brown*, 130 Cal. 591).
3. To rebut a claim of insanity by showing the rational nature of defendant's actions (*People v. Donlan*, 135 Cal. 489).
4. To remove doubt as to the identity of the perpetrator (*People v. Wright*, 144 Cal. 161).
5. To help determine the degree of the crime (*People v. Soeder*, 150 Cal. 12).
6. To help determine the issue of justification or excusability of the act (*People v. Soeder*, 150 Cal. 12).

3.10 INTOXICATION AS AFFECTING INTENT

In California, drunkenness, whether voluntary or involuntary, is never an excuse for the commission of a crime. However, in considering the effect upon the guilt of a defendant the law makes a distinction between intoxication which is voluntary, and that which is involuntary. Both voluntary and involuntary intoxication are explained in more detail below.

Voluntary Intoxication—PC 22. Voluntary intoxication includes the voluntary ingestion, injection, or taking by any other means of any intoxicating liquor, drug, or other substance.

Intoxication of a person is voluntary if it results from his willing use of any intoxicating liquor, drug or other substance, knowing that it is capable of an intoxicating effect or when he willingly assumes the risk of that effect (*People v. Wyatt*, 22 Cal. App. 3d 671). Voluntary intoxication from drugs or alcohol, is not grounds for exemption from criminal responsibility. Exceptions are (a) where intoxication has produced insanity, in which case the exemption is based on insanity and not on intoxication, and (b) where a specific intent is essential to constitute the crime, in which case the fact of intoxication may negate its existence.

Evidence of voluntary intoxication shall not be admitted to negate the capacity to form any mental states for the crimes charged, including, but not limited to (1) purpose, (2) intent, (3) knowledge, (4) premeditation, (5) deliberation, or (6) malice aforethought, with which the accused committed the act.

Evidence of voluntary intoxication is admissible solely on the issue of whether or not the defendant actually formed a required specific intent, or, when charged with murder, whether the defendant premeditated, deliberated, or harbored express malice aforethought.

Intoxication and Intent. While drunkenness itself is not an excuse for committing crime, it may be a defense when a particular purpose, or intent constitutes a necessary element of the *corpus delicti* of the crime. If the defendant was in such an intoxicated state that he did not form that requisite state of mind necessary to the commission of the crime, such could be a defense. Thus, in the case of burglary, where specific intent is a part of the *corpus delicti*, one who was in such an intoxicated state that he did not form the specific intent could raise a defense to the crime based on inability to form the specific intent necessary.

When specific intent is an element of a crime, it is a matter for the jury to determine whether defendant was so intoxicated that he did, or did not, form a criminal intent (*People v. Sutton*, 17 Cal. App. 2d, 561).

Involuntary Intoxication. Intoxication is said to be involuntary when a person does not willingly and knowingly consume intoxicants, but is either fraudulently induced to partake of intoxicants, or does so in such a manner that he is not aware of such a fact. Where a person becomes involuntarily intoxicated, the law recognizes the fact that such a person cannot be held criminally responsible for his acts. Rather, he is placed in the category of those who, under Penal Code Section 26, are incapable of committing crimes because they are not fully conscious thereof.

However, depending on the extent or degree of intoxication, a person who is involuntarily intoxicated may, or may not, have the ability to realize what he is doing. In such cases, the degree of intoxication is a question of fact for the judge or jury to decide.

3.11 DIMINISHED CAPACITY

The defense of "diminished capacity" was abolished by passage of Proposition 8. Defendants utilizing this defense in the past maintained that due to intoxication, trauma, mental illness, or the effect of too much blood sugar on the brain, they did not have the capacity to form the necessary criminal intent to commit the crime of which they were accused.

PC 25(a) abolished the defense of diminished capacity in any criminal action and any juvenile court proceeding as it relates to capacity to form the particular purpose, intent, motive, malice aforethought, knowledge, or other mental state required for the commission of crime.

Evidence of diminished capacity or of a mental disorder may still be considered by the court, but only at the time of sentencing or other disposition or commitment after the issue of guilt or innocence has already been determined (PC 25(c)).

STUDENT REVIEW

TERMINOLOGY DEFINED—CHAPTER 3

Please see Terminology Quiz at the end of this chapter.

1. Abet: encourage or assist another in committing a crime.
2. Accessory: aiding or concealing a felon after the crime.
3. Accomplice: one who aids a principal in committing a crime.
4. Concurrent: at the same time, e.g., concurrent sentences.
5. Confession: statement including acknowledgment of guilt, including an admission of every element of the crime.
6. Constructive (transferred) intent: liability for unintended consequences of an act.
7. Consummated: completed, accomplished.
8. Crime: a public offense for which punishment is provided.
9. Embezzlement: theft by one to whom property is entrusted.
10. Extrajudicial: outside the court.
11. Intent: mental purpose of, or resolve to do an act.
12. *Mens rea*: a guilty mind or wrongful purpose.
13. Motive: reason for or moving cause.
14. Omission: failure to act when required by law.
15. Perpetrator: active participant or person responsible.
16. *Prima facie*: valid on its face, literally, "first face."
17. Principal: anyone involved in the initial commission of a crime.
18. Proximate cause: direct or contributing cause.
19. Specific intent: a particular mental purpose.
20. Theft: stealing with intent to permanently deprive.

TRUE-FALSE QUIZ—CHAPTER 3

After reading this chapter, you should be able to correctly answer the following items.

___ 1. Before a defendant can be convicted of a crime, the prosecution must first establish the *corpus delicti* of the offense.

___ 2. A defendant may be convicted solely on the basis of a confession without first establishing the *corpus delicti* by independent evidence.

___ 3. In order for conduct to constitute a crime, there must be a unity of act and intent or criminal negligence.

___ 4. A person can legally be found guilty of theft if he intended to steal another's property, but accidentally took his own.

___ 5. In some cases a mere omission to act may constitute a crime.

___ 6. An act may take place outside this state which will result in a crime within this state.

___ 7. Punishment for two offenses arising from the same criminal act is prohibited by the U.S. and State Constitutions.

___ 8. A proximate cause need not exist between the defendant's act and the result which constitutes a crime.

___ 9. A person who intentionally commits an unlawful act, and inflicts unforeseen injury on another, is criminally liable for such injury.

___10. The terms "specific intent" and "constructive intent" are synonymous.

___11. General intent is that type which is presumed from the mere doing of an act prohibited by law.

___12. The law presumes that a person intends the necessary and direct consequences of his acts.

___13. Burglary is a good example of a crime which requires constructive intent.
___14. Even though no criminal intent is present, one may still be guilty of a crime if criminal negligence is present.
___15. Motive is an essential part of the *corpus delicti* of a crime.

ESSAY-DISCUSSION ITEMS—CHAPTER 3

After reading this chapter, you should be able to answer the following items.

1. What is the prosecution's responsibility relative to the *corpus delicti* in obtaining a conviction for any crime?
2. Can a *corpus delicti* be proven by a confession or admission of a defendant? Briefly explain.
3. A "unity" between what factors must exist in order to constitute a crime?
4. Give a brief example of omission to act as it constitutes a crime.
5. May one be charged and convicted of several crimes for one criminal act? Explain.
6. Briefly explain "proximate cause" and its importance to a defendant's criminal act.
7. Briefly explain the "felony-murder rule" as discussed in your text.
8. Define "intent" and describe the types of intent which must exist to constitute a crime.
9. What is meant by the term "criminal negligence" and what is its relationship to intent?
10. Briefly explain how intent may be proven and give a short example.
11. Give an example of a crime which involves each of the types of intent.
12. List three of the five elements to consider in order to find intent in cases involving criminal negligence.
13. Briefly distinguish between motive and intent.
14. Under what circumstances, if any, is voluntary intoxication an excuse for committing a crime?

TERMINOLOGY QUIZ—CHAPTER 3

Match terms and definitions by writing the number preceding the correct term between the appropriate brackets.

Terms	*Definitions*
1. Abet	[ ] Outside of court
2. Accessory	[ ] Aiding a felon after the crime
3. Accomplice	[ ] One who aids a principal in a crime
4. Concurrent	[ ] Direct or contributing cause
5. Confession	[ ] A particular mental purpose in mind
6. Constructive intent	[ ] Theft by one to whom property entrusted
7. Consummated	[ ] Completed, accomplished
8. Crime	[ ] Reason for or moving cause
9. Embezzlement	[ ] Statement acknowledging guilt
10. Extrajudicial	[ ] Valid on its face
11. Intent	[ ] Liability for unintended consequences
12. Mens rea	[ ] Mental purpose or resolve to do an act
13. Motive	[ ] Failure to act, especially when required
14. Omission	[ ] Active participant or person responsible
15. Perpetrator	[ ] A guilty mind or wrongful purpose
16. Prima facie	
17. Principal	
18. Proximate cause	
19. Specific intent	
20. Theft	

CHAPTER 4

CAPACITY TO COMMIT CRIME—INSANITY DEFENSE

4.1 PERSONS CAPABLE OF COMMITTING CRIME

Penal Code Section 26, states that: "All persons are capable of committing crimes except those belonging to the following classes:

1. Children under the age of fourteen, in the absence of clear proof that at the time of committing the act charged against them, they knew its wrongfulness.
2. Persons who are mentally incapacitated.
3. Persons who committed the act or made the omission charged under an ignorance or mistake of fact, which disproves any criminal intent.
4. Persons who committed the act charged without being conscious thereof.
5. Persons who committed the act or made the omission charged through misfortune or by accident, when it appears that there was no evil design, intention, or culpable [wrongful] negligence.
6. Persons (unless the crime be punishable with death) who committed the act or made the omission charged under threats or menaces sufficient to show that they had reasonable cause to and did believe their lives would be endangered if they refused."

Theory of Criminal Responsibility. The law assumes capacity upon the part of all persons, except those in certain exempted classes named above, to comply with the standards of conduct set by the criminal law. Criminal responsibility simply means liability to legal punishment. In certain situations the law exempts persons from criminal responsibility who are not entirely blameless, but who, by reason of circumstances beyond their control, are not sufficiently blameworthy to be punished.

4.2 CHILDREN UNDER AGE FOURTEEN

The common law rule regarding the criminal responsibility of children and the fact that they are conclusively presumed to be mentally incapable of committing any crime, is completely nonexistent in this state. The age referred to in the California statute (under 14 years) refers to chronological and not mental age.

All persons in this state who are under eighteen years of age are subject to the provisions of the juvenile court law specifically, and penal law generally. The primary jurisdiction for criminal cases involving persons under the age of eighteen years (juveniles) rests entirely with the juvenile court. It is highly unlikely that a juvenile under the age of even sixteen years, who has committed a crime less than a felony, would ever be subject to the formal adversarial judicial proceedings which are reserved for adults. This is not to say that children under eighteen years are not given rights equal to adults. On the contrary, the Supreme Court, particularly in the case of *In re Gault*, spells out the fact that juveniles are to have many of the same inherent constitutional rights as their elders (juveniles have no right to bail).

Status of Juveniles. Juveniles are not considered to have committed crime, but rather have a unique status of criminality which is euphemistically called "juvenile delinquency." As previously stated, the juvenile court has primary jurisdiction in this state in cases involving youthful offenders under eighteen years of age. The juvenile court may, as a discretionary matter, find a juvenile unfit for juvenile court in the case of any juvenile who is at least sixteen years of age (fourteen in some cases) and who committed what would have amounted to a serious felony had the same offense been committed by an adult. Thus, it can be seen that the provision of PC 26.1, relating to children under fourteen years, is more applicable to juvenile court proceedings than to the adult criminal court process.

For more information on juvenile crime, go to the National Criminal Justice Reference Services (NCJRS) Web Site at: **http://virlib.ncjrs.org/JuvenileJustice.asp.** Select (click on) "Juvenile Justice" on the left of your computer screen. Next, select topics of interest under Juvenile Justice. You must have Acrobat Reader installed on your computer to read PDF Files; otherwise click on HTML or ASCII files.

Capacity to Commit Crime. The question of the capacity of a minor under fourteen to commit a crime was the subject of a California Supreme Court opinion in *In re Gladys R.*, 1 Cal. 3d 855. Twelve-year-old Gladys had been charged in a juvenile court petition with violating PC 647a (child annoyance). The juvenile court judge had sustained the petition after hearing, but no showing had been made that Gladys had understood the wrongfulness of her act at the time she committed it.

Knowledge of Wrongfulness of Act. On appeal, the Supreme Court reversed the wardship finding and held that whenever a juvenile court conducts a 602 hearing involving conduct by a minor under fourteen years of age, the court should require evidence that the minor had an appreciation of the wrongfulness of her conduct at the time the offense was committed.

Before a juvenile offender can be held accountable, it must be shown that he or she knew the wrongfulness of his or her illegal conduct. *Courtesy of John Neubauer/PhotoEdit*

This decision suggests that more extensive questioning would have created a stronger court case. It also points out that in cases of minors under fourteen, clear proof must be shown that at the time of the offense, the youngster knew the wrongfulness of the act. Relevant areas of inquiry would include the minor's age, intelligence, education, experience and prior police contacts. In addition, questioning the minor's parents, teachers and friends would possibly produce evidence helpful in proving the question. It should be noted that the same factors listed above are relevant in proving a *Miranda* waiver for a minor of any age.

4.3 MENTALLY INCAPACITATED

A person who is "mentally incapacitated" is defined as one who is virtually without mentality—one who is without understanding. This defense is clearly separated from that of an insanity plea and represents the defendant's mental status from birth. Such a person is said to be incapable of appreciating the character and significance of his or her acts. The mentally incapacitated, as characterized by the Binet intelligence classification, appears lowest on the scale, having been said to possess an I.Q. of from ten to twenty-four. Mental retardation does not necessarily come within the purview of this defense unless it can be clearly shown that the defendant was incapable of knowing the wrongfulness of his or her acts.

4.4 IGNORANCE OR MISTAKE OF FACT

One who honestly and mistakenly commits or omits an act which would ordinarily result in a crime were it not for the lack of a criminal intent, may usually introduce a defense under paragraph 3, of PC 26. This must, however, be an honest and reasonable mistake of fact, which is a question for the judge or jury to resolve.

For example, the California Appellate Court held in a case of unlawful sexual intercourse (PC 261.5), that such crime is defensible when criminal intent is lacking. The case involved sexual intercourse between an eighteen year old male and a female seventeen years and some months of age. She voluntarily engaged in the act with the defendant. The Appellate Court held that it was reversible error to refuse to permit defendant to present evidence showing that he had a good faith reasonable belief that the female was eighteen years of age or more at the time (*People v. Hernandez*, 61 Cal. 2d, 529). The conviction was reversed.

In the *Hernandez* case, the court said, however, that criminal intent would exist in cases where the perpetrator proceeds with utter disregard of, or without any grounds for, a belief that the female has reached the age of consent.

Ignorance of the Law. While ignorance of the law is no defense to a criminal prosecution, a penalty may be avoided upon proof of ignorance or mistake of fact (*People v. McLaughlin*, 111 Cal. App. 2d 781). However, where one does an unlawful act voluntarily and willfully, he is presumed to have intended what he did as well as all natural, probable, and usual consequences of such act (*People v. Wade*, 71 Cal. App. 2d 646).

One cannot claim a defense of mistake of fact where his immediate act constitutes the requisites of crime (i.e., act and intent or criminal negligence), which proximately results in additional harm to others. Thus, setting fire to a home to defraud the insurer wherein homicide is committed inadvertently is nonetheless murder. Or, an officer using hollow-point bullets, in violation of departmental orders, who inadvertently shoots a bystander while seeking to arrest a fleeing felon, could be guilty of manslaughter if the innocent victim should die.

4.5 UNCONSCIOUSNESS OF ACT

One may present a defense to his acts under the provision of PC 26, paragraph 4, where he can show that such acts were not voluntarily done by him, but were caused by an irrational response of which he was unconscious. Such a defense has no reference to insanity or mental disease, but relates to those cases in which there is no functioning of conscious mind and the person's acts are controlled solely by the subconscious mind (*People v. Denningham*, 82 Cal. App. 2d 119).

The testimony of a medical doctor may sometimes be necessary for the defendant to meet his burden of proving himself unconscious of a criminal act. *Courtesy of AP/Wide World Photos*

Unconscious Act Defined. An unconscious act applies to persons who are not conscious of acting. Examples are: performing acts while asleep or while suffering from a delirium of fever or because of an attack of epilepsy, a blow on the head, the involuntary taking of drugs, the involuntary consumption of intoxicating liquor, or any similar cause. Unconsciousness of an act does not require that a person be incapable of movement (*People v. Alexander*, 182 Cal. App. 2d 281).

Involuntary Intoxication. It is apparent that in cases where a person is subjected to involuntary intoxication without being conscious thereof, such a person might utilize this defense.

Burden of Proof. The burden is on the defendant to prove his unconscious state, through medical testimony if necessary (*People v. Coston*, 82 Cal. App. 2d 23).

Voluntary Intoxication. Unconsciousness caused by voluntary intoxication is not a defense when a crime requires only a general criminal intent (*People v. Conley*, 64 Cal. App. 321).

Absence of Free Will. An act done in the absence of the will is not any more the behavior of the actor than is an act done contrary to his will (*People v. Freeman*, 61 Cal. App. 2d 110). PC 26, paragraph 4, does not refer to cases of unsound mind, but only to cases of persons of sound mind who suffer from some force that leaves their acts without choice or self will (*People v. Hardy*, 33 Cal. 2d 52).

4.6 ACCIDENT AND MISFORTUNE

A defense under PC 26, paragraph 5, is based upon the absolute lack of the requisites of a crime, i.e., a lack of criminal act, intent, negligence, or evil design on the part of the defendant. Such a defense is often offered in cases of homicide, either excusable or justifiable. For example, if a person were to drive a car within the speed limit, and a child runs into the path of the vehicle in pursuit of a ball, the death of such child would have been unintentional, with no evil design on the part of the driver, assuming that the vehicle was operationally sound and there was no negligence.

However, in the same case, if the driver was traveling at a high rate of speed, driving recklessly or under the influence of a drug or intoxicant, such a defense could obviously not be used.

The majority of cases in which "accident and misfortune" have been used as a defense generally have to do with bodily injury or homicide. The killing of a human being is excusable and not unlawful when committed in doing any lawful act by lawful means and without any unlawful intent.

Examples of such include (1) lawfully correcting a child who, following a mild swat, ran and was fatally injured falling down stairs (*People v. Forbs*, 62 Cal. 2d 847); (2) in defending oneself from an unprovoked attack, where a single blow to an assailant's chin causes him to fall back against a sharp object which causes his death (no undue advantage or deadly weapon was used). Excusable homicide is discussed in detail in text Section 11.10.

4.7 CRIMES COMMITTED UNDER THREATS

When a person is forced to commit a crime because of threats or menaces sufficient to show that such person had reasonable cause to, and did believe their life would be endangered if they refused, they may be able to use the defense provided by PC 26, paragraph 6.

Thus, where one forces another to rob a liquor store with an unloaded gun by threatening to shoot the perpetrator if he fails to comply, the innocent perpetrator who committed the crime under threat of certain death would not be responsible for the commission of such a crime. Threats of future danger of loss of life is no defense. The danger must be real and immediate (*People v. Otis*, 174 Cal. App. 2d 119).

On the other hand, if "A" threatens to kill "B" if the latter fails to commit a homicide upon "C," this defense is not applicable. Penal Code 26, paragraph 6, does not apply to the commission of capital (death penalty) crimes. In the commission of any crime, evidence as to whether a person was coerced and forced to assist the perpetrator due to fear for their life, and whether such person resisted such coercion, is a question of fact for the jury to resolve (*People v. Ellis*, 137 Cal. App. 2d 408).

Where the crime committed is punishable by the death penalty, no amount of threats, coercion, or duress will relieve a person who cooperates in the commission of the offense (*People v. Petro*, 13 Cal. App. 2d 245).

4.8 INSANITY AS A DEFENSE

The purpose of a legal test for insanity is to identify those persons who, owing to mental illness, should not be held criminally responsible and so punished for their crime. The question, then, is what constitutes insanity?

Insanity Defined—PC 25(b). Under Proposition 8, the test for legal insanity is now whether a criminal defendant proves by a preponderance (greater weight or majority) of the evidence that he or she was incapable (1) of knowing or understanding the nature and quality of his or her act, and (2) of distinguishing right from wrong at the time of the commission of the offense.

M'Naghten Test Restored. Essentially, Proposition 8 reinstates the traditional M'Naghten Rule on insanity (often referred to as the "right-wrong" test). The M'Naghten Rule was in effect since first adopted by the California Supreme Court in 1864, until overturned by the California Supreme Court in 1978 in *People v. Drew*, (22 Cal. 3d 333).

Current Insanity Test. The M'Naghten test for insanity in California now requires the defendant to clearly prove by a preponderance of evidence that at the time of committing the act, the defendant (1) was laboring under such a defect of reason as not to know the nature and quality of his or her act; or (2) if the defendant did know it, that he or she did not know that what they were doing was wrong. This, in essence, is the M'Naghten "right-wrong" rule.

Burden of Proof. Insanity is a *defense* to crime. The law presumes every person to be sane and free from mental illness. This means the burden of proof is on the defendant. The accused person must prove by a preponderance of the evidence that he or she was incapable of knowing or understanding the nature and quality of his or her act and of distinguishing right from wrong at the time of the commission of the offense (PC 25(c)). It is the defendant's responsibility to prove an inability to distinguish "right from wrong" because of some form of mental disorder (*People v. Kelly*, 10 Cal. 3d 565).

Temporary Insanity. Legal insanity of a short duration (temporary insanity) if existing at the time of the commission of the offense, is as fully recognized as a defense as that of insanity for a longer duration. For drug intoxication to be legal insanity, however, it must be "settled insanity" and not merely a temporary mental condition produced by the recent use of intoxicants (*People v. Kelly*, above). A defense of insanity cannot be based solely on a personality or adjustment disorder, seizure disorder, or addiction to or abuse of intoxicants (PC 25.5).

STUDENT REVIEW

TERMINOLOGY DEFINED—CHAPTER 4

Please see the Terminology Quiz at the end of this chapter.

1. Abortion: procuring or causing miscarriage, may be legal or illegal.
2. Accusation: any complaint, indictment, or information.
3. Admission: statement by accused, which tends to connect him to the crime, but which falls short of a confession.
4. Adultery: sexual relations with married person, not one's spouse.
5. Affidavit: a sworn declaration in writing.
6. Affirmation: declaration by witness that he will speak truthfully.
7. Arraignment: court appearance, defendant advised of charges and rights.
8. Arrest: taking a person into custody in a manner authorized by law.
9. Asportation: movement of things from one place to another as in theft.
10. Assault: an unlawful attempt to inflict injury or force on another.
11. Attempt: a "try" to commit a crime, frequently punishable as a crime.
12. Capital crime: one punishable by death.
13. Contradistinction: by contrast, having opposite qualities.
14. Chronological age: actual age in years since birth.
15. Imminent: immediate, without delay.
16. Insanity: incapable of knowing right from wrong.
17. Interpose: to put forth, to place between.
18. Prosecutrix: female victim, especially in rape cases.
19. Requisites: necessary requirements or conditions.
20. Subornation: procuring another to commit a crime.

TRUE-FALSE QUIZ—CHAPTER 4

After reading this chapter, you should be able to correctly answer the following items.

___ 1. Criminal responsibility means liability to legal punishment.
___ 2. In certain instances the law exempts persons from punishment even though they are not entirely blameless.
___ 3. In all cases, children under fourteen years are held incapable of committing a crime in California.
___ 4. The Supreme Court has held that most constitutional rights do not apply to juvenile proceedings.
___ 5. A child under fourteen can be convicted of a crime only if it can be proven he knew the wrongfulness of his act.
___ 6. A person who is "mentally incapacitated" is legally defined as one whose mental age does not match his chronological age.
___ 7. In California, the test of insanity is based on the M'Naghten Rule.
___ 8. The burden of proof is on the defendant if insanity is his defense.
___ 9. A defense of "mistake of fact" is a question for a jury to decide (if a jury trial).
___10. Generally, criminal intent is missing in a true "mistake of fact" defense.
___11. When one does an unlawful act involuntarily and willfully, he is presumed to have intended all natural, probable, and usual consequences of such an act.
___12. Unconsciousness caused by voluntary intoxication is not a defense for crimes requiring only general intent.

___13. Irresistible and uncontrollable impulses and "moral insanity" constitute defenses to crime in California.
___14. The defense that one committed a crime under imminent threat of great bodily harm is applicable to misdemeanors only.
___15. Where a crime is punishable by the death penalty, no amount of threats, coercion, or duress will relieve a defendant who cooperates in the commission of the offense.
___16. A juvenile aged 16 or older may sometimes be legally tried as an adult.
___17. A misunderstanding of the law is a defense to certain crimes under Penal Code Section 26.
___18. The law presumes every person charged with a crime to be sane.
___19. The prosecution has the burden of proving a defendant either sane or insane.
___20. Temporary insanity existing at the time of the crime is no longer a defense under the M'Naghten Rule.

ESSAY-DISCUSSION ITEMS—CHAPTER 4

After reading this chapter, you should be able to correctly answer the following items.

1. List four of the six exceptions to the rule that all persons are capable of committing crimes.
2. What are the practical aspects regarding the commission of crimes by persons under fourteen years of age? Are they capable of committing a crime?
3. Is a mentally retarded person legally considered a person who is "mentally incapacitated?" What I.Q. is applicable in such defenses?
4. What legal rule is applied to "insane" persons who commit crimes?
5. Briefly define and give an example of a case involving a "mistake of fact." Is this a defense or an element of the crime?
6. What may be the legal effect of voluntary intoxication in crimes involving specific intent?
7. Briefly discuss "accident and misfortune" as a defense to a crime. In what types of cases is this defense most applicable?
8. What are the defenses to crime which fall under the category of lack of capacity?
9. Discuss the legal aspects of crimes committed under threats and coercion. Is this a defense to all crimes? What will constitute a legal threat in such cases?
10. Who has the burden of proof in an insanity defense and how much evidence must be presented to establish same?

TERMINOLOGY QUIZ—CHAPTER 4

Match terms and definitions by writing the number preceding the correct term between the appropriate brackets.

Terms	*Definitions*
1. Abortion	[ ] A complaint, indictment, or information
2. Accusation	[ ] A sworn declaration in writing
3. Admission	[ ] Defendant advised of rights and charges in court
4. Adultery	[ ] Procuring another to commit a crime
5. Affidavit	[ ] Female victim, especially in rape cases
6. Affirmation	[ ] Incapable of knowing right from wrong
7. Arraignment	[ ] Incriminating statement by accused, short of confession
8. Arrest	
9. Asportation	[ ] Declaration by witness to tell the truth
10. Assault	[ ] Necessary requirements or conditions
11. Attempt	[ ] Movement of things from place to place

12. Capital crime	[ ] To put forth, to put between
13. Contradistinction	[ ] Actual years since birth
14. Chronological age	[ ] Crime punishable by death
15. Imminent	[ ] Immediate, without delay
16. Insanity	[ ] By contrast, having opposite qualities
17. Interpose	
18. Prosecutrix	
19. Requisites	
20. Subornation	

CHAPTER 5

PARTIES TO CRIME

5.1 COMMON LAW PARTIES TO CRIME

Under the old common law, the person who overtly and actually committed the criminal act was known as a *principal in the first degree.* One who knowingly and willfully assisted the actual perpetrator was known as a *principal in the second degree*. One who was not present when the crime was committed, but procured, counseled, or abetted the actual perpetrator was known as an *accessory before the fact.* Finally, one who assisted the perpetrator to escape arrest and punishment after the crime was committed was known as an *accessory after the fact.*

These distinctions no longer exist, as will be discussed below. Sometimes, however, the old terms are still used occasionally to more accurately define the role or relationship of an individual to a particular crime.

5.2 PRINCIPALS DEFINED

Who Are Principals—PC 31. This section states: "All persons concerned in the commission of a crime, whether it be felony or misdemeanor, or whether they directly commit the act constituting the offense, or aid and abet in its commission, or not being present, have advised and encouraged its commission, and all persons counseling, advising, or encouraging children under the age of fourteen years, or persons who are mentally incapacitated, to commit any crime, or who, by fraud, contrivance, or force, occasion the drunkenness of another for the purpose of causing him to commit any crime, or who, by threats, menaces, command, or coercion, compel another to commit any crime, are principals in any crime so committed."

Distinctions Nullified—PC 971. This section eliminates the old common law distinctions. PC 971 reads: "The distinction between an accessory before the fact and a principal, and between principals in the first and second degree is abrogated [repealed, nullified]; and all persons concerned in the commission of a crime, who by the operation of other provisions of this code are principals therein, shall hereafter be prosecuted, tried and punished as principals and no other facts need be alleged in any accusatory pleading against any such persons than are required in an accusatory pleading against a principal."

Principals—Elements of Offense. As noted in PC 31, above, all persons involved in any way in the planning, preparation or carrying out of any crime become principals. This is true even if they are not present at the time the crime is committed. The key elements are:

1. Aids and abets in the commission of a crime.
2. Advises and encourages its commission (even if not present).
3. Fraudulently gets another person drunk for the purpose of causing that person to commit a crime.
4. Compels another to commit a crime by threats, menaces, or coercion.

The first sentence of PC 31, which reads: "All persons concerned in the commission of crime, whether it be felony or misdemeanor," means that the designation "principal" applies to all crimes—misdemeanors, infractions and felonies. The next portion of that sentence, "whether they directly commit the act, or aid and abet in its commission," will be explained in more detail below.

5.3 PENAL CODE PROVISIONS

In addition to PC 31, (Principal Defined) and PC 32, (Accessory Defined), there are several other sections of the California Penal Code which will help give a clearer picture of who are parties to a crime and the various acts which can make them such. These additional sections are discussed below.

Persons Liable to Punishment—PC 27. This section tells us that the following persons are liable to punishment under the laws of this state:

1. All persons who commit, in whole or in part, any crime within this state;
2. All who commit any offense without this state which, if committed within this state, would be larceny, [theft] robbery, or embezzlement under the laws of this state, and bring the property stolen or embezzled, or any part of it, or are found with it, or any part of it within this state:
3. All who, being without this state, cause or aid, advise or encourage, another person to commit a crime within this state, and are afterwards found therein.
4. Perjury is punishable, also, when committed outside of California as provided in PC 118, which is the section defining perjury.

Bringing Stolen or Embezzled Property Into the State—PC 497. "Every person who, in another state or country, steals or embezzles the property of another, or receives such property knowing it to have been stolen or embezzled, and brings the same into this state, may be convicted and punished in the same manner as if such larceny, or embezzlement, or receiving had been committed in this state."

Acts Punishable Under Foreign Law—PC 655. "An act or omission declared punishable by this Code is not less so because it is also punishable under the laws of another state, government or country, unless the contrary is expressly declared."

Foreign Conviction or Acquittal—PC 656. "Whenever, on the trial of an accused person, it appears that upon a criminal prosecution under the laws of another state, government, or country, founded upon the act or omission in respect to which he is on trial, he has been acquitted or convicted, it is a sufficient defense." This means, for example, if a person is tried in federal court for a crime also triable under state law, the federal conviction or acquittal would be a sufficient defense to another trial for the same act under state law.

Aiding in Misdemeanor—Punishment—PC 659. "Whenever an act is declared a misdemeanor, and no punishment for counseling or aiding in the commission of such act is expressly prescribed by law, every person who counsels or aids another in the commission of such act is guilty of a misdemeanor."

General Liability—Jurisdiction—PC 777. Every person is liable to punishment by the laws of this state for a public offense committed by him therein (except for federal crimes), and except as otherwise provided by law, the jurisdiction of every public offense is in any competent court within the jurisdictional territory in which the crime is committed (section briefed).

Out-of-State Aider and Abettor—PC 778b. "Every person who, being out of this state, causes, aids, advises, or encourages any person to commit a crime within this state, and is afterwards found within this state, is punishable in the same manner as if he had been within this state when he caused, aided, advised, or encouraged the commission of such crime."

Principal Innocent—Accessory Guilty—PC 972. It is interesting to note that an accessory to the commission of a felony may be tried, and convicted, even though the principal may be neither prosecuted nor tried, and though the principal may even have been acquitted.

5.4 AID AND ABET DEFINED

A person aids and abets the commission of a crime if, with knowledge of the unlawful purpose of the perpetrator of the crime, he or she promotes, encourages, assists or instigates by act or advice the commission of such crime (*People v. Ponce*, 96 Cal. App. 2d 327). A person aids and abets the commission of a crime when he or she:

1. with knowledge of the unlawful purpose of the perpetrator; and
2. with the intent or purpose of committing, encouraging, or facilitating the commission of the target offense,
3. by act or advice aids, promotes, encourages or instigates the commission of the crime (*People v. Beeman,* 35 Cal. 3d 547).

In the *Beeman* case, the supreme court ruled that persons may be found guilty of aiding and abetting a crime *only* if it can be shown they share the same criminal intent as the perpetrator. This does not mean that the aider/abettor must necessarily intend to participate personally (e.g., have sex with a rape victim or share in the burglary loot), only that he or she knowingly supported the perpetrator's intent and purpose. "If the mens rea of the aider and abettor is more culpable than the actual perpetrator's, the aider and abettor may be guilty of a more serious crime than the actual perpetrator." *(People v. McCoy,* 25 Cal.4th 1111.*)*

Responsibility of Aider and Abettor—A Case PI Study. A striking example of the responsibility of one who aids and abets is contained in *People v. Hopkins,* 101 Cal. App. 2d 704. In this case one Richard Hopkins delivered a friend, Herbert Caro, who was quite ill, to the Park Emergency Hospital in San Francisco. Caro was diagnosed as having narcotic poisoning, and Hopkins informed the doctor in attendance that Caro had taken heroin earlier that day. Caro died that afternoon.

Hopkins made a statement to an inspector of the San Francisco police department, identifying himself as a merchant sailor. He stated that he had left his ship in San Francisco in early afternoon and visited a tavern in Marin County where he met Caro, whom he had known for about three years. He said decedent Caro, asked him if he would "like to get high tonight," to which he agreed. They left in Hopkins' car. Hopkins gave Caro $13.00 and Caro left. About fifteen minutes later Caro returned to the car, having purchased some heroin.

They then drove out to Funston Avenue where they stopped. They opened the package, and Caro produced an eyedropper, which he filled with water at a service station. They drove around a few blocks and then parked on 14th Avenue where they took a "cap" of heroin and heated and mixed it in a spoon. After they had it mixed, Hopkins said he took a shot in the arm, and then Caro took a shot. Hopkins wrapped a handkerchief around Caro's arm to force his veins out. Hopkins took another shot and then assisted Caro in taking his second shot in the same manner by wrapping the handkerchief around Caro's arm, as he had when he took the first shot.

After Caro took the second shot, he told Hopkins he felt sick. He got out of the car and attempted to vomit, but wasn't able to do so. Hopkins got out and walked around the car to Caro who was, by then, practically unconscious. Hopkins then placed Caro in the back seat of the car and took him to the Park Emergency Hospital.

When the decedent injected the heroin into his own arm he violated Sections 11721 and 11009 of the Health and Safety Code and when Hopkins manipulated the handkerchief-tourniquet around decedent Caro's arm, he assisted him in the commission of an unlawful act not amounting to a felony. As a result of these acts, decedent died.

In reviewing the case the District Court of Appeal said: "The help which Hopkins gave decedent brings him within the provisions of Section 31 of the Penal Code [principals defined]. That he aided is clear, that he abetted is clear, since he and decedent set out together with the purpose of doing that which Section 11721 of the Health and Safety Code denounced."

In order to charge Hopkins with manslaughter it was not necessary for testimony before the grand jury to show that he injected heroin, since Section 31 draws no line between persons who directly commit the act constituting the offense and those who aid and abet in its commission.

Not Being Present—Advised and Encouraged—PC 31. The District Court of Appeal, in the case of *People v. Lewis*, said: "To be a principal it is not necessary that the person be present at the commission of the crime."

Case Study—*People v. Lewis.* In the Lewis case the defendant was charged with the crime of rape upon a child under the age of sixteen years. The jury returned a verdict of guilty as charged. Defendant appealed from the order denying his motion for a new trial and from the final judgment of conviction.

The victim was the stepdaughter of the defendant. There was no evidence that defendant had sexual intercourse with her or that he was present at the commission of the crime. However, there was abundant evidence that he aided and abetted its commission by one Alan Wheeler, a youth of seventeen years of age. Defendant's contention was that since he was not present when the crime was committed, the evidence must be held to be insufficient to justify the verdict.

The evidence was that defendant on several occasions solicited Wheeler to have sexual intercourse with the defendant's stepdaughter. He brought them together under circumstances calculated to arouse their "animal passions" and to bring about his "wicked design." He advised Wheeler to procure Vaseline to be used in the act of coition (sexual intercourse), if necessary. He also procured medicated capsules or suppositories, gave them to the girl, and instructed her in Wheeler's presence how to use them to prevent conception.

There was evidence that defendant took his stepdaughter and Wheeler to San Francisco, for the purpose of encouraging them to have sex. The first night they occupied a small room which had only one bed, and all three slept in it. The second night they occupied a different room in which were two beds. The defendant slept in one, and Wheeler and the girl slept in the other. The Court held that there was ample evidence to convict Lewis of unlawful sexual intercourse (PC 261.5), as a principal.

Case Study—*People v. Wood.* In the case of *People v. Wood,* 56 Cal. App. 2d 431, the court said, "Where a person knowingly provides a room for another to commit unlawful sexual intercourse, both are guilty as being principals to the crime." In this case, defendant and one James Moore were jointly charged with the crime of committing statutory rape (now unlawful sexual intercourse). The case was dismissed against Moore, but not Wood, who was an adult. Upon trial, Wood was convicted. He appealed his conviction and nine months sentence in the county jail.

Wood's chief contention was that the verdict was not warranted by the evidence. It is conceded that Wood did not have sexual intercourse with the girl involved. However, it conclusively appears from the evidence that one evening Wood met Moore and the girl together, and that he, Wood, at the request of Moore, procured a room for their use. Wood took Moore and the girl to the room where the two spent the remainder of the night. In the morning, as agreed, Wood returned and awakened them. As shown by the evidence, Wood knew the illegal purpose for which the room was to be used and knowingly both aided and abetted Moore in the commission of the crime. The conviction was sustained. We see, therefore, that a person may be convicted as a principal even though not present at the actual commission of the offense.

Encouraging Children to Commit Crime. Again, going back to PC 31, we read: "... and all persons counseling, advising, or encouraging children under the age of fourteen years, ... to commit any crime ..." This part of PC 31 defines a situation where the person who commits the act, such as a child under the age of fourteen, may not be guilty of any crime, yet the person who counseled, advised, or encouraged them to perform the prohibited act would be subject to prosecution as a principal. PC 26 describes those people who are generally incapable of committing a crime, which includes children under age 14 (see text Section 4.1).

Use of Fraud or Force. Again looking at PC 31, we read in part: "All persons ... who, by fraud, contrivance, or force, occasion the drunkenness of another for the purpose of causing him to commit a crime ..." Examples would include causing a person to become intoxicated by means of fraud, contrivance, or force for the purpose of causing him or her to participate in an act of sex perversion or to illegally use controlled substances, or to cause him or her to commit theft, robbery or burglary, etc.

Uses of Threats. PC 31, also reads, in part: "... or who by threats, menaces, command, or coercion, compels another to commit any crime, are principals in any crime so committed." It's possible the actual perpetrator of the offense under these circumstances (unless the offense be punishable with death), would have a defense under PC 26 (criminal capability), previously discussed. Again, the person who compels another to perform a criminal act (or omission) would be just as guilty as he would have been had he committed the crime himself.

Shared Criminal Intent. In order to convict one for aiding and abetting the perpetrator of an offense, there must be proof that the accused not only aided the perpetrator, but at the same time shared in the criminal intent (*People v. Butts,* 236 Cal. App. 2d 817).

Evidence that the defendant aided and abetted in the commission of a robbery, although he did not strike the blows with the rolled-up kit of automobile tools, sustained his conviction as a principal in the crime (*People v. Crowl,* 28 Cal. App. 2d 299). However, mere presence at the scene of the crime and failure to take steps to prevent a crime do not establish aiding and abetting (*Pinell v. Superior Court,* 232 Cal. App. 2d 284).

Criminal Street Gang Liability. All gang members who knowingly promote, further or assist in felonious activity by the gang are guilty of a felony. Punishment may range from 16 months to life in prison, depending upon the crime and the circumstances (PC 186.22). After conviction (or after having a juvenile court petition sustained), the gang member must register with the sheriff or police chief as a gang member, for a period of 5 years (PC 186.30, 186.32). Failure to register within 10 days of release or change of address is a misdemeanor and, if a new felony is committed while the person is in violation of the registration requirement, additional imprisonment up to 3 years applies (PC 186.33).

5.5 CO-PRINCIPALS EQUALLY GUILTY

All parties who are legally principals under the law are equally guilty. For example, a person who serves as "lookout" for a burglary or robbery is as guilty of the offense as his confederates who entered and completed the crimes (*People v. Navarro*, 212 Cal. App. 2d 299). Further, all parties to the crime are responsible for the natural, reasonable, and probable consequences of the acts of anyone of the others during the commission of the crime (*People v. Goldstein*, 146 Cal. App. 2d 268).

Exception: "Non-triggermen" Principals. On July 2, 1982, the United States Supreme Court struck down the death penalty for "non-triggerman" criminals who did not intend to take part in a killing, but whose crimes resulted in death (*In re Enmund,* 458 U.S. 782). The sharply divided court ruled that the imposition of death under such circumstances violates the Constitution's ban on "cruel and unusual punishment." The ruling still stands today.

A Question of Intent. The *Enmund* decision overturned the death penalty imposed on Florida death-row inmate Earl Enmund, for participation in a robbery during which an elderly couple was slain. Justice Byron R. White wrote: "Putting Enmund to death to avenge two killings that he did not commit and had no intention of committing or causing does not measurably contribute to the retributive end of ensuring that the criminal gets his just deserts." White said that it must be shown that defendants like Enmund "intended or contemplated that life would be taken."

Enmund said he helped plan the robbery of Thomas and Eunice Kersey's home near Wauchula, Florida, but he did not know that his accomplices would gun down the couple. Mrs. Kersey, age 74, was shot six times. Her husband, age 86, was shot three times. Trial testimony indicated that Enmund was not in the Kersey home when the killings occurred, but was waiting in a get-away car. Most of Justice White's opinion, because of the way state death penalty statutes are fashioned, was devoted to so-called "non-triggerman" criminals who took part in a robbery resulting in death.

However, the opinion strongly indicates that it would be applicable to all non-triggerman defendants in "felony-murder" cases. Examples are those who take part in a rape or kidnapping during which another participant kills the victim. Justice Sandra Day O'Connor strongly disagreed with the decision. She stated, "I dissent from this holding not only because I believe that it is not supported by our previous decisions, but also because today's holding

All participants in a crime are jointly punishable as principals, and will normally be charged together as codefendants in a criminal case. *Courtesy of AP/Wide World Photos*

interferes with the state criteria for assessing legal guilt by recasting intent as a matter of federal law."

The Florida Supreme Court rejected Enmund's appeal, ruling that the Constitution does not prevent imposition of the death penalty just because the evidence does not show that the criminal defendant intended to kill anyone. The United States Supreme Court overturned that ruling and ordered a resentencing of Enmund.

"For the purposes of imposing the death penalty, Enmund's criminal culpability [guilt] must be limited to his participation in the robbery, and his punishment must be tailored to his personal responsibility and moral guilt," Justice White said. He also noted that only a handful of states allow the imposition of the death penalty for so-called "felony-murders" during a robbery like the one for which Enmund was convicted (*In re Enmund* 458 U.S. 782).

5.6 ACCESSORY DEFINED

Penal Code section 32, describes an accessory as: "Every person who, after a felony has been committed, harbors, conceals, or aids a principal in such felony, with the intent that said principal may avoid or escape from arrest, trial, conviction, or punishment, having knowledge that said principal has committed such felony or has been charged with such felony or convicted thereof, is an accessory to such felony."

As has been stated, there is no longer an accessory "before" or "after" the fact in California. We only have one type of accessory as defined in PC 32, above. Therefore we rarely use the terms "accessory before the fact" (now a principal) or "accessory after the fact," now merely an "accessory."

After Felony Committed. Note the language used in this section which reads: "Every person who, *after a felony* has been committed . . ." PC 32 applies only to *felonies* and only *after* they have been committed. There is no such thing as an accessory to a misdemeanor.

Knowledge Required. Note that PC 32 requires the accessory to have knowledge that the principal (felonious suspect) has either committed a felony or has been charged with or convicted of a felony. Mere general rumors and common talk that a party has committed a felony are wholly insufficient to constitute "having knowledge" (*People v. Gamett,* 129 Cal. 364).

Harboring Defined. To "harbor" a person means to receive that person secretly or covertly and without lawful authority for the purpose of concealing him so that another having the right to lawful custody of such person shall be deprived of same. It may be aptly used to describe the furnishing of shelter, lodging, or food surreptitiously or with concealment. (*United States v. Grant,* 55 F 415).

Concealing Defined. The word "conceal," as used in PC 32, means more than a simple withholding of knowledge possessed by a party that a felony has been committed. The concealment necessary to constitute a crime includes some affirmative act upon the part of the person doing the concealing. Mere silence after knowledge of a felony's commission is not sufficient to constitute the crime.

Charged Defined. The word "charged," as used in this section, means a formal complaint, indictment, or information has been filed against the person being concealed. It is not necessary that a warrant have been issued.

Proof Required. We find, then, that in order to successfully prosecute a person for the crime of accessory, we will have to establish the following: (1) that the principal's crime was a felony; (2) that the accessory had actual knowledge that the principal had committed a felony, or had been charged with a felony, or had been convicted thereof; (3) that the accessory either harbored, concealed, or aided such principal; (4) with intent of assisting the principal in avoiding arrest, trial, conviction, or punishment.

Jurisdiction—PC 791. "In the case of an accessory, as defined in Section 32, in the commission of a public offense, the jurisdiction is in any competent court within the jurisdictional territory of which the offense of the accessory was committed, notwithstanding the principal offense was committed in another jurisdictional territory."

Therefore, if a felony is committed in San Francisco, and the perpetrator flees to Los Angeles, where someone performs any act making him an accessory to such felony, the accessory would be prosecuted in Los Angeles county, even though the principal would be prosecuted in the city and county of San Francisco.

Punishment—PC 33. This section makes being an accessory a felony "wobbler," punishable by imprisonment in the state prison, or in the county jail not exceeding one year, or by a fine not exceeding five thousand dollars ($5,000), or both.

5.7 ACCOMPLICE DEFINED

Penal Code section 1111, defines an accomplice as ". . . one who is liable to prosecution for the identical offense charged against the defendant on trial in the cause in which the testimony of the accomplice is given."

To be an accomplice, the person must have aided, promoted, encouraged, or instigated by act or advice the commission of an offense with knowledge of the unlawful purpose of the person who committed the offense.

A person who knowingly, voluntarily, and with common intent with the principal offender unites in the commission of the crime is an accomplice (*People v. Sieffert,* 81 Cal. App. 195). He or she is, in effect, a principal in the crime. One can be an accomplice to felonies, misdemeanors or infractions.

Corroboration Required. PC 1111 states: "A conviction cannot be had upon the testimony of an accomplice unless it be corroborated by such other evidence as shall tend to connect the defendant with the commission of the offense; and the corroboration is not sufficient if it merely shows the commission of the offense or the circumstances thereof."

Corroboration Defined. Corroboration is *independent evidence* that tends to connect the defendant with the commission of the offense. This independent evidence must be something other than the testimony of an accomplice—or even more than one accomplice.

Juveniles—Exception. There is an exception to the above rule on corroboration in juvenile court hearings. In the case of *In re Darrell A.* (90 Cal. App. 3d 325), the Supreme Court held that in a juvenile court hearing, a statement by an accomplice is sufficient to convict a minor for an alleged offense. Corroboration of an accomplice's statement, is therefore not required in juvenile court hearings.

Discussion. There are some situations in California where a participant in crime cannot be an accomplice. In unlawful sexual intercourse, PC 261.5, for example, the prosecutrix (victim), being under the statutory age of consent, cannot be an accomplice (*People v. Hamilton*, 88 Cal. App. 2d 398).

The victim of a violation of PC 288 (lewd acts against children), being under age of fourteen years, cannot be an accomplice. If the offense is also a violation of PC 288a (oral copulation) and the child, under fourteen, was a willing participant in forcing another to participate, and it could be proved satisfactorily by the evidence that he knew the wrongfulness of the act at the time he committed it, he would then be an accomplice insofar as the 288a was concerned (*People v. Williams*, 12 Cal. App. 2d 207).

The test of being an accomplice, therefore, is whether one can be prosecuted as a principal. He must be liable himself for the identical crime for which the principal is on trial.

5.8 FEIGNED ACCOMPLICE

A feigned accomplice is one who participates in a crime for evidence gathering and prosecution purposes only. A feigned accomplice, therefore, lacks criminal intent. The feigned accomplice's testimony need not be corroborated because he or she is not a true accomplice. Such person may be working under the direction of a law enforcement officer, or upon his or her own initiative. As such, there is no criminal intent on the part of a feigned accomplice, nor does his or her activity generally constitute entrapment (See Entrapment, Chapter 7).

A feigned accomplice is distinguished from a true accomplice in that the true accomplice is one who knowingly, voluntarily, and with common intent with a principal offender, unites in the commission of a crime. Whereas a feigned accomplice may cooperate in the commission of a crime for the purpose of apprehending or securing evidence against the guilty party and is not guilty of the offense committed.

For "plain-English" explanations of legal terms, answers to questions on criminal law, landlord-tenant and neighborhood disputes and child custody matters, go to the Web Site: **www.nolo.com.** Here you will also find an excellent legal encyclopedia, law dictionary and access to laws and Supreme Court cases.

STUDENT REVIEW

TERMINOLOGY DEFINED—CHAPTER 5

Please see the Terminology Quiz at the end of this chapter.

1. Abrogate: abolish, nullify, repeal.
2. Autopsy: dissection or testing of a body to determine cause of death.
3. Bailiff: officer assigned to keep order in the court.
4. Battery: unlawful use of force on another.
5. Bench warrant: issued by judge for contempt or failure to appear.
6. *Certiorari:* order from appellate court to hear an appeal.
7. Circumstantial evidence: that from which other facts may be concluded.
8. Coition: sexual intercourse, also coitus.
9. Commitment: court order sending person to jail, hospital, etc.
10. Complaint: a criminal charge made to a court.
11. Compounding: accepting a reward not to prosecute, a crime in itself.
12. Conspiracy: crime of two or more persons planning to commit a crime.
13. Contempt: disregard of court order or disrespect toward court.
14. Contraband: goods forbidden by law to possess, import, etc.
15. Coroner's jury: appointed by coroner to hear evidence as to cause of death.
16. Corroboration: evidence which confirms, supports, substantiates.
17. Court trial: jury waived; judge determines guilt or innocence.
18. Culpable: deserving the blame, guilt or censure.
19. Decedent: one who is dead, the deceased.
20. Subpoena: court order commanding witness to appear in court.

TRUE-FALSE QUIZ—CHAPTER 5

After reading this chapter you should be able to correctly answer the following items.

___ 1. Under the old common law, the person who assisted the actual perpetrator in a crime was known as an accessory after the fact.
___ 2. The distinctions of accessory before and after the fact have now been eliminated.
___ 3. One cannot be guilty of being a principal to a crime if he was not present when the crime was committed.
___ 4. The term "principal to a crime" applies to felonies only.
___ 5. One can be a principal to a crime merely by advising and encouraging its commission by another.
___ 6. The word "abet" generally signifies guilty knowledge and wrongful purpose.
___ 7. If "A" helps "B" to voluntarily take a shot of heroin, and "B" dies from an overdose, "A" can be charged with manslaughter as being a principal to the death.
___ 8. One who advised and aided a friend to have sexual relations with a 16-year old girl could be guilty of unlawful sexual intercourse even though he was not present when the act was committed.
___ 9. It is possible for the one who commits an act not to be guilty of a crime, but the one who aids and encourages such act to be guilty.
___10. If during a liquor store robbery, one person remains outside in a car, the one remaining in the car is guilty of being an accessory.
___11. There is no such crime as being an accessory to a misdemeanor.
___12. One can be guilty of being an accessory by helping another to plan a robbery.

___13. To be guilty of being an accessory, the accused must have actual knowledge that the principal has committed a felony.
___14. An accomplice is liable to prosecution for the identical offense as that charged against the principal.
___15. Except for juveniles, the testimony of an accomplice must be corroborated in all cases.
___16. In those instances where required, an accomplice's testimony must be corroborated to a greater degree than merely showing that a crime was committed.
___17. A "feigned accomplice" is one who did not know the wrongfulness of the act committed.
___18. Feigned accomplices are guilty as principals providing they are over fourteen years of age.
___19. The punishment for an accessory is one-half of that for a principal.
___20. The test as to whether one is an accessory is whether the latter could be prosecuted as a principal.

ESSAY-DISCUSSION ITEMS—CHAPTER 5

After reading this chapter you should be able to correctly answer the following items.

1. What elements make one a principal to a crime in California?
2. Briefly describe how the definition of "principal" applies to felonies and to misdemeanors.
3. How does California law regarding two or more principals differ from the old common law provisions as it applies to their participation?
4. Briefly explain the responsibility of a principal who aids another in taking drugs as described in *People v. Hopkins*.
5. What elements constitute the crime of accessory?
6. How does an accessory differ from a principal?
7. How does an accomplice's culpability compare with that of a principal?
8. Briefly discuss the applicable factors when using an accomplice as a witness against a principal.
9. Briefly define corroboration.
10. What is a "feigned accomplice" and what would be the motive of such a person?

TERMINOLOGY QUIZ—CHAPTER 5

Match terms and definitions by placing the number preceding the correct term between the appropriate brackets.

Terms	*Definitions*
1. Abrogate	[ ] issued by a judge for failure to appear
2. Autopsy	[ ] a criminal charge made to a court
3. Bailiff	[ ] goods forbidden by law to possess
4. Battery	[ ] court order for witness to appear
5. Bench warrant	[ ] to abolish, nullify, repeal
6. Certiorari	[ ] accepting a reward not to prosecute
7. Circumstantial evidence	[ ] two or more persons planning a crime
8. Coition	[ ] disregard of court order, disrespect to court
9. Commitment	[ ] deserving of blame, guilt, censure
10. Complaint	[ ] one who is dead
11. Compounding	[ ] evidence which confirms, supports, substantiates
12. Conspiracy	[ ] court order sending person to jail, hospital, etc.
13. Contempt	[ ] appellate court order to hear an appeal
14. Contraband	[ ] sexual intercourse

15. Coroner's jury [ ] that from which other facts may be concluded
16. Corroboration
17. Court trial
18. Culpable
19. Decedent
20. Subpoena

CHAPTER 6

ATTEMPTS—SOLICITATION—OBSTRUCTING JUSTICE—CONSPIRACY

6.1 ATTEMPT DEFINED

Attempt—PC 664. An attempt to commit a crime is a crime in itself. Every person who attempts to commit any crime, but fails, or is prevented or intercepted in the perpetration thereof, is guilty of an attempt to commit the crime.

Elements of Attempt—PC 21a. The two elements which form attempt are:

1. a specific intent to commit the target crime; and
2. a direct but ineffectual act toward the commission of the crime.

Act Defined. The act must come dangerously close to completion of the crime. It must come close enough so that the crime apparently would have been completed except for being interrupted by some circumstance not intended in the original plan (*People v. Dillon*, 34 Cal. 3d 441).

Punishment for Attempted Offenses—PC 664. Punishment for an attempt is usually half the sentence (state prison or county jail or fine) of the target crime. Exceptions to this are attempted murder, which can be punished by life imprisonment with the possibility of parole, and attempted premeditated murder of a safety officer, punishable by a minimum term of fifteen years of a 15-to-life sentence.

Crimes Divided Into Degrees—PC 664(d). If a crime is divided into degrees, an attempt to commit the crime may be of any such degree, and the punishment for such an attempt shall be determined as provided by this section.

Attempts—Commission of a Different Crime—PC 665. This section provides that a person who, in attempting unsuccessfully to commit one crime, accomplishes the commission of another and different crime, whether more or less serious, is guilty of the crime committed. In such cases the perpetrator could be tried for both the crime attempted and the crime committed. For example, if in attempting unsuccessfully to snatch a purse, a suspect injures the victim, the perpetrator could be tried for both attempted grand theft from person and battery.

Discussion. An attempt consists of an act done by a perpetrator, with specific intent to commit a particular crime (*People v. Rupp*, 41 Cal. 2d 527). Such act must go beyond mere preparation, and come close to accomplishment. It must, nevertheless, fall short of completion of the intended crime to be an attempt. If an attempt is successfully completed, obviously the perpetrator would be charged with the crime committed. In order to constitute an attempt there must be a direct, ineffectual act, done toward the ultimate commission of the crime.

Mere agreement to commit a crime will not constitute an attempt to commit that particular crime in the absence of some overt physical act. The perpetrator's conduct must be more than mere preparation. Thus, where a man buys a gun and some cartridges to be used in a robbery, such actions, at this point, would not satisfy the requirements of an attempted offense (*People v. Stites*, 75 Cal. 2d 570). Some appreciable fragment of the crime sought to be committed must have been accomplished (*People v. McEwing*, 216 Cal. App. 2d 33).

Where a suspect hired an "assassin" (in reality, an undercover officer) to murder his sister and her friend, gave detailed information on their daily routines and paid a down payment of $5000, the California Supreme Court held that these acts constituted not merely a solicitation for murder but an attempt to commit murder by the suspect. *People v. Decker*, 41 Cal.4th 1.

Examples. Entering a car without the owner's permission and operating the starter in an apparent effort to start the motor, for example, is an attempt to commit theft of the car (*People v. Carter*, 73 Cal. App. 3d 495). Other examples are: sawing a lock on a warehouse door, starting to remove the screen from a house window, and piling lawn furniture against a backyard fence for pick-up by an accomplice parked in the alley (*People v. Gibson*, 94 Cal. App. 2d 468).

Attempts as Separate Crimes. In some instances, an attempt is directly declared by another Penal Code section to be a crime. Some examples are attempted escape, PC 107, and attempted arson, PC 455. It could be noted that assault, PC 240, is in effect, an attempted battery, PC 242.

6.2 ABANDONMENT OF ATTEMPT

When the defendant commits acts toward the commission of a crime which thereby satisfy the *corpus delicti* of an "attempt to commit an offense," he cannot thereafter avoid responsibility by abandoning his original purpose. Assume, for example, that a perpetrator specifically intends to commit a certain crime but is interrupted during the crime. Assume, also, that had he not been interrupted, he could have completed the crime. He cannot rely on the interruption to negate his criminal act. He is, in effect, guilty of an attempt to commit a crime.

Abandonment is a defense only if the attempt to commit a crime is freely and voluntarily abandoned before the act is in the process of final execution, and when there is no outside cause prompting such abandonment (*People v. Von Hecht*, 133 Cal. App. 2d 25).

6.3 POSSIBILITY OF COMPLETION

There can be no crime of attempt if there is an impossibility of its consummation. There are those cases where it would appear that the defendant was in a physical position to commit a crime, but was unable to complete the act because of a legal ramification or technicality.

Thus, where one throws red pepper in the eyes of another with the intent to blind him (PC 203, mayhem), and it can be shown that the material thrown was not pepper and would not destroy the eye or eyesight, the perpetrator cannot be guilty of attempted mayhem. The assailant could, however, be charged with simple assault (PC 240) or battery (PC 242).

In another case, an adult male attempted to have voluntary sex with his adult adopted daughter, but was interrupted by his wife. The question is: is either guilty of attempted incest (PC 285)? Since PC 285 and Civil Code section 59 prohibit marriage or fornication (sexual intercourse) *only* between blood relatives, the crime of incest, and therefore the attempt, could not have been committed as a matter of law.

In order to determine whether a crime is apparently possible to commit or absolutely impossible to commit, it is necessary to look to court decisions. As previously stated, if the crime can apparently be consummated, then it can be attempted. Cases have held that the defendant's lack of knowledge of the impossibility of carrying out his intention, is quite immaterial. For example, a defendant could be found guilty of attempting to steal money from an empty cash register, or from the person of another who has no money in his pockets (*People v. Fiegelman*, 33 Cal. App. 2d 100).

In another case, the court held that defendant could reasonably attempt to possess contraband in violation of the Health and Safety Code when he paid a large sum of money for common talcum powder, thinking it to be narcotics (*People v. Siu*, 126 Cal. App. 2d 41). The courts have said that if a person attempts to shoot another with an unloaded gun, there can be no assault because of the impossibility of completing the crime by virtue of the gun being incapable of projecting a missile (*People v. Sylva*, 143 Cal. 62). But where a defendant fired a pistol through a roof at a location where he believed the intended victim to be, although the victim, a police officer, was some distance away, the court held this to be an assault because of the possibility of completion of the act (*People v. King*, 97 Cal. 666).

Impossibility of Completion. Physical or factual impossibility of completing the crime is not a defense unless the conditions were known in advance to the perpetrator. For example, if a pickpocket reaches into a victim's pocket but finds it empty, he is guilty of attempted grand theft from the person. If an assailant shoots at a cashier in a glass booth, not knowing the glass is bulletproof, he is guilty of assault with a deadly weapon (ADW) (*People v. Valdez*, 175 Cal. App. 3d 103).

Legal impossibility, on the other hand, is a defense. For example, trying to kill a person who is known to be dead cannot legally constitute attempted murder. Likewise, intending to have sexual intercourse with a person known to be dead is not attempted rape (*People v. Thompson,* 12 Cal. App.4th 195).

6.4 SOLICITATION TO COMMIT CRIME

Soliciting Commission of Certain Crimes—PC 653f. "(a) Every person who, with intent that the crime be committed, solicits another to offer or accept or join in the offer or acceptance of a bribe, or to commit or join in the commission of carjacking, robbery, burglary, grand theft, receiving stolen property, extortion, perjury, subornation of perjury, forgery, kidnapping, arson, or assault with a deadly weapon or instrument or by means of force likely to produce great bodily injury or, by the use of force or a threat of force, to prevent or dissuade any person who is or may become a witness from attending upon, or testifying at, any trial, proceeding, or inquiry authorized by law, is punishable by imprisonment in the county jail not more than one year or in the state prison, or by a fine of not more than ten thousand dollars ($10,000), or . . . by both such fine and imprisonment.

(b) Every person who, with the intent that the crime be committed, solicits another to commit or join in the commission of murder is punishable by imprisonment in the state prison. . . .

(c) Every person who, with intent that the crime be committed, solicits another to commit rape by force or violence, sodomy by force or violence, oral copulation by force or violence, or any violations of PC 264.1 [rape], PC 288 [lewd act on child under fourteen] or PC 289 [penetration of genital or anal openings by foreign object], is punishable by imprisonment in a state prison. . . .

(d) Every person who, with the intent that the crime be committed, solicits another to commit . . . [various crimes relating to controlled substances, e.g., transporting, importing, selling, furnishing, manufacturing, etc., is guilty of a misdemeanor (first offense), or a wobbler (subsequent offenses)].

(e) Every person who, with the intent that the crime be committed, solicits another to commit an offense specified in Section 14014 of the Welfare and Institutions Code [relating to falsified health care claims] shall be punished [by up to six months jail (first offense) or by state prison or one year in jail (subsequent offenses)].

(f) An offense charged in violation of PC 653f subdivision (a), (b), or (c) must be proven by the testimony of two witnesses or by one witness and corroborating circumstances."

Discussion. To ask a person to "commit or join," etc., in itself consummates the crime of solicitation. In other words, the solicitation itself completes the crime. No overt act toward committing the crime is necessary (People v. Burt, 45 Cal. 2d 311).

The crime is complete whether the person solicited responds favorably or not. It also doesn't matter if the person solicited was already contemplating or planning to commit the crime himself before the solicitation. Thus, it has been held a crime to solicit a public officer to take a bribe, or to solicit any of those felony offenses enumerated in the statute. Soliciting one to offer a bribe is a crime separate and distinct from the crime of bribery or the crime of attempted bribery (*People v. Litt*, 221 Cal. App. 2d 543).

Note that most all of the solicited crimes listed in PC 653f are felonies. If the crime solicited is committed, the offense of solicitation is merged in the greater offense and the solicitor becomes an accomplice (and thus a principal) in the crime.

How Proved. The crime of solicitation must be proved by corroboration which consists of the testimony of two witnesses, or of one witness and corroborating circumstances. An accomplice is a "witness" within the meaning of this section (*People v. Rissman*, 154 Cal. App. 2d 265). Proof that other persons were also solicited to commit the same crime has been held to be sufficient corroboration.

In a prosecution for willfully, unlawfully, and feloniously soliciting certain persons to join in the commission of the crime of robbery, testimony of the person so solicited was amply sufficient to make it appear that the offense had been committed and that there was probable cause to believe the one soliciting had committed it (*Kind v. Superior Court*, 143 Cal. App. 2d 100).

Soliciting Street Gang Members. Any person who solicits another to join a gang, with the intent that the person solicited will participate in felonious gang activities, is guilty of a felony. Threatening or using violence to recruit or coerce another to join the gang results in an additional three years imprisonment, consecutive to the term imposed for the solicitation itself (PC 186.26).

6.5 OBSTRUCTING JUSTICE—COMPOUNDING CRIMES

The administration of justice may be obstructed in many ways. For purposes of this section, however, we are limiting the term to include:

1. compounding crimes,
2. perjury,

3. subornation of perjury,
4. bribery, and
5. falsification of evidence.

Compounding or Concealing Crimes—PC 153. "Every person who, having knowledge of the actual commission of a crime, takes money or property of another, or any gratuity or reward, or any engagement, or promise thereof, upon any agreement or understanding to compound or conceal such crime, or to abstain from any prosecution thereof, or to withhold any evidence thereof, except in the cases provided for by law, in which crimes may be compromised by leave of court, is punishable as follows:

1. By imprisonment in the state prison or in the county jail not exceeding one year, where the crime was punishable by death or imprisonment in the state prison for life;
2. By imprisonment in the state prison or in the county jail not exceeding six months, where the crime was punishable in the state prison for any other term than for life;
3. By imprisonment in the county jail not exceeding six months, or by fine not exceeding one thousand dollars ($1,000), where the crime was a misdemeanor."

Discussion. The offense of compounding a crime is committed where one who knows that it has been committed agrees, for a consideration (fee or something of value), not to prosecute. In order for the crime to be committed, it is necessary that a criminal offense shall first have actually been committed and that the defendant shall have knowledge of such an offense.

However, the mere reimbursement to a person who has been injured by the commission of a crime is not necessarily a violation of the section. For example, where one settles out of court in respect to an injury caused through the commission of a crime, such as an assault and battery, the victim violates no law in accepting some compensation for such injury.

However, where a person who has knowledge of the actual commission of a crime agrees for a fee to compound or conceal such a crime, or to abstain from any prosecution thereof, he is guilty of violating this section (*Bowyer v. Burgess*, 54 Cal. 2d 97).

Under Penal Code Sections 1377 through 1379, provision is made for misdemeanors to be "compromised" (dismissed upon payment of damages to victim) under certain circumstances. PC 1378, provides that the court may stay proceedings when compensation for injury sustained by an individual as a result of a crime has been made to the victim.

Penal Code Section 1379 expressly prohibits the compounding or compromising of any offense, misdemeanor or felony, except as provided for in Penal Code Sections 1377 and 1378.

6.6 PERJURY

Perjury Defined—PC 118(a). "Every person who, having taken an oath that he or she will testify, declare, depose, or certify truly before any competent tribunal, officer, or person, in any of the cases in which the oath may by California law be administered, willfully and contrary to the oath, states as true any material matter which he or she knows to be false, and every person who testifies, declares, deposes, or certifies under penalty of perjury in any of the cases in which the testimony, declarations, or certification is permitted by California law under penalty of perjury and willfully states as true any material which he or she knows to be false, is guilty of perjury."

Discussion—Elements. The crime of perjury involves:

1. knowingly making of a false statement, either oral or written,
2. either under oath or "under penalty of perjury,"
3. with respect to a fact which is "material,"
4. before a competent legal tribunal, proceeding or person.

In perjury cases, testimony is "material" if it could *probably* have influenced the trier of act, not just when it in fact had an effect or influence (*People v. Sagehorn*, 140 Cal. App. 2d 138). Testimony must be knowingly false to constitute perjury (*People v. Dixon*, 99 Cal. App. 2d 94). An honest mistake does not constitute perjury (*People v. Von Tiedeman*, 120 Cal. 128).

An unqualified statement of that which one does not know to be true is equivalent to a statement of that which one knows to be false (PC 125). Also, stating under oath that one doesn't remember a material fact, when in truth they do, is perjury (*People v. Gusati*, 220 Cal. App. 2d 456).

False Affidavit—PC 118a. Any person who, in any affidavit (written statement) taken before any person authorized to administer oaths, swears, affirms, declares, deposes, or certifies that he will testify truthfully, and in such affidavit willfully and contrary to such oath, states as true any material (important, relevant) matter which he knows to be false, is guilty of perjury [section briefed].

After a witness has taken an oath, giving knowingly false testimony on a material fact can result in a prosecution for perjury. *Photograph by John Neubauer, courtesy of PhotoEdit*

Oath Defined—PC 119. The term "oath," as used in PC 118 and 118a, includes an affirmation and every other mode authorized by law of attesting the truth of that which is stated.

Oath of Office—PC 120. The typical "oath of office," administered to an elected or appointed official, is not an "oath" as defined in PC 119.

Incompetency of Witness No Defense—PC 122. "It is no defense to a prosecution for perjury that the accused was not competent to give the testimony, deposition, or certificate of which falsehood is alleged. It is sufficient that he did give such testimony or make such deposition or certificate."

Witness's Knowledge of Materiality of Testimony—PC 123. "It is no defense to a prosecution for perjury that the accused did not know the materiality [importance] of the false statement made by him, or that it did not, in fact, affect the proceedings in or for which it was made. It is sufficient that it was material, and might have been used to affect such proceeding."

When Deposition Deemed Complete—PC 124. "The making of a deposition, affidavit, or certificate is deemed to be complete, within the provisions of this chapter, from the time when it is delivered by the accused to any other person, with the intent that it be uttered or published as true."

False Statement Under Oath—PC 129. "Every person who, being required by law to make any return, statement, or report, under oath, willfully makes and delivers any such return, statement or report, purporting to be under oath, knowing the same to be false in any particular, is guilty of perjury, whether such oath was in fact taken or not."

Punishment For Perjury—PC 126. Perjury is a felony, punishable by imprisonment in state prison.

6.7 SUBORNATION OF PERJURY

Procuring Perjury—PC 127. "Every person who willfully procures another person to commit perjury is guilty of subornation of perjury, and is punishable in the same manner as he would be if personally guilty of the perjury so procured."

Discussion. The crime of subornation of perjury has two essential elements: (1) that one person shall willfully procure another person to commit perjury, and (2) that such other person shall commit perjury.

To violate the provisions of this section, it is necessary that some person shall have committed the crime of perjury and that the perjury was committed through the procurement of the person charged with its subornation. In addition, the accused must know that the testimony given was untrue.

Procuring Execution of Innocent Person—PC 128. "Every person who, by willful perjury or subornation of perjury, procures the conviction and execution of any innocent person, is punishable by death or life imprisonment without possibility of parole. The penalty shall be determined pursuant to Sections 190.3 and 190.4." ***Note:*** these two sections (PC 190.3 and 190.4) define "mitigating" and "special" circumstances for punishment purposes.

6.8 BRIBERY

The crime of bribery is unique in that it involves several individual laws, each of which defines the giving, offering, or receiving of a bribe by specific classification of individuals. Common bribery elements include:

1. Asking, giving, accepting, or offering anything of value or advantage, or the promise of same;
2. To or by the class of persons named in each specific bribe statute;
3. With specific intent to corruptly influence any act, decision, vote, opinion, or other official function or duty of such person.

Bribing Executive Officers—PC 67. "Every person who gives or offers any bribe to any executive officer of this state with intent to influence him in respect to any act, decision, vote, opinion, or other proceeding as such officer, is punishable by imprisonment in the state prison . . . and is disqualified from holding any office in this state." ***Note:*** The term "executive officer," as used here, includes peace officers (*People v. Buice*, 230 Cal. App. 2d 324).

Offering or Giving Bribe to Public Officers—PC 67.5. Every person who gives or offers as a bribe to any ministerial officer [includes peace officers], employee, or appointee of the State of California, county or city therein or political subdivision thereof, anything the theft of which would be petty theft, is guilty of a misdemeanor; if the theft of the thing so given or offered would be grand theft, the offense is a felony.

Asking or Receiving Bribe by Public Officers—PC 68. "Every executive or ministerial officer [includes peace officers], employee or appointee of the State of California, county or city therein, . . . who asks, receives, or agrees to receive, any bribe, upon any agreement or understanding that his vote, opinion, or action upon any matter then pending, or which may be brought before him in his official capacity, shall be influenced thereby, is punishable by imprisonment in the state prison . . . and is forever disqualified from holding any office, employment or appointment in this state." Restitution fines of $2,000 to $10,000 must also be imposed.

Offering a Bribe. The offense of offering a bribe is complete once it is evident that the officer is being bribed. There need not be any actual tender, presentation, showing or transfer of money (*People v. Sweeney*, 55 Cal. 2d 27).

Giving a Bribe. The offense of giving a bribe is complete when the bribe is actually delivered to the person being bribed (*People v. Guillory*, 178 Cal. App. 2d 854).

Receiving a Bribe. The offense of receiving a bribe is complete once the accused asks, receives, or agrees to receive or accept any bribe in consideration of an unlawful act of influence. The person solicited need not consent to giving a bribe. One is guilty of "receiving" a bribe either by (1) asking, (2) agreeing to accept, or (3) actually accepting a bribe.

Outside employment of peace officers, such as providing private security services at sporting events, is governed by Penal Code § 70. *Photograph © Reuters NewMedia Inc., courtesy of CORBIS*

Discussion. Under the above sections, bribery or attempted bribery or any attempt to corruptly influence official action of police officers constitutes the crime (*Oppenheimer v. Clifton's*, 98 Cal. App. 2d 403). The crime is complete when a police officer is offered a bribe to allow gaming to continue, whether such illegal activity does in fact continue, and the officer is guilty of "accepting" a bribe merely by agreeing to receive a bribe (*People v. Markham*, 64 Cal. 157).

It is not an essential element of the crime of bribery that the bribe be offered to an official with actual authority as long as the official's act falls within the general scope of duties of the person being bribed.

Peace Officers—Unauthorized Gratuities—PC 70. "(a) Every executive or ministerial officer, employee or appointee of the State of California, county or city therein or political subdivision thereof, who knowingly asks, receives, or agrees to receive any emolument, gratuity, or reward, or any promise thereof excepting such as may be authorized by law for doing an official act, is guilty of a misdemeanor."

Employment Outside Department. Notwithstanding PC 70, above, "Because of the nature of their employment, public officers are under a special duty at all times to use their best efforts to apprehend criminals." (*People v. Hooker*, 254 Cal. App. 2d 878.) "A peace officer has a continuing responsibility to keep the peace at all hours, whether or not officially on duty." (*People v. Corey*, 21 Cal. 3d 738, Clark dissenting.) Therefore, peace officers are allowed to accept off-duty employment while retaining their peace officer status, with certain conditions.

Discussion. PC 70 (c), which applies when an officer is employed as security or patrol *for a public entity* outside regular employment, confers peace officer status if "a police uniform" is worn and the officer is subject to department rules and regulations during such employment. Any civil or criminal liability from this secondary employment is the responsibility of the *secondary employer*—not the department.

PC 70 (d), which applies when an officer is employed as security or patrol *by a private employer* while off-duty, confers peace officer status if

1. the officer is in his or her police uniform,
2. the department has approved the wearing of the uniform and equipment,
3. the officer is subject to department rules, and
4. the secondary employment is approved by the employing agency.

Any civil or criminal liability from this secondary employment is the responsibility of the *department*—not the secondary employer (although the department may require an indemnity agreement with the private employer).

Officers may also engage in off-duty employment that does not involve security or policing activities, subject to reasonable restrictions by the employing agency and collective bargaining agreements. An employer withholding consent to outside employment must provide the officer with written reasons for denial (PC 70(e)).

Peace officer powers are not permitted for private employment in a labor dispute, and cross-jurisdictional authority would require a reciprocal-consent agreement per PC 830.1 (a)(2), or applicability of the exception under PC 830.1 (a)(3).

A peace officer properly employed under PC 70 who is clearly identifiable as a peace officer in the performance of his or her duties could apply the special protections of such statutes as PC 148, PC 241, and PC 243, where applicable.

6.9 OTHER BRIBERY STATUTES

Under the Penal Code sections indicated, each of the following bribery statutes are felonies:

1. Giving or offering a bribe to members of the Legislature (PC 85).
2. Asking for or receiving a bribe by members of the Legislature (PC 86).
3. Giving or offering a bribe to a judge, juror, referee, arbitrator, or umpire (PC 92).
4. Asking for or receiving a bribe by a judge, juror, referee, arbitrator, or umpire (PC 93).
5. Corruptly attempting to influence a juror's decision (PC 95).
6. Offering or give a witness a bribe to withhold true or give false testimony (PC 137).
7. Receiving or offering to receive a bribe by a witness for the purpose set forth in PC 137 (PC 138).
8. Giving or offering a bribe to any member of a council, board of supervisors, board of trustees (PC 165).
9. Giving or offering a bribe to any participant in any athletic or sporting event (PC 337b).
10. Soliciting someone else to offer or accept a bribe (PC 653f).

6.10 FALSIFICATION CRIMES

Offering False Evidence—PC 132. This section provides that: "Every person who upon any trial, proceeding, inquiry, or investigation whatever, authorized or permitted by law, offers in evidence as genuine or true, any book, paper, document, record, or other instrument in writing, knowing the same to have been forged or fraudulently altered or antedated [before in time], is guilty of a felony." It should be noted that this section applies to written evidence only, and not to all types of evidence.

Deceiving a Witness—PC 133. This misdemeanor offense provides that: "Every person who practices any fraud or deceit, or knowingly makes or exhibits any false statement, representation, token, or writing, to any witness or person about to be called as a witness upon any trial, proceeding, inquiry or investigation whatever, authorized by law, with intent to affect the testimony of such witness, is guilty of a misdemeanor."

Preparing False Evidence—PC 134. This felony section provides that: "Every person guilty of preparing any false or antedated [dated earlier] book, paper, record, instrument in writing, or other matter or thing, with intent to produce it, or allow it to be produced for any fraudulent or deceitful purpose, as genuine or true, upon any trial, proceeding, or inquiry whatever, authorized by law, is guilty of a felony."

Planting Evidence—PC 141. Any person who knowingly and willfully alters, modifies, plants, places, manufactures, conceals or moves physical matter with the intent to cause a person to be charged with a crime or with the intent to cause false evidence to be offered as genuine is guilty of a misdemeanor (PC 141(a)). If the acts are done by a peace officer, the crime is a felony (PC 141(b)).

Destroying Evidence—PC 135. This section provides that: "Every person who, knowing that any book, paper, record, instrument in writing, *or other matter or thing* [italics added for emphasis], is about to be produced in evidence upon any trial, inquiry, or investigation whatever, authorized by law, willfully destroys or conceals same, with intent thereby to prevent it from being produced, is guilty of a misdemeanor."

Dissuading Witness—PC 136.1.a. Maliciously threatening or dissuading a victim or witness from testifying, or from making a report of a crime, is a wobbler. If accomplished by threats of force or violence, or as part of a conspiracy or for financial gain, such crime is a felony, as are subsequent convictions for the same offense.

Threatening Witnesses or Families—PC 139. This section provides that if any person who has been convicted of any felony offense listed in PC 12021.1 ("violent crimes"), willfully and maliciously communicates a "credible threat" to use force or violence on the witness or that person's family, they are guilty of a felony (wobbler). This section is applicable even if the perpetrator is incarcerated at the time of making the threat.

"Credible threat," as used in this section, means one made with the intent and apparent ability to carry it out so as to cause the target of the threat to reasonably fear for his or her safety or the safety of his or her immediate family.

Threatening a Crime Witness—PC 140. This section makes it a "wobbler" to willfully threaten to use force or violence upon the person of a crime witness, victim, informant or one who has provided information or assistance to the authorities.

False Citizenship Documents. Making or selling false citizenship documents is a felony punishable by five years' imprisonment or $75,000 fine (PC 113). Use of such documents is a felony punishable by five years' imprisonment or $25,000 fine (PC 114).

Misusing 911 Line for Non-emergency Calls—PC653y. Any person who knowingly allows the use of or who uses the 911 telephone system for any reason other than because of an emergency is guilty of an infraction, with penalties ranging from written warnings (first two offenses) to graduated fines of $50 to $200 for subsequent offenses. Parents of offending minors are jointly and severally liable for paying the fines.

False Amber Alert–PC 148.3. It is a misdemeanor to knowingly make a false report of a missing child that causes activation of the Amber Alert system.

Falsely Reporting Crime—PC 148.5. It is a misdemeanor to knowingly make a false report of a crime to any grand jury, peace officer, or other police agent in the performance of official duty. A person 18 or older who is convicted of making a false crime report may be held liable for the costs of emergency response (Govt. Code 53153.5).

Falsely Reporting Police Misconduct—PC 148.6. It is a misdemeanor to knowingly file a false accusation of official misconduct against any officer. Any person filing a misconduct complaint is required to read and sign a notice as to this provision (language specified in PC 148.6(a)). The California Supreme Court upheld this statute (*People v. Stanistreet*, 29 Cal.4th 497); however, the Ninth Circuit declared it unconstitutional (*Chaker v. Crogan*, 428 F.3d 1215), making it unenforceable, as a practical matter. Knowingly filing a false lien or civil claim against a peace officer to harass or dissuade the officer from official duty is a misdemeanor PC 148.6(b).

Giving False Identification—PC 148.9. It is a misdemeanor to give a false identity, upon lawful detention or arrest, to evade proper ID or process of the court.

Crimes While Impersonating Another—PC 529. It is a wobbler to impersonate another person, and to commit a forgery or do some act which could subject the impersonated person to damages or prosecution.

Obtaining False DMV Documents—PC 629.7 Any person who fraudulently obtains or assists another in obtaining a driver's license, identification card, vehicle registration certificate, or other official document of the Department of Motor Vehicles is guilty of a misdemeanor.

Identity Theft—PC 530.5. It is a wobbler to obtain personal identifying information about another (including name, address, license number, social security number, mother's maiden name, account numbers, etc.), and to use that information for any unlawful purpose. A person who learns or reasonably suspects that he or she is the victim of identity theft may make a report to the local law enforcement agency, which must take the report and initiate an investigation (PC 530.6). Jurisdiction of identity theft cases is wherever the theft of the identifying information occurred, or wherever it was unlawfully used (PC 786).

Impersonating an Officer—PC 538d. It is a misdemeanor for a person to wear a uniform or display a badge or ID of a peace officer to fraudulently induce another to believe the person is a peace officer. Violation of this provision during the commission of a felony adds one year of imprisonment to the felony sentence. (PC 667.17). Those who sell law enforcement uniforms must verify the ID of purchasers. Failure to do so is a misdemeanor, punishable by $1000 fine (PC 538d(d).)

False Information—VC 31. It is a misdemeanor to knowingly give false information to a peace officer while in the performance of his or her duties under the Vehicle Code.

Discussion. An example of a violation of VC 31 might be a false statement about ownership or use of vehicle, or about license or registration status, or required equipment or records. *People v. Millar*, 97 Cal. App. 3d Supp. 1. A violation of PC 148.9 typically occurs when a stopped motorist gives a fictitious name because he knows he has outstanding arrest warrants. See *People v. Cole*, 23 Cal. App. 4th 1672. A violation of PC 529 would occur if, for example, a motorist gave the name of his brother or some other person, and signed a written promise to appear under that name, potentially causing an FTA warrant to be issued when the unsuspecting third party failed to appear. *People v. Robertson*, 223 Cal. App. 3d 1277.

Concealing Accidental Death—PC 152. It is a misdemeanor to actively conceal or attempt to conceal an accidental death, such as by concealing the body, destroying evidence of the body, or destroying or concealing the instrumentality of death.

6.11 CONSPIRACY

Conspiracy Defined—PC 182. Conspiracy may be defined as two or more persons agreeing to commit *any* crime, where at least *one* of them does an *overt act* in furtherance of the conspiracy. Conspiracy is a felony.

The term "overt act," means any step taken or act committed which goes beyond mere planning or agreement to commit the crime. Examples of what constitutes an overt act are given in Section 6.12, below. The crime of conspiracy may be committed in any one of the following six ways.

Elements of the Crime—PC 182. "If two or more persons conspire:

1. To commit any crime.
2. Falsely and maliciously to indict another for any crime, or to procure another to be charged or arrested for any crime.
3. Falsely to move or maintain any suit, action, or proceeding.
4. To cheat and defraud any person of any property, by means which are in themselves criminal, or to obtain money or property by false pretense or by false promises with fraudulent intent not to perform such promises.
5. To commit any act injurious to the public health, to public morals, or to pervert or obstruct justice or the due administration of the laws.
6. To commit any crime against the person of the President or Vice President of the United States, the governor of any state or territory, any United States justice or judge, or the secretary of any of the executive departments of the United States."

Specific Intent Required. Conspiracy is a specific intent crime, requiring the accused to have the intent to commit the offense which is the object of the conspiracy (*People v. Jones*, 228 Cal. App. 2d 74).

To sustain a conviction of conspiracy there must be proof that the accused entered into a criminal agreement with specific intent to commit an unlawful act or to do a lawful act in an unlawful manner (*People v. Smith*, 63 Cal. 2d 779).

Discussion. The two or more persons who must agree or conspire together may include husband and wife (*People v. Pierce*, 61 Cal. 2d 879).

If an undercover officer is involved, there must be at least two other persons involved. The undercover officer is, of course, not one of the conspirators. It is not necessary that the accused know all the parties to the conspiracy. Each accused need know and enter into the unlawful agreement with only one other member of the conspiracy.

The target crime or object of the conspiracy does not have to be completed, or even attempted, to sustain a conspiracy conviction. Criminal conspiracy is a corrupt agreement between two or more persons to commit an offense prohibited by statute and which is accompanied by some overt act in furtherance of such agreement (*People v. Danielson*, 203 Cal. App. 2d 498).

Punishment for Conspiracy—PC 182. The crime of conspiracy, including a conspiracy to commit a misdemeanor, is a felony. Specific penalties, as given in PC 182, vary with the offense the conspirators plan to commit.

"All cases of conspiracy may be prosecuted and tried in the superior court of any county in which an overt act tending to effect such conspiracy shall be done [PC 182]."

Discussion. Conspiracy is actually an agreement between two or more persons to do an act which is unlawful in itself or to do a lawful act by some unlawful means. It is essential to the commission of the crime of conspiracy that there be an agreement or understanding between two or more persons that they shall act together. It is not necessary that the agreement be a formal one. It is sufficient if the minds of the parties meet understandingly so as to bring about an intelligent and deliberate agreement.

6.12 OVERT ACT IN CONSPIRACY

Overt Act Required—PC 184. "No agreement amounts to a conspiracy, unless some act, besides such agreement, be done within this state to effect the object thereof, by one or more of the parties to such agreement and the trial of cases of conspiracy may be had in any county in which any act be done."

Both the buyer and the seller of illicit drugs will generally also be guilty of conspiracy to engage in an unlawful transfer of narcotics. *Courtesy of Brand X Pictures*

Criminal conspiracy exists when two or more persons agree to commit a crime and then do some overt act in furtherance of the agreement (*People v. Cockrell*, 63 Cal. 2d 779).

Discussion. The term "overt act" means any step taken or act committed by one or more of the conspirators that goes beyond the mere planning or agreement to commit a public offense and which step or act is done in furtherance of the accomplishment of the object of the conspiracy.

To be an "overt act," the step taken or act committed need not, in and of itself, constitute the crime or even an attempt to commit the crime which is the ultimate object of the conspiracy. However, it must be a step or act which is taken in furtherance of accomplishing the object of the conspiracy. For example, buying a gun, tools, or supplies necessary for the job would constitute an overt act, thus satisfying that element of the crime.

Before the agreement amounts to a conspiracy, at least one of the conspirators must perform some overt act, lawful or unlawful, evidencing that the parties have gone beyond mere agreement and that the conspiracy has begun an active existence. It is not necessary that the overt act amount to an attempt to perform the conspiracy, although such would clearly constitute an overt act.

6.13 AGREEMENT NECESSARY IN CONSPIRACY

It is not necessary that each conspirator should know all of the details of the project or that the agreement should require each conspirator to participate in carrying out every detail of the conspiracy. It is sufficient that there should be a common understanding of the end to be achieved and an agreement to do whatever may be necessary to the achievement of such end (*People v. Buckman*, 186 Cal. App. 2d 38).

An agreement to commit a crime, as an element of criminal conspiracy, may be inferred from the conduct of defendants in mutually carrying out a common purpose in violation of the statute defining conspiracy (*People v. Cockrell*, cited above).

The essence of criminal conspiracy is the formation of a combination with others to do an unlawful act or to do a lawful act by unlawful means. Conspiracy is a separate and distinct offense from the crime which is the target or object of the conspiracy (*People v. Marrone*, 210 Cal. App. 2d 299).

Proof that two or more individuals conspired to commit a crime and engaged in overt acts leading to its commission will sustain a conviction of conspiracy even though they failed to accomplish the object of their intrigue (*People v. Buono*, 191 Cal. App. 2d 203). For example, three defendants who acted in concert with each other in transporting stolen property with an ultimate objective of disposing of it in some manner were guilty of conspiracy even though they were unable to sell the property (*People v. Wells*, 187 Cal. App. 2d 324).

Husband and Wife as Conspirators. Husband and wife could not, at common law, enter into a conspiracy between themselves without a third party being involved. Such is not the case in California today. Husband and wife can conspire between themselves, without a third party, and can no longer claim immunity from prosecution for conspiracy on the basis of their marital status (*People v. Pierce*, 61 Cal. 2d 879).

6.14 ABANDONMENT OF CONSPIRACY

It is possible to legally withdraw from a criminal conspiracy after once having met the requirements of a coconspirator. However, the abandoning conspirator must not only withdraw from all further activity, but must remain away from the scene at the time the crime is committed by other conspirators. Further, one who intends to withdraw from a conspiracy must make this fact known to his confederates. He must indicate his desire to entirely sever his relationship and no longer be a partner to the illegal enterprise (*People v. Beaumaster*, 17 Cal. App. 3d 996).

One who has joined a criminal conspiracy can effectively withdraw from it *only* by some affirmative act bringing home the fact of his withdrawal to his confederates. Unless this is done, the person will be presumed to have continued until the ultimate purpose of the conspiracy is established. Remaining silent or discontinuing further participation does not constitute "effective withdrawal" from a conspiracy (*People v. Moran*, 166 Cal. App. 2d 410).

For a veritable gold mine of answers to frequently asked questions (FAQ) about criminal conspiracy, specific intent, criminal procedure, search and seizure laws, laws of arrest and much more, go to Nolo Press' Web Site at: **http://www.nolo.com.** In the upper right corner of your computer screen, select "Search Entire Site." Then type "criminal law" and hit enter.

6.15 CRIMINAL LIABILITY IN CONSPIRACY

All parties to the conspiracy are equally responsible for the actions of all other parties taken in furtherance of the conspiracy. This includes any crimes, whether planned or not, which are committed during preparation for, or during commission of the crime. It also includes acts committed after the objective has been accomplished, such as during an escape or arrest. However, it does not include independent crime *not* committed in furtherance of the conspiracy by individual members of the conspiracy (*People v. Smith*, 63 Cal. 2d 779).

All coconspirators are liable for the consequences that naturally flow from the conspiracy and for the acts of all who participate with them in executing the unlawful purpose. Each conspirator is said to be the agent of the other, and the acts done are, therefore, the acts of each and every coconspirator. Even if one knowing of a conspiracy, without intending to join the agreement, nevertheless aids in carrying out such a conspiracy, he becomes equally guilty with the other conspirators.

Conspirators need not all join in the agreement at the same time. Those who join in a conspiracy previously formed, and who thereafter assist in its execution, become conspirators. As such they are equally liable with the others, not only for acts done thereafter, but for the original agreement and for all acts done in furtherance thereof (*People v. Brawley*, 1 Cal. 3d 277).

All members of a criminal conspiracy are bound by all of the acts of the members thereof in furtherance of an agreed-upon purpose (*People v. Scott*, 224 Cal. App. 2d 146). In addition, one who joins a conspiracy after its formation is liable as a conspirator just as those who originated it (*People v. Cornell*, 188 Cal. App. 2d 668).

Once a defendant's participation in a conspiracy is shown, it will be presumed to continue unless he is able to prove that he effectively withdrew from the conspiracy before acts toward the conspired crime commenced (*People v. Crosby*, 58 Cal. 2d 713).

A member of a criminal street gang, as defined in PC 186.22(f), who, with knowledge of the gang's criminal activity, promotes, furthers, assists, or benefits from any felonious criminal conduct by gang members, is guilty of conspiracy to commit that felony (PC 182.5).

STUDENT REVIEW

TERMINOLOGY DEFINED—CHAPTER 6

Please see the Terminology Quiz at the end of this chapter.

1. Abstain: to refrain from, refusing to participate.
2. Attest: to bear witness, to certify as true.
3. Compromise: settlement of a dispute by agreement of the parties.
4. Contusion: a bruise or similar injury however slight.
5. Cross-examination: examination of a witness by the opposing side.
6. Cumulative: additional evidence to the same point.
7. Deposition: sworn testimony given out of court to proper official.
8. e.g.: means "for example."
9. Element: identifiable segment of the crime.
10. i.e.: means "that is," or "in other words."
11. Immaterial: not important, does not alter anything.
12. Impanel: the process of selecting and seating a jury.
13. Impotent: lacking in sexual ability.
14. Incompetent: unfit, legally inadmissible.
15. Irrelevant: not to the point, does not apply.
16. Oath: promise or affirmation, attesting the truth.
17. Overt act: a physical act, usually toward completing a crime.
18. Perjury: giving false evidence or testimony under oath.
19. q.v.: means "which see" or "see reference."
20. Solicitation: crime of offering a bribe or asking another to participate in certain crimes.

TRUE-FALSE QUIZ—CHAPTER 6

After reading this chapter, you should be able to correctly answer the following items.

___ 1. An act of preparation is sufficient to make one guilty of an attempted crime.
___ 2. Entering a car without the owner's consent and operating the starter with a stolen key constitutes an attempted theft.
___ 3. One who abandons his original purpose after committing acts toward the commission of a crime is not guilty of any crime.
___ 4. There can be no crime of attempt if there is an impossibility of its consummation.
___ 5. If one attempts to shoot another with an unloaded gun, he is guilty of an assault.
___ 6. A person could be guilty of attempting to steal money from an empty cash drawer if at the time he thought it contained money.
___ 7. If one shoots another, not knowing the person he shot was already dead, he is not guilty of assault.
___ 8. Merely asking another to accept a bribe legally consummates the crime of solicitation.
___ 9. The crime of solicitation must be corroborated by two witnesses or by one witness and corroborating circumstances.
___10. Soliciting one to commit a misdemeanor is a crime under PC 653f.
___11. The offense of solicitation does not require an overt act other than the initial solicitation.
___12. If one offers an officer a bribe, but the officer refuses, the one offering the bribe is still guilty of the crime of solicitation.
___13. One is not guilty of perjury if he falsely testifies as to some immaterial fact.
___14. If "A" takes money from "B" to commit perjury, but instead "A" tells the truth, "B" is still guilty of subornation of perjury.
___15. Offering a teacher something of value in order to receive a better grade constitutes the crime of bribery under PC 67.5.

___16. Because of their marital status, husband and wife cannot commit the crime of conspiracy in California.
___17. Mere agreement by two or more persons to commit a felony constitutes conspiracy.
___18. Conspiracy to commit a misdemeanor is a felony under PC 182.
___19. If "A" and "B" plan a burglary, and "A" buys a prybar as a result, both are then guilty of conspiracy even though they are arrested before they actually do anything else toward commission of the burglary.
___20. All coconspirators are liable for the consequences of the acts of any one of the group in carrying out the conspiracy.

ESSAY-DISCUSSION ITEMS—CHAPTER 6

After reading this chapter, you should be able to correctly answer the following items.

1. How is an attempt defined? How far must it go toward completion to constitute a crime?
2. At what point is abandonment of an attempt a defense to the crime?
3. List any six of the several crimes for which one may be guilty of solicitation under PC 653f.
4. What are the elements of conspiracy?
5. Explain the overt act discussed in your text relative to conspiracy.
6. What are the elements of compounding a crime? Under what circumstances is it a felony and when a misdemeanor?
7. What is the essence of the crime of perjury? Must the witness know he is lying and must his statement be material to the case?
8. What are the elements of subornation of perjury? How does it differ from perjury?
9. What are the elements of bribery? What effect, if any, does the value of the bribe have on the offense?
10. How does bribery of a witness differ from subornation of perjury?

TERMINOLOGY QUIZ—CHAPTER 6

Match terms and definitions by writing the number preceding the correct term in the appropriate brackets.

Terms	*Definitions*
1. Abstain	[ ] giving false evidence or testimony under oath
2. Attest	[ ] promise or affirmation, attesting the truth
3. Compromise	[ ] to bear witness, to certify as true
4. Contusion	[ ] settlement of a dispute by agreement of the parties
5. Cross-examine	[ ] not to the point, does not apply
6. Cumulative	[ ] a bruise or similar injury
7. Deposition	[ ] unfit, legally inadmissible
8. e.g.	[ ] lacking in sexual ability
9. Element	[ ] additional evidence to the same point
10. i.e.	[ ] sworn testimony given out of court
11. Immaterial	[ ] Latin: "for example"
12. Impanel	[ ] the process of selecting and seating a jury
13. Impotent	[ ] identifiable segment of the crime
14. Incompetent	[ ] not important, does not alter anything
15. Irrelevant	[ ] Latin: meaning "that is" or "in other words"
16. Oath	
17. Overt act	
18. Perjury	
19. q.v.	
20. Solicitation	

CHAPTER 7

LAWS OF ARREST

7.1 ARREST DEFINED

PC 834 defines an arrest as follows: "An arrest is taking a person into custody, in a case and in the manner authorized by law. An arrest may be made by a peace officer or by a private person."

Method of Arrest. PC 835 defines how an arrest is made and what restraint is permitted. "An arrest is made by an actual restraint of the person or by submission to the custody of an officer. The person arrested may be subjected to such restraint as is reasonable for his arrest and detention."

Judges May Order Arrest. PC 838 states that: "A magistrate may orally order a peace officer or private person to arrest anyone committing or attempting to commit a public offense in the presence of such magistrate."

Summoning Assistance to Make Arrest. PC 839 provides that: "Any person making an arrest may orally summon as many persons as he deems necessary to aid him therein."

Following Arrest—Delay in Arraignment. A proper and lawfully executed arrest will generally not be rendered illegal should there be a delay in arraigning the arrestee (*People v. Jablon*, 153 Cal. App. 2d 456). However, criminal and civil liability for such delay on the part of the arresting officer or citizen is discussed in Sections 7.18 and 7.19 of this text.

7.2 ENCOUNTERS AND DETENTIONS

There is a legal difference as to what actually constitutes an arrest and what amounts to a temporary detention for questioning. There are obviously innumerable contacts between police and citizens that do not amount to arrests. California courts have recognized and distinguished between these situations as cited in the following case. "There are many contacts between police and citizen which are in no way related to crime, but from which evidence of crime may result. They arise from the police officer's duty

Whether an officer is engaged in a *detention* or a *consensual encounter* depends on whether a reasonable person would have felt free to leave. *Courtesy of Hulton Getty/Liason Agency, Inc.*

to maintain peace and security, to protect citizens from harm or annoyance and to do all those innumerable miscellaneous tasks which society calls upon the police to perform which have nothing to do with the detection of crime." (*Batts v. Superior Court*, 23 Cal. App. 3d 435).

Such contacts are not governed by the statutory rules of arrest, but by the Fourth Amendment requirement that governmental (includes police) search or seizure activity must not be "unreasonable." When an officer takes action which amounts to a "seizure" of an individual (detention or arrest), the Fourth Amendment safeguards come into play.

Even when an officer acts for the sole or primary purpose of uncovering or investigating criminal activity, such actions are not subject to the Fourth Amendment unless they amount to some sort of "search or seizure." To determine whether a contact between an officer and an individual amounts to a Fourth Amendment "seizure," it is necessary to examine the United States Supreme Court definitions.

A "search" occurs when governmental action infringes an expectation of privacy that society is prepared to consider reasonable (*US v. Jacobsen*, 466 US 109).

A "seizure" of *property* occurs when there is some meaningful interference by the government with an individual's possessory interests in that property (*Soldal v. Cook County*, 121 L.Ed. 2d 450).

A *person* has been "seized" within the meaning of the Fourth Amendment where the government, by show of force or other assertion of official authority, communicates to an individual that he or she is not free to disregard police presence and go about his or her business, and the individual is thereby caused to submit (*Florida v. Bostick*, 502 US 429; *California v. Hodari D.*, 499 US 621).

Given this definition of what is—and what is not—a "seizure" of a person under the Constitution, police contacts with citizens can be categorized in the following three ways:

1. **Consensual Encounters:** may properly be initiated by police even if they lack any "objective justification."
2. **Detentions:** may be undertaken by police if they have articulable suspicion.
3. **Arrests:** are constitutionally permissible only if police have probable cause.

The significance of these definitions lies in the fact that many police-citizen interactions fall into the first two categories and do not require "probable cause" for their initiation. This is important because under the court-created "exclusionary rule," any evidence resulting from an unreasonable search or seizure is subject to exclusion from a defendant's trial. This means that every seizure (including both "detentions" and "arrests") must be justified by a corresponding level of suspicion in order to be held constitutionally reasonable for exclusionary rule purposes.

Police officers, attorneys and judges must analyze the circumstances and events surrounding police contacts of those who eventually become criminal defendants. The purpose is to determine the point at which a "consensual encounter" occurred (if at all), the point at which an encounter progressed from being "with consent" into a "detention" (if at all), and the moment at which a detention was elevated to an "arrest."

Once the facts are known and analyzed, the parties can examine whether "articulable suspicion" existed as of the time of detention, and whether "probable cause" was established by the time an arrest was made. If each step the officer took was supported by the required level of justification, the exclusionary rule will not force the loss of resulting evidence. Also, the officer will not suffer civil liability for depriving the defendant of his or her Fourth Amendment rights.

Consensual Encounters. Typical examples of encounters which require no justification, include:

1. an officer walking up to a pedestrian and requesting (not demanding) to see identification (*United States v. Mendenhall*, 446 US 544),
2. officers asking a person if he would mind stepping aside and answering a few questions (*Florida v. Rodriquez*, 469 US 1), and
3. officers approaching the occupants of parked cars and engaging them in conversations (*People v. Jones*, 96 Cal. App. 3d 820 and *People v. Sandoval*, 164 Cal. App. 3d 958).

An encounter is still considered to be consensual even though the officer may be in uniform and driving a marked patrol car, as long as no force, commands or other manifestations of official authority are used to require the contacted person to remain. The court said: "The fact that most citizens will respond to a police request does not eliminate the consensual nature of the response" (*INS v. Delgado*, 466 US 210).

Under the Fourth Amendment test, a police officer is free to approach individuals on the streets or in other public places and make plain-view observations, engage in consensual conversation, and even request identification. The individual does not have to remain, or reply, or cooperate. And, his or her refusal to do so does not, in itself, constitute sufficient cause for detention. However, if the person voluntarily engages in a consensual encounter with an officer, any evidence resulting from this encounter will be unaffected by the exclusionary rule.

Temporary Detentions. The two most common examples of temporary detentions are the pedestrian stop and the traffic stop. Under the *Mendenhall* definition, a pedestrian has been "detained" when police use a show of force or authority, or order a person to stop or remain for questioning.

For such a detention to be "reasonable" under the Fourth Amendment, the officer must have "articulable (be able to state it) suspicion" that the pedestrian may be involved in criminal activity. This means that the officer must be able to articulate (state) exactly what the circumstances were that led him or her to suspect that the suspect may have been involved in criminal activity.

Safety and control permitting, therefore, an officer should ordinarily attempt a *consensual encounter* (by means of *requests*) before resorting to a *detention* (through *commands*). If the individual resists an encounter and the officer can articulate reasonable suspicion, a detention can then be employed.

Traffic Stops. The traffic stop, another example of a temporary detention, also can be made on the basis of articulable suspicion. Though many people often speak of "probable cause," or "PC," for a car stop, this is *not* the proper legal standard under the Fourth Amendment test.

What makes a traffic stop a form of detention is the display of red/blue lights or sirens (show of authority), or a command by an officer for a motorist to "pull over." Since a reasonable person should know he or she was not free to leave under these circumstances, a detention would have occurred as soon as the individual yielded. If the person flees, no detention occurs until he or she finally submits or is physically restrained (*California v. Hodari D.*, 499 US 621).

Detention Examples. The courts have also found a detention where police blocked the defendant's vehicle, even though no red lights were used. Where an officer pulled up behind a parked car and turned on red lights to signal the car not to pull away, a detention has occurred (*People v. Bailey*, 176 Cal. App. 39 402).

On the other hand, the use of a white spotlight for illumination of a vehicle does not create a detention. The court said that white lights do not legally compel a person to remain, and reasonable people know this (*People v. Franklin*, 192 Cal. App. 3d 935).

Articulable Suspicion. Unfortunately, there are few clear-cut formulas for determining whether facts and inferences amount to articulable suspicion to justify a detention. The court held that a traffic violation or equipment defect is sufficient to justify a car stop in *People v. Franklin*, 171 Cal. App. 3d 627. A wanted flyer for a vehicle's occupant was held sufficient in *United States v. Hensley*, 469 US 221.

Other factors that may contribute to articulable suspicion may include:

1. Observations of the suspect's activity.
2. Time of day.
3. Nature of the location.
4. The officer's knowledge of criminal activity in the area.
5. Information received through official channels and civilian informants.
6. Reasonable inferences that a trained and experienced police officer would be warranted in drawing.

Note: Compare the above articulable suspicion factors with probable cause under Section 7.9.

Length of Detention. Since a detention is, by definition, only a temporary seizure, it cannot be prolonged any longer than reasonably necessary to accomplish the purpose of the initial stop. However, if new facts become evident and justify further investigation, it can be extended (*People v. McGaughran*, 25 Cal. 3d 577).

If the initial detention serves to dispel the officer's suspicion, the detainee must be released to continue on his or her way. On the other hand, if the detention produces further grounds for suspicion, further detention is justified. If suspicion rises to the level of "probable cause," an arrest would then be warranted.

Cursory Search Upon Detention. Under the holding of *Terry v. Ohio*, an officer engaged in a temporary detention may conduct a cursory "pat down" search of a detainee's outer clothing, to discover offensive weapons, if the officer has articulable suspicion that the suspect may be armed and potentially dangerous. This same level of justification permits a cursory examination of the passenger compartment of a vehicle during a traffic detention (*Michigan v. Long*, 463 U.S. 1032). In all cases, however, the officer must be able to articulate (specifically describe) the reason for his or her suspicion.

Vehicle Occupants. During a lawful traffic stop, police are permitted to routinely order all occupants of a vehicle to get out of the car and remain in a neutral location. Furthermore, this order need not be justified by any particular suspicion of criminal activity (*Pennsylvania v. Mimms*, 434 US 106; and *Maryland v. Wilson,* 137 L Ed 2d 41).

Also during a lawful traffic stop, the officer is entitled to inspect the vehicle identification number (*New York v. Class*, 475 US 106), and if the driver indicates that driver's license or registration is in the vehicle, the officer is permitted to retrieve these items personally. The officer need not allow the driver to gain access to possible weapons by entering the vehicle (*People v. Faddler*, 132 Cal. App. 3d 607).

Officer's Intent Not a Factor. The peace officer's intent—whether to attempt a consensual encounter, make a detention, or make an arrest—is *not* a controlling factor in a Fourth Amendment analysis. The Fourth Amendment test which must be applied is an objective one. The inquiry focuses on what a reasonable person in the suspect's position would have believed, given the officer's actual behavior. Therefore, a contact will be judged, not on intentions, but objectively on the facts.

The court said, "Whether a Fourth Amendment violation has occurred turns on an objective assessment of the officer's action in light of the facts and circumstances confronting him at the time, and not on the officer's actual state of mind at the time the challenged action was taken" (*Maryland v. Macon*, 472 US 463).

7.3 PEACE OFFICER DEFINED

Chapter 4.5 of the California Penal Code, Sections 830 and 831 (with their many subsections), defines who are peace officers in this state. PC 830, which defines "peace officer," specifically reads: "Any person who comes within the provisions of this chapter and who otherwise meets all standards imposed by law on a peace officer is a peace officer, and notwithstanding any other provision of law, no person other than those designated in this chapter is a peace officer."

Designated Peace Officers—PC 830.1. "(a) Any sheriff, undersheriff, or deputy sheriff, employed in that capacity, of a county, any police officer of a district . . . authorized by statute to maintain a police department, any marshal or deputy marshal of a municipal court, or any constable or deputy constable, employed in that capacity, of a judicial district, or any inspector or investigator, employed in that capacity, in the office of a district attorney, is a peace officer. The authority of these peace officers extends to any place in the state:

1. As to any public offense committed or which there is probable cause to believe has been committed within the political subdivision which employs the peace officer.
2. Where the peace officer has the prior consent of the chief of police, or person authorized by him or her to give consent, if the place is within a city or of the sheriff, or person authorized by him to give such consent, if the place is within a county.
3. As to any public offense committed or which there is probable cause to believe has been committed in the peace officer's presence, and with respect to which there is immediate danger to person or property or of the escape of the perpetrator of the offense.

(b) The Deputy Director, assistant directors, chief, assistant chiefs, special agents and narcotics agents of the Department of Justice and such investigators who are designated by the Attorney General, are peace officers. The authority of these peace officers extends to any place in the state as to a public offense committed or which there is probable cause to believe has been committed within the state."

7.4 PEACE OFFICER STATUS PRIMARY DUTY

Authority of California Highway Patrol—PC 830.2(a). This section designates members of the California Highway Patrol as peace officers whose authority extends to any place in the state; provided, that their primary duty shall be enforcement of the provisions of the Vehicle Code or of any other law relating to the use or operation of vehicles upon the highways, as that duty is set forth in the Vehicle Code.

University of California Police—PC 830.2(b). Defines a member of the University of California Police as a peace officer pursuant to Section 92600 of the Education Code, provided that the primary duty of any such peace officer shall be the enforcement of the law within the area specified in the above Education Code section.

State College Police—PC 830.2(c). Defines members of a state university police department as peace officers pursuant to Education Code Section 89560 with the same authority and limitations given to University of California police described above.

Miscellaneous Police—PC 830.2, 830.3. These sections grant peace officer powers to the following agencies' investigators:

- Department of Alcoholic Beverage Control investigators.
- Department of Consumer Affairs investigators.
- Department of Forestry volunteer fire wardens.
- Department of Motor Vehicle investigators.
- California Horse Racing Board investigators.
- State Fire Marshal and deputy fire marshals.
- Food and Drug Section investigators.
- Division of Labor Standards Enforcement investigators.
- State Department of Health and Social Service investigators.
- California Exposition and State Fair marshals and police.
- Department of Insurance investigators.
- Department of Housing and Community Development investigators.
- State Controller's Office investigators.
- Department of Corporations investigators.
- State Contractors' License Board investigators.
- Franchise Tax Board officers.
- Specified officers of other executive departments. Peace officers under this section are not permitted to carry firearms unless their agency has adopted a policy on the use of deadly force, and the officers qualify with their firearms at least semi-annually.

Correctional, Parole, Probation Officers—PC 830.5. This section grants peace officer status to correctional officers, parole officers, probation officers, and California Youth Authority officers for the purpose of carrying out their primary function. Except as specified, these peace officers may carry firearms only if authorized and under the terms as specified by their employing agency. Persons permitted to carry firearms under PC 830.5, either on or off duty, shall meet the training requirements of PC 832 and shall qualify with the firearm at least quarterly.

Reserve Officers and Deputies—PC 830.6. This section pertains to reserve and auxiliary officers, deputy sheriffs, regional park districts, etc. Such special, reserve or auxiliary officer is a peace officer only during his or her specific assignment or tour of duty.

Limited Peace Officer Authority. It should be noted that the authority of all peace officers listed in PC 830.1 through PC 830.8 and PC 831 through 831.6 is limited to some degree. In most cases, these persons' peace officer jurisdiction is limited geographically to the property their employing agencies administer or have jurisdiction over (with the exceptions noted).

In other instances, firearms may not be carried without the express approval of the employing agency. Chapter 4.5 of the Penal Code also lists several peace officer categories where the officer is generally limited to exercising peace officer powers to his or her primary duty, such as is the case with state hospital security officers, and Alcoholic Beverage Control and Department of Motor Vehicle investigators.

One should also note that PC 832 requires that every person described and designated as a peace officer must complete a course of training (including use of firearms, if carried) certified by the Commission on Peace Officer Standards and Training within 90 days after being employed. Peace officer status is not granted until the required course is successfully completed.

Required Identification Badge—PC 830.10. This section requires the wearing of nameplate or badge clearly bearing the name or identification number of a uniformed peace officer.

Powers in Other Jurisdictions. Agreements, by letter or by a form entitled "Notice of Consent," may exist between municipalities with the cooperation of the county sheriff. The notice of consent grants that all regularly sworn, salaried peace officers of one jurisdiction shall have the authority of a peace officer at all times within the other jurisdiction.

Status of Off-Duty Police Officers. The Attorney General has ruled that a police officer may be paid on the basis of a regularly assigned forty-hour week by a city and nevertheless be charged at all times with the performance of the duties of a peace officer.

He or she is in fact a police officer twenty-four hours a day and subject to call both during his or her regularly assigned duty period and while he or she is off duty, and also at the termination of his or her regularly assigned duty hours (*AG Memo Opinion*, 21 December 1960).

A California Appellate Court decision tends to reinforce the above-stated opinion. The court said: "Peace officers such as policemen, deputy sheriffs, constables, etc., are under a special duty at all times, because of the nature of their employment, to use their best efforts to apprehend criminals . . ." (*People v. Derby*, 177 Cal. App. 2d 626).

Carrying Concealed Weapons Outside of Jurisdiction. The carrying and possession of concealed weapons is regulated by the Dangerous Weapons Control Law (PC 12000 et seq.). Section 12002 authorizes peace officers, special police officers, or law enforcement officers to carry various weapons and other equipment authorized by their agency for the enforcement of the law. Members of a police department are authorized to carry concealed weapons outside the city for which they are employed. Carrying concealed weapons in other states is controlled by the laws of each state.

Off-Duty Status and Private Employment. The Attorney General has ruled that off-duty peace officers who seek private employment as an incidental supplement to their public duties (such as working as security officers for a public entity), do not forfeit their status as peace officers. They retain such status while privately employed to keep the peace at specific public functions, and it necessarily follows that the commission of an assault or battery against such a peace officer is a felony offense as defined in PC 241 and PC 243.

Injuries suffered by a peace officer while off duty, but while performing a general duty of his office, have been held to be covered under workmen's compensation laws (*AG Opinion 66148 March 1966*). See PC 70, Section 6.8 of this text for additional details.

Status of Reserve Peace Officers. Section 24401 of the Government Code states, "Every county or district officer, except a supervisor or judicial officer, may appoint as many deputies as are necessary for the prompt and faithful discharge of duties of his office."

Section 7 of the Government Code, provides that: "Whenever a power is granted to, or a duty is imposed upon, a public officer, the power may be exercised or the duty may be performed by a deputy of the officer or by a person authorized, pursuant to law, by the officer, unless this code expressly provides otherwise."

Therefore, a special deputy sheriff or a special or reserve police officer is included within the exemption contained in subsection (a) of 12027 of the Penal Code. When so authorized by their superior officer, such officers may, therefore, carry concealed weapons (*AG Memo Opinion, October 1960*).

Reserve sheriff's deputies or police officers, while performing services as employees of a private patrol operator, may not wear any uniform, badge, or insignia which would give them the appearance of being deputy sheriffs or would create the impression that they are connected with a governmental agency.

Status of Federal and Private Police. Federal officers, such as FBI agents, Federal Narcotics Agents, Border Patrolmen, etc., are not peace officers when acting to enforce state laws.

Private patrol officers, private patrol operators, and private detectives or investigators are not peace officers. In making arrests they must follow the provisions as outlined in PC 837 relative to arrests by private persons (27 *Opinions, Attorney General*, 213).

7.5 ARRESTS BY PEACE OFFICERS WITHOUT WARRANT

The majority of arrests made by law enforcement officers are made without warrant and frequently under circumstances where thoughtful and effective judgment may be hampered by emotional conflicts. The officer stands in a cross-fire between the obligation to bring offenders to justice and the equally binding obligation of not violating a suspect's constitutional rights in so doing. This dilemma is a familiar occupational hazard in police work, and when faced with such a circumstance, the defense is a level head, and a thorough knowledge of the laws of arrest.

Warrantless Arrest in Home. Both the United States Supreme Court, in *Payton v. New York*, and the California Supreme Court, in *People v. Ramey*, 16 Cal. 3d 263, have held that police entry into a private home to make an arrest must either be by warrant, or with consent, or under "exigent (urgent) circumstances."

Such exigencies include life-threatening or dangerous crimes in progress, such as murder, robbery, rape, aggravated assault or kidnap. Substantial property-threatening emergencies would include arson, bombs, toxins, etc. Other exigencies would include "hot pursuit" of a dangerous offender, and imminent destruction of evidence.

In *United States v. Santana*, 427 US 38, the United States Supreme Court noted that even though an entry to make an arrest would be subject to the *Payton* restrictions, if the arrest were already being attempted outside, the suspect could not avoid arrest by retreating into private premises.

In other words, if the suspect is already inside a home when police arrive to arrest him, they must have a warrant, consent, or exigent circumstances. However, if police contact a suspect outside and inform him he is under arrest, he may be lawfully pursued wherever he flees for refuge.

Entry into a home to make an arrest is permissible only with warrant, consent, or exigent circumstances. *Photograph © Reuters NewMedia, Inc., courtesy of CORBIS*

Peace Officer Powers of Arrest—PC 836. A peace officer may make an arrest in obedience to a warrant, or may, pursuant to the authority granted by provisions of Chapter 4.5 (commencing with Section 930) of Title 3 of Part 2, without a warrant, arrest a person:

1. Whenever the officer has reasonable cause to believe that the person to be arrested has committed a public offense in the officer's presence.
2. When a person to be arrested has committed a felony, although not in the officer's presence.
3. Whenever the officer has reasonable cause to believe that the person to be arrested has committed a felony, whether or not a felony has in fact been committed.

In analyzing the subsection 1, above, three factors must be considered:

1. reasonable cause,
2. officer's presence, and
3. public offense.

A peace officer may make an arrest without a warrant if he or she has "reasonable cause" to believe that the arrestee has committed a felony. PC 836, subsection 1, includes misdemeanor arrests and is the only definitive portion of the Penal Code covering this area.

To the general rule that an officer may make a misdemeanor arrest only for offenses occurring in his or her presence, the legislature has made several specific exceptions. Under PC 836.1, a misdemeanor arrest may be made based on "reasonable cause" to believe the arrestee has assaulted or battered a firefighter or paramedic (PC 241(b) or 243(b)). Per PC 12031(a)(4), an officer may arrest on reasonable cause for a misdemeanor violation of PC 12031, carrying a loaded firearm in a vehicle or in public.

Vehicle Code 40300.5 authorizes a DUI arrest on reasonable cause in cases of traffic accidents, vehicles blocking the roadway, the person will not be apprehended unless immediately arrested, injury or damage may result if no arrest is made, or evidence may be destroyed or concealed without immediate arrest. And Welfare & Institutions Code section 625 permits a minor to be taken into custody on reasonable cause as to any offense, felony or misdemeanor. Also, in domestic violence cases, an officer shall make a misdemeanor arrest on reasonable cause to suspect violation of a restraining order (PC 836 (c)(1)), and may, as soon as probable cause arises, arrest for an assault or battery against a cohabitant, relative 65 or older, or child (PC 836 (d)).

Officer's Presence Defined. An officer must have reasonable cause to believe that the person to be arrested has committed a misdemeanor in the officer's presence. The term "*in the officer's presence*" is not limited to immediate physical proximity but relates to the person's senses, i.e., what is perceived by the person making the arrest (*People v. Lavender*, 137 Cal. App. 582). Thus, regardless of the distance between the officer and the person to be arrested, conduct on the part of the arrestee may very well be apparent through one of the officer's appropriate senses such as sight (includes using binoculars), smell, or hearing.

Public Offense Defined. Under subdivision 1, the term "public offense" includes felonies, misdemeanors and infractions. Although citations are normally issued in infraction cases, both the US and California Supreme Courts have held that a custodial arrest for a fine-only traffic infraction is reasonable under the Fourth Amendment, if supported by probable cause (*Atwater v. City of Lago Vista, Texas,* 532 U.S. 318; *People v. McKay,* 27 Cal.4th 601).

Felony Not in Officer's Presence. Subsection 2, of PC 836, is applicable only to those felonies which have actually been committed by the person who is arrested. A peace officer may, without a warrant, arrest a person for a felony not committed in the officer's presence (*People v. Poole*, 27 Cal. 572).

Reasonable Cause. Subsection 3, of PC 836 is the most practical in regard to arrests for felony offenses. This provision deals with felony arrests whether within or out of the officer's presence. The officer, of course, must have reasonable cause to believe that the arrestee has committed a felony, whether or not a felony has in fact been committed. A verbal complaint by a citizen, for example, could constitute the "reasonable cause" requirement. Reasonable cause factors are discussed more fully in Section 7.9 of your text.

Arrest Without a Warrant on Reasonable Cause—PC 836.5(a). "A public officer or employee, when authorized by ordinance, may arrest a person without a warrant whenever he has reasonable cause to believe that the person to be arrested has committed a misdemeanor in his presence which is a violation of a statute or ordinance which such officer or employee has the duty to enforce."

Civil Liability—Self Defense—PC 836.5(b). "There shall be no civil liability on the part of, and no cause of action shall arise against, any public officer or employee acting pursuant to subdivision (a) and within the scope of his authority for false arrest or false imprisonment arising out of any arrest which is lawful or which the public officer or employee, at the time of the arrest, had reasonable cause to believe was lawful. No such officer or employee shall be deemed an aggressor or lose his right to self-defense by the use of reasonable force to effect the arrest, prevent escape, or overcome resistance."

Written Notice to Appear—PC 836.5(c). "In any case in which a person is arrested pursuant to subdivision (a) and the person arrested does not demand to be taken before a magistrate, the public officer or employee making the arrest shall prepare a written notice to appear and release the person on his promise to appear, as prescribed by . . . Section 853.6 of this title. The provisions of such chapter shall thereafter apply with reference to any proceeding based upon the issuance of a written notice to appear pursuant to this authority."

7.6 DUTY FOLLOWING ARREST

Duty to Take Accused Before Magistrate—PC 849(a). "When an arrest is made without a warrant by a peace officer or private person, the person arrested, if not otherwise released, shall without unnecessary delay, be taken before the nearest or most accessible magistrate in the county in which the offense is triable, and a complaint stating the charge against the arrested person shall be laid before such magistrate."

Release From Custody—PC 849(b). This subsection provides that "Any peace officer may release from custody, instead of taking such person before a magistrate, any person arrested without a warrant whenever:

1. He or she is satisfied that there are insufficient grounds for making a criminal complaint against the person arrested.
2. The person arrested was arrested for intoxication only, and no further proceedings are desirable.
3. The person was arrested only for being under the influence of a controlled substance or drug, and such person is delivered to a facility or hospital for treatment and no further proceedings are desirable."

Record of Release—Detention—PC 849(c). "Any record of arrest of a person released pursuant to paragraphs (1) and (3) of subdivision (b) shall include a record of release. Thereafter, such arrest shall not be deemed an arrest, but a detention only."

Appearance Before Magistrate—Time Extension PC 825. The defendant must in all cases be taken before the magistrate without unnecessary delay, and in any event, within 48 hours after his arrest, excluding Sundays and holidays; provided, however, that when the 48 hours expire at a time when the court in which the magistrate is sitting is not in session, such time shall be extended to include the duration of the next regular court session on the judicial day immediately following; provided further, that a person arrested on a Wednesday must be arraigned on Friday (unless either the Wednesday or Friday is a court holiday).

Right to Attorney—PC 825(b). "After such arrest, any attorney at law entitled to practice in the courts of record of California, may, at the request of the prisoner or any relative of such prisoner, visit the person so arrested."

Refusing Attorney Visit—Penalty—PC 825(b). "Any officer having charge of the prisoner so arrested who willfully refuses or neglects to allow such attorney to visit a prisoner is guilty of a misdemeanor. Any officer having a prisoner in charge, who refuses to allow any attorney to visit the prisoner when proper application is made therefor, shall forfeit and pay to the party aggrieved the sum of five hundred dollars ($500), to be recovered by action in any court of competent jurisdiction."

Foreign National Advisement—PC 834c. Upon arrest and booking, or detention for more than two hours, a known or suspected foreign national must be advised of the right to communicate with a consular official from his or her country. If the arrestee requests it, police must contact the consulate and allow communications or visits with a consular official.

Certificate Describing Arrest as Detention—PC 851.6. This section provides that when a person is arrested and released pursuant to paragraph (1) or (3) of subdivision (b) of PC 849 (see Release From Custody, above), the person shall be issued a certificate, signed by the releasing officer or his superior officer, describing the action as a detention.

Any reference to the action as an arrest shall be deleted from the arrest records of the arresting agency and of the Bureau of Criminal Identification and Investigation of the Department of Justice. Thereafter, any such record of the action shall refer to it as a detention.

7.7 PRIVATE PERSON ARRESTS

Private Persons—Authority to Arrest—PC 837. "A private person may arrest another:

1. For a public offense committed or attempted in his presence.
2. When the person arrested has committed a felony, although not in his presence.
3. When a felony has been in fact committed, and he has reasonable cause for believing the person arrested to have committed it."

An officer responding to a domestic violence call is required to "make a good faith effort to inform the victim of his or her right to make a citizen's arrest" (PC 836(b)).

Felony Must Be Committed. A private citizen, unlike a peace officer, may not arrest solely on reasonable cause to believe that the person to be arrested has committed a felony not in his presence, unless a felony has in fact been committed (*People v. Martin*, 225 Cal. App. 2d 91).

In Presence Defined. The subject of a citizen's arrest is reviewed in *People v. Burgess*, 170 Cal. App. 2d 36, and the court discusses what circumstances must exist for the offense to have been committed "in the presence" of the arresting citizen. The term as used in PC 837 is liberally construed much the way it is for police officers. "In his presence," as used in this section, does not refer merely to physical proximity. It includes anything within the reception of the arresting person's senses. This means, for example, that a crime can be committed in the presence of one's sense of hearing and smell, as well as sight (*Ogulin v. Jeffries*, 121 Cal. App. 2d 211).

Use of Force. A private person is justified in using only reasonable force (as is a peace officer) in making an arrest. The citizen making an arrest may not use any more force than is absolutely necessary to overcome resistance, if any. Of course, if the person being arrested does not resist, then no force may be used. A private citizen is not justified in using lethal force in making an arrest for crimes against property, unless his or another person's life is in immediate danger. Even in felony crimes, deadly force may be used to stop a fleeing felon only if the fleeing felon is at the moment an actual threat to other persons' lives. An example might be a fleeing robber who is firing a gun as he runs from the scene.

Resistance to Private Person Arrest. A private person making an arrest has the right to use reasonable force in effecting an arrest if such arrest is lawful. If the person being arrested physically resists the arrest, the arrestee is committing an assault upon the person making the arrest providing the latter is acting in a lawful capacity.

Duty After Arrest—PC 847. "A private person who has arrested another for the commission of a public offense must, without unnecessary delay, take the person arrested before a magistrate or deliver him to a peace officer. There shall be no civil liability on the part of, and no cause of action shall arise against, any peace officer acting within the scope of his authority, for false imprisonment arising out of any arrest when:

a. Such arrest was lawful or when such peace officer, at the time of such arrest, had reasonable cause to believe such arrest was lawful; or
b. When such arrest was made pursuant to a charge, upon reasonable cause, of the commission of a felony by the person to be arrested; or
c. When such arrest was made pursuant to the requirements of Penal Code Sections 142, 838, or 839."

Duty of Officer to Receive Arrested Persons—PC 142. "(a) Any peace officer who has the authority to receive or arrest a person charged with a criminal offense and willfully refuses to receive or arrest such person shall be punished by a fine not exceeding ten thousand dollars ($10,000), or by imprisonment in the state prison or in a county jail not exceeding one year, or by both such fine and imprisonment."

"(c) This section shall not apply to arrests made pursuant to Section 837."

Inquiry Into Legality of Private Person Arrest. Although PC 142 makes it a felony to refuse to receive a person charged with a criminal offense, this provision does not apply to arrests made by private persons. To avoid civil liability, the federal courts have insisted that probable cause support any arrest made or accepted by a peace officer—including a citizen's arrest (*Arpin v. Santa Clara Valley Transportation Agency,* 261 F. 3d 912). Therefore, officers who are asked to receive a private person's arrest may either refuse to do so, or may inquire into the probable cause for the arrest, and to minimize liability risks, should accept it, if at all, only if satisfied it is supported by probable cause. In borderline cases, the officer may advise the private person that the arrest has been accepted, but then immediately release the arrestee per PC 849(b), and refer the matter to the prosecutor for a decision on whether or not to file charges. Local policy advice should be sought on this issue.

Detention of Suspect—PC 490.5(f). A merchant, theater owner or librarian may detain a suspect based on probable cause to believe the suspect is attempting to take merchandise, an unauthorized recording, or library materials; reasonable nondeadly force may be used for protection against the suspect or to prevent escape, and to conduct a search if items are not voluntarily surrendered.

7.8 MISDEMEANOR CITATIONS

Several California codes authorize the issuance of a citation in lieu of taking an arrestee into custody, and in some instances, such as most traffic violations and violations of the Alcohol Beverage Control Act, a citation must be issued. The citation, often referred to as a summons, is simply a form directing the defendant to appear at a specified time and place to answer a specific charge in a court of competent jurisdiction.

PC 853.6(a) provides that when a person is arrested for any misdemeanor offense not involving domestic violence and does not ask to be taken before a magistrate, the arresting officer may, instead of taking such person before a magistrate, receive from him his written promise to appear in court. An officer may use the written notice to appear (1) for any misdemeanor offense which he has reasonable cause to believe the person to be arrested has committed in his presence, or (2) for any misdemeanor offense in which a private person made the arrest and delivered the arrested person to the officer.

Miscellaneous Citation Provisions—PC 853.6. The following subsections of PC 853.6 further regulate the issuance of citations as indicated:

(b) Specifies that the court appearance date shall be at least 10 days after arrest.

(c) Specifies the court before whom the person must appear.

(d) Provides that the arrestee shall be given one copy of the notice to appear (citation).

(e) Provides that the officer shall file the duplicate notice to appear with the court or prosecuting attorney.

(f) States that no warrant shall issue on the charge for the arrest of a person who has given written promise to appear unless he or she fails appear.

(g) Provides for pre-release booking, or citation to the department for booking and fingerprinting prior to the specified court appearance.

(h) Provides that a police officer may use the written notice to appear procedure for any misdemeanor offense under PC 836 or PC 847 (Citizen's arrest).

Reasons for Nonrelease—PC 853.6(i). This subsection provides that whenever any person is arrested by a peace officer for a misdemeanor, and is not released with a written notice to appear in court according to this chapter, the arresting officer shall indicate on a form, provided by his or her agency, which of the following was a reason for the nonrelease:

1. The person arrested was so intoxicated that he could have been a danger to himself or to others.
2. The person arrested required medical examination or medical care or was otherwise unable to care for his own safety.
3. The person was arrested for one or more of the offenses listed in Section 40302 and 40303 of the Vehicle Code (no ID, failure to sign citation).
4. There were one or more outstanding arrest warrants for the person.
5. The person could not provide satisfactory personal identification.
6. The prosecution of the offense(s) for which the person was arrested or the prosecution of any other offense(s) would be jeopardized by immediate release of the person arrested.
7. There was a reasonable likelihood that the offense(s) would continue or resume, or that the safety of persons or property would be imminently endangered by release of the person arrested.
8. The person arrested demanded to be taken before a magistrate or refused to sign the notice to appear.
9. There is reason to believe that the person would not appear at the time and place specified in the notice. The basis for this determination must be specifically stated by the officer.

Voiding Citations—PC 853.6(j). Once a citation has been delivered to the person cited, it is a misdemeanor for any officer or his agency to "alter, cancel, modify, nullify or destroy" the citation. Any voiding or cancellation of a citation, once issued, can only be done in court, by the magistrate.

Vehicle Code Violations—VC 40500. This section of the California Vehicle Code provides for the issuance of a citation in triplicate with generally the same requirements as for criminal offenses. There are, however, exceptions in this case where a mandatory appearance by the arrestee is necessary by law, such as (1) failure of arrestee to exhibit an operator's license or other satisfactory evidence of identity; (2) failure of arrestee to sign the citation; (3) when the arrestee demands to be taken forthwith to a magistrate; and (4) when the person arrested is charged with certain other Vehicle Code Violations such as VC 20001 (failure to stop at the scene of an accident involving bodily injury).

Voiding Traffic Citations. As with PC 853.6(j), voiding or altering a traffic or parking citation is likewise a misdemeanor under VC 40202(c) and 40500(d).

Citations for Alcoholic Beverage Control Violations. Section 24209 of the Business and Professions Code (Alcoholic Beverage Control Act) states in part that . . . "when an arrest is made of any person for a violation of Sections 23000 through 26004, the arresting officer shall release such licensee or employee without taking him before a magistrate, upon such licensee or employee signing an agreement to appear in court or before a magistrate at a place and time designated by an arresting officer."

7.9 PROBABLE CAUSE TO ARREST

Under the test of Fourth Amendment "reasonableness," an arrest must be based on "probable cause." Though this concept has not proven easy to describe, probable cause is obviously more than "articulable suspicion" sufficient to justify a detention. For example, a driver's weaving and speeding would constitute articulable suspicion to justify a traffic detention. Once an officer had added this degree of suspicion to the driver's intoxicated appearance, admission to drinking, and poor performance on field sobriety tests, the initial suspicion would have grown into sufficient probable cause to support a DUI arrest.

Probable Cause Defined. Probable cause (sometimes referred to as "reasonable cause") has been judicially defined on many occasions since 1984 as ". . . such a state of facts as would lead a person of ordinary care and prudence to believe and conscientiously entertain an honest and strong suspicion that the person is guilty of a crime." (*People v. Kilvington*, 104 Cal. 86.)

The United States Supreme Court has further explained the "probable cause" standard as follows: "While an effort to fix some general, numerically precise degree of certainty corresponding to probable cause may not be helpful, it is clear that only the probability, and not a *prima facie* showing, of criminal activity is the standard of probable cause." (*Illinois v. Gates*, 462 U.S. 213.)

The Supreme Court also said, ". . . when used by trained law enforcement officers, objective facts, meaningless to the untrained, can be combined with permissible deduction from such facts, to form a legitimate basis for suspicion of a particular person and for action on that suspicion." (*United States v. Cortez*, 449 US 411.)

The courts will generally inquire into two aspects of reasonableness to arrest:

1. Probable cause to believe that a crime was *prima facie* committed, based on the establishment of a *corpus delicti*, and
2. Probable cause to believe that the person arrested is the perpetrator of the crime committed.

Probable Cause Factors. The kinds of factors, previously mentioned as possible ingredients of articulable suspicion, are normally the same kinds of factors constituting probable cause. This is true because the difference between articulable suspicion and probable cause is not the *nature* of the underlying information, but the *amount* of it. The more information an officer has, the greater the suspicion that will be warranted. As the United States Supreme Court has noted: "In making a determination of probable cause, the relevant inquiry is not whether particular conduct is 'innocent' or 'guilty,' but the

Warrantless arrest requires *probable cause* to believe the suspect is guilty of some criminal offense. *Photograph by Robert Brenner, courtesy of PhotoEdit*

degree of suspicion that attaches to particular types of noncriminal acts." (*Illinois v. Gates*, 462 US 213.)

Thus, innumerable factors could operate to establish probable cause for arrest including:

1. suspect's activity and statements,
2. attempts at concealment,
3. flight,
4. manner of dress,
5. location,
6. time of day or night,
7. number of suspects,
8. prior criminal record,
9. recent reports of criminal activity in the area,
10. official information such as broadcasts, flyers, etc.,
11. information from informants,
12. historical patterns of criminal activity,
13. suspect's physical appearance and demeanor such as speech, injection "tracks", etc.,
14. telltale odors, such as alcohol, marijuana, ether, and
15. facts gained by the officer's senses of sight, smell, touch, hearing and taste.

As the court said in *People v. Marshall*, 69 Cal. 2d 51, ". . . an officer may rely upon all his senses in determining whether there is probable cause to believe that a crime has been committed or that contraband may be present."

When a police officer considers the particular information available to him or her in light of training and experience and draws reasonable inferences of criminal activity such that any reasonable officer would have been warranted in drawing—and this combination of factors and their implications creates a strong suspicion the person has committed or is committing a crime—a probable cause finding is justified.

Obviously, each case must be judged on the totality of the circumstances confronting the officer in each particular case. There is no "secret formula" for probable cause. There are no "magic words" (such as "furtive gestures" or "evasive conduct") which will automatically justify an officer's conduct. Specific facts—not hunches—are the requirement of the probable cause standard.

Insufficient Probable Cause. The arresting officer must be in a position to articulate (state) specific facts that constitute probable cause for an arrest. In *Cunba v. Superior Court*, 2 Cal. 3d 352, the court held there was no probable cause to make an arrest where a plain-clothes officer observed the defendant and a companion look around to see if anyone was watching. When they stopped walking, it appeared that they exchanged money. The officer testified that the defendant was arrested to see if a narcotics sale had occurred.

Re-arrest of Probationer or Parolee—PC 1203.2. This section provides for the re-arrest of a person on probation by a probation officer or peace officer *without* warrant or other process, at any time until final disposition of the probationer's case. Rearrest must be based on probable cause to believe the probationer has violated a condition of probation, or the criminal law.

Regarding parolees, the Adult Authority has full power to suspend, cancel, or revoke any parole without notice and to order the return to prison of any prisoner under parole. The *written* order of any member of the Adult Authority shall be sufficient warrant for any peace officer to return to actual custody any conditionally released or paroled prisoner (PC 3060).

Discussion. As a condition of obtaining probation or parole, most convicts have agreed to a "search and seizure condition." This is a provision that makes the person subject to search and seizure by peace officers anytime, anyplace, whether or not there is probable cause or articulable suspicion to believe the person is violating the law. (*People v. Reyes*, 19 Cal. 4th 229).

The California Supreme Court has upheld these conditions, provided police officers do not use them to harass the probationer or parolee (*People v. Bravo*, 43 Cal. 3d 600).

7.10 ENTRAPMENT

Entrapment Defined. *Black's Law Dictionary* defines entrapment as an act by the police of inducing a person to commit a crime not contemplated by the suspect, for the purpose of prosecuting him. In one of the leading cases in California, the court stated, "The law does not tolerate a person, particularly a law enforcement officer, generating in the mind of a person who is innocent of any criminal purpose, the original intent to commit a crime, entrapping such person into the commission of a crime which he would not have committed or even contemplated but for such inducement." (*People v. Galvan*, 208 Cal. App. 2d 443.)

California Supreme Court Ruling. The California Supreme Court made a major change in the law of entrapment with its decision in *People v. Barraza*, 23 Cal. 3d 675. That decision set forth an entirely new standard for determining whether activities of law enforcement officers and their agents will be considered entrapment.

Origin of Intent Rule Overruled. The California Supreme Court, in overruling Barraza's conviction, discussed entrapment and the "origin of intent" rule, which had been the legal standard used in California to determine entrapment for many years.

The court rejected this former rule. It stated that the reason for having entrapment as a defense is to deter police misconduct. The court felt that the defense should thus focus itself on the police conduct, not on the defendant and his particular predispositions toward crime. The court stated that no matter how bad the defendant's prior record or present inclinations toward criminality were, police conduct to ensnare him into further crime could not be tolerated.

Current Entrapment Test. The court then formulated the following test on whether police actions are, or are not, entrapment. The test is: was the conduct of the law enforcement agent likely to induce a normally law-abiding person to commit the offense?

Official conduct that does no more than offer that opportunity to the suspect—for example, a decoy program—is therefore permissible. However, it is impermissible for the police or their agents to pressure the suspect by overbearing conduct such as badgering, cajoling, or other affirmative acts likely to induce a normally law-abiding person to commit the crime.

Setting Traps. Officers may set reasonable traps in an effort to apprehend criminals. This is best illustrated by an early California case in which a constable disguised himself and feigned drunkenness by lying in an alley in an effort to apprehend suspects who were "rolling" drunks in the area. The court held that there is no entrapment where an officer disguises himself, feigns drunkenness, and makes no objection when (marked) money is taken from his person (*People v. Hanselman*, 76 Cal. 460).

Use of Decoy. When officers of the law are informed that a person intends to commit a crime against the property or person of another, the law permits them to afford opportunities for its commission and to lay traps which may result in the detection of the offender. To this end a decoy may pretend to be a participant in a crime. The decoy may be present with the suspect at the time the crime is to be committed. If the accused commits the overt acts necessary to complete the offense, he will not be protected from punishment by reason of the fact that when the acts were done by him the decoy was present, with acknowledgment and approval of the authorities—even if the decoy aided in and encouraged their perpetration.

Use of Deception. The courts have held, for example, that the loaning of a truck to the defendants by a police officer to facilitate the commission of a burglary is not entrapment, even though the officer knew from his conversation that they intended to commit the crime (*People v. Malone*, 117 Cal. App. 629).

Use of Informants. Use of informants both to detect crime and to gather evidence against suspects of crime is considered almost essential for detection of crimes such as narcotics, prostitution, gambling, illegal liquor sales, etc. Such offenses usually involve no victim who will complain to the police.

Inevitably, the use of police informers and undercover agents involves police deception, false friendships and sometimes the buying of information against an accused. The courts have condoned such activities on the grounds of sheer necessity as long as police practices were kept within reasonable bounds as discussed in this section.

In *Hoffa v. United States*, 385 US 293, the Supreme Court rejected most of the constitutional challenges to the use of informers and upheld a conviction based on incriminating statements made by the accused to an apparent colleague (who was actually an informer). The court held that defendant's expectations that his statements would be kept confidential by the "colleague" were not entitled to constitutional protection. The defendant, in effect, was held to have "assumed the risk" that his apparent colleague might turn out to be an informant.

The courts have also held that paid informers are an indispensable part of law enforcement and that relevant evidence obtained by them is admissible (*People v. Finkelstein*, 98 Cal. App. 2d 545).

Juvenile Informants. No person under age thirteen may be used as a police informant. Minors aged thirteen to eighteen may be used only with a court order. An "informant" is a minor who is cooperating for consideration on his or her own pending petition in juvenile court (PC 701.5).

In-custody Informants. When one prisoner is used as an informant on another, this fact must be disclosed to the jury at trial (PC 1127a). If the informant is granted leniency on his case for cooperating, this fact must be disclosed to the victim in the informant's case (PC 1191.25). No cash payment over $50.00 may be paid to an in-custody informant for his testimony (PC 4001.1).

Informant "Wired for Sound." The use of an informer who is wearing a "wire" or body transmitter, raises issues under the Fourth and Sixth Amendments, as well as under state and federal statutes regulating governmental use of electronic surveillance.

The United States Supreme Court has generally found no search and seizure problem under the Fourth Amendment in "wired informant" cases. This on the theory that a wrongdoer's misplaced trust in a feigned confidant does not qualify as a legitimate expectation of privacy. Just as the informant would have been free to testify to what he had heard the suspect say, he is free to transmit the conversation simultaneously to police receivers, or to record it for evidentiary purposes (*United States v. White*, 401 US 745).

Tape recordings, as a practical matter, are more trustworthy than an individual's recollection.

Surreptitious Surveillance Limitation. Once the suspect has been formally charged (by indictment or arraignment) and has retained or requested an attorney, surreptitious recording of statements elicited by a wired informant violates the Sixth Amendment right to the assistance of counsel and would be inadmissible as evidence of the crime charged (*United States v. Henry*, 447 US 264).

Custodial Surveillance. Both the US Supreme Court (*Lanza v. New York,* 370 US 139) and the California Supreme Court (*People v. Lloyd,* 27 Cal.4th 997 and *People v. Davis,* 36 Cal.4th 510) have ruled that there is no legitimate expectation of privacy in a jail or prison cell or waiting room. This means that surreptitious monitoring or recording of inmates' unprivileged conversations in a custodial setting will not violate the Fourth Amendment. *Note:* State law prohibits monitoring or recording confidential conversations between a prisoner and his attorney, religious adviser or physician (PC 636).

Need for Legal Consultation. Because these statutory restrictions are constantly changing, and because violations by police officers can carry heavy civil and criminal penalties, police use of wires, beepers, pen registers, and other devices for receiving or tracking communications must be made only in close consultation with departmental legal advisors.

To be sure that planned use of electronic surveillance will not violate the Fourth Amendment restrictions of *Katz v. United States*, 389 U.S. 347, nor the Sixth Amendment restrictions of *Massiah v. United States*, 377 U.S. 201, it is desirable to obtain the advice of local prosecutors, wherever possible.

7.11 ACCOMPLISHING THE ARREST

An arrest is made by an actual restraint of the person or by submission to the custody of an officer. The person arrested may be subjected to such restraint as is reasonable for his arrest and detention (PC 835).

Under this section, an arresting officer or private citizen has the right to pursue an arrestee or an escapee and use whatever force may be necessary for his arrest as long as such means are reasonable.

An officer or citizen is never justified in using deadly force on one guilty of a misdemeanor in order to effect an arrest (unless in self-defense to counter deadly force). An officer properly engaged in attempting to make an arrest on a misdemeanor charge, has the right to resist attack made upon him, and being rightfully there and not being legally considered the aggressor, he may in his own defense take a human life (*People v. Wilson*, 36 Cal. App. 589).

Advising Cause and Authority for Arrest—PC 841. The person making the arrest must inform the person to be arrested (1) of the intention to arrest him, (2) of the cause of the arrest, and (3) the authority to make it.

So advising is not required when (1) the person making the arrest has reasonable cause to believe that the person to be arrested is actually engaged in the commission of or an attempt to commit an offense, or (2) the person to be arrested is pursued immediately after its commission or after an escape.

The person making the arrest must, if requested by the person he is arresting, inform the latter of the offense for which he is being arrested.

An officer does not have to notify the accused of his official capacity before making an arrest, when it is known to the accused or when by the exercise of ordinary reason, the accused should know it. For example, notification of authority to arrest is not needed where the officers are in uniform, with their badges displayed (*Allen v. McCoy*, 135 Cal. App. 500).

When the arrestee insists on knowing the specific charge on which he is being arrested, it is the officer's obligation to so advise the arrested person. However, the statutory declaration of intention can be dispensed with if the circumstances are such that the arrestee knows he is about to be arrested (*People v. Scott*, 170 Cal. App. 2d 446).

Actual and Constructive Custody. Custody is generally defined as the detention of a person against his will. Actual custody and constructive custody differ in that, as previously stated, one comes into actual custody through physical restraint or through submission to custody. On the other hand, constructive custody implies a status. Constructive custody would thus apply to a county jail "trusty" or an honor farm inmate.

Use of Reasonable Force—PC 835a. Any peace officer who has reasonable cause to believe that the person to be arrested has committed a public offense may use reasonable force to effect the arrest, to prevent escape, or to overcome resistance. A peace officer who makes or attempts to make an arrest need not retreat or desist from his or her efforts by reason of the resistance or threatened resistance of the person being arrested. Also, the officer shall not be deemed the aggressor or lose his or her right to self-defense by using reasonable force to effect the arrest, to prevent escape, or to overcome resistance.

Use of Deadly Force. Homicide is never justifiable in making an arrest for a misdemeanor or preventing escape of a misdemeanor arrestee (*People v. Newsome*, 51 Cal. App. 42). (See also text Section 7.13, Escape and Fresh Pursuit.)

Although reasonable force may include deadly force in some cases, the United States Supreme Court has held that police use of deadly force to apprehend or prevent escape may violate the Fourth Amendment and create civil liability under federal law. Exceptions could apply to dangerous offenses with indications that the suspect presents a grave danger to public safety unless immediately apprehended (*Garner v. Tennessee*, 471 US 1). Departmental policy on use of deadly force should be consulted for more specific guidelines.

Unlawful Use of Force—Penalty—PC 149. "Every public officer who, under color of authority without lawful necessity, assaults or beats any person, is punishable by a fine not exceeding ten thousand dollars ($10,000) or by imprisonment in the state prison, or in a county jail not exceeding one year, or by both such fine and imprisonment."

Inhumanity to Prisoners—Penalty—PC 147. "Every officer who is guilty of willful inhumanity or oppression toward any prisoner under his care or in his custody, is punishable by a fine not exceeding four thousand dollars ($4,000) and by removal from office."

7.12 RESISTING ARREST

Resisting Arrest—Duty to Refrain—PC 834a. This section, while not describing a crime, clearly states that if a person has or should have knowledge that he or she is being arrested by a peace officer, it is that person's duty to refrain from using force or any weapon to resist arrest.

Resisting or Obstructing Peace Officer, Public Officer, Emergency Medical Technician; Removal of Officer's Firearm—PC 148(a). "Every person who willfully resists, delays, or obstructs any public officer, peace officer, or an emergency medical technician . . . in the performance of his or her office or employment, when no other punishment is prescribed, is punishable by a fine . . . or by imprisonment in the county jail . . . or by both a fine and imprisonment."

Discussion. The above describes the misdemeanor portion of PC 148. There is no violation of this section unless the perpetrator actually impedes the officer. Merely shouting obscenities, or throwing one's ID on the ground, for example, is not sufficient. A violation requires some obstructive conduct, such as physically blocking a doorway (*People v. Pool*, 42 Cal. 3d 105).

The U.S. Supreme Court has held that a person may be convicted of delaying or obstructing an officer for refusing to identify himself, where the circumstances of a detention require the officer to determine the person's identity in order to complete the investigation (*Hiibel v. Sixth Judicial District of Nevada,* 124 S.Ct. 2451).

Felony Resisting. However, with the addition of any one of the following elements, the crime becomes a felony (PC 148.10):

(1) Whenever the willful resistance of a person proximately causes death or serious bodily injury to a peace officer, the person violating the subdivision shall be punished by imprisonment in the state prison . . . or a fine . . . or both the fine and imprisonment or by imprisonment in the county jail . . . or by a fine . . . or by both a fine and imprisonment.

(2) For purposes of paragraph (1), the following facts shall be found by the trier of fact:

(a) That the peace officer's action was reasonable based on the facts or circumstances confronting the officer at the time.

(b) That the detention and arrest was lawful and there existed probable cause or a reasonable cause to detain.

(c) That the person who willfully resisted, delayed, or obstructed any peace officer knew or reasonably should have known that the other person was a peace officer engaged in the performance of his or her duties.

(3) Paragraph (1) shall not apply to conduct which occurs during labor picketing, demonstrations, or disturbing the peace.

(4) For purposes of this subdivision, "serious bodily injury" is defined in paragraph (5) of subdivision (f) of Section 243.

Discussion. It is a felony (wobbler) under PC 148(b) and (d) for a person, during the commission of any offense described in PC 148(a), to:

(1) take or remove any weapon *other than a firearm or*

(2) to *attempt* to remove or take a *firearm* from the person of or immediate presence of a peace officer or public officer.

It is a felony under PC 148(c), to actually take or remove a firearm from the person of or immediate presence of a peace officer or public officer.

In order to prove a violation involving a firearm, the prosecution must establish that the defendant had *specific intent* to remove or take the firearm by demonstrating that any of the following direct, but ineffectual acts occurred. That the defendant:

(1) unfastened the officer's holster strap,
(2) partially removed officer's gun from its holster,
(3) released the gun's safety,
(4) stated to an independent witness that he or she intended to take or remove the firearm and the defendant actually touched the gun,
(5) had his or her hand on the gun and tried to take it away from the officer who was holding it, or
(6) attempted to pick up the officer's firearm after it fell in the course of any struggle,
(7) touched the firearm, as evidenced by fingerprints or other scientific evidence.

Giving False Identification—PC 148.9. It is a misdemeanor to give false identification to a peace officer when lawfully detained or arrested.

Resisting Executive Officer—PC 69. This section makes it a felony (wobbler) to deter or prevent an "executive officer" (which includes peace officers) from doing their legal duty by threatening or knowingly resisting with force or violence.

Posting Officials' Addresses on the Internet—GC 6254.21. No person shall knowingly post the home address or phone number of a public official (includes judges, prosecutors, public defenders, elected officials and peace officers) on the internet, intending to cause imminent great bodily harm or threatening to cause imminent great bodily harm. Violation is a misdemeanor if no harm results, or a felony (wobbler) if the official or household dependent suffers bodily injury.

7.13 THE MIRANDA ADMONISHMENT

The Fifth Amendment to the United States Constitution includes a provision that "no person shall be compelled in any criminal case to be a witness against himself." In the five-to-four 1966 landmark decision in *Miranda v. Arizona* (384 US 436), the United States Supreme Court held that compulsion is *inherent* (built-in) in the process of custodial interrogation.

The court reasoned that whenever a person is arrested and held in isolation by police, the stress of

Recommended procedure is to read the Miranda admonishment from a standard card or form before custodial interrogation, to insure that nothing is inadvertently omitted or materially modified. *Photograph © Monkmeyer/Conklin*

the police-dominated atmosphere and the knowledge that one is under arrest, tend to undermine the person's free will. When this custodial compulsion is then *combined* with the additional compulsion of being subjected to police interrogation, the arrestee loses the ability to choose for himself whether to speak or remain silent. Any statement given under such circumstances, said the court, is *necessarily compelled,* and its use in the prosecution's case would violate the Fifth Amendment.

Having reached this conclusion, the Supreme Court established a judicial exclusionary rule under the Fifth Amendment (as it had previously done in Fourth Amendment search-and-seizure cases, such as *Mapp v. Ohio*). The court declared that the prosecution could not use any statement made by a criminal defendant to prove guilt whether incriminating or not—resulting from custodial interrogation, unless adequate safeguards were taken to neutralize the "inherent compulsion." Physical evidence discovered by interrogation lacking Miranda compliance is not made inadmissible by Miranda (*People v. Whitfield*, 46 Cal. App. 4th 947).

Procedures For Admonishment. The Court approved a technique of admonishing the suspect of his Fifth Amendment rights and giving the suspect the option of agreeing to answer questions, or remaining silent. In the later decision of *California v. Prysock* (453 U.S. 355), the Supreme Court explained that no "talismanic incantation" of any particular words or magic Miranda formula was required. However, the following admonishment has generally been held to meet *Miranda* requirements:

- You have the right to remain silent.
- Anything you say may be used against you in court.
- You have the right to have a lawyer with you before and during questioning.
- If you cannot afford to hire a lawyer, one will be appointed for you without charge before questioning, if you wish.

Steps Following Admonishment. After the admonishment is given, the suspect should be asked if he understands his rights, and whether he wants to discuss the case. Any ambiguity or lack of understanding should be resolved before proceeding further. For example, if the suspect seems confused about any of the rights, or if his responses don't clearly show whether he intends to waive or invoke his rights, further clarification should be attempted.

Before the prosecution can offer a suspect's responses to custodial interrogation into evidence, the prosecutor has the burden of proving that the suspect (1) was timely and properly advised, (2) understood his rights, and (3) voluntarily waived his rights.

Invocation of Rights. If the suspect invokes his or her rights, any custodial statement obtained thereafter will be inadmissible in the prosecution, unless the suspect himself initiates further discussions and waives his rights (*Smith v. Illinois*, 469 US 91; *Edwards v. Arizona*, 451 US 477).

When Miranda Admonishment Required. Since the Miranda warning was specifically designed to neutralize the inherent compulsion of custodial interrogation, it is only required when the two elements of *custody* and *interrogation* are present. Thus, a volunteered statement made by a suspect in custody is *not* subject to Miranda because it was not prompted by *interrogation.* Likewise, telephonic interrogation of a suspect while he is at home or at work, for example, is not subject to Miranda because the suspect is not in *custody.*

When and Where *Not* to Admonish. The following is recommended relative to administration of the Miranda warning:

1. No suspect in custody should be warned of his or her rights and a waiver solicited unless an interrogation is to follow within a short period of time. Conversely, if a suspect is given a warning and a waiver obtained, he or she should be interrogated promptly thereafter. All too often, arrest reports indicate that a suspect was advised of his or her rights and a waiver obtained and no interrogation followed. In some cases, a warning is given and no waiver solicited. In such cases, the officer who gave the Miranda warning has engaged in an idle act.
2. Where the suspect appears unlikely to waive Miranda rights, he or she should *not* be warned and questioning should be deferred to a later time. This will usually occur where the suspect appears to be obviously uncooperative or belligerent.
3. Where the suspect appears likely to waive Miranda rights and talk about the case, questioning should begin as soon as possible. Compliance with Miranda rules must, of course, precede the interrogation.
4. Questioning should be deferred, together with warning of Miranda rights, where the arresting officer is unfamiliar with the case. For example, it often happens that an officer making an arrest upon a warrant or pursuant to instructions will be unfamiliar with the case.
5. Law enforcement agencies should adopt, wherever feasible, procedures whereby investigating officers may be promptly alerted of the fact that a suspect is in custody so that an interrogation can be begun as soon as possible. Procedures should also be adopted so that investigating officers will be available to conduct an interrogation as soon as possible after the arrest of a suspect.
6. It should be remembered that a person in custody need not be warned of Miranda rights and a waiver solicited, unless he or she is to be interrogated.
7. Any officer hearing a volunteered statement made by a suspect in conversation initiated by the suspect, should make notes of the statements and advise his supervisor or the investigating officer. A report of the volunteered statement and the circumstances should be included in the case file. This policy should apply to any officer, whether or not he is familiar with the case.
8. In all cases, an officer should promptly notify his supervisor or the investigating officer of the fact that the suspect has stated that he desires to talk about the case. The investigating officer should be immediately informed of the suspect's request.
9. A suspect who initiates a conversation about the case, need not be warned of his rights until police custodial interrogation commences.

Note: Neither custody nor interrogation alone will trigger the need for a Miranda warning. It is only the combination of custody and interrogation together that creates the kind of psychological compulsion triggering the need for neutralizing warnings. This fact makes it necessary for officers to be aware of the Supreme Court's definitions of "interrogation" and "custody," which follow.

What Constitutes Interrogation. In *Rhode Island v. Innis* (446 US 291), the United States Supreme Court responded to this question thusly: "The term 'interrogation' under Miranda refers not only to express questioning, but also to any words or actions on the part of the police (other than those normally attendant to arrest and custody) that the police should know are reasonably likely to elicit an incriminating response from the suspect." Typical booking questions, such as asking the suspect's name, date of birth, address, etc., would not be subject to Miranda warning or exclusionary provisions.

Also, if officers are conversing between themselves in the suspect's presence, but without intent to provoke a response from the suspect, any statement he volunteers would not be the product of interrogation.

What Constitutes Custody. In the years immediately following the *Miranda* decision, California appellate courts, struggling to interpret Miranda in light of the *Dorado* and *Escobedo* decisions, sent out conflicting signals as to how the courts (and, therefore, peace officers) should determine the existence of "custody." For example, some officials were of the view that custody occurred whenever a suspect was interrogated inside a police station.

Another view held that custody was dependent upon the officer's focus of suspicion on a suspect. Still another interpretation was that custody attached as soon as police developed probable cause to arrest. Finally, a different theory held that a person was in custody as soon as he was no longer free to leave.

One by one, these assorted definitions of Miranda "custody" have been rejected by the United States Supreme Court. In *Minnesota v. Murphy* (465 US 420) the court said, "The mere fact that an investigation has focused on a suspect does not trigger the need for Miranda warnings in noncustodial settings."

In *Oregon v. Mathiason* (429 US 492) the court had this to say about Miranda warnings: "Police officers are not required to administer Miranda warnings to everyone whom they question. Nor is the requirement of warnings to be imposed simply because the questioning takes place in the station house, or because the questioned person is one whom the police suspect."

Current Objective Test of "Custody." Recognizing that earlier state decisions had misconstrued the "custody" element of Miranda, later appellate decisions have declined to rely on such subjective factors as focus, probable cause or intent to detain, to determine "custody."

In *Stansbury v. California,* 128 L Ed 2d 293, the United States Supreme Court finally settled the question of when a suspect is in custody. Quoting its earlier decision in *California v. Beheler*, 463 US 1121, the court said: "Although the circumstances of each case must certainly influence a determination of whether a suspect is 'in custody' for purposes of receiving Miranda protection, the ultimate inquiry is simply whether there is a formal arrest or restraint on freedom of movement of the degree associated with a formal arrest."

When Miranda Does Not Apply. Under the *Beheler* concept that custody depends on an announced arrest or equivalent restraints (such as handcuffs, drawn weapons, or lock-ups), and not on what the officer or the suspect happened to be thinking, the Supreme Court held that Miranda did *not* apply to police interrogation in the following circumstances:

- A burglary suspect voluntarily agreed to come to the station and answer questions, having been advised that he was suspected, but not under arrest (*Oregon v. Mathiason*).
- A murder suspect was asked to accompany officers to the station, where he was told he was not under arrest, and was not subjected to any physical restraint (*California v. Beheler*).
- A temporary pedestrian detention or car traffic stop, even though the suspect would obviously not be free to leave. Such persons are not "in custody" for Miranda purposes (*Berkemer v. McCarty*, 468 US 420).
- A DUI suspect was questioned about his drinking, even though the officer making the stop had already made up his mind that the suspect would be arrested (but hadn't told this fact to the suspect) (*Berkemer v. McCarty*).
- A tax fraud suspect was questioned in his home by IRS agents, even though the agents advised the suspect he was the focus of a criminal investigation (*Beckwith v. United States*, 426 US 341).

Custody a Critical Factor. The critical factor in each of these cases was that a reasonable person in the suspect's position would not have felt that he was *under arrest* at the time the interrogations occurred. In the absence of either a formal arrest or its equivalent restraints, the compulsive element of *custody* was not present; therefore, Miranda did not apply.

Miranda and "Independent State Grounds." Prior to the passage of Proposition 8 in 1982, California courts had occasionally refused to follow United States Supreme Court decisions in the Miranda area. They decided, instead, to place greater restrictions on police and prosecutors in this state, on the basis of "independent state grounds" of the state constitution.

In a significant reversal of this trend, the California Supreme Court held in its 1988 opinion of *People v. May*, 44 Cal. 3d 309, that the voters, in enacting Proposition 8's "Truth-in-Evidence" provision, intended to rescind the state-grounded exclusionary decisions.

In the *May* decision, the court reasoned that "Proposition 8 was crafted for the very purpose, among others, of abrogating [nullifying] state court decisions which had elevated the procedural rights of the criminal defendant above the level required by the federal Constitution, as interpreted by the United States Supreme Court." On the basis of this holding, the California Supreme Court approved of a decision by the lower trial court to follow the United States rule of *Harris v. New York*. This rule made non-Mirandized statements admissible for impeachment of the defendant, thereby abandoning the contrary holding of *People v. Disbrow*.

Independent State Grounds Abolished. In the *May* decision, relating to admissibility of a suspect's statement, like the earlier decision of *In re Lance W.*, on the admissibility of evidence resulting from search-and-seizure activity, the United States Supreme Court declared the California courts could no longer (after Proposition 8) apply different exclusionary rules than those prescribed by the U.S. Supreme Court. As a result of this holding, the following California decisions have been abrogated (nullified, repealed) in favor of the corresponding federal rules.

- **Abrogated.** *People v. Pettingill*, 21 Cal. 3d 231, which had held that once an arrestee had invoked his rights, no officer could attempt to question him, even about unrelated crimes.

- **Current.** *Michigan v. Mosley*, 423 US 96. The United States Supreme Court held that as long as police "scrupulously honor" the arrestee's invocation of silence as to the first crime, it is permissible to request a waiver and obtain a statement regarding a separate crime being investigated.

- **Abrogated.** *People v. Johnson*, 70 Cal. 2d 541, which had held that if an arrestee is initially questioned in violation of Miranda, any subsequent statements he makes—even after a warning and waiver—would be presumed to be tainted by the initial error and would be inadmissible.

- **Current.** In *Oregon v. Elstad*, 470 US 298, the United States Supreme Court held that even though an initial Miranda error would render the initial statements inadmissible, this would not prevent the police from later giving a valid warning, obtaining a voluntary waiver, and getting an admissible statement.

- **Abrogated.** California cases such as *People v. Braeseke*, 25 Cal. 3d 691, applied a *Wong Sun* "fruit of the poisoned tree" theory to Miranda violations. This suppressed not only the defendant's non-Mirandized statements, but also any physical evidence or other so called "fruit of the poisoned tree" disclosed by the statements.

- **Current.** The United States Supreme Court, in *U.S. v. Patane,* 124 S.Ct. 262, specifically limited the *Miranda* exclusionary rule to unwarned statements themselves, and refused to extend exclusion to cover the "fruits" of a Miranda error.

- **Abrogated.** In *People v. Rucker*, 26 Cal. 3d 368, the California court held that after an arrestee had invoked Miranda, any answers he might give to routine booking questions would be inadmissible, on the ground that such questions would constitute "interrogation."

- **Current.** In *Rhode Island v. Innis,* 446 US 291, which defined "interrogation" for purposes of the Miranda warning, the United States Supreme Court limited the definition to questions "other than those normally attendant to arrest and custody." Thus, booking questions would not be subject to Miranda warnings (*United States v. Avery*, 717 Fed. 2d 1020).

In addition to the specific cases listed above, all of the earlier California cases attempting to equate "custody" with such concepts as focus of suspicion, probable cause to arrest, or intent to detain, are no longer controlling. These cases conflict with the

United States Supreme Court holding in *California v. Beheler* (discussed earlier) that "custody," for purposes of the Miranda warning, essentially means a formal arrest or use of that degree of restraints normally associated with arrest.

Frequency of Miranda Warnings. In apparent overreaction to the *Miranda* decision, some peace officers have followed a practice of warning the suspect repeatedly, each time an interrogation resumes, or each time the interrogating officer changes. Giving repeated warnings sometimes prompts individuals to request an attorney and invoke their right to remain silent. Therefore, it is not desirable to "over-Mirandize." Nor, according to the courts, is it necessary to do so. "A Miranda warning is not required before each custodial interrogation. One warning, if adequately and contemporaneously given, is sufficient." (*People v. Braeseke*, above.)

Miranda Warnings for Juveniles. The United States Supreme Court has never held that juveniles should receive any different advice under Miranda than is required before custodial interrogation of adults. Although some printed versions of the "advice of rights cards" used by some agencies contain a special admonition that juveniles have a "right" to consult parents and have parents present at interrogation, this admonition is not constitutionally required. The court said: "There is no requirement that a minor be advised of and waive the opportunity to speak to a parent or to have a parent present during police questioning" (*In re Jessie L.*, 131 Cal. App. 3d 202).

The United States Supreme Court did suggest, in *Fare v. Michael C.*, 442 U.S. 707, that a minor's request to talk to a parent or probation officer might be an attempt to invoke the right to remain silent (and should be clarified before proceeding with interrogation). The court held, however, that such a request was *not* a direct invocation of the right to counsel.

Therefore, whenever a juvenile in custody affirmatively requests to speak to relatives or other advisers before answering questions, it is advisable for the officer to clarify with the minor whether he or she is asserting the Fifth Amendment right to remain silent. However, it is not legally necessary (or tactically wise) to gratuitously invite a problem by erroneously advising the juvenile of a "right" to talk to parents.

Welfare and Institutions Code section 625 creates a statutory duty on the part of officers to advise a minor of certain rights "in any case where" a minor is taken into temporary custody for a W & I 602 violation. This statute does not refer to Miranda, and there is no statutory exclusionary remedy attached. For purposes of admissibility of a minor's statements, therefore, W & I 625 has no effect. Admissibility will be determined by constitutional standards, including Miranda compliance. Officers are best advised to consult local policy on W & I 625 application for other purposes.

The Miranda Waiver. The *Miranda* decision established that the prosecution bears a "heavy burden" of demonstrating a knowing and voluntary waiver of its protections before a resulting statement is admissible. This does not necessarily require an express statement by the suspect that he is waiving his rights, and it is not legally necessary for officers to ask a suspect whether he wishes to give up his rights and discuss the case. Both the United States and California Supreme Courts have held that neither an express written or oral statement of waiver is invariably necessary (*North Carolina v. Butler*, 441 U.S. 369; *People v. Whitson,* 17 Cal. 4th 229). The *Whitson* case held that a suspect's acknowledgment that he understood his rights, followed by a statement, would indicate that he knowingly chose to waive his rights and to speak.

In *People v. Peevy*, 17 Cal. 4th 1184, the California Supreme Court unanimously ruled that a voluntary statement obtained from a custodial suspect who has requested an attorney, while inadmissible to prove guilt, is nevertheless admissible to impeach the suspect if he testifies inconsistently at trial. In *dicta*, the court voiced its disapproval of the practice of questioning "outside Miranda". Departmental policies on the use of such questioning may vary, and should be consulted for guidance.

As a matter of practice, it is not uncommon for defendants to contradict police testimony, falsely asserting either that they were not properly warned, or did not waive, or did not make the statements attributed to them. Most prosecutors recommend that, whenever possible, officers use tape recorders, or written waivers and confessions, to overcome courtroom recanting by defendants.

Volunteered Statements. Regardless of Miranda, a suspect's *volunteered* statements are always admissible. And even though a suspect has once invoked his rights to cut off interrogation, the suspect himself remains free to change his mind, initiate further discussion with police, and waive the rights he had previously invoked.

Nothing in the Miranda line of cases prevents police from overhearing a volunteered statement. "Volunteered statements of any kind are not barred by the Fifth Amendment and their admissibility is not affected by our holding today." (*Miranda v. Arizona*, 384 US 436.)

Other Constitutional Restrictions. When the admissibility of a confession is at issue, most people think automatically of the Fifth Amendment test of Miranda. Law enforcement professionals must bear in mind, however, that a statement can also be held inadmissible under the Fourth, Sixth and Fourteenth Amendments, in situations having nothing to do with Miranda.

Fourth Amendment Rights. Under such Fourth Amendment cases as *Wong Sun v. United States*, 371 US 471 and *Brown v. Illinois*, 422 US 590, even a statement preceded by full Miranda warning and waiver can be suppressed if it resulted from an unreasonable search, seizure or entry.

Sixth Amendment Rights. The Sixth Amendment right to counsel will be violated—requiring exclusion of a resulting statement—if police initiate interrogation of an accused (whether in or out of custody) after he has been indicted or arraigned on the case and has requested or obtained an attorney. This was the ruling of such cases as *Massiah v. United States*, 377 U.S. 201. Therefore, once judicial proceedings have begun and the accused asserts his right to counsel, police may no longer initiate interrogation on this case in the absence of counsel. Volunteered statements and discussion initiated by the accused are still permissible. Because the Sixth Amendment is "offense specific," it does not prohibit questioning on other cases where no indictment or arraignment has occurred (but if the suspect is in custody, Miranda still applies).

Fourteenth Amendment Rights. The "Due Process Clause" of this amendment may compel exclusion of a suspect's statements if such statements resulted from improper police influences, including force, threats, or express or implied promises of leniency. Thus, when an officer suggests to the suspect that things will "go harder" on the suspect unless he confesses, any resulting statement may be inadmissible.

Likewise, if an officer promises to get the suspect some sort of help, or work out a "deal," or offers to exchange any kind of benefit for a statement (such as an "own recognizance" release, lowering bail, dropping some charges, releasing a relative or arranging preferential treatment for the suspect), any statement obtained thereby would probably be found to be legally "involuntary" and inadmissible, despite Miranda compliance (*Mincey v. Arizona*, 437 U.S. 385 and *People v. Jimenez*, 21 Cal. 3d 595).

7.14 ARREST PURSUANT TO WARRANT

Affidavit for Arrest Warrant. In order to secure arrest warrants, the courts require an affidavit to accompany the complaint. The affidavit must state, under oath, the facts constituting the probable cause for the arrest, in order to comply with the Fourth Amendment of the United States Constitution. If such affidavit is not used, any evidence found as a result of a search incidental to that arrest might not be admitted into evidence.

Of course, if the defendant is already in custody, no affidavit is needed with the complaint. Each court has forms for the affidavit that may be used by that particular court.

However, in a case in which an officer in good faith obtains a warrant for the arrest of the accused, and has personal knowledge constituting probable cause for the arrest, even if the warrant is otherwise invalid on federal grounds, the arrest is still lawful. The fruits of a search incidental to that arrest are admissible under such circumstances (*US v. Leon*, 468 US 897).

Hearsay evidence is admissible in these affidavits because it is being used to establish probable cause for the arrest, not the truth of the matter of the offense (*Chimel v. California*, 396 US 752).

The Formal Complaint. The filing of a complaint will normally precede the issuance of a warrant of arrest. The complaint, like an indictment or information, is an accusatory pleading (PC 691). The complaint is a written document, sworn to under oath, subscribed (signed) by the complainant, and filed with a competent court, charging a person with a criminal offense. Where there is no one available who has positive knowledge of all the facts of the alleged offense, such complaint may be made upon information and belief.

"Ramey Warrant"—PC 817. In *People v. Ramey*, 16 Cal. 3d 263, the court held that a nonconsensual, non-exigent entry into a home to make an arrest requires a warrant. Section 817 sets forth a procedure by which an arrest warrant can be obtained in a case where no complaint has yet been filed by the prosecutor or indictment returned by the grand jury. A statement of probable cause for arrest may be submitted to a magistrate by written affidavit, or by telephone or facsimile, to get a "Ramey Warrant."

Nature of Arrest Warrant. A warrant of arrest is a written order, signed by a magistrate, and directed to a peace officer, commanding the arrest of a person. If the complaint satisfies the magistrate that the offense complained of has been committed and there are reasonable grounds to believe the defendant committed it, he has a duty to issue a warrant to arrest the defendant (PC 813). The warrant may also be issued upon indictment by the Grand Jury, or to arrest a bail-jumping fugitive from another state (PC 847.5).

Form of the Arrest Warrant. The form of an arrest warrant is set forth by statute—PC 814 for felony warrants—PC 1427 for misdemeanor warrants. The following must be included in the arrest warrant:

1. Name of defendant, but if unknown he may be designated by any name. If a fictitious name (e.g., John Doe) is used, the warrant must contain a description or some means of identifying the person intended, otherwise the warrant is void.
2. Time of issuance.
3. City and county where issued.
4. Signature of issuing magistrate or judge with the title of his office.
5. The bail as set by the magistrate, if the offense is bailable (PC 815-815a).

Warrant—To Whom Directed. A warrant of arrest must be directed generally to any peace officer in the state and may be executed by any of those officers to whom it may be delivered (PC 816).

Although no one other than a peace officer may execute a warrant of arrest, the law provides that any person making an arrest may orally summon as many persons as he deems necessary to aid him therein (PC 839).

Nighttime Service of Warrant. An arrest for the commission of a felony may be made on any day and at any time of the day or night. An arrest for the commission of a misdemeanor or an infraction cannot be made between the hours of 10 o'clock p.m. of any day and 6 o'clock a.m. of the succeeding day, unless:

1. The arrest is made without a warrant pursuant to Section 836 or 837 (which cover arrests without warrants).
2. The arrest is made in a public place.
3. The arrest is made when the person is in custody pursuant to another lawful arrest, or
4. The arrest is made pursuant to a warrant which, for good cause shown, directs that it may be served at any time of the day or night (PC 840).

Misdemeanor Offense Warrant. PC 818 provides that where a misdemeanor warrant is served at night upon a person at his place of residence, and the warrant is for a traffic offense, and such warrant on its face authorizes said procedure, the arresting officer may release the defendant on a notice to appear instead of booking him.

Warrant Not in Officer's Possession. An arrest by a peace officer acting under a warrant is lawful even though the officer does not have the warrant in his possession at the time of the arrest, but if the person arrested so requests it, the warrant shall be shown to him as soon as practicable (PC 842).

Either a telegraphic copy or an abstract of a warrant may be sent by teletype or telegraph, and in the hands of the receiving officer, he must proceed as though he had the original warrant (PC 850). A proper abstract must contain the following:

- The charge, and whether a felony or a misdemeanor.
- The court of issuance.
- The subject's name, address, and description.
- The bail.
- The name of the issuing magistrate.
- The warrant number.

Disposition of Arrestee in County Where Warrant Issued. If the offense charged is a felony, and the arrest occurs in the county in which the warrant was issued, the officer making the arrest must take the defendant before the magistrate who issued the warrant or some other magistrate of the same county (PC 821).

Disposition of Arrestee in a County Other Than Where Warrant Issued (Felony or Misdemeanor). An officer must inform the defendant in writing of his right to be taken before a magistrate in the county where arrested and must note on the warrant that he has so informed the defendant and, if required by the defendant, must take him before a magistrate in that county.

The defendant may post bail in the amount set on the warrant (or set by bail schedule if bail not set on a misdemeanor warrant) either with the magistrate, or with the officer in charge of the jail without appearing before the magistrate. The magistrate or officer in charge of the jail may release the arrested person and set a time and place for his appearance in the proper court of the county where the warrant was issued.

If a defendant is admitted to bail by a local magistrate, the magistrate must certify that fact on the warrant, deliver it to the officer, and the officer must then discharge the defendant from arrest and deliver the warrant to the Clerk of the issuing court.

If a felony warrant has no bail set thereon, or if in any case the defendant does not demand to be taken before a local magistrate, or if he does not post bail, the arresting officer must notify the law enforcement agency requesting the arrest in the county where the warrant was issued and that agency must take custody of the defendant within five days and take him before the magistrate who issued the warrant, or another magistrate in the same county (PC 821, 822, 823 and 1296b).

Weapons Taken From Arrested Person. Any person making an arrest may take from the person arrested all offensive weapons which he may have about his person and must deliver them to the magistrate before whom he is taken (PC 846).

Return of Warrant After Service. The arresting officer has the duty of endorsing and subscribing his "return" (verification of service) on the warrant and delivering it to the magistrate at the time he delivers the arrestee. Penal Code Section 828, prescribes the procedure for endorsing the warrant upon proper service.

Officer's Liability in Serving Warrant. There shall be no liability on the part of, and no cause of action shall arise against, any peace officer who makes an arrest pursuant to a warrant of arrest regular upon its face if such peace officer in making the arrest, acts without malice and in the reasonable belief that the person arrested is the one referred to in the warrant (Civil Code, Section 43.5a).

7.15 ESCAPE, PURSUIT, AND RETAKING

Escape. A person who has knowingly been lawfully arrested by a peace officer commits a misdemeanor by escaping or attempting to escape custody. If the escapee uses force or violence and thereby causes serious bodily injury to the peace officer, the crime is a wobbler (PC 836.6).

Escapes by booked or sentenced prisoners are covered by Penal Code sections 4530 through 4536. Also, a person who brings or sends escape devices to prisoners to aid an escape is guilty of a felony (PC 4535).

Fresh Pursuit—PC 852.2. "Fresh pursuit" means close pursuit, or as it is sometimes called, "hot pursuit" of a suspect by a police officer. PC 852.2 authorizes a peace officer from another state to continue in fresh pursuit of a felony suspect into this state with the same authority thereafter as a peace officer of this state.

If an arrest is made in this state by a peace officer from another state, the arresting officer must take the arrestee without unnecessary delay before a magistrate of the county in which the arrest was made. If the magistrate determines the arrest was lawful, he shall commit the person arrested to await a reasonable time for the issuance of an extradition warrant or admit him to bail. If the arrest is deemed unlawful, the magistrate shall discharge the arrestee (PC 852.3).

Bail Fugitive Recovery—PC 1299. A bail agent who apprehends fugitives must meet training and licensing requirements spelled out in PC 1299.02 and 1299.04, must carry proper paperwork, may not wear a law enforcement look-alike badge or uniform, and must generally notify local authorities at least six hours before attempting arrest. Forcible entry must comply with PC 844 restrictions (PC 1299.09). Bail agents may not carry firearms or weapons except as permitted by law (PC 1299.10). Violation of these provisions is a misdemeanor (PC 1299.11).

7.16 *POSSE COMITATUS*

The term *posse comitatus* means "power of the county" and in this case relates to the authority of the sheriff (or any other law enforcement officer) to command any able-bodied person over eighteen years of age to aid and assist in arresting any person against whom there may be issued any process, or to prevent breach of the peace or any criminal offense.

Refusing to Aid—Penalty. PC 150 states in part that any able-bodied person over eighteen years of age who refuses to join the *posse comitatus*, by neglecting or refusing to aid and assist in taking or arresting any escapee, or neglecting or refusing to aid and assist in preventing any breach of the peace or criminal offense, is punishable by a fine of not less than $50 or more than $1,000.

PC 723, states, "When a sheriff or other public officer authorized to execute process finds, or has reason to apprehend that resistance will be made to the execution of the process, he or she may command as many able-bodied inhabitants of the officer's county as he or she may think proper to assist him or her in overcoming the resistance, and, if necessary, in seizing, arresting, and confining the persons resisting, their aiders and abettors."

The above sections, while of general interest, are rarely directly invoked or enforced.

7.17 THREATENED OFFENSES

Security to Keep the Peace. PC 701, provides that "An information may be laid before any of the magistrates mentioned in Section 808, that a person has threatened to commit an offense against the person or property of another." This is sometimes known as a "peace bond."

When the information is presented to the judge, he must examine, under oath, the informer and any witness he may produce and must have their statements taken in writing and have them signed by the parties making them (PC 702).

Arrest Warrant Issued. If the judge is convinced that the threatened danger is real, he may issue a warrant for the person complained of. PC 703 provides for the issuance of a warrant for the arrest of a person who threatens the commission of a criminal offense. The person who has threatened the commission of a crime may then be arrested by any peace officer and brought before the judge.

If it appears that there is no reason to fear such commission on the part of the arrestee, he must be discharged (PC 705).

Bail May be Required—PC 706. If there is just reason to fear the commission of the offense, the person complained of may be required to enter into an undertaking (post a bond) in such sum, not exceeding five thousand dollars ($5,000), as the magistrate may direct, . . . to keep the peace towards the people of this state, and particularly towards the complainant.

The undertaking is valid and binding for six months, and may, upon the renewal of the information, be extended for a longer period, or a new undertaking be required.

Effect of Giving or Refusing Security. If the undertaking required by PC 706 is given, the party informed of must be discharged. If he does not give it, the magistrate must commit him to prison . . . (PC 707).

Breach of the Peace. If a person who has been released on the undertaking (cash or bond) as described above, is convicted of a breach of the peace, the court must order the district attorney to bring "forfeiture" action against the undertaking in the name of the people of this state. The subject in question then loses his money (PC 711 and 712).

7.18 DIPLOMATIC IMMUNITY

The United States is signatory to the Vienna Convention on Diplomatic Relations, which creates immunities from arrest and prosecution for specified members of a foreign country's diplomatic officers and their family members. Such persons must carry with them credentials issued by the US Department of State, with their appropriate level of immunity printed on the back of their ID cards. Status can be verified by telephoning the State Department at 202–647–7277.

Vehicles used by the diplomatic corps will have license plates issued by the State Department with identifying prefixes ("D" for diplomats, "C" for consuls and "S" for administrative staff members. The State Department also issues drivers licenses, which can be suspended if drivers get too many "points" on their records. Diplomatic immunity does not prevent traffic tickets, and does not prevent necessary police intervention to keep the peace or prevent injury or serious crime. In such cases, prosecutors can request a waiver of immunity from the sending country, in order to prosecute the offending individual.

7.19 ARRESTED PERSON'S RIGHTS

Arrestee's Right to Phone Calls—PC 851.5. Immediately upon being booked, and, except where physically impossible, no later than three hours after arrest, an arrested person has the right to make at least three completed phone calls as follows:

- At no expense if the *completed* numbers called are within the local dialing area.
- At his or her own expense if the calls are outside the local area.
- The three calls may be to a private attorney, the public defender (whose number must be posted), a bail bondsman or a relative or other person.

The person arrested may divide his or her three calls (or more, if permitted by custodial authorities) any way he or she wishes among the above possible parties. The right to at least three completed phone calls arises immediately after booking and lasts an indefinite time, until the person arrested has no more need thereof.

If it is determined during booking that the person is a custodial parent of one or more minor children, the person is entitled to two additional completed calls to arrange child care.

If the person is a juvenile, he or she is entitled to make two calls within one hour of being taken into custody, or immediately upon lodging, whichever occurs first (W&I 627(b)).

The arrested person has the right to complete his calls from any place where he is temporarily detained or confined, if not taken promptly to the police station or a lock-up. If the arrestee requires hospitalization, he must be permitted to make his calls from there, if he so requests and is physically able.

PC 851.5(1) specifically prohibits monitoring, recording or eavesdropping on an arrestee's call to an attorney. Any public officer or employee who willfully deprives an arrested person of the rights granted by this section is guilty of a misdemeanor (PC 851.5(e)).

Time Within Which Accused Must Be Taken Before Magistrate—PC 825. Every person arrested who isn't otherwise released, must be taken before a magistrate without unnecessary delay, and in any event within 48 hours following the arrest, excluding Sundays and holidays.

Provided, however, that when the two days prescribed herein expire at a time when the court in which the magistrate is sitting is not in session, such time shall be extended to include the duration of the next regular court session on the judicial day immediately following. A person arrested on a Wednesday must be taken before a magistrate by Friday (unless either Wednesday or Friday is a holiday).

Right to Attorney. After such arrest, any attorney at law entitled to practice in the courts of record of California, may, at the request of the prisoner or any relative of such prisoner, visit the person so arrested.

Any officer, having charge of the prisoner so arrested, who willfully refuses or neglects to allow such attorney to visit a prisoner is guilty of a misdemeanor. Any officer, having a prisoner in charge, who refuses to allow any attorney to visit the prisoner when proper application is made therefor, shall forfeit and pay to the party aggrieved the sum of five hundred dollars ($500), to be recovered by action in any court of competent jurisdiction.

7.20 LAW ENFORCEMENT AND CIVIL LIABILITY

There is always a possibility that a police officer can be held liable to the person whom he has arrested in either a criminal or civil action, or possibly both. The best defense to either civil or criminal action is knowledge of the laws of arrest.

Nature of Civil Action Against Police Officers. The following are the more common legal actions brought against individual officers by citizens.

- Assault, battery, use of unnecessary force.
- False arrest and false imprisonment (e.g., delay in arraignment).
- Negligence, failure to exercise due care (e.g., directing traffic, etc.).
- Wrongful death, excessive force (e.g., shootings).

Defense to Civil Actions. The following are typical defenses to civil actions brought against police officers.

1. **Probable cause for the arrest.** Probable cause has been defined as "such a state of facts as would lead a person of ordinary care and prudence to believe or entertain an honest and strong suspicion that the person arrested is guilty of the offense charged."

   In considering the question of probable cause, the court will look only at the facts and circumstances presented to the officer at the time he was required to act. The fact that an officer stops a person and asks reasonable questions under certain circumstances does not mean that the person is arrested.

Reasonable cause to effect an arrest may consist of information from others. In one case the arresting officer properly relied on information from his superior officer, who in turn had received the information from the defendant's probation officer, who in turn had received it from the defendant's wife.

2. **Reasonable force in effecting arrest.** If the force used by a police officer is reasonably necessary to effect a lawful arrest, then such police officer is not liable for any injuries that might result from the use of such force (*People v. Adams*, 83 Cal. 231).

   The United States Supreme Court held that police could be sued in federal court under the civil rights statute (Title 42, United States Code, section 1983) for using deadly force to stop a fleeing burglar. The court further held that deadly force could only be employed, consistent with the Fourth Amendment, when reasonably necessary to apprehend a fleeing suspect when the suspect was dangerous and likely to harm the officer or others (*Garner v. Tennessee*, 471 U.S. 1).

3. **Self-defense.** Any necessary force may be used to protect the person or property of oneself from wrongful injury (Civil Code, Section 50). While a peace officer, when attempting an arrest, may use all necessary force to effect it, or may take the life of the supposed offender, if *necessary* to save his own, there must be a real or apparent necessity to justify resorting to such measure for his own safety or protection (*People v. Newsome*, 51 Cal. App. 42).

4. **Coercive interrogation claims.** For many years, the Ninth Circuit Federal Court of Appeals ruled that officers could be subject to suit under the Fifth Amendment for intentionally failing to comply with Miranda and persisting with questioning. In such cases as *Cooper v. Dupnik, CACJ v. Butts* and *Martinez v. Oxnard,* that court allowed suits for claimed coercive interrogation to be brought. However, these opinions were overturned by the U.S. Supreme Court in *Chavez v. Martinez,* 123 S.Ct. 1994.

   In the *Chavez* case, the Supreme Court ruled that police officers do not violate the Fifth Amendment by Miranda non-compliance, because the Fifth Amendment privilege against compelled self-incrimination is a *trial* right, which officers are not capable of violating. The court also said that a failure to comply with Miranda procedures, while it may result in the suppression of evidence, does not itself violate the Fifth Amendment.

   Actual coercion, such as using force, threats, mistreatment or overbearing promises of leniency, can cause civil liability under the Fourteenth Amendment due process clause, if the coercion is so egregious as to "shock the conscience." Moreover, as discussed above, involuntary statements produced by actual coercion are never admissible, for any purpose. Avoiding both suppression of evidence and civil liability risks would require officers to be scrupulous in insuring that a prisoner is not denied adequate rest, sleep, food, water, or restroom access, and that no threatening language or promised leniency occurs.

STUDENT REVIEW

TERMINOLOGY DEFINED—CHAPTER 7

Please see the Terminology Quiz at the end of this chapter.

1. Admonish: to advise of rights.
2. Appellant: one who appeals to a higher court.
3. Ambiguous: not clear, more than one meaning.
4. Covert: secretive, clandestine, disguised.
5. Cursory: superficial, a cursory search.
6. Defendant: one against whom legal action is brought.
7. Demurrer: an answer to a legal accusation claiming it is defective.
8. Diplomatic immunity: freedom from prosecution under international law.
9. Direct examination: testimony of witness for side that calls him.
10. Entrapment: inducing one to commit a crime not previously contemplated.
11. Flagrant: openly corrupt or criminal.
12. Fresh pursuit: continuous pursuit of suspect.
13. Heinous: hateful, repulsive, brutal.
14. Incriminating: tending to show guilt.
15. Indigent: destitute, without means.
16. Information: formal accusation of crime.
17. Manifest: clear, plain, apparent.
18. Pursuant: as a result of, in accordance with.
19. Scrutinize: to inspect closely, examine.
20. Subsequent: occurring after some other event.

TRUE-FALSE QUIZ—CHAPTER 7

After reading this chapter you should be able to correctly answer the following items.

___ 1. A traffic violator is legally under arrest from the time he is stopped until released on his written promise to appear.

___ 2. The Penal Code specifically gives officers the right to stop and detain suspicious persons.

___ 3. Evidence seized when there is articulable suspicion to detain but not arrest, will be rendered inadmissible if an arrest is made.

___ 4. If the detention is proper, the courts will approve a search without articulable suspicion for weapons which could endanger the officer.

___ 5. If a frisk is used as an excuse to conduct an exploratory search, any evidence found is inadmissible.

___ 6. PC 830 (along with its sub-sections) grants full peace officer status to all those enumerated.

___ 7. The Penal Code requires all uniformed peace officers to wear either a numbered badge or name-plate.

___ 8. Generally speaking, members of a police department are authorized to carry concealed weapons outside of the city by which they are employed.

___ 9. A peace officer may arrest a person whenever he has reasonable cause to believe the person arrested has committed a public offense in his presence.

___10. A peace officer may make an arrest when he has reasonable cause to believe the person arrested committed a felony, whether or not a felony in fact has been committed.

___11. Once a peace officer has arrested someone, he may not legally release the arrested person without first taking him before a magistrate.

____12. If an officer arrests someone for a misdemeanor and subsequently releases him due to insufficient grounds to prosecute, the arrest thereafter is legally deemed a detention only.

____13. Except for serving warrants, a private person has the identical powers of arrest as does a peace officer.

____14. An officer may legally release a citizen-arrested misdemeanant on a signed citation rather than taking him directly to jail or court.

____15. No arrest without a warrant may legally be made except on probable cause.

____16. Entrapment is inducing someone to commit a crime he didn't otherwise contemplate for the purpose of arresting and prosecuting the subject.

____17. If a citizen knows he is being arrested by an officer, but believes the arrest is unlawful, he is legally justified in resisting such arrest.

____18. Generally, the Miranda Warning should be given just before custodial interrogation of a suspect.

____19. Before a legal warrant can be issued, the suspect's true name must be determined and included on the warrant.

____20. If an arrested person escapes from the police car shortly after being arrested, he may be charged with the crime of escape in addition to the crime for which he was initially arrested.

ESSAY-DISCUSSION ITEMS—CHAPTER 7

After reading this chapter you should be able to correctly answer the following items.

1. What are three typical defenses to a civil action for false arrest?
2. Define "arrest." Is arrest synonymous with "detention" in California?
3. In determining "probable cause" for making an arrest, into what two aspects will the court generally inquire?
4. What are the four "elements" of the *Miranda* decision warning? When should it be given?
5. What are three instances where a peace officer may make an arrest without a warrant?
6. What does *posse comitatus* mean? What is its practical application in law enforcement?
7. What is the essence of entrapment? How does it differ from "setting traps" or using decoys for the purpose of apprehending suspects?
8. May a suspect who has just been arrested in the field for a crime be charged with escape if he breaks and runs from the officer? What are the elements of the crime of escape?
9. Under what three circumstances may a private person make an arrest and what must he do with the suspect immediately following an arrest?
10. What is the arrestee's right relative to phone calls following his arrest?
11. Is it constitutionally permissible to make a custodial arrest of a person for a fine-only infraction? Would such an arrest support a search incident to arrest?
12. Under what circumstances might a law enforcement officer be civilly liable for conducting a coercive interrogation of an arrested person? Is mere non-compliance with Miranda procedures enough to generate civil liability?

TERMINOLOGY QUIZ—CHAPTER 7

Match terms and definitions by writing the number preceding the correct term in the appropriate brackets.

Terms

1. Admonish
2. Appellant
3. Ambiguous
4. Covert
5. Cursory
6. Defendant
7. Demurrer
8. Diplomatic immunity
9. Direct examination
10. Entrapment
11. Flagrant
12. Fresh pursuit
13. Heinous
14. Incriminating
15. Indigent
16. Information
17. Manifest
18. Pursuant
19. Scrutinize
20. Subsequent

Definitions

[ ] one who is destitute
[ ] a repulsive crime, brutal
[ ] superficial
[ ] to inspect closely
[ ] occurring after some other event
[ ] exempt from prosecution under international law
[ ] clear, plain, apparent to the sight
[ ] one who takes an appeal to a higher court
[ ] as a result of, in accordance with
[ ] tending to show guilt
[ ] doubtful, having more than one meaning
[ ] secretive, clandestine, disguised
[ ] an answer to a legal accusation
[ ] formal accusation of a crime by the DA
[ ] to advise of rights, Miranda warning

CHAPTER 8

OFFENSES AGAINST THE PUBLIC PEACE

8.1 DISTURBING THE PEACE

Introduction—Disturbing the Peace. At common law, any willful and unjustifiable disturbance of the public peace was a crime. The offense consisted of disturbing a neighborhood or a number of people assembled in a public meeting, or of disturbing an individual in such a manner or to such an extent as to provoke a breach of the peace.

In California, offenses against the public peace are defined in several code sections. They cover fighting, unreasonable noise, disturbance of various public meetings, damaging property, rioting, trespassing, terrorism, and disturbance on school campuses and of college classes, to name a few.

Disturbing the Peace Defined—PC 415. "Any of the following persons shall be punished by imprisonment in the county jail for a period of not more than 90 days, a fine of not more than four hundred dollars ($400), or both such imprisonment and fine.

1. Any person who unlawfully fights in a public place or challenges another person in a public place to fight.
2. Any person who maliciously and willfully disturbs another person by loud and unreasonable noise.
3. Any person who uses offensive words in a public place which are inherently likely to provoke an immediate violent reaction."

Disturbing the Peace at Schools—PC 415.5. This section is very similar to PC 415, above, except that it applies only to buildings and grounds of any school, community college, state college, state university, etc., as defined in PC 626. The elements are otherwise the same as in PC 415, except that PC 415 refers to a "public place" and PC 415.5 refers to the "buildings and grounds of any school," etc.

It should be noted that PC 415.5 does not apply to any person who is a registered student of the school or college where the disturbance took place. The difference between PC 415.5 and PC 415, is that PC 415.5 provides increased punishment for previous convictions of this and other school disturbance laws beginning with PC 626. (See Section 8.10 of your text for additional school disturbance laws.) PC 415, defining disturbing the peace is divided into three general areas:

Fighting or Challenging to Fight. This part of PC 415 (and PC 415.5) applies to persons who fight or challenge another to fight. It may be difficult to apply this portion of the statute in cases not observed by the officer. At times both participants in a fight will be guilty if they are mutually involved. On other occasions, one may be a victim of an assault or battery.

This Internet site provides information on preventing crime: what works; what doesn't; what's promising. See **http://www.ncjrs.org/works/index.htm.**

Loud and Unreasonable Noise. In determining what constitutes "loud and unreasonable noise," the officer must first determine if it can be considered "communication." Communication is words, shouting, or cheering that is intended to convey ideas, and is generally protected by First Amendment (freedom of speech) rights.

On the other hand, a noise such as a loud motorcycle engine at 3:00 a.m., is not communication. Neither is shouting which is done for the purpose of disruption. A loud family quarrel during the night would also fit into the disturbance category. Although the latter technically involves communication, it is not the type protected by the First Amendment.

If the noise is not a communication and, based on the time, place or manner in which it is made, is the kind of noise that would disturb a reasonable person, an arrest is justified if someone was disturbed by it.

Disturbing the normal activities of a business, a bank in this case, by singing and other disruptive conduct to the annoyance, disturbance, and obstruction of patrons with normal business to transact, indicated beyond a reasonable doubt the existence of a disturbance of the peace as defined in PC 415 (*People v. Green*, 234 Cal. App. 2d 871).

Offensive Words. The United States Supreme Court recognizes the existence of "fighting words," which is applicable to PC 415(3). These are defined as: ". . . those words which by their very utterance inflict injury or tend to incite an immediate breach of the peace." The utterance of fighting words is not protected by the First Amendment guarantee of free speech. Later cases support the view that it is not merely the words themselves, but also the context in which they are uttered, that qualify them as "fighting words." And there is often a further requirement that words be spoken with intent to have the effect of inciting the hearer to an immediate breach of the peace.

Two cases have interpreted what kind of language qualifies as "inherently likely to provoke an immediate violent reaction," under PC 415(3). In *John V*, (167 Cal. App. 3d 761), the words "fucking bitch," screamed by the defendant at his neighbor as she drove by, were found to be a violation of the statute. However, in *People v. Callahan*, (168 Cal. App. 3d 631), the characterization "fucking asshole," directed at a police officer by a hostile motorist at an accident scene, was held insufficient because the officer was neither offended by the language nor provoked to react violently.

Offensive Signs. In *Cohen v. California*, (403 U.S. 15), the United States Supreme Court held that the California statute on disturbing the peace was not violated where a defendant walked through a courthouse corridor wearing a jacket bearing the words "FUCK THE DRAFT." The court reasoned that no person who viewed the jacket could regard the words as a direct personal insult, and there was no showing that anyone was, in fact, violently aroused. Therefore, no violation was committed.

Discussion. The offense known as "disturbing the peace" or breach of the peace embraces a great variety of conduct destroying or menacing public order and tranquility. PC 415 limits this conduct to fighting, offering to fight, loud and unreasonable noise, and offensive words in a public place. Note that challenging to fight or fighting or use of offensive words in private is not a violation of PC 415.

We should also note that PC 415(2), limits disturbing an individual's peace to *loud and unreasonable noise*. What is loud and unreasonable could be further described as that which agitates or arouses from a state of repose, or molests or interrupts. The circumstances surrounding the incident are very important. The amount of noise which would be disturbing in a quiet residential neighborhood would be much less than that required to disturb someone in a noisy public place.

A complaining witness who observed the disturbance prior to the arrival of police officers has every right to make a private person arrest upon the suspect, assuming that he has legal cause to do so (*People v. Cove*, 228 Cal. App. 2d 466).

Joint tenants have no authority to enter and take possessions from the licensee of a premises by using force and violence, by pounding upon licensee's door, and by using abusive language. Such activity is clearly a violation of PC 415 (*People v. Verdier*, 152 Cal. App. 2d 348).

Amplification Devices—Vehicle Code Section 27007. "No driver of a vehicle shall operate . . . any sound amplification system which can be heard outside the vehicle from 50 feet or more when the vehicle is being operated upon a highway, unless that system is being operated to request assistance or warn of a hazardous situation."

This statute makes it illegal to use an outside loudspeaker or stereo "boom" system on a highway except as stated. Emergency and public utility vehicles are exempted. The law, also, does not apply to vehicles in parades, etc., if being operated with a city or county permit.

Obscene or Harassing Phone Calls—PC 653m. It is a misdemeanor to telephone or contact by electronic means (including computers, video recorders, fax or pagers), with intent to annoy, and use obscene language or make threats of injury to the person or property of the person addressed, or a family member.

It is also a misdemeanor to make repeated phone calls or electronic contacts to another's residence, with intent to annoy, even if no conversation ensues (hang-up calls, or "breathers," for example).

These two provisions do not apply to calls made in good faith.

Making repeated calls or electronic contacts to another at his or her workplace, with intent to annoy, is a misdemeanor if in violation of a restraining order, or if more than ten in twenty-four hours are made to a former spouse or relationship partner.

The offenses are committed either where transmitted or where received, and the violations also occur when committed in response to a requested return call.

Discussion. Note that PC 653m requires proof of *specific intent to annoy* and covers both obscene language calls and calls threatening to inflict injury. Subdivision (b) covers repeated calls and does not require that any conversation take place. Subdivision (e) makes it an offense to leave a request, with a person or on an answering machine, to call back-providing that when the person calls back, the perpetrator makes threats or uses obscene language. The call-back number is often a telephone booth.

Annoying 911 Calls—PC 653x. It is a misdemeanor to telephone the 911 emergency line with intent to annoy or harass another person. Such intent may be proven by repeated calls that are unreasonable under the circumstances.

Terrorist Threats—PC 422. Any person who wilfully threatens the life or safety of another, intending that the threat be taken seriously and thereby causing sustained fear for individual or family safety, is guilty of a wobbler, if the threat is so clear and immediate as to convey a serious and imminent prospect of being carried out. The unlawful threat may be made verbally, in writing, or by electronic communication, including telephone, fax, pager or e-mail.

8.2 UNLAWFUL ASSEMBLY

Unlawful Assembly Defined—PC 407. "Whenever two or more persons assemble together to do an unlawful act, or do a lawful act in a violent, boisterous, or tumultuous manner, such assembly is an unlawful assembly."

Penalty—PC 408. "Every person who participates in any rout or unlawful assembly is guilty of a misdemeanor."

Discussion. In a prosecution for violation of PC 407, there are two distinct types of conduct. One is assembly to do an *unlawful* act. The other is assembly to do a *lawful* act in a violent, boisterous or tumultuous manner. Each is defined below.

Assembly to Do an Unlawful Act. The statutory language that there must be an assembling to do an unlawful act only requires that there be an assembly for an unlawful purpose by those who knowingly participate. Those in the assembly must intend to commit an unlawful act or engage in an unlawful purpose.

Doing a Lawful Act in a Violent, Boisterous, or Tumultuous Manner. In a prosecution for a violation of this part of the statute, the courts have said that not every meeting where violent or boisterous conduct occurs may be called an unlawful assembly. The statute is intended to prevent a tumultuous disturbance of the public peace by two or more persons, having no avowed, legal, or constitutional objective, to assemble and act in such a manner which produces danger to the public peace and tranquility, and which excites terror, alarm, or consternation in the neighborhood.

Evidence—Assembly to Do an Unlawful Act. Evidence of joint or common unlawful purpose, as manifested by signs, chants, statements, conduct, etc., is necessary to support a *prima facie* case. A single act of misconduct by one person in an otherwise lawful assembly would not convert the assembly into an unlawful one.

Evidence—Assembly to Do a Lawful Act by Unlawful Means. The same evidence as indicated above is necessary. However, additional evidence of conduct which terrorizes the community or places the inhabitants in fear is necessary. Such fear is measured in such terms as would reasonably impart fear to an average person. In testing this, it is necessary to take into account the hours at which the parties meet, the language used by them, and the act(s) done.

Unlawful Assembly—Paramilitary Organization PC 11460(a). "Any two or more persons who assemble as a paramilitary organization for the purpose of practicing with weapons shall be punished by imprisonment in the county jail for not more than one year or by a fine of not more than one thousand dollars ($1,000), or by both.

As used in this subdivision, 'paramilitary organization' means an organization which is not an agency of the United States Government or of the State of California, or which is not a private school meeting the requirements set forth in Section 12154 of the Education Code, but which engages in instruction or training in guerrilla warfare or sabotage, or which, as an organization, engages in rioting or the violent disruption of, or violent interference with, school activities."

8.3 FAILURE TO DISPERSE

There are several statutes which provide peace officers with adequate authority to suppress major disturbances, unlawful assemblies, routs and riots. The more common such statutes are given below:

Refusing to Disperse Upon Lawful Command—PC 416. "(a) If two or more persons assemble for the purpose of disturbing the public peace, or committing any unlawful act, and do not disperse on being desired or commanded so to do by a public officer, persons so offending are severally guilty of a misdemeanor."

Liability for Damages, Clean-up—PC 416(b). This subdivision provides that any person who, as a result of violating PC 416(a), personally causes damage to real or personal property, whether publicly or privately owned, shall make restitution for the damage caused, including, but not limited to, the cost of cleaning up, repairing, replacing, or restoring the property. The burden of proof on this issue rests with the prosecuting agency or claimant.

Remaining Present at Scene of Riot, Rout, or Unlawful Assembly—PC 409. "Every person remaining present at the place of any riot, rout or unlawful assembly, after the same has been lawfully warned to disperse, except public officers and persons assisting them in attempting to disperse the same, is guilty of misdemeanor."

Arrest for Failure to Disperse—PC 727. "If the persons assembled do not immediately disperse, such magistrates and officers must arrest them, and to that end may command the aid of all persons present or within the county."

Discussion. If a group assembles with no other apparent motive than to disturb the public peace, i.e., an unlawful purpose, this section is violated. If the group is assembled for a lawful purpose, this section does not apply. A willful disturbance of the peace for no lawful purpose, or to commit an unlawful act, are the chief prohibitions of this section.

Police Authority to Close Area During Emergency—PC 409.5. "(a) Whenever a menace to the public health or safety is created by a calamity such as flood, storm, fire, earthquake, explosion, accident, or other disaster, officers of the California Highway Patrol, California State Police, police department, or sheriffs office, . . . may close off the area where the menace exists for the duration thereof by means of ropes, markers, or guards to any and all persons not authorized by such officer to enter or remain within the closed area.

If such a calamity creates an immediate menace to the public health, the local health officer may close the area where the menace exists pursuant to the conditions which are set forth above in this section.

(b) Officers of the California Highway Patrol, police departments, or sheriffs office . . . may close the immediate area surrounding any emergency field command post . . . to any and all unauthorized persons. . . .

(c) Any unauthorized person who willfully and knowingly enters an area closed pursuant to subdivision (a) or (b) and who willfully remains within such area after receiving notice to evacuate or leave, shall be guilty of a misdemeanor.

(d) Nothing in this section shall prevent a duly authorized representative of any news service, newspaper, or radio or television station or network from entering the areas closed pursuant to this section."

Discussion. An assembly may be unlawful even if it consists of a "sit-in." As the court has said, "There can be little doubt that Section 409 can encompass, under applicable circumstances, activity which consists in the occupying of an area, place, or establishment for the purpose of an organized protest against some grievance."

Penal Code, Section 409, making it a misdemeanor to remain at the place of any riot, rout, or unlawful assembly after being lawfully warned to disperse, can encompass, under applicable circumstances, activity that consists in the occupying of an area, place, or establishment for the purpose of an organized protest against some grievance (*In re Bacon*, 240 Cal. App. 2d 34).

In the *Bacon* case, students protesting university regulations knowingly remained in a university building after it became closed to the public. They remained after being fairly and adequately notified to leave by the chancellor and by a police captain going from floor to floor announcing over a portable loudspeaker that persons gathered were participating in an unlawful assembly and were free to leave. They were also told that those who remained would be arrested for trespass. The court held that they violated PC 409 in failing to disperse even though they may not have participated in the protest assembly.

Under PC 407, the illegal purpose of a group in assembling to view an illegal "hot-rod" race renders the action of the group knowingly participating therein an unlawful assembly (*Coverstone v. Davies*, 38 Cal. 2d 315).

8.4 ROUT AND RIOT DEFINED

Rout Defined—PC 406. "Whenever two or more persons, assembled and acting together, make any attempt or advance toward the commission of an act which would be a riot if actually committed, such assembly is a rout."

Discussion. A rout may be described as the preparatory stage of a riot. It is as the statute says an ". . . attempt or advance toward the commission of an act which would be a riot if actually committed . . ." Thus, in every riot, which involves use of force and violence, disturbing the public peace, or a threat to do so, with apparent power available, a rout has necessarily preceded such an offense.

A rout is evidenced by an overt act beyond mere assembly. It is possible for a group to have been lawfully assembled, but suddenly depart from its lawful purpose. It may proceed to embark on the execution of an unlawful purpose to be accomplished by force and violence. Any act committed toward the consummation of that unlawful purpose constitutes a rout. Thus, it has been said that when an unlawful assembly begins to move toward the execution of the common unlawful purpose for which it came together, but before any acts of violence or disorder have occurred, then a rout has been committed. The legislative intent of PC 406, is to provide law enforcement officers a means by which to control any willful and malicious obstruction of the citizen's free use of a public way (*Rees v. City of Palm Springs*, 188 Cal. App. 2d 339).

Riot Defined PC 404. "(a) Any use of force or violence, disturbing the public peace, or any threat to use such force or violence, if accompanied by immediate power of execution, by two or more persons acting together, and without authority of law, is a riot.

(b) As used in this section, disturbing the public peace may occur in any place of confinement. Place of confinement means any state prison, county jail, industrial farm, or road camp, or any city jail, industrial farm or road camp."

Unlawful use of force or violence to disturb the peace is a riot. *Courtesy of The Liason Agency, Inc./Getty Images, Inc.*

Discussion. To constitute a riot, the objective need not be unlawful, provided the acts are done in a manner calculated to inspire terror. Even if the original coming together was lawful and for the carrying out of a lawful purpose, still, if after coming together, the persons proceed to execute either a lawful or an unlawful purpose in such a violent and unlawful manner as to terrorize the populace, it is a riot.

The chief element in riot is the use of force and violence, or threat to use force and violence to disturb the public peace. It is essential to a violation of this section that there be a concurrence of at least two persons, acting together, in the use, or threatened use, of force or violence. No previous agreement to use force and violence is necessary as long as there is a common purpose to use force and violence. Even if the original purpose was a lawful one, but afterwards the purpose becomes unlawful, the original peaceful purpose is no defense.

8.5 INCITING A RIOT

Urging a Riot—PC 404.6. Every person who with the intent to cause a riot does an act or engages in conduct which urges a riot, or urges others to commit acts of force or violence, or the burning or destroying of property, and at a time and place and under circumstances which produce a clear and present and immediate danger of acts of force or violence or the burning or destroying of property, is guilty of a misdemeanor punishable by a fine not exceeding $1000, or by imprisonment in a county jail not exceeding one year, or by both. Inciting a riot in a confinement facility with resultant serious bodily injury is a wobbler.

Discussion. Under the Unlawful Assembly, Rout, and Riot sections of the Penal Code, one of the chief elements is a common purpose by two or more persons to do an unlawful act. But under this section (PC 404.6), a single suspect, acting alone, can commit the unlawfully prescribed conduct. It must be shown that the perpetrator's acts or conduct was with the specific intent to cause a riot.

8.6 LYNCHING—PRISONER RESCUE

The term "lynching" often causes one to think of someone strung up by a hangman's noose to the nearest oak tree in the old "Wild West" image. Or we might think of an angry "lynch mob," intent on taking the law into their own hands and administering "justice!" to an accused without benefit of a trial. By statute, the crime is defined quite differently.

Lynching Defined—PC 405a. "The taking by means of a riot of any person from the lawful custody of any peace officer is a lynching."

Lynching Penalty—PC 405b. "Any person who participates in any lynching is punishable by imprisonment in the state prison. . . ."

Prisoner Rescue—PC 4550. "Every person who rescues or attempts to rescue, or aids another person in rescuing or attempting to rescue, any prisoner from . . . any officer or person having him in lawful custody, is punishable as [a felony]."

Discussion. There is a requirement in PC 405a, that the person must be in "lawful" custody of the officer, otherwise there would be no crime. The offense of lynching is usually committed during rout or riot. As the statute indicates, whenever two or more persons act together (requisites of both a riot and a violation of this section) and take a legally arrested person, or other person in the lawful custody of an officer, they are in violation of this section. Neither actual nor intended harm of the person taken is an element of this offense.

In the crime of rescuing a prisoner (PC 4550), only one person need be involved and there is no requirement that the rescue be by "means of riot," as there is in PC 405a.

8.7 DISTURBING PUBLIC AND RELIGIOUS MEETINGS—HATE CRIMES

Disturbance of Assembly or Meeting—PC 403. "Every person, who, without authority of law, willfully disturbs or breaks up any assembly or meeting, not unlawful in its character, other than such as is mentioned in Section 302 of the Penal Code [religious meetings] and Section 29440 of the Elections Code [see below], is guilty of a misdemeanor."

Disturbing Political Meetings—Elections Code 29440. "Every person who, by threats, intimidations, or unlawful violence, willfully hinders or prevents electors from assembling in public meetings for the consideration of public questions is guilty of a misdemeanor."

Discussion. Not every interruption of a speaker is a disturbance. The meeting itself must be thrown into such disorder that the business under discussion cannot effectively continue. Thus, the character and nature of the meeting are relevant in determining whether the disturbance is a violation of this section. For example, an extemporaneous "soapbox" speaker should expect to be interrupted from time to time. Free speech cannot be used as an excuse to justify converting an orderly meeting into bedlam, but some assemblies can be expected to be somewhat disorderly, e.g., political conventions.

Disturbing Religious Meetings—PC 302. "Every person who willfully disturbs or disquiets any assemblage of people met for religious worship, by profane discourse, rude or indecent behavior, or by any unnecessary noise, either within the place where such meeting is held, or so near it as to disturb the order and solemnity of the meeting, is guilty of a misdemeanor. . . ." (briefed)

Discussion. This statute prohibits any serious disruption of the solemnity of a religious meeting and requires less evidence than the preceding section relative to political meetings. The concluding phrase of the statute prohibits noise inside as well as outside the building, and the disturbance must be willful and intentional.

In one case, large numbers of people picketed in front of a particular church during services. They expressed vile epithets to those entering and departing, thereby provoking wrath and indignation. Under the circumstances described, the perpetrators would likely be in violation of PC 302.

Disrupting Sporting Events—PC 243.83. It is an infraction to throw objects onto the playing field or court during a sporting event with the intent to interfere with play or distract a player, or to enter onto the playing field or area during an event, without permission.

Cemetery Vandalism—PC 594.35. It is a wobbler to destroy, injure or deface any cemetery or mortuary property, graves, tombs, vaults, etc., or to interfere with a funeral service or procession.

Hate Crime—PC 422.6. Use of force or threats to interfere with another's civil liberties because of race, color, religion, ancestry, national origin, disability, gender or sexual orientation is a wobbler. Hate-crime victims and witnesses who may be illegal immigrants may not be detained or reported to the INS (PC 422.93).

Access to Clinics and Religious Facilities—PC 423.2. It is a misdemeanor (punishable by jail and fines up to $50,000) to intimidate, obstruct or interfere with those coming or going from reproductive services facilities or places of worship, subject to constitutionally protected free speech activities.

8.8 TRESPASSING

Trespass—Threat to Cause Serious Bodily Injury—PC 601. This section makes it a felony (wobbler) to make a credible threat to cause "serious bodily injury," as defined in PC 417.6(a), to another and then within 30 days of the threat to: (1) enter into a residence contiguous to the residence of the person threatened with the intent to execute the threat or (2) knowingly enter the threatened person's workplace with the intent to execute the threat.

This law does not apply if the residence or workplace entered is the residence or workplace of the person making the threat. Also, this section is not applicable to persons engaged in certain agricultural labor union activities.

Trespassing in General—PC 602. This section is comprised of approximately 20 very specific subsections, each with its own elements which must be proved to be enforceable. Those subsections rarely used by law enforcement have been omitted.

"Notwithstanding Section 602.8, every person who willfully commits a trespass by any of the following acts is guilty of a misdemeanor:

(a) Cutting down, destroying, or injuring any kind of wood or timber standing or growing upon the lands of another.

(b) Carrying away any kind of wood or timber lying on such lands.

(c) [omitted]

(d) Digging, taking, or carrying away from any lot situated within the limits of any incorporated city, without the license of the owner or legal occupant thereof, any earth, soil, or stone.

(e) [omitted]

(f) Maliciously tearing down, damaging, mutilating, any [roadway] sign upon any property belonging to the state, city or county . . . or putting up or painting any . . . notice, advertisement . . . on any property belonging to the state, city or county . . .

(g) [omitted]

(h) Entering posted lands where listed animals are raised for human consumption, or carrying animals away.

(i) Willfully opening, tearing down, or otherwise destroying any fence on the enclosed land of another, or opening any gate, bar or fence of another and willfully leaving it open without the written permission of the owner, or maliciously tearing down, mutilating, or destroying any sign, signboard, or other notice forbidding shooting on private property.

(j) Building fires upon any lands owned by another where signs forbidding trespass are displayed at intervals not greater than one mile along the exterior boundaries and at all roads and trails entering such lands, without first having obtained written permission from the owner of such lands or his agent, or the person in lawful possession thereof.

(k) Entering lands, whether unenclosed or enclosed by a fence, for the purpose of injuring any property . . . or with intention of interfering with or obstructing any lawful business carried on . . . by the person in lawful possession.

(l) Entering any lands . . . where signs forbidding trespass are displayed . . . without the written permission of the owner of such land, his agent or of the person in lawful possession and

1. Refusing or failing to leave such lands immediately upon being requested by the owner of such land, his agent or by the person in lawful possession to leave such lands, or
2. Tearing down, mutilating or destroying any sign, signboard, or notice forbidding trespass or hunting on such lands, or
3. Removing, injuring, unlocking, or tampering with any lock on any gate on or leading into such lands, or
4. Discharging any firearm.

(m) Entering and occupying real property or structures of any kind without the consent of the owner, the owner's agent, or the person in lawful possession thereof.

(n) Driving any vehicle, as defined in Section 670 of the Vehicle Code, upon real property belonging to or lawfully occupied by another and known not to be open to the general public, without the consent of the owner, the owner's agent, or the person in lawful possession thereof.

(o) Refusing or failing to leave land, real property, or structures belonging to or lawfully occupied by another and not open to the general public, upon being requested to leave

1. by a peace officer at the request of the owner, the owner's agent, or the person in lawful possession, and upon being informed by the peace officer that he or she is acting at the request of the owner, the owner's agent, or the person in lawful possession, or
2. the owner, the owner's agent, or the person in lawful possession. . . .

(p) [omitted]

(q) Refusing or failing to leave a public building of a public agency during those hours of the day or night when the building is regularly closed to the public upon being requested to do so by a regularly employed guard, watchman, or custodian of the public agency owning or maintaining the building or property, if the surrounding circumstances are such as to indicate to a reasonable man that the person has no apparent lawful business to pursue.

(r) Knowingly skiing in an area or on a ski trail which is closed to the public and which has signs posted indicating such closure.

(s) Refusing or failing to leave a hotel or motel, where he or she has obtained accommodations and has refused to pay for those accommodations, upon request of the proprietor or manager. . . .

(t) Entering private property . . . or structures thereon . . . whether or not generally open to the public, after having been informed by a peace officer or the owner . . . or owner's agent, that the property is not open to that particular person; or refusing or failing to leave the property upon being asked to leave. . . ."

(u) [omitted]

(v) Failing to submit to screening at airport sterile area.

(w) Refusing to leave a battered women's shelter after being asked to do so by the manager.

(x) Entering or remaining in a posted neonatal unit or maternity ward, without lawful business.

(y) Except as permitted by federal law, intentionally avoiding security screening at a courthouse or public building where entrances have given notice that prosecution may result from such avoidance.

Peddling on Airport Property—PC 602.4. "Every person who enters or remains on airport property owned by a city, county . . . sells, peddles, or offers for sale any food, merchandise, property or services of any kind . . . without express written consent of the governing board . . . is guilty of a misdemeanor."

Unauthorized Entry of Property—PC 602.5. "Every person other than a public officer . . . who enters or remains in any noncommercial dwelling house, apartment, or other such place without the consent of the owner, the owner's lawful possession thereof, is guilty of a misdemeanor."

If the resident or a guest of the entered premises is present at any time during the unauthorized entry incident, the offense becomes an "aggravated trespass," punishable by up to one year in jail and/or a fine of not more than $1000. In addition, a sentencing court can issue a restraining order against the person convicted of aggravated trespass, valid for up to 3 years (PC 602.5(b),(d)).

Obstruction Easement—PC 420.1. It is an infraction, punishable by $500 fine, to prevent a person from entering or leaving land where the person has a right of entry or passage.

Obstruction of Street or Sidewalk—PC 647c. "Every person who willfully and maliciously obstructs the free movement of any person on any street, sidewalk, or other public place or on or in any place open to the public is guilty of a misdemeanor."

Discussion. Regarding PC 602(1) (entering and occupying real property), it should be noted for enforcement purposes that transient, noncontinuous possession is not "occupation" for purposes of this section (*People v. Catalano,* 29 Cal. 3d 1).

PC 602(n) (refusing to leave private property), also has been modified by the courts. The mere presence on another's real property is not a trespass. The property owner, or a peace officer at the owner's request, must first ask the intruder to leave. The court said in *People v. Medrano,* (78 Cal. App. 3d 198): "Refusal to leave is the gist of this offense. Indispensable preconditions of that refusal are *dual* requests to leave; one from a peace officer, the other from the property possessor."

There can be no trespass unless the land involved is either (1) not open to the public, or (2) open to the public but being used by the suspect in some manner not related to the purpose for which the owner holds it open (*People v. Lundgren,* 189 Cal. App. 3d 381).

Demonstrators often temporarily block entrances to public buildings. If the inconvenience to others is slight, little action need be taken. But when a building is intentionally blocked so that passage in and out is willfully impaired for an unreasonable length of time (e.g., "sit-ins") officers can invoke PC 602(j), PC 407 (unlawful assembly), and PC 602(k).

No one has the right to willfully and intentionally block the right of citizens to enter and move through public buildings under the circumstances outlined, and they are subject to arrest for failing to disperse after a proper order is given.

Under PC 602(p), (refusal to leave a public building at closing hour), persons such as demonstrators, etc., should be warned by the person in charge of the building. If the persons fail to heed this order, police may be called, whereupon they too should give a dispersal command. If the parties still refuse to leave, they may be arrested for violating this statute. Demonstrators who refuse to leave a college or university building upon being commanded to do so, and after ample warning, are also subject to arrest under this section (*In re Bacon,* 240 Cal. App. 2d 34).

8.9 FORCIBLE ENTRY AND DETAINER

The statutes discussed below are similar to those described in trespassing, except that they involve the additional element of forcible entry or damage of property inside.

Forcible Entry and Detainer—PC 418. "Every person using or procuring, encouraging, or assisting another to use any force or violence in entering upon or detaining any lands or other possessions of another, except in cases and in the manner allowed by law, is guilty of a misdemeanor."

Destruction of Property—PC 603. "Every person other than a peace officer engaged in the performance of his duties as such who forcibly and without the consent of the owner, representative of the owner, lessee or representative of the lessee thereof, enters a dwelling house, cabin, or other building occupied or constructed for occupation by humans, and who damages, injures, or destroys any property of value in, around or appertaining to such dwelling house, cabin, or other building, is guilty of a misdemeanor."

Discussion. Forcible detainer is the possession of property by the use of force and violence. It may occur where the original entry was forcible or where it was peaceable. Forcible entry occurs where a person violently enters upon real property occupied by another, with menaces, force and arms and without the authority of law.

In order that there may be a forcible entry, it must appear that the peaceable possession of someone has been interfered with. It is not necessary that the person in possession should have been actually present at the time of the entry, if at that time he or she had control and authority of the premises.

8.10 SCHOOL DISTURBANCE LAWS

Crimes Against Public and School Officials—PC 71. "Every person who, with intent to cause, attempts to cause, or causes, any officer or employee of any public or private educational institution or any public officer or employee to do, or refrain from doing, any act in the performance of his duties, by means of a threat, directly communicated to such person, to inflict an unlawful injury upon any person or property, where it reasonably appears to the recipient of the threat that such threat could be carried out, is guilty of a public offense . . . [felony wobbler]."

Disturbing Campus Peace—PC 415.5. "(a) Any person who (1) unlawfully fights within any building or upon the grounds of any school, community college, state college, or state university, or challenges another person within any such buildings or upon such grounds to fight, or (2) maliciously and willfully disturbs another person within any such buildings or upon such grounds by loud and unreasonable noise or (3) uses offensive words within any such building or upon such grounds which are inherently likely to provoke an immediate violent reaction is guilty of a misdemeanor. . . ."

Obstructing Students' or Teachers' Access to Classes—PC 602.10. "Every person who, by physical force and with the intent to prevent attendance or instruction, willfully obstructs or attempts to obstruct any student or teacher seeking to attend or instruct classes at any . . . [community college, state college or university] campuses or facilities . . . [is guilty of a misdemeanor].

As used in this section, 'physical force' includes, but is not limited to, use of one's person, individually or in concert with others, to impede access to or movement within or otherwise to obstruct the students and teachers of the classes to which the premises are devoted."

Entry on Campus After Suspension—PC 626.2. This section makes it a misdemeanor for any student or employee to willfully and knowingly enter the campus or buildings of any school, college, state university, etc., without written permission, after such person has been suspended or dismissed.

Notice of Consent Withdrawal—PC 626.4. This section authorizes school or college administrators to notify any person, who has disrupted the orderly operation of the campus or facility, that consent for them to remain on campus has been withdrawn. Entering campus following such notification is a misdemeanor.

Nonstudents on Campus—PC 626.6. In any case in which a person, who is not a student or officer or employee of a community college, state university, or a school, and who is not required by his or her employment to be on the campus or any other facility owned, operated, or controlled by the governing board on any such school, and it appears . . . that such person is committing or likely to interfere with peaceful conduct thereon, that person may be ordered off the campus and failure to comply with the order is a misdemeanor [section briefed].

This section makes it a misdemeanor to remain on or reenter a campus after having been asked to leave by the chief administrative official or the official's designee. Further, the person requested to leave may not reenter the campus for seventy-two hours.

Unauthorized Reentry—PC 626.7. After an unauthorized person is directed to leave a school facility because of a perceived likelihood that he or she will commit an act that interferes with the peaceful conduct of the school, it is a misdemeanor for such person to reenter the school campus or facility outside of the common areas where public business is conducted without following the posted requirements to contact the schools's administrative offices.

Sex Offender on School Grounds—PC 626.8. "(a) Any person who comes into any school building or upon any school ground or street, sidewalk, or public way adjacent thereto, without lawful business thereon, and whose presence or acts interfere with the peaceful conduct of the activities of such school or disrupt the school or its pupils or school activities, or any specified sex offender [one required to register under PC 290] who comes into any school building or upon any school ground or public way adjacent thereto, unless the person is a parent or guardian of a child attending that school or is a student at the school or has prior written permission for the entry from the chief administrator of that school, is guilty of a misdemeanor if he or she:

(1) Remains there after being asked to leave by the chief administrator of the school or his designee,

School grounds receive special protection under the law, because of society's strong interest in the protection of children. *Photograph by John Gillis, courtesy of AP/Wide World Photos*

or by a school security officer, or a city police officer, deputy sheriff or California Highway Patrol officer;

(2) Reenters or comes upon such place within 72 hours of being asked to leave by a person named in (1), above; or

(3) Has otherwise established a continued pattern of unauthorized entry . . . "[section briefed].

> ***Note:*** "School" under this section means any preschool or school having any grades from kindergarten through grade twelve (PC 626.8(5)). The obvious purpose of this statute is to protect younger students against sex offenders. The crime here is in the failure to leave or the reentering of the areas described within seventy-two hours after being asked to leave by the chief administrative official (or designee), plus conduct or activities which interfere with the peaceful conduct of the school.

Drug Offender at School—PC 626.85. Persons who have been convicted within the past three years of specified drug offenses, who remain on or repeatedly reenter school grounds or adjacent streets, are guilty of a misdemeanor.

Possession of Firearms—PC 626.9. This section makes it a felony (wobbler) to bring or possess a firearm upon the grounds of any public school, or within 1000 feet of a school, without written permission of the head administrator. This prohibition includes all public schools in the state. This section does not apply to peace officers, those assisting the police and the military.

Possession of Other Weapons—PC 626.10. This section makes it a misdemeanor to bring or possess any of the following on to any public school campus:

- Dirk or dagger
- Knife having a blade longer than 3.5 inches
- Folding knife with locking blade
- Razor with unguarded blade
- Taser, or stun gun as defined in PC 244.5(a)

Exceptions are made for possession of the above items for lawful purpose within the scope of one's employment, teaching purposes, for police officers and anyone assisting them and for military personnel.

Exclusion of Unauthorized Persons—PC 627.2. "No outsider shall enter or remain on school grounds during school hours [one hour before classes begin and one hour after they end] without first registering with the principal or his designee, except to proceed expeditiously to the office . . . for the purpose of registering . . . " (PC 627.2).

An "outsider" is defined in PC 627.1, as anyone other than current students, parents and guardians, employees, elected officials and public employees (includes police officers) whose employment re-quires them to be on campus.

8.11 DISORDERLY CONDUCT

This statute provides police officers with a most effective "weapon" in dealing with many street problems. More arrests are likely to be made under this statute's several subsections, than any other section of the Penal Code.

Disorderly Conduct Defined—PC 647. "Every person who commits any of the following acts shall be guilty of disorderly conduct, a misdemeanor:

(a) Who solicits anyone to engage in or who engages in lewd or dissolute conduct in any public place or in any place open to the public or exposed to public view.

(b) Who solicits or who agrees to engage in or who engages in any act of prostitution. A person agrees to engage in an act of prostitution when, with specific intent to so engage, he or she manifests an acceptance of an offer or solicitation to so engage, regardless of whether the offer or solicitation was made by a person who also possessed the specific intent to engage in prostitution. No agreement to engage in an act of prostitution shall constitute a violation of this subdivision unless some act, beside the agreement, be done within this state in furtherance of the commission of an act of prostitution by the person agreeing to engage in the act. As used in this subdivision, prostitution includes any lewd act between persons for money or other consideration.

(c) Who accosts other persons in any public place or any place open to the public for the purpose of begging or soliciting alms.

(d) Who loiters in or about any toilet open to the public for the purpose of engaging in or soliciting any lewd or lascivious or any unlawful act.

(e) Who lodges in any building, structure, vehicle or place, whether public or private, without the permission of the owner or person entitled to the possession or in control of it.

(f) Who is found in any public place under the influence of intoxicating liquor, any drug, controlled substance, toluene, or any combination of any intoxicating liquor, drug, controlled substance or toluene, in such condition that he or she is unable to exercise care for his or her own safety or the safety of others, or by reason of his or her being under the influence of intoxicating liquor, any drug, controlled substance, or any combination of any intoxicating liquor, drug, toluene, interferes with or obstructs or prevents the free use of any street, sidewalk, or other public way.

(g) When a person has violated subdivision (f) of this section, a peace officer, if he or she is reasonably able to do so, shall place the person, or cause him or her to be placed, in civil protective custody. Such person shall be taken to a facility designated pursuant to Section 5170 of the Welfare and Institutional Code, for the 72-hour treatment and evaluation of inebriates. A peace officer may place a person in civil protective custody with that kind and degree of force which would be lawful were he or she effecting an arrest for a misdemeanor without a warrant. No person who has been placed in civil protective custody shall thereafter be subject to any criminal prosecution or juvenile court proceeding based on the facts giving rise to such placement. This subdivision shall not apply to the following persons:

1. Any person who is under the influence of any drug, or under the combined influence of intoxicating liquor and any drug.
2. Any person who a peace officer has probable cause to believe has committed any felony, or who has committed any misdemeanor in addition to subdivision (f) of this section.
3. Any person who a peace officer in good faith believes will attempt escape or will be unreasonably difficult for medical personnel to control.

(h) Who loiters, prowls, or wanders upon the private property of another, at any time, without visible or lawful business with the owner or occupant thereof. As used in this subdivision, 'loiter' means to delay or linger without a lawful purpose for being on the property and for the purpose of committing a crime as opportunity may be discovered.

(i) Who, while loitering, prowling, or wandering upon the private property of another, at any time, peeks in the door or window of any inhabited building or structure located thereon, without visible or lawful business with the owner or occupant thereof.

(j) (1) Anyone who [looks through a peep-hole or uses a device to view a bathroom, dressing room, or other place subject to a reasonable expectation of privacy, with intent to invade privacy]."

(2) "Any person who [use photo or recording devices to secretly film or record the undergarments worn by an identifiable person, without consent or knowledge, with the intent to gratify sexual desire and to invade privacy, wherever the person has a reasonable expectation of privacy]."

Discussion—PC 647(a). The California State Supreme Court rendered a decision clarifying certain terms used in, and acts constituting, a violation of this subsection in *Pryor v. Municipal Court*, (25 Cal. 3d 238). The court defined "solicitation" as tempting, seeking to induce, or trying to obtain the commission of lewd criminal conduct such as the touching of the genitals, buttocks, or female breast for the purpose of sexual arousal, gratification, or annoyance. The court ruled that the offense must occur in a public place, a place open to the public or a place exposed to public view. The court also ruled that to be a crime the suspect must know or should know there may be persons present who might be offended by the conduct.

Such acts as masturbation in public, groping of the genitals, and solicitation of lewd acts to occur in public, are offenses as long as there are others present who could be offended by them.

Maintaining a massage parlor for the purpose of prostitution and soliciting or engaging in lewd or dissolute conduct in a public place is a violation of this subdivision (*Hora v. City and County of San Francisco*, 233 Cal. App. 2d 375).

PC 647(b). This subsection pertains to soliciting, agreeing to engage in or engaging in any act of prostitution. To facilitate undercover investigations of prostitution, the legislature amended the original statute to add the crime of "agreeing" to engage in prostitution. This change makes it irrelevant who first proposes the illicit exchange of sex for money (subject to the guidelines of entrapment).

A prostitute (male or female) now violates PC 647(b) even if the vice officer initiates the solicitation, as long as the prostitute agrees to the proposition and does some "act in furtherance" of the agreement. As it now stands, any act taken by the suspect to facilitate or carry out the agreed upon prostitution would suffice to complete the crime.

Such acts might include, for example, getting into the officer's car, directing the officer to a particular motel or other location, accepting money, opening or removing either party's clothing, obtaining or producing condoms, or any physical touching or exposure to promote arousal.

In the case of *Gaylord v. Municipal Court*, (196 Cal. App. 3d 1348), the court ruled that when the prosecution charges a defendant with violating PC 647(b) for *agreeing* to an act of prostitution, at least one specific "act of furtherance" must be alleged in the complaint and supported by evidence provided by the arresting officer's report.

The "act in furtherance" can be mere words, as in directing the undercover officer where to park, or giving the officer instructions to undress or to put on a condom (*Kim v. Superior Court*).

Note that the "act in furtherance" requirement applies only to an *agreement* to engage in prostitution. There is no need for any act in furtherance if the suspect is first to *solicit* officers, or if an actual act of engaging in prostitution occurs.

PC 647(c). This subdivison does not prohibit passive solicitation of money or goods (such as sitting or standing near passers-by with a sign that says "Will work for food"), since such activity may be protected under the First Amendment (*Blair v. Shanahan*, 775 F. Supp. 1315). However, where the beggar actively *accosts* another (such as by blocking a person's path and asking for spare change), the statute may be constitutionally applied (*People v. Zimmerman*, 15 Cal. App. 4th Supp. 7).

PC 647(d). This subsection was enacted to preclude persons from loitering about public toilet facilities for the purpose of engaging in or soliciting lewd or lascivious or unlawful acts. The legislative intent of the section is to prevent persons from being accosted and solicited to participate in primarily homosexual acts, and to prevent public toilets from being used for this purpose.

The terms "lewd" or "lascivious" are defined as lustful, vulgar, indecent, obscene, sexually impure, or tending to depress the morals in respect to sexual relations.

Police generally make arrests under this law in response to specific complaints, such as allegations that unwilling adults or children are being accosted in restrooms. The law covers any one who loiters about any toilet open to the public for the specific intent and purpose of engaging in or soliciting the conduct prohibited. This subsection was upheld as constitutional by the United States Supreme Court in August, 1988.

PC 647(e). This subdivision has been declared unconstitutional by the United States Supreme Court (*Kolender v. Lawson*, (cited above) and is not currently enforceable.

PC 647(f). This subsection is applicable to persons who appear in public under the influence of intoxicating liquor, any drug, or the combined influence of intoxicants and drugs and are unable to exercise care for their own safety or the safety of others.

Under the influence: is defined as "when the brain is so far affected by alcohol or drugs or both that intelligence, sense perceptions, judgment, continuity of thought or of speech and physical coordination is impaired and not under normal control."

Public place: has been defined to be a place where the public has a right to go and be, and includes public streets, roads, highways, and sidewalks (*People v. Belanger*, 243 Cal. App. 2d 819). Webster defines a public place as one "open to common or general use, participation, enjoyment, and specifically, open to the free and unrestricted use of the public."

A barber shop is a "public place" for the criminal aspects of being intoxicated in a public place (*Ex parte Zorn*, 59 Cal. 2d 650). A person in an automobile parked on a public street is in a "public place" as contemplated by Section 647f (*People v. Belanger*, 243 Cal. App. 2d 819).

As arrests can only be made for a violation of PC 647f in public places, the clear implication is that no arrests can be made for drunkenness on obviously private premises, such as homes or apartments (*People v. De Young*, 228 Cal. App. 2d 334). Arrests cannot be made in places merely "exposed to public view" (*In re Koehne*, 59 Cal. 2d 646).

Automobiles. It is proper for police officers to investigate cases of persons sleeping in automobiles on public streets. The officer does not know at the time of such investigation what the condition of the person may be . . . and the officer in making his investigation is doing so in order to protect the individual involved and also the general public. It is certainly not improper or onerous to ask an individual to step out of an automobile in order to fully determine why or under what circumstances a person may have been asleep in an automobile parked on a public street (*People v. Superior Court*, 267 Cal. App. 2d 363).

It is reasonable for an officer to request a person to alight in order to ascertain his condition or to engage him, if possible, in intelligible conversation (*People v. Manning*, 33 Cal. App. 3d 586).

Under these authorities, officers investigating persons suspected of being passed out in automobiles due to drugs or intoxication, would be justified in having the person(s) get out, or in entering the vehicle to remove or check on the person, if unresponsive.

PC 647(g). This subdivision requires the officer to place anyone found to be in violation of PC 647(f), into protective custody, i.e., in a treatment facility for inebriates except: (1) persons who are under the influence of any drug or (2) under the combined influence of liquor and any drug, or (3) persons believed to have committed some other crime, or (4) persons the officer believes will escape or be unreasonably difficult for medical personnel to control.

PC 647(h). This subsection covers prowling or loitering on private property by one who has no lawful business with the owner or occupant and without consent of the owner or occupant. The offense can be committed at any time of the day or night.

PC 647(i). This subsection obviously deals with "window peeking" while on private property by one who has no visible or lawful business with the owner or occupant. It is not necessary that anyone be home at the time, and the peeking may be via a door as well as a window.

PC 647(j). This subsection covers problems arising as a result of persons who lodge, occupy, sleep in, etc., any building, structure, vehicle or place, whether public or private, without the permission of the owner, occupant, or person entitled to the possession or in control thereof.

C 647(k). This subsection outlaws both peephole voyeurism and secret taping or filming beneath the dress, skirt or other clothing, as specified. Subsection (2) appears to be a legislative response to reported incidents of the use of concealed video cameras at such places as parades, amusement parks and outdoor events to obtain photographs of women's and girls' underwear, for posting on the internet or for sale or personal viewing. Note that it does require an identifiable victim.

Obstructing Movement—PC 647c. This section makes it a misdemeanor to willfully and maliciously obstruct the free movement of any person on a street, sidewalk, or other public place or in any

Soliciting customers for prostitution is punishable under Penal Code § 647(b). *Courtesy of Stock Boston*

place open to the public such as, airports. This section can be used to control aggressive beggers and solicitors.

Loitering for Prostitution—PC 653.22. It is a misdemeanor to loiter in any public place with intent to commit prostitution. This intent is shown by acting in a manner and under circumstances that openly demonstrate a purpose of inducing, enticing, soliciting or procuring prostitution. Relevant circumstances in establishing unlawful intent may include (1) repeated beckoning to or conversations with passerby or occupants of vehicles, (2) prior convictions within five years, (3) circling an area in a vehicle and repeatedly signalling or talking to pedestrians or other motorists, (4) similar behavior within six months, (5) area known for prostitution activities, and any other pertinent facts.

Aiding Prostitution—PC 653.23. It is a misdemeanor for any person to direct, supervise, recruit or otherwise assist an act of prostitution, or to receive any of the proceeds of an act of prostitution. One who derives ongoing support or maintenance from prostitution is guilty of the felony of pimping (PC 266h).

8.12 PUBLIC SECURITY AND SAFETY

Public Nuisance Defined—PC 370. "Anything which is injurious to health, or is indecent, or offensive to the senses, or an obstruction to the free use of property, so as to interfere with the comfortable enjoyment of life or property by an entire community or neighborhood, or by any considerable number of persons, or unlawfully obstructs the free passage or use, in the customary manner, of any navigable lake, or river, bay, stream, canal, or basin, or any public park, square, street, or highway, is a public nuisance."

"Any person who maintains or commits any public nuisance, . . . or who willfully omits to . . . [remove] a public nuisance, is guilty of a misdemeanor [PC 372]."

Smoking on Playground—Health and Safety 104495. It is an infraction ($100 fine) to smoke on playgrounds at schools or parks, to dispose of cigarette butts there, or to threaten or intimidate those who report violators.

Weapons in Vehicles—PC 417.3. "Every person who, except in self defense, in the presence of any other person who is an occupant of a motor vehicle proceeding on a public street or highway, draws or exhibits any firearm, whether loaded or unloaded, in a threatening manner against another person in such a way as to cause a reasonable person apprehension or fear of bodily harm is guilty of a felony. . . ."

Street Gang Participation-PC186.22. Any person who actively participates in any criminal street gang with knowledge that its members engage in or have engaged in a pattern of criminal gang activity, and who willfully promotes, furthers, or assists in any felonious criminal conduct by members of that gang, is guilty of a felony ("wobbler"). Only listed violent and serious crimes qualify as a "pattern of criminal gang activity" (see PC 186.22(e)).

Dangerous Animals—PC 399. Any person owning or having control of an animal with known mischievous propensities who allows it to go at large and attack persons who are exercising reasonable precautions for their safety is guilty of a felony if a death results, or a wobbler in case of serious bodily injury.

Public Transportation—Disturbance or Damage—PC 640. Any of the following acts committed on or in the facilities or vehicles of a public transportation system . . . is punishable [as a misdemeanor].

1. Evasion of the payment of fares.
2. Misuse of transfers, passes, tickets or token with the intent to evade the payment of fares.
3. Playing sound equipment on or in system facilities or vehicles.
4. Smoking, eating, or drinking in or on system facilities or vehicles . . . where prohibited by that system.
5. Expectorating [spitting] upon system facilities or vehicles.
6. Willfully disturbing others on or in system facilities or vehicles by engaging in boisterous or unruly behavior.
7. Carrying explosives or toxins.
8. Urinating or defecating.
9. Blocking another's movement.
10. Skateboarding, roller skating or rollerblading.
11. Unauthorized use of a discount ticket.

Damage to Jails or Prisons—PC 4600. This section makes it a crime to willfully and intentionally injure or destroy any jail, prison, or public property therein. If the damage amounts to $400 or less, the offense is a misdemeanor. If the damage is more than $400, the crime is a felony.

Racial or Religious Terrorism—PC 11411(c). "Any person who burns or desecrates [mistreats] a cross or other religious symbol, knowing it to be a religious symbol, or places or displays a sign, mark, symbol, emblem, . . . including but not limited to a Nazi swastika on the private property of another without authorization for the purpose of terrorizing another or in reckless disregard of the risk of terrorizing another shall be punished by imprisonment in the county jail . . . or by a fine . . . or both . . . "

(d) "As used in this section, 'terrorize' means to cause a person of ordinary emotions and sensibilities to fear for personal safety."

Terrorism Generally—PC 11413. "(a) Any person who explodes, ignites, or attempts to explode or ignite any destructive device or any explosive, or who commits arson, in or about any of the places listed by subdivision (b), for the purpose of terrorizing another or in reckless disregard by terrorizing another is guilty of a felony. . . .

(b) Subdivision (a) applies to the following places: (1) Any licensed health care facility. (2) Any church, temple, synagogue, or other place of worship. (3) The buildings, offices, and meeting sites of organization that counsel for or against abortion. (4) Any place at which a lecture, film-showing or other private meeting . . . with respect to abortion practices or policies . . . is taking place [and other designated facilities].

(d) As used in this section, 'terrorizing' means to cause a person of ordinary emotions and sensibilities to fear for personal safety."

Electronic Tracking—PC 637.7. It is a misdemeanor for any person or entity to use an electronic tracking device (such as a beeper or transponder) to determine the location or movement of a person, except with the consent of a vehicle owner or lessee. Lawful use by law enforcement is exempt.

STUDENT REVIEW

TERMINOLOGY DEFINED—CHAPTER 8

Please see the Terminology Quiz at the end of this chapter.

1. Dissolute: loose of morals and conduct.
2. Double jeopardy: tried a second time for charge previously adjudicated.
3. *Duces tecum:* Latin: "bring with," a subpoena for papers, etc.
4. Duress: Coercion of a person to do something against his will.
5. Emancipation: free from another's custody, age of majority.
6. Execution: carrying out court order, e.g., warrants, death penalty.
7. Extortion: "blackmail," taking property via illegal threats.
8. Extradition: process of returning an accused from another jurisdiction.
9. False pretense: deceit used to unlawfully gain property from another.
10. *Habeas corpus:* Latin: "have body," order to bring person to court.
11. Hearsay: a statement repeated in court as proof of its truth.
12. Homicide: killing of one human being by another, may be legal or illegal.
13. Inquest: inquiry into cause of violent or unusual death.
14. Judgment: official declaration of results of a lawsuit or court ruling.
15. Lascivious: lustful, lewd, indecent, obscene.
16. Lynching: taking a person from custody of police by riot.
17. *Posse comitatus:* Latin: "power of the county," legal right of police to require assistance.
18. Preempt: supersede, take precedence over, prior jurisdiction.
19. Rout: preparatory stages of a riot.
20. Tumultuous: boisterous, disorderly, disturbing.

TRUE-FALSE QUIZ—CHAPTER 8

After reading this chapter you should be able to correctly answer the following items.

___ 1. The courts do not recognize the existence of "fighting words" as a basis for disturbing the peace.
___ 2. The use of offensive words other than in a public place does not constitute disturbing the peace.
___ 3. If two or more persons assemble together and advance toward the commission of an act which would be a riot if committed, such is legally an unlawful assembly.
___ 4. It is a crime to remain at the scene of a riot after having been warned to disperse, even if one is only an observer.
___ 5. A rout is simply defined as the preparatory stage of a riot.
___ 6. To constitute a riot, the object of the assembly need not necessarily be unlawful.
___ 7. Taking soil from another's vacant lot without permission constitutes the crime of trespass.
___ 8. Tearing down a "no hunting" sign on another's property constitutes the crime of trespass.
___ 9. The taking by means of riot of any person from the lawful custody of an officer constitutes a crime of rout.
___10. One who engages in lewd or dissolute conduct in a public place is guilty of disorderly conduct.
___11. Loitering around a public toilet for the purpose of engaging in any unlawful act is in violation of PC 647(d), disorderly conduct.
___12. Begging money in a public place is no longer a crime in California.
___13. No agreement to engage in an act of prostitution is a crime unless some act, besides the agreement is done.
___14. One can be guilty of prowling only if the act was done at night under PC 647(h).
___15. If no one is home at the time, a subject cannot be guilty of window-peeking under PC 647(i).
___16. A "public place" is any place such as an office building, movie house, department store, etc., generally open to the public.

___17. One who solicits or agrees to engage in an act of prostitution is guilty of disorderly conduct under PC 647(b).
___18. PC 647(g) requires an officer to place one who is found under the influence of drugs in a public place in civil protective custody.
___19. To be guilty of window peeking, the building must be inhabited under PC 647(i).
___20. A building is considered inhabited if it is customarily used as a dwelling even if the resident is temporarily absent.

ESSAY-DISCUSSION ITEMS—CHAPTER 8

After reading this chapter you should be able to correctly answer the following items.

1. What are the three different types of illegal activity which constitute disturbing the peace under PC 415?
2. List the elements of "failure to disperse" as defined under PC 416.
3. What are the two elements of unlawful assembly as under PC 407?
4. Under what circumstances, if any, is it unlawful to be present at the scene of any rout or riot?
5. Briefly describe the difference between rout and riot.
6. What type of activity or element constitutes violation of PC 404.6, inciting a riot?
7. What constitutes a (1) public place and (2) a place open to the public under PC 647?
8. List five of the acts or activities which constitute a violation of PC 647, disorderly conduct.
9. To what extent must a meeting be disrupted to constitute a violation of PC 403, Disturbing a Public Meeting?
10. List the elements of PC 647(h) and (i), Prowling and Window Peeking.

TERMINOLOGY QUIZ—CHAPTER 8

Match terms and definitions by writing the number preceding the correct term between the appropriate brackets.

Terms	*Definitions*
1. Dissolute	[ ] boisterous, disorderly, disturbing
2. Double jeopardy	[ ] court order to bring "body" to court
3. Duces tecum	[ ] loose of morals and conduct
4. Duress	[ ] preparatory stages of a riot
5. Emancipation	[ ] deceit used to gain property of another
6. Execution	[ ] process for returning accused from another jurisdiction
7. Extortion	[ ] a subpoena requiring papers, etc., be brought to court
8. Extradition	[ ] coercing a person to act against his or her will
9. False pretense	[ ] supersede, take precedence over
10. Habeas corpus	[ ] taking a person from police custody by riot
11. Hearsay	[ ] free from another's legal custody
12. Homicide	[ ] lustful, lewd, indecent, obscene
13. Inquest	[ ] blackmail, taking property by illegal threats
14. Judgment	[ ] carrying out court orders
15. Lascivious	[ ] inquiry into cause of violent or unusual death
16. Lynching	
17. Posse comitatus	
18. Preempt	
19. Rout	
20. Tumultuous death	

CHAPTER 9

DANGEROUS WEAPONS CONTROL LAWS

9.1 PROHIBITED WEAPONS

Dangerous Weapon Manufacture Sale Possession—PC 12020. This section makes it a felony (wobbler), to:

1. possess,
2. lend, give, sell, manufacture, import, or
3. carry concealed on the person certain deadly or dangerous weapons, or materials listed below.

Gun violence, firearm injury and death from crime and dangerous weapons use by offenders is an increasingly serious threat to society.

Possession Unlawful. Mere possession of any of the following (other than the exceptions noted) is a felony. It is also a felony to manufacture, cause to be manufactured, import into the state, keep for sale, offer or expose for sale, give or lend any of the following (other than the exceptions noted):

Altered Rifle or Revolver. See Sawed-off shotgun, below.

Ballistic Knife Defined. This is a device that propels a knife-like blade as a projectile by means of a spring, elastic or compressed gas. Such devices as crossbows and underwater spear guns are not included in this definition and are not illegal.

Belt Buckle Knife Defined. A knife which is made an integral part of a belt buckle and has a blade of at least two and a half inches long.

Billy Defined. A billy is defined as a club or a bludgeon. A bludgeon is a short club-like weapon with one end usually loaded and thicker than the other end. The courts have included certain articles, such as loaded pool cues, tire irons, police batons, pieces of pipe, etc., to fall within the terms of this section (*People v. Grubb,* 63 Cal. 2d 614).

Blackjack Defined. A blackjack is a small leather-covered club or billy weighted at one end and having an elastic shaft.

A large number of steel washers strung on a rawhide thong was held to be a blackjack or slingshot within the meaning of this act (*People v. Mulherin,* 140 Cal. App. 212). In another case, a flat steel wrench with a leather thong attached was also held to be a blackjack or slingshot (*People v. Williams,* 100 Cal. App. 149).

Camouflaged Firearm Container. This includes any container designed to enclose a firearm which: (1) allows the gun to be fired by external controls while the firearm is in the container and (2) is not readily recognizable as containing a firearm.

Cane Gun Defined. A cane gun means any firearm mounted or enclosed in a stick, rod, crutch, or similar device, designed to be or capable of being used as an aid in walking, if such firearm may be fired while mounted or enclosed therein.

Disguised Firearm Defined. This includes any firearm or firearm-type device which is not immediately recognizable as such. Possession is a felony.

Fléchette Dart Defined. As used in this section, a "fléchette dart" means a dart, capable of being fired from a firearm, which measures approximately one inch in length, with tail fins which take up five-sixteenths inch of the body. Possession is a felony.

Metal Knuckles Defined. This device is variously defined as a device made wholly or partly of metal which is worn in or on the hand. It is likened to four large rings welded together and is often referred to as a "knuckle duster" or "brass knuckles." The courts have held that the use of alternate strips of lead and friction tape, fashioned into a bracelet to fit over four knuckles, is within the term "metal knuckles" (*People v. Quinones,* 140 Cal. App. 2d 609).

Nunchaku Defined. A nunchaku is an instrument consisting of two or more sticks, clubs, bars or rods to be used as handles, connected by rope, cord, wire, or chain, in the design of a weapon used in connection with the practice of a system of self-defense such as karate.

Exception. It is not a crime to manufacture nunchakus for the purpose of selling them to a school which holds a regulatory license and teaches the arts of self-defense. It is also not a violation to possess a nunchaku on the premises of a self-defense school providing the school holds a proper business license.

Sandbag or Sandclub Defined. These articles may be simply defined as "hard bag full of sand." Such devices are typically home-made and resemble a blackjack.

Sawed-off Shotgun—Altered Rifle or Revolver. As used in this section, a sawed-off shotgun means any firearm (including any revolver) manufactured, designed, or converted to fire shotgun ammunition having a barrel (or barrels) of less than 18 inches in length, or a rifle having a barrel less than 16 inches in length, or any weapon made from a rifle or shotgun (whether altered, modified, or otherwise) if the weapon has an overall length of less than 26 inches.

Thus a rifle or shotgun would be illegal if its overall length is less than 26 inches, regardless of the length of the barrel. It could also be illegal if its barrel length is less than 18 inches (in the case of a shotgun) or 16 inches (in the case of a rifle) regardless of its overall length.

Exceptions—Altered Shotgun. The manufacture or possession of sawed-off shotguns for use with blank cartridges solely as props for teaching institutions, motion picture or television program production when authorized by the Department of Justice (see PC 12095) is not a violation of law.

Suriken Defined. An instrument, without handles, consisting of a metal plate having three or more radiating points with one or more sharp edges in any geometric shape for use as a throwing weapon.

Slungshot Defined. A slungshot is defined as a small mass of metal or stone fixed on a flexible handle, strap, or other similar contrivance. There are relatively few case decisions which reflect the use of a slungshot. However, any object such as a mace, which is suspended by rope, wire, chain, etc., and which can be swung about will generally fit within the meaning of this section.

Law enforcement officers regularly encounter a variety of illegal weapons.
Courtesy of Reuters/Corbis Images

Special Ammunition Defined. This includes any ammunition which contains or consists of any fléchette dart, or any bullet containing or carrying an explosive agent. Possession is a felony.

Throwing Stars Defined. This is an instrument, without handles, consisting of a metal plate having three or more radiating points with one or more sharp edges and designed in the shape of a polygon, trefoil, cross, star, diamond, or other geometric shape for use as a weapon for throwing.

Wallet Gun Defined. A wallet gun means any firearm mounted or enclosed in a case, resembling a wallet, designed to be or capable of being carried in a pocket or purse, if such firearm may be fired while mounted or enclosed in such case.

Other Prohibited Weapons. Also included in the category of unlawful weapons are the following: explosive bullets, cane swords, multiburst trigger activators, leaded canes, zip guns, lipstick knives, shobizues, air gauge knives, writing pen knives, and unconventional pistols. Manufacture or transfer of large capacity magazines (more than ten rounds) is also prohibited.

Miscellaneous Exceptions. It is not against the law to possess any of the following:

1. **Antique Firearms.** For purposes of this section, the term "antique firearm" means any firearm not designed or redesigned for using rim fire or conventional center fire fixed ammunition and manufactured in or before 1898. This also includes matchlock, flintlock or similar type firearms whether manufactured in or before 1898.
2. **Tracer Ammunition.** Tracer ammunition manufactured for shotguns is also exempt from the provisions of PC 12020(a) and possession of such is not a crime in California.
3. **Relics and Curios.** Any firearm or ammunition which is a curio or relic, as defined in Section 178.11 of the Code of Federal Regulations, is exempt from the provisions of PC 12020(a) and possession of such is not a crime in California.

Possession Defined. The law recognizes two kinds of possession: (1) actual possession and (2) constructive possession. A person who knowingly has direct physical control over a thing is then in *actual* possession of it. A person who, although not in actual possession, knowingly has the right of control over a thing, either directly or through another person or persons, is then in *constructive* possession of it. The law recognizes that one person may have possession alone, or that two or more persons jointly may share actual or constructive possession.

Carrying Concealed Upon the Person—PC 12020(a). It is a felony (wobbler) to carry, concealed on the person, any explosive substance or a dirk or dagger.

Explosive Substance Defined. This includes any substance, with the exception of fixed ammunition, which, as the term implies, is capable of being exploded. Note that such materials must be carried on the person in a concealed manner to constitute a crime.

Dirk or Dagger Defined. "Dirk" or "dagger" means a knife or other instrument with or without a handguard capable of ready use as a stabbing weapon that may inflict great bodily injury or death, excluding an unlocked folding knife (PC 12020(c)(24)).

Switchblade Knife—on Person or in Vehicle—PC 653k. It is a misdemeanor to possess a switchblade knife having a blade *over* two inches in length:

1. in the passenger or driver area of any motor vehicle in any public place or place open to the public, or
2. to carry same on the person, or
3. to sell, offer to sell, loan, or give same to any other person.

Switchblade Knife Defined—PC 653k. For purposes of this section a "switchblade knife" is one having the appearance of a pocketknife, and shall include a spring blade knife, snap-blade knife, gravity knife, or any other similar type knife, the blade or blades of which are two or more inches long and which can be released automatically by a flick of a button, pressure on the handle, flip of the wrist or other mechanical device, or is released by the weight of the blade or by any type of mechanism whatsoever. A knife opened by thumb pressure against the blade or a thumb stud is not a switchblade, provided resistance must be overcome.

For purposes of this section "passenger's or driver's area" means that part of a motor vehicle which is designed to carry the driver and passengers, including any interior compartment or space therein.

Undetectable Knife—PC 12001.1. It is a misdemeanor to make, import, offer or keep for sale any undetectable knife. Such devices are defined the same as dirks or daggers, with the added element that they be undetectable by a metal detector set at standard calibration. There are exceptions for law enforcement, military and institutional entities.

Hard Plastic Knuckles—PC 12020.1. It is a misdemeanor to manufacture commercially, import for commercial sale, or offer, keep or expose for commercial sale any hard plastic knuckles. The prohibited device is anything made wholly or partially of hard plastic, worn for the purposes of offense or defense, that either protects the wearer's hand or increases the injury to the person struck, including fist supports and shields and studs or projections.

9.2 FIREARM CONCEALED ON PERSON OR IN VEHICLE

Pistol-Revolver-Concealable Firearm Defined—PC 12001. As used in the Deadly Weapons Control section of the Penal Code, the terms "pistol," "revolver," and "firearm capable of being concealed upon the person" apply to and include any device, designed to be used as a weapon, from which is expelled a projectile by any form of explosion or combustion and which has a barrel length of *less* than 16 inches. These terms also apply to any device which has a barrel length of *more* than 16 inches, which is designed to be *interchanged* with a barrel of *less* than 16 inches.

Firearm—Expanded Definition—PC 12001(d). In addition to the definition in PC 12001, above, the term "firearm" also includes any rocket, rocket propelled projectile launcher or similar device containing any explosive or incendiary material. This includes any device designed for emergency or distress signaling purposes.

Concealed Firearm in Vehicles—PC 12025(a)(1). Except as otherwise provided, any person who carries concealed within any vehicle which is under his control or direction, any pistol, revolver or other firearm capable of being concealed (one with barrel less than 16 inches in length) without having a license to carry such firearm is guilty of a misdemeanor. Note: Also see Transporting Firearms, PC 12026.1, below.

Degree of Concealment. The firearm need not be, completely hidden in a vehicle in order for it to be deemed concealed. In one case the officer saw a butt of a gun protruding from beneath two pillows on the front seat of defendant's car after stopping him for drunk driving. The gun was held to be "concealed" within the meaning of PC 12025 (*People v. Linden,* 185 Cal. App. 2d 752).

It should be noted that PC 12025 does not prohibit the carrying of a concealable firearm in a vehicle so long as the weapon is in plain view and is not loaded. The Attorney General has ruled: "It appears quite clear that a concealable firearm carried on the seat of a vehicle is legally carried under PC 12025, so long as the weapon is in plain view and is not loaded. It further appears that a concealable weapon may be carried anywhere else in the vehicle, again provided it remains in plain view and is not loaded [38 *Opinions Atty.* Gen. 199]."

Possession of Weapons in Vehicles. Suppose officers stop a vehicle in order to issue the driver a traffic citation. During the course of this lawful detention, they spot a concealed pistol under the front seat between the driver and his passenger. The driver tells the officer that the firearm belongs to the passenger. May the driver be arrested for carrying a concealed firearm? May the passenger be arrested for the same charge?

Under PC 12025(a)(1), the driver may be arrested, because a firearm is being carried concealed in a vehicle that is under his control or direction. And if the circumstances (e.g., proximity, statements of the driver and passenger, location of clips or ammo, or indicia of ownership) indicate that the passenger placed or concealed the firearm in the vehicle, the passenger can be arrested under PC 12025(a)(3), which prohibits causing a concealed firearm to be carried in a vehicle in which the person is an occupant.

Concealed Weapon Upon Person—PC 12025(a)(2). Any person who carries concealed upon his or her person any pistol, revolver or other firearm capable of being concealed (same barrel length as above) upon the person without having a license to carry such firearm, is guilty of a misdemeanor. ***Note:*** a second conviction under either of the above sections is a felony.

A violation is also a felony if the firearm is stolen and this is known to the suspect, or where the person is an active gang member or has a prior felony conviction, or is not in lawful possession of the firearm. Violation by a person with a prior conviction for a crime against a person or property, or for narcotics violations, is a felony (wobbler), as is violation by a person who is not the registered owner of the firearm with the Department of Justice and who also has matching ammunition immediately available.

Degree of Concealment. A firearm does not have to be completely hidden in order to be held to be concealed for the purposes of PC 12025. In *People v. May* (33 Cal. App. 3d 888), a police officer observed the defendant walking along an alley in a high-crime area. He noticed a bulge in the defendant's pocket and saw that the top of the object which caused the bulge was silver. While detaining the defendant briefly for questioning, the officer saw that the object in the defendant's pocket was a derringer. The defendant argued that since the gun was partially exposed to view, it could not be considered concealed. The court disagreed with *May's* argument since that logic would enable a defendant to ". . . immunize himself from prosecution on a charge of possessing a concealed weapon merely by intentionally or unintentionally permitting an occasional glimpse of the weapon which would otherwise remain concealed from sight."

Firearms Carried Openly—PC 12025(e). Firearms carried openly in belt holsters are *not* concealed within the meaning of this section. The same is true of hunting knives carried openly in sheaths suspended from the waist of the wearer. ***Note:*** PC 12031 (below) prohibits the carrying of *loaded* firearms in public places.

Transporting Firearms in Vehicles—PC 12026.1. This section modifies PC 12025, discussed above. It is now legal for a person over the age of 18 (who is not a convicted felon or narcotic addict as described in PC 12021), to carry or transport a pistol, revolver or other firearm capable of being concealed, in a vehicle provided the following applies:

1. The firearm is locked in the vehicle's trunk, or
2. It is locked in a container (not the utility or glove compartment) which may then be in the vehicle.
3. The firearm is in a locked container while being carried for lawful purposes directly to or from the vehicle.

Locked Container Defined. A locked container as used here means a secure container which is fully enclosed and locked by a padlock, key lock, combination lock, or similar locking device (PC 12026.l(c)).

Loaded Firearm in Public Place—PC 12031. This section makes it a misdemeanor to carry a *loaded* firearm on the person or in a vehicle in any public place or on any public street in an incorporated city or in any "prohibited area" of any unincorporated territory. A "prohibited area" is any place it is unlawful to discharge a firearm. This section does not apply to peace officers and others legally carrying a firearm in the line of duty.

A violation of PC 12031 is a felony if the firearm is stolen and this is known by the suspect, or if the person is an active gang member, or where the person is not in lawful possession of the firearm, or where the person has a prior conviction for any felony or any weapons offense of this chapter. Violation by a person with a prior conviction of a crime against a person or property, or of a narcotics violation, is a wobbler, as is violation by a person who is not the registered owner of the firearm with the Department of Justice.

Discussion. No specific intent is necessary to violate any of these sections—general intent will suffice. The mere manufacturing, importation, sale, possession, giving or lending of prohibited weapons, or carrying concealed upon the person or loaded in public those weapons listed is sufficient to sustain a conviction, in the absence of a legitimate defense.

Also, a person is said to be in possession of an article when it is under his or her dominion and control. It is absolutely essential that the person have knowledge of the fact that he or she has possession (*People v. Patterson*, 102 Cal. App. 2d 675).

Exceptions, Home or Business. California law provides that concealable firearms may be kept in one's home or place of business without a license providing the owner is a citizen of the United States, over the age of 18, and not an addict or ex-felon (PC 12026).

PC 12025 does not apply to peace officers, members of the armed forces when on duty, licensed hunters when they are hunting or on their way to or from hunting, and certain guards and messengers (PC 12027).

It is a defense to a PC 12021 or PC 12025 charge that the person possessed the firearm only for the purpose of taking it to a law enforcement station for disposal, provided the person has given advance notice to the law enforcement agency and follows the procedure specified in PC 12026.2 (PC 12021(h); PC 12026.2(a)(17) and (18)).

Receipt and Return—PC 12028.7. Except as otherwise specifically provided, where an officer takes custody of a firearm, a receipt must be issued to the person from whom the firearm is taken, listing the description and serial number, and indicating where and when the firearm may be recovered. The firearm must be held at least 48, but no more than 72 hours, unless retention is authorized by other statutes.

9.3 DEADLY WEAPONS

Certain objects such as blackjacks, sawed-off shotguns, metal knuckles, nunchakus and throwing stars are considered deadly weapons ordinarily associated with criminal activity and therefore the California Legislature has made their possession unlawful (PC 12020). There are other objects and instruments, such as a garden hoe, canes or hat pins, which are not considered weapons when used for the purpose normally intended. However, if two men begin to fist fight and one of them picks up a garden hoe and advances on the other, that garden hoe may very well become a deadly weapon depending on how it is used.

Whenever an object has the capacity for being used to inflict death or great bodily injury, and its possessor intends such a use should the circumstances require it, that object may be considered a deadly weapon. In addition, being armed with a deadly weapon can elevate a simple assault to an assault with a deadly weapon or increase the penalty of other crimes.

The Test for Being Armed. In *People v. Moran* (33 Cal. App. 3rd 274), the defendant was convicted of rape while armed with a deadly weapon. At the time he committed the crime, he was armed with a "metal three-pronged instrument" (throwing star). On appeal defendant argued that this object could not be considered a deadly weapon. The court disagreed with the defendant and said: "When it appears that such an instrument is capable of being used in a dangerous or deadly manner, and it may be fairly inferred from the evidence that its possessor intended on a particular occasion to use it as a weapon should the circumstances require, we believe that its character as a 'dangerous or deadly weapon' may thus be established, at least for the purpose of that occasion."

The court in the *Moran* case ruled that a perpetrator may be held to have been armed with a deadly weapon if (1) the object in question was capable of being used to cause death or great bodily injury, and (2) the facts indicate that he intended such a use if the circumstances required it.

9.4 PROHIBITED WEAPONS AND DEVICES

Policy and Purpose. A major purpose of the regulation of weapons is to outlaw the classic instruments normally used only for criminal purposes. In particular, the Legislature has attempted to minimize the danger to public safety arising from the free access to firearms that can be used for crimes of violence. This approach has been upheld as a valid exercise of the "police power" of the State for the protection of the lives and property of citizens (*People v. Billon,* 26 Cal. App. 2d 537).

Possession Alone Sufficient. For prohibited weapons and devices, proof of possession alone is sufficient to convict in most cases. It is not necessary to prove malicious intent or wrongful use of the instrument (*People v. Odegard,* 203 Cal. App. 2d 427). Where the offense is defined as mere possession, the only knowledge required is knowledge of the character of the object possessed (*People v. Mendoza,* 251 Cal. App. 2d 835).

Handguns With Altered Numbers—PC 12094. It is a misdemeanor to possess any pistol or revolver that does not bear identification numbers or has missing or altered make, model, serial numbers, etc. Furthermore, alterations of such numbers is a felony (PC 12090). There is a rebuttable presumption that one possessing such an altered handgun made the alteration.

Possession of a Silencer—PC 12520. It is a felony to possess any device commonly known as a silencer for firearms. A silencer is any device or attachment designed, used or intended for use in silencing the report of a firearm (PC 12500).

Destructive Devices—PC 12301. It is a felony to possess any "destructive device" which includes hand grenades, tracer or incendiary ammunition (except for shotgun tracer ammunition), grenade launchers, rocket type devices and their launchers,

"Molotov cocktails," and any weapon greater than sixty caliber which fires fixed ammunition.

Terrorist Weapons—PC 11418. Any person who makes, transfers or possesses any weapon of mass destruction (biological, nuclear, etc.), or who uses such a weapon against stock, crops, natural resources or the food or water supply, is guilty of a felony; use against a person in a form that could cause widespread injury or death is punishable by life in prison, or if death results, by life in prison without possibility of parole (or may be sentenced to death under PC 190.2) (PC 11418). An intentional threat to use a weapon of mass destruction that causes sustained fear and quarantine is a wobbler (PC 11418.5). Unauthorized possession of specified biological agents is punishable by fine or imprisonment; any officer who encounters restricted agents must immediately notify the local public health officer (PC 11419). Sending or placing a facsimile weapon of mass destruction with intent to create fear is a misdemeanor if no one is placed in fear, and a felony if someone is (PC 11418.1). Cross-jurisdictional attacks by terrorists using weapons of mass destruction may be prosecuted in any jurisdiction where any one or more violations occur (PC 787).

Shotgun Restrictions—F&G Code 2010. Other prohibited firearms include a shotgun bore larger than ten gauge, or any shotgun capable of holding more than six shells at one time (Fish and Game Code).

Constitutionality. The Second Amendment of the United States Constitution reads: "A well-regulated militia being necessary to the security of a free state, the right of the people to keep and bear arms shall not be infringed." This amendment applies, however, only to the exercise of power by the *federal* government. It does *not* restrict against the state government's passing weapons laws. It has been held that the right of the people to keep and bear arms is not a right granted by the constitution (*In re Ramirez,* 193 Cal. 633). Furthermore, even where the State Constitution includes the same sort of provision as the Second Amendment, it is interpreted to apply only to the bearing of arms by citizens in defense of a common cause and not to their use in private brawls (*In re Ramirez*). The Supreme Court of the United States has also held, for example, that a shotgun having a barrel less than eighteen inches in length has no reasonable relation to the preservation of a well regulated militia and is not within the meaning of that provision (*United States v. Miller,* 307 U.S. 174).

9.5 TEAR GAS POSSESSION

Tear Gas For Self-Defense—PC 12403.7. Citizens are permitted to purchase, possess and carry tear gas (aerosol spray type only) for self-defense purposes subject to the following requirements:

- Must be at least 16 years of age (minors need parental approval).
- Has not been convicted of a felony.
- Is not addicted to any narcotic drug.

The citizen may then purchase a special "civilian" aerosol spray canister of a specific size, only. It must bear the words: "The use of this substance or device for any purpose other than self-defense is a crime under the law. The contents are dangerous—use with care." ***Note:*** no person shall possess or use any tear gas weapon which expels a projectile under this law, nor any weapon that has not been approved by the Department of Justice (PC 12450).

Pepper Spray. Oleoresin Capsicum (pepper spray) is legal to possess following its approval by the California Department of Justice.

Penalty for Misuse—PC 12403.7. Any person who has a valid permit, who uses tear gas or tear gas weapons except in self-defense or for authorized training purposes, is guilty of a public offense (felony wobbler).

9.6 ILLEGAL USE OF FIREARMS

The mere pointing of an unloaded firearm at someone, accompanied by a threat to shoot him, but without an attempt to use the gun as a bludgeon, is not considered an assault of any type in California (*People v. Sylva,* 143 Cal. 62). However, the pointing of an unloaded firearm at another in a "rude, angry or threatening manner" may constitute a violation of PC 417, which makes brandishing a firearm in such a manner a misdemeanor (see Chapter 10, Types of Assaults).

The California assault statute (PC 240) requires a showing of "present ability" to do harm, and the courts have held that pointing an unloaded firearm does not imply the present ability to do harm and therefore does not amount to an assault unless the a firearm is used as a bludgeon.

Penal Code 12022(a), provides for a penalty enhancement (increase) of one additional consecutive year in prison upon conviction of committing or attempting to commit any felony if one or more of the perpetrators was armed with a firearm. The firearm in such cases may be of any type. Whether or not the firearm was concealed or concealable is not an element. The fact that it was not used or even displayed is not important if, in fact, one of the perpetrators was armed.

PC 12022(b) provides that if any person personally uses a deadly or dangerous weapon (includes knives, (clubs, guns, etc.) during commission of a felony, the one year enhancement applies unless the use of the dangerous or deadly weapon is an element of the crime charged (such as carrying a concealed weapon).

PC 12022.5 provides that any person who uses a firearm to commit or attempt to commit a felony, shall be subjected to a two-year consecutive and additional penalty enhancement unless the use of a firearm is an element of the offense charged. ***Note:*** The additional term provided by this section may also be imposed in cases of assault with a deadly weapon under PC 245.

The so-called "10-20-life" sentencing law, effective as to specified serious felonies committed on or after January 1, 1998, adds a mandatory, consecutive enhancement of ten years for personal use of a firearm, twenty years for personal discharge, and life imprisonment (minimum twenty-five years) for discharge resulting in great bodily injury, during the commission of the specified crimes.

The courts have held that even an unloaded gun is at least a "dangerous weapon" in its natural state, and has a potential to be used as a club or bludgeon. Penalty enhancements, therefore, would apply in a robbery or burglary committed with an unloaded firearm. It is not necessary to show that the defendant intended to use the gun (*People v. Aranda,* 63 Cal. 2d 518).

If the defendant was armed with a loaded firearm during the perpetration of a burglary or robbery, penalty enhancements would be proper even if the gun was not drawn or in any way exposed to the victim (Burglary: *People v. Moore,* 143 Cal. App. 2d 333; Robbery: *People v. Hall,* 105 Cal. App. 2d 359).

It is well settled in California that a firearm is a "deadly weapon" even if unloaded and not operable (*People v. Torres,* 19 Cal. App. 2d 724).

9.7 FIREARMS—CONCEALABLE WEAPON RESTRICTIONS

Felons, Addicts, Prohibited From Possessing—PC 12021. Subdivisions (a) and (b) of this section make it a felony for any person who has been previously convicted of any felony or any crime involving the violent use of a firearm, or who is addicted to the use of any narcotic drug, to own or have under their possession or control any firearm. Subdivision (c) makes it a misdemeanor for any person who has been convicted of a misdemeanor violation of several other sections of the Penal Code involving firearms violations, within 10 years of the conviction, to own or have any firearm under their control.

Subdivisions (d), (e) and (g) make punishable the possession of firearms by those prohibited from doing so by a probation condition, by persons under age thirty who were guilty of an offense under W&I 707(b) (specified serious crimes by juveniles), or by persons subject to certain protective orders.

At sentencing, the judge is required to serve written notice on those who are prohibited from owning or possessing firearms. The failure to provide this notice is not a defense to a charge of unlawful possession.

Minors. It is a wobbler for a minor to possess a concealable firearm, and a misdemeanor to possess live ammunition, unless he has either written permission of his parent or guardian or is accompanied by the parent or guardian at the time and place of possession and is engaged in such activities as target shooting, hunting, or dramatic acting (PC 12101). Selling or otherwise furnishing any BB device to a minor is restricted (PC 12551, 12552).

Mental Patients. Mental patients are not allowed to possess any firearms. The same restriction applies to people who have been adjudicated by a court to be a danger to others as a result of mental illness.

Exceptions. Peace officers are exempted from most, though not all, of the restrictions applicable to deadly and dangerous weapons control. Certain weapons, to be legally possessed by peace officers, must be authorized by their employing agency and in many cases, the officer must possess a certificate showing special training in the use of the weapon, e.g., firearms and tear gas.

Also, certain weapons such as metal knuckles cannot be authorized by an employing agency or legally possessed by a peace officer except when being held for evidence.

Inoperable Weapons. The rule is that the prohibition on a weapon remains no matter how disabled it may be if it still retains its efficiency to such an extent that it may in some manner be used as originally intended (*People v. McCloskey,* 76 Cal. App. 2d 227). Thus, its essential character is not changed even by dismemberment, if the parts may be easily assembled so as to become effective (*People v. Ekstrand,* 28 Cal. App. 2d 117).

Sale of Concealable Firearms. It is a misdemeanor for anyone employed in the business of selling firearms to sell or transfer a concealable firearm without a license to do so (PC 12020 and PC 12071). In addition, there are restrictions on the eligibility of the buyer (must be 18 or over), the time of delivery (must not be delivered within 5 days of the purchase), method of delivery (gun must be unloaded and securely wrapped) and the dealer must register the sale (PC 12072). In the case of a firearm sale between two private parties, where neither party holds a dealer's license, the sale must be handled through a licensed dealer (PC 12072(d)). It is an infraction (first or second offense) or a misdemeanor (third or subsequent offense) to apply to purchase more than one handgun in any thirty day period (PC l2072(a)(9)(A)).

9.8 FIREARMS IN PUBLIC PLACES

With certain exceptions, it is a misdemeanor to carry a loaded firearm on one's person or in a vehicle while in any public place or street in an incorporated city or in a prohibited area of an unincorporated territory (PC 12031). Exceptions to this prohibition include on-duty members of the military, and those who are licensed to carry concealed firearms, among others (PC 12031(a)).

Police May Inspect Firearms—PC 12031(e). This section authorizes officers to examine any firearm carried openly in a public place in order to determine whether or not it is loaded. In fact, refusal to allow a peace officer to inspect a firearm pursuant to the provisions of this section constitutes probable cause for arrest for violation of this section. A firearm will be deemed loaded for purposes of this section if there is any unexpended cartridge or shell in or in any way attached to the firearm, including the firing chamber, the magazine or the clip (PC 12031(e)). It is not necessary to prove that the defendant knew the gun was loaded in order for him to be convicted of violating PC 12031 (*People v. Harrison,* 1 Cal. App. 3d 115). This section does not prevent a person from keeping a loaded firearm on his private property or place of business (PC 12031).

Loaded Rifles and Shotguns in Vehicles—F&G 2006. The Fish and Game Code makes it unlawful to have a loaded rifle or shotgun in or on any vehicle on a public highway. For purposes of this section, the firearm is considered loaded only when there is an unused shell or cartridge in the chamber. This section does not apply to peace officers or members of the armed forces while on duty.

Discharging Firearms from Vehicles—PC 12034. It is a wobbler to permit another to discharge a firearm from a vehicle, and it is a felony to discharge a firearm at another person from a vehicle; it is a misdemeanor for the driver or owner of a vehicle to allow another to bring a firearm into a vehicle in violation of PC 12031 or Fish and Game 2006.

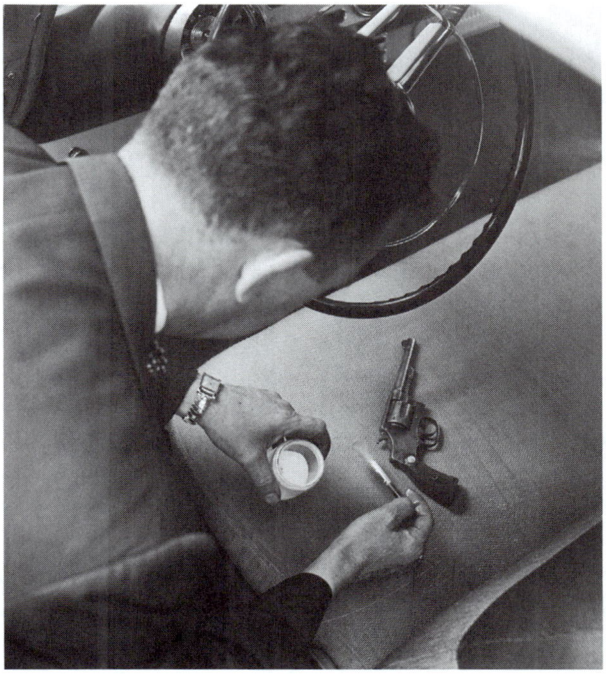

It is unlawful to carry a loaded firearm in a vehicle on the public streets. *Courtesy of Hulton Getty/Liason Agency, Inc.*

Firearms in the State Capitol—PC 171c. It is a felony to carry a loaded firearm into the State Capitol area. This includes the grounds, offices and hearing rooms. It should be noted that in this context, a firearm is considered loaded whenever the gun and the ammunition are in possession of the same person.

Prohibited Weapons at Airports—PC 171.5. It is a misdemeanor to possess listed firearms, weapons and ammunition in an "airport sterile area," or "passenger vessel terminal," meaning the security zone around an airport or port facility as specified in federal regulations. In addition to firearms, prohibited weapons and devices include certain knives, box cutters, grenades, unauthorized tear gas, tasers, BB guns, imitation firearms and grenades, and component parts of firearms. This section does not apply to current or retired peace officers who are authorized to carry firearms.

9.9 RELATED CODE SECTIONS

Armed Criminal Action—PC 12023. It is a wobbler to carry a loaded firearm with intent to commit any felony.

Return of Seized Firearms—PC 12021.3. A person seeking the return of a firearm that is in the custody of a law enforcement agency must submit an application to DOJ to have his or her eligibility to possess the firearm confirmed, and must pay a processing fee. The agency must enter a report into the automated firearms system, recording the identity of the person to whom the firearm is returned.

Destruction of Weapons as Nuisances—PC 12028. This section provides for the destruction of those weapons mentioned in Sections 653k, 12020 and 12025. Also included are weapons used in the commission of, or attempt to commit, a felony, including those cases where the defendant is found guilty of a lesser included offense or a misdemeanor. Such destruction is to take place between the 1st and 10th days of July each year (briefed).

License to Carry Firearms—PC 12050. The sheriff of a county, or the chief or other head of a municipal police department of any city or city and county, upon proof that the person applying is of good moral character, that good cause exists for the issuance, and that the person applying is a resident of the county or spends substantial business time there, and who has completed the designated training course, may issue to such person a license to carry concealed a pistol, revolver, or other firearm for a period of two years from the date of license.

Tampering with Marks on Firearms—PC 12090. Any person who changes, alters, removes, or obliterates the make, model, manufacturer's number, or other mark of identification, including any distinguishing number or mark assigned by the State Bureau of Criminal Identification and Investigation, on any pistol or revolver, without first having secured written permission from the bureau to make such change, alteration, or removal shall be punished by imprisonment in the state prison.

Machine Gun Defined—PC 12200. The term "machinegun" means any weapon that shoots, is designed to shoot, or can readily be restored to shoot, automatically, more than one shot, without reloading, by a single function of the trigger. The term also includes the frame or receiver, parts used to convert a weapon into a machinegun, and parts that can be assembled into a machinegun, as well as any weapon deemed by the federal BATF as readily convertible to a machinegun.

This section exempts law enforcement officers and the military from any provisions prohibiting private citizens from any transporting or possessing machine guns (briefed).

Transporting or Possession of Machine Gun—PC 12220. Any person, firm, or corporation who within this state possesses, or knowingly transports a machine gun, except as authorized by this chapter, is guilty of a public offense and upon conviction thereof shall be punished by imprisonment in the state prison or by a fine . . . or by both such fine and imprisonment.

Ban on Assault Weapons—PC 12280. The sale, distribution, manufacture, transportation or possession of prohibited assault weapons is a felony, except that these weapons lawfully possessed prior to June 1, 1989, and properly registered, may be lawfully possessed under prescribed circumstances (PC 12285). Assault weapons are listed in PC 12276 and 12276.1.

Criminal Storage of Firearm—PC 12035. A person who keeps a loaded firearm in premises where

DEADLY WEAPONS CONTROL LAW CHART

WEAPONS	MERE POSSESSION	CONCEALED ON PERSON OR IN VEHICLE	CARRIED OPENLY OR VISIBLY
Blackjack, slingshot, billy, sandclub, sandbag, metal knuckles, nunchaku, throwing stars, cane gun, explosive ammo, wallet gun	Felony to possess, offer for sale or keep for sale. (12020 PC)	Mere possession a felony. (12020 PC)	Mere possession a felony. (12020 PC)
Machine guns	Felony or misdemeanor to possess. (12220 PC)	Mere possession a felony or misdemeanor. (12220 PC)	Mere possession a felony or misdemeanor. (12220 PC)
Firearm silencers	Felony to possess. (12520 PC)	Felony to possess. Does not have to be concealed (12520 PC)	Mere possession a felony. (12520 PC)
Dirk or Dagger	Legal	Concealed on person, felony (wobbler) (12020 PC)	Legal
Handguns (concealable weapons)	Felony or misdemeanor if person has previously been convicted of a felony or is addicted to narcotic drugs. (12021 PC) Misdemeanor if possessed by minor not accompanied by parent or guardian or without written permission of parent or guardian. (12101 PC)	Misdemeanor to carry concealed on the person or concealed in any vehicle under person's direction or control without license or permit to carry concealed (12025 PC)* Felony if stolen, unlawfully possessed, or carried by active gang member or person with specified priors or non-registered owner with matching ammo. *See exceptions to 12025 PC in 12027 PC.	Misdemeanor to carry loaded on person or in vehicle while in public place, public street within incorporated city, or public place or public street in an unincorporated area where it would be unlawful to discharge a weapon. Felony if stolen, unlawfully possessed, or carried loaded by non-registered owner active gang member or person with specified priors. Defines a "loaded" firearm for purposes of enforcement as that which has an unexpended cartridge or shell in, or attached in any manner to the firearm, including, but not limited to, the firing chamber, magazine or clip thereof attached to the firearm. (12031 PC)* Felony to carry loaded on person or in vehicle within the state capitol and other legislative offices, or upon the grounds of or within any residence of the governor or any state legislator, or upon the grounds of or within any public school. Defines a firearm as being "loaded" for purposes of enforcement whenever both the firearm and unexpended ammunition are in the possession of the same person. (171c, 171d and 171c PC)* Peace Officers are authorized to examine any such weapon for the purpose of determining if a violation exists. Refusal to allow such examination constitutes probable cause to arrest. *See exceptions in this chapter.
Rifles	Felony to possess only if barrel is less than 16" in length or if overall length is less than 26" (12020 PC)	Misdemeanor if cartridge is in chamber when the rifle is in a vehicle on any public highway or other way open to the public (2006 Fish and Game Code).	
Shotguns	Felony to possess only if barrel is less than 18" in length or if overall length is less than 26". (12020 PC)	Misdemeanor if cartridge is in chamber when the shotgun is in a vehicle on any public highway or other way open to the public (2006 Fish and Game Code).	
Switch-blade Knife (blade over 2")	Legal to own, misdemeanor to sell, loan, give away, etc.	Misdemeanor to possess in vehicle, carry on person.	

a minor gains access to the firearm and uses it to commit an injury, or carries it to a public place, is guilty of a misdemeanor, except that if the minor causes death or great bodily injury, the person is guilty of a felony.

Sale of BB Device to Minor—PC 12551. Every person who sells to a minor under the age of eighteen years any BB device is guilty of a misdemeanor.

Sale of Firearm to Minor—PC 12072(a)(3)(A). It is a felony to sell, loan, or transfer a firearm to a minor, or to sell a handgun to a person under 21. This statute does not apply to one who furnishes a non-concealable firearm to a minor, for 30 days or less, for a lawful purpose (e.g., hunting, target shooting), with parental consent (PC 12078(p)(1)).

Furnishing Weapon to Minor—PC 12552. Every person who furnishes any BB device, to any minor under the age of eighteen years, without the express or implied permission of the parent or legal guardian of the minor is guilty of a misdemeanor.

Ammunition Sold To/Possessed by Minor—PC 12316. It is a misdemeanor to knowingly sell ammunition to a minor under the age of eighteen (PC 12316(a)), and it is a misdemeanor for a minor who is prohibited from possessing a firearm to possess ammunition (PC 12316(b)).

Laser Pointer Sold to Minor or Misused—PC 417.27. It is an infraction to knowingly sell a laser pointer to an unaccompanied minor, or to shine a laser into the eyes of an occupant of a moving vehicle or a guide dog or K-9 with intent to annoy, or for a student to possess a laser pointer at primary or secondary school except for valid purposes.

Firearms Possession by Former Mental Patient—W&I 5153. The Welfare and Institutions Code prohibits any person who was involuntarily committed after October 1, 1955, to any mental hospital or sanitarium for a period of thirty days or more from having in his possession, custody, or control any firearm, unless such person has been issued a certificate as set forth in that section, and unless such person has not, subsequent to the issuance of such certificate, again been involuntarily committed for a period of thirty days or more in any such hospital or sanitarium. A violation of this section constitutes a misdemeanor.

Felon with Body Armor—PC 12370. It is a felony for a person who has been convicted of a violent felony to purchase, own or possess body armor.

Distribution of Imitation Firearms—PC 417.2. Commerce in “imitation firearms” is subject to a civil fine of up to $10,000 per violation. An imitation firearm is one that is so similar to a real firearm that a reasonable person might conclude that it was real. Exceptions are made for theatrical, military, and athletic uses. Excluded from the definition of imitation firearms are devices that are bright orange or bright green, BB guns, and pellet guns.

Any person who commercially makes, distributes or receives (etc.) a real firearm that is colored bright orange or bright green is liable for a civil fine of up to $10,000 (PC 12020.3). It is a misdemeanor to alter imitation firearms to make them look real (PC 12553).

Falsifying Purchase Eligibility—PC 12076. A person who is prohibited by law from possessing firearms who knowingly falsifies any information provided in connection with a purchase or attempt to purchase a firearm is guilty of a felony and is punishable by imprisonment for 8, 12 or 18 months.

STUDENT REVIEW

TERMINOLOGY DEFINED—CHAPTER 9

Please see the Terminology Quiz at the end of this chapter.

1. Asphyxiate: to smother, unable to breathe.
2. Blackjack: small, leather-covered, flexible-handled club.
3. Dirk: a fixed blade knife designed for stabbing.
4. Evidence: means by which facts are established in court.
5. False imprisonment: any unlawful restraint of one's liberty.
6. Hung jury: one unable to reach unanimous verdict.
7. Lethal: capable of causing death, deadly.
8. Penologist: an authority on prisons or rehabilitation.
9. Possession: under one's control or custody.
10. *Post mortem:* examination to determine cause of death.
11. Presumptive evidence: assumed true until contrary proved.
12. Recidivist: repeat offender, habitual criminal.
13. *Res gestae:* acts and words just before and after a crime.
14. Restitution: payment for loss or damage, repayment.
15. Summons: a writ requiring an answer in a civil suit.
16. Verdict: the decision in a jury or court trial.
17. *Versus:* against, e.g., People v. Jones.
18. Warrant: a court order commanding an arrest or a search.

TRUE-FALSE QUIZ—CHAPTER 9

After reading this chapter you should be able to correctly answer the following items.

___ 1. Other than for peace officers, mere possession of a blackjack is a crime.
___ 2. A sawed-off shotgun is one having a barrel less than 18 inches long.
___ 3. Possession of a rifle with a barrel less than 16 inches long is a crime.
___ 4. Possession of a shotgun or rifle with an overall length of 28 inches is a crime.
___ 5. Peace officers are legally permitted to carry "metal knuckles" as part of their regular equipment.
___ 6. A "nunchaku" is an instrument with handles and sharp points used for throwing.
___ 7. To be guilty of possession of an illegal weapon it must be proven the defendant knew he had same under his custody and control.
___ 8. Whether or not an item is a dangerous weapon depends on its nature and its intended use.
___ 9. It is a misdemeanor to carry a switchblade knife with a blade over 2 inches.
___10. The Second Amendment of the United States Constitution restricts the State from passing gun control laws, allocating this power to the Federal Government.
___11. The Constitutional phrase "right of the people to keep and bear arms" has been held to apply to an individual's right to own a gun.
___12. If one knowingly possesses "brass knuckles," but doesn't know such is illegal, it is a good defense to the crime.
___13. Possession of tear gas (license no longer required) for one's own personal defense is not a crime.
___14. It is a misdemeanor to possess a pistol or revolver which does not bear identification numbers.
___15. Mere possession of a dirk or dagger is a crime.
___16. It is legal to carry a loaded revolver in a public place provided it is carried openly in a belt holster.
___17. A "concealable firearm" is one having a barrel length of less than 12 inches.
___18. If a defendant was armed with a loaded weapon during a robbery, the penalty would be more severe even if he never drew the gun or exposed it to the victim.

___19. Aliens may not legally own concealable firearms in California.
___20. It is a felony to possess a disguised firearm-type device which is not immediately recognizable as a firearm.

ESSAY-DISCUSSION ITEMS—CHAPTER 9

After reading this chapter you should be able to correctly answer the following items.

1. What is the legal definition of a concealable firearm?
2. Under what conditions is the possession of a dirk or dagger a crime under the provisions of PC 12020?
3. Is a .22-caliber rifle, previously 33 inches in overall length but cut down to a 26 inch overall length, still a legal firearm? Explain.
4. What type of intent is necessary to violate the provisions of the Deadly Weapons Control Law? Are there exceptions?
5. When is a person said to be "in possession" of an illegal weapon? Need he be the owner to be guilty of illegal possession?
6. Under what circumstances may a minor be sold a firearm?
7. Is a previously convicted felon in violation of the law if he possesses a shotgun for hunting purposes? Explain.
8. Who issues permits (city and county) to carry a concealed weapon? Where and for what length of time are these permits valid?
9. Is a person who possesses a concealable firearm, the serial number of which is missing, removed or altered, guilty of any crime?
10. What loaded firearms are illegal to possess in a vehicle? Define the term "loaded" within the meaning of the statute.

TERMINOLOGY QUIZ—CHAPTER 9

Match terms and definitions by writing the number preceding the correct term between the appropriate brackets.

Terms	*Definitions*
1. Asphyxiate	[ ] writ requiring answer to a civil suit
2. Blackjack	[ ] payment for loss or damage
3. Criminology	[ ] capable of causing death, deadly
4. Deadly weapon	[ ] a repeat offender, habitual criminal
5. Dirk	[ ] to smother, unable to breathe
6. Evidence	[ ] a fixed blade knife designed for stabbing
7. False imprisonment	[ ] court order commanding an arrest or search
8. Hung jury	[ ] means by which facts are established in court
9. Lethal	[ ] the decision in a jury or court trial
10. Penology	[ ] Latin meaning "against"
11. Possession	[ ] examination to determine cause of death
12. *Post mortem*	[ ] acts and words just before and after a crime
13. Presumptive evidence	[ ] under one's custody and control
14. Recidivist	[ ] small, leather-covered, flexible-handled club
15. *Res gestae*	[ ] an unlawful restraint of one's liberty
16. Restitution	
17. Summons	
18. Verdict	
19. Versus	
20. Warrant	

CHAPTER 10

TYPES OF ASSAULT

10.1 SIMPLE ASSAULT

Assault Defined—PC 240. "An assault is an unlawful attempt, coupled with a present ability, to commit a violent injury on the person of another."

Elements of Assault. The three elements necessary to prove an assault are:

1. An unlawful attempt (to commit a battery)
2. Coupled with a present ability
3. To commit a violent injury (on the person of another).

"Unlawful" Defined. Not all assaults are unlawful. Self defense against an assailant, for example, is legal. The necessary force used in making a lawful arrest is also legal. The acts of force used in various athletic events such as in a boxing match or a football game are examples of "legal assaults."

"Attempt" Defined. It is important to realize that an assault is basically an attempt to commit a battery (PC 242) in most cases. To be guilty of assault, it is not necessary that the force or injury intended need actually be inflicted. There need be no contact with the victim and the victim need not be injured for the crime of assault to be complete (such as throwing a rock which misses).

The same rules apply to an assault as for other attempts. There must be more than mere intention and/or preparation or words or threats. While no actual touching is necessary, if such does occur, the crime of battery (PC 242) is committed.

"Present Ability" Defined. Present ability means that the act attempted is physically capable of being carried out by the assailant. It means that so far as the assailant is personally concerned, the methods he intends to use and the manner in which he or she threatens or intends to use them, will, in fact, inflict the injury intended.

Such present ability relates solely to the ability of the person attempting the unlawful injury. It does not refer to the fact that by some reason or some condition not controlled by the assailant, the intended injury cannot be inflicted (see "Discussion," below).

"Violent Injury" Defined. The words "violent injury" as used in defining the crime of assault do not mean that the injury attempted must be a severe one or cause great physical pain, but merely mean the unlawful application of physical force upon the person of another.

The terms "violence" and "force" are synonymous when used in relation to assault and include any application of force even though it entails no pain or bodily harm and leaves no mark (*People v. James*, 9 Cal. App. 2d 162).

Punishment for Assault—PC 241(a). Simple assault is a misdemeanor. The penalty for assaults against private persons is a fine not exceeding $1000, or imprisonment in the county jail not exceeding six months, or both such fine and imprisonment.

When an assault is committed against a peace officer, firefighter, emergency medical technician, paramedic, doctor or nurse (outside a hospital) while engaged in the performance of their duties, and the assailant knows or reasonably should know that the person being assaulted is one of the above, the penalty is a fine not exceeding $2,000, or imprisonment in the county jail not exceeding one year, or both such fine and imprisonment (PC 241(c)). Assault against a parking control officer performing official duty is punishable by fine of $2000 and/or six months in jail (PC 241(b)).

"Simple Assault" Defined. The term "simple assault" has come, by common usage, to mean a violation of PC 240. The term is frequently used to differentiate from the more serious Assault With a Deadly Weapon (ADW), a violation of PC 245.

The financial cost to assault victims and their families for doctors, hospitalization and lost wages, to say nothing of their pain and suffering and perhaps life-long disability, is a brutal burden to bear. For a series of current articles on victims of assault and other crimes, see Web Site: **http://virlib.ncjrs.org/VictimsOfCrime.asp**.

Assault Against Peace Officers—FireFighters, Other Special Classes. The Legislature has made it a more serious offense to assault certain classes of persons while such persons are engaged in the performance of their duties. These laws were passed in response to an increase in public and group violence and riot-like activities used as problem-solving or attention getting techniques by some groups.

Special Classes Described—PC 241. The special classes against whom an assault carries a more severe penalty are as follows:

- Peace officer, firefighter, emergency medical technician, mobile intensive care paramedic, physician or nurse (engaged in rendering emergency care outside of a hospital).
- Custodial officer (jailor), a felony (PC 24 1.1).
- Teacher, school administrator or security officer (PC 241.2).
- Bus or cab driver, streetcar operator, etc. (PC 241.3).
- School district peace officer, a felony (PC 241.4).
- School employee (PC 241.6).
- Juror (PC 241.7).
- Armed forces member (PC 241.8).

Elements Defined. The elements of assault against these certain classes of persons is the same as for any other assault, except for the addition of three elements as follows:

1. The person assaulted must be a peace officer, firefighter, paramedic, school teacher, administrator, or security officer, bus driver, etc.
2. The person assaulted must be engaged in the performance of his or her duties at the time of the assault.
3. The assailant knows, or reasonably should know, that the victim is one of the classes of persons named (such as a peace officer).

Penalty. The penalty for assault against the above special class of persons is generally a fine of $2,000, or one year in the county jail, or both. In the case of custodial officers (jailors) and school district peace officers, the crime is a felony (wobbler) punishable by either one year in the county jail or by imprisonment in the state prison.

Discussion of Assault. Where the unlawful attempt to injure another has been made, the fact that the assailant failed in his attempt, or was prevented or desisted from actually inflicting the injury he was attempting, does not affect his guilt.

The attempt to injure in many cases of assault is usually very evident, especially when actual injury results. In other cases an attempt to injure may be inferred from the circumstances. Where the assailant threatened to kill the victim and seized an axe and started toward her and she fled and escaped, his act was held to be an assault.

The attempt need not be apparent to the victim. The victim may be unconscious. In one case gunpowder, to which was attached a burning fuse, was left near the person to be assaulted, although the person intended to be injured was not aware of such attempt.

An assailant need not have been in striking distance to inflict the blow he threatened; it is enough if he comes sufficiently near to the person threatened to warrant the belief that the blow will be instantly struck unless the intended victim defends or flees.

Since an assault is an attempt, the rules generally applicable to the law of attempts apply to both misdemeanor and felony assaults. To constitute an assault there must be more than intention or preparation or words of threat; there must be an *overt act* from which the inference can be drawn that violent injury to the person of another was intended.

The attempt, coupled with the present ability to inflict an unlawful injury, constitute the essential elements of the offense (*People v. Roder*, 24 Cal. App. 477). The term "violent injury," merely means the application of physical force on the person of another. The kind of physical force is immaterial; it may consist of taking indecent liberties with a woman or taking hold of her and kissing her against her will (*People v. Whalen*, 124 Cal. App. 2d 713).

Attempted Assault. There is no such offense as attempted assault in California because assault is itself an attempt (*In Re James M.,* 9 Cal. 3d 517).

Examples of Assault. Firing at a person through a door at the place where the assailant believed the potential victim to be, even though he had moved and was not hit, is an assault. Where an assailant pointed an unloaded gun and attempted to fire at the victim, there was no assault because "present ability" did not exist. ***Note:*** had the assailant then thrown the gun at the victim who was nearby, an assault would have been complete. Also, had the gun been an automatic with bullets in the clip (even though no shell was in the firing chamber) the crime would have been complete because putting a shell into the chamber (present ability) would have been fast and simple (*People v. Bennett*, 37 Cal. App. 646). In cases where heavy objects are thrown, whether or not it is an assault depends largely on whether the victim was close enough to have been hit.

10.2 BATTERY

Battery Defined—PC 242. Battery is rather simply defined as ". . . any willful and unlawful use of force or violence upon the person of another."

Battery includes and implies an assault, for there can be no battery without an assault, but there can be assault without a battery. Battery is a completed assault and the offense of simple assault is a necessarily included offense where battery is charged.

Elements of Battery. The three elements which constitute battery are:

1. Any willful and unlawful
2. Use of force or violence
3. On the person of another.

"Willful and Unlawful" Defined. These words refer to the intent with which the act is committed. This simply means that the act was not accidental. General or constructive intent will suffice to sustain a conviction. Proof of willingness to do the unlawful act is proof of the intent to commit the battery.

Gross negligence constituting a reckless disregard for other persons is also sufficient. One who is grossly and wantonly negligent or reckless in exposing others to danger is presumed to have intended the natural consequences of his negligence.

"Force or Violence" Defined. The amount of force applied is immaterial because the gist of the offense is its unlawfulness. It need not cause any pain. Every touching or laying hold of another, or his clothing, in an angry, revengeful, rude, insolent, or hostile manner, is a battery.

Discussion. Battery is any willful and unlawful use of force or violence upon the person of another. Battery includes an assault, but there can be an assault without a battery. Therefore, battery is a consummated assault and assault is a necessarily included offense where battery is charged.

It is not necessary that an assailant *directly* apply the force in battery. It would be battery to

Bar fights account for a substantial number of assault and battery arrests. *Courtesy of Hulton Archive*

strike or frighten a horse, causing it to bolt with its rider, or to drive a car against a person, or for one automobile driver to force another off the road, or to set a dog on a person if the dog actually bites or touches him, if the act is willful and unlawful.

Force and violence are synonymous and mean any wrongful application of physical force against the person of another, even though it causes no pain or bodily harm or leaves no mark, and even though only the feelings of such person are injured by the act. The slightest unlawful touching, if done in an insolent, rude, or angry manner, is sufficient (*People v. Flummerfelt*, 153 Cal. App. 2d 104).

Examples of Battery. To help differentiate between simple assault and battery, it has often been said that if one takes a swing at another and misses, he has committed an assault. If he connects with the other person's nose, it's battery. Other examples are spitting on another, running into them with a bicycle, squirting them with water, slapping someone's face, shoving another off a sidewalk, etc. Note that the amount of force used is not too important, except that causing very serious injury or using dangerous or deadly force can result in increased punishment or a more serious charge.

Battery—Punishment. Battery is a misdemeanor punishable by a fine not exceeding $2,000, or by imprisonment in the county jail not exceeding six months or by both fine and imprisonment (PC 243(a)). If the battery is committed against a present or former spouse or mate, or against a peace officer or other designated official or emergency worker performing apparent duty or giving aid, or against a member of the armed forces, the maximum jail term is one year (PC 243(b), (e), 243.10).

Felony Battery. Battery is a felony "wobbler" when committed upon specified officers and emergency personnel, while they are on duty or rendering aid, and injury is inflicted (PC 243(c)(1)).

Battery with injury on a peace officer performing official duty, when the perpetrator should reasonably know that the victim is a peace officer in the performance of duty, is a "wobbler" carrying a maximum $10,000 fine and up to three years in prison (PC 243(c)(2)).

When battery against any person results in great bodily injury, the crime is a felony "wobbler," with punishment ranging up to four years in prison (PC 243(d)).

Battery against operators, passengers and agents of specified transportation vehicles or entities is a misdemeanor, with a maximum fine of $10,000 and up to one year in jail. If injury is inflicted, a transportation battery is a "wobbler", with a $10,000 fine and up to three years in prison as punishment (PC 243.3).

Injury Defined—PC 243(f)(5). "Injury," for purposes of the above means any physical injury which requires professional medical treatment.

Serious Bodily Injury Defined—PC 243(f)(4). "Serious bodily injury" means a serious impairment of physical condition, including, but not limited to the following:

1. Loss of consciousness;
2. Concussion;
3. Bone fracture;
4. Protracted loss or impairment of any bodily member or organ;
5. A wound requiring extensive suturing;
6. Serious disfigurement.

Assault With Stun Gun—PC 244.5. This section makes it a felony (wobbler) to commit an assault on the person of another with a stun gun or a taser. A "stun gun" is any item, except a taser, capable of temporarily immobilizing a person by the infliction of an electrical charge (PC 12650).

Sexual Battery—PC 243.4. Any person who touches an intimate part of another person while that person is unlawfully restrained by the accused or an accomplice, or is institutionalized or disabled, or is unconscious of the nature of the act because of the perpetrator's fraudulent misrepresentation that the touching serves a professional purpose, and if the touching is against the will of the person touched and is for the purpose of sexual arousal, gratification, or abuse, is guilty of sexual battery. Such act is punishable as a felony (wobbler). Sexual battery, as described above, against a minor, by a person with a prior felony conviction for such offenses, is a felony, punishable by up to four years in prison (PC 243.4(i)). Sexual battery without restraint or incapacity is a misdemeanor (PC 243.4(d)(1)).

"Intimate Part," "Touches" Defined—PC 243.4. As used here, "intimate part" means the sexual organ, anus, groin, or buttocks of any person, and the breast of a female. "Touches" means physical contact with another person whether accomplished directly, through the clothing of the person committing the offense, or through the clothing of the victim.

Lawful Resistance to Crime (PC 692). Lawful resistance to the commission of a public offense may be made:

1. By the party about to be injured;
2. By other parties.

Where an attack is sudden and personal danger is imminent, a person may stand his or her ground and subdue his or her attacker even though it be proven that he or she might have more easily gained safety by flight (*People v. Dawson*, 88 Cal. App. 2d 85). ***Note:*** One could slay their attacker only if threatened with life-threatening or serious bodily harm, not just "danger."

Resistance sufficient to prevent the offense may be made by the party about to be injured (PC 693):

1. To prevent an offense against his person, his family, or some member thereof.
2. To prevent an illegal attempt by force to take or injure property in his possession.

The owner of property is justified in using force or a deadly weapon to eject a trespasser only when it is apparent to one, as a reasonable person, that physical injury is contemplated. The owner is then entitled to use only such force as is reasonably necessary to repel attack or to protect property. (*People v. Miller*, 72 Cal. App. 2d 602).

Many replica firearms are so difficult to distinguish from the real thing that it has been made illegal to exhibit a replica in a threatening manner. The real gun, top, is a .357 Desert Eagle. *Photograph by Kim D. Johnson, courtesy of AP/Wide World Photos*

Defense of Others—PC 694. Any other person, in aid or defense of the person about to be injured, may make resistance sufficient to prevent the offense.

Discussion. A person cannot set up his own standards of reasonableness or belief of injury, or of the amount of force necessary. He is limited to that which the ordinary reasonable and prudent person, placed in the same position, would be warranted in considering reasonable and necessary under the circumstances.

10.3 EXHIBITING DEADLY WEAPON

Exhibiting Firearm in Threatening Manner—PC 417. Except in self-defense, every person who draws, or exhibits any firearm, whether loaded or unloaded, or any other deadly weapon in a rude, angry, or threatening manner, or who unlawfully uses such a weapon in a fight or quarrel, is guilty of a misdemeanor.

Note: PC 417 covers the use of *any* deadly weapon and in the case of firearms, the gun need *not* be loaded.

Exhibiting in Presence of Peace Officer—PC 417(c). This subsection makes it a felony (wobbler) for any person who, in the immediate presence of a peace officer, draws or exhibits any firearm, whether loaded or unloaded, in a rude, angry, or threatening manner, and who knows or reasonably should know that such victim is a peace officer engaged in the performance of his or her duties, and such peace officer is in fact engaged in the performance of his or her duties.

As used in this section "peace officer" refers to any person designated as a peace officer by PC 830.1, subdivisions (a) to (e) and PC 830.2 and 830.5. It also covers reserve and auxiliary peace officers.

Exhibiting Firearm Replica—PC 417.4. It is a misdemeanor, except in self-defense, to draw or exhibit a firearm replica in a threatening manner against another person in such a way as to cause a reasonable person fear of bodily harm.

"Firearm replica," means any device with the apparent capability of expelling a projectile by force of air or explosion and which is reasonably perceived by the victim to be an actual firearm. This definition includes blank starter pistols and air guns.

Firearm Drawn at Motor Vehicle Occupant—PC 417.3. This section was passed by the legislature in response to shootings at vehicles on our streets and highways. It provides that every person who, except in self-defense, in the presence of any other person who is an occupant of a motor vehicle proceeding on a public street or highway, draws or exhibits any firearm, whether loaded or unloaded, in a threatening manner or in such a way as to cause a reasonable person apprehension or fear of bodily harm is guilty of a felony (wobbler).

This section covers pointing a firearm (whether loaded or unloaded), at a driver or passenger of a motor vehicle, whether the perpetrator is in another vehicle or on foot.

Pointing a Laser—PC 417.25-417.26. Aiming or pointing a laser scope or laser pointer at another in a threatening manner with intent to cause fear of bodily harm is a misdemeanor (30-day maximum sentence). If the victim is a peace officer and the perpetrator should reasonably know it, the jail term may be up to six months (first offense) or one year (second or subsequent offense).

Deadly Weapon Possession With Intent to Assault—PC 12024. "Every person having upon him or her any deadly weapon with intent to assault another, is guilty of a misdemeanor."

This section includes any of the "deadly weapons" defined in the Penal Code. It requires the prosecution to prove that the perpetrator was carrying a deadly weapon with the *specific* intent to assault another.

10.4 ASSAULT WITH A DEADLY WEAPON

ADW Defined—PC 245. Every person who commits an assault upon the person of another with a firearm or other deadly weapon or instrument, or by any means of force likely to produce great bodily injury is guilty of a felony (wobbler).

The penalty is more severe if the weapon used is a firearm. The penalty is also more severe if the victim is a peace officer or firefighter engaged in the performance of his or her duties (PC 245(c)).

Discussion—Assault With Deadly Weapon or Instrument. Where no direct evidence as to the nature of the weapon used is obvious, it may be established by circumstantial evidence. Thus, where the victim suffered a severe wound such as might have been caused by a sharp instrument the jury is warranted in concluding that a deadly weapon was used (*People v. Lee*, 23 Cal. App. 2d 168).

Whether or not a particular object or instrument is a deadly weapon depends not upon the use for which it was originally suited or intended but upon whether it was used in a manner likely to produce death or great bodily injury (*People v. Robertson*, 217 Cal. 671).

Where defendant intentionally accelerated his automobile and steered directly at the victim, striking the latter on the legs, a conviction of assault was sustained (*People v. Flummerfelt*, 153 Cal. App. 2d 104). In a case in which defendant drove his automobile at night without lights on a public highway and struck a pedestrian it was held that the jury was warranted in finding that the defendant, by such conduct on his part, intended the natural and probable consequence of his acts (*People v. Vasquez*, 85 Cal. App. 575).

Pointing a loaded gun in a threatening manner at the back of another, and lowering it when the latter's wife screamed is, regardless of the defendant's reason for not firing, an assault with a deadly weapon (*People v. Dodini*, 51 Cal. App. 179).

Discussion—Assault by Means Likely to Produce Bodily Injury. To commit this form of felonious assault it is not necessary that the defendant shall have used a weapon or other instrument as the means of the assault. It is the violence and likelihood of the assault to produce great bodily injury that is the essence of this offense (*People v. Tallman*, 27 Cal. 2d 209). Convictions of this offense have been sustained where the means used were the hands and knees; throwing a person out of a window; knocking a person down and kicking him; choking the victim; vicious assaults with the fists alone; and pushing the victim so his head hit a parking meter.

Where, after being stopped for questioning by officers, defendant fled in his car and, in departing from the scene, his left front fender struck one of the officers standing in the street, throwing him against another car and inflicting minor injuries, the conviction was sustained (*People v. Conley*, 110 Cal. App. 2d 731).

Intent Required in ADW. The required intent for the commission of an assault with a deadly weapon is the intent to commit a battery. Reckless conduct alone does not generally constitute a sufficient basis for assault or for battery even if the assault results in an injury to another. However, when an act inherently dangerous to others is committed with a conscious disregard of human life and safety, the act goes beyond recklessness, and the intent to commit a battery is presumed (*People v. Lathus*, 35 Cal. App. 3d 466).

Hazing—PC 245.6. It is a misdemeanor to engage in initiation hazing at an educational institution. If death or serious bodily injury results, the crime is a felony (wobbler).

HIV Exposure—H&S 120291. Any person who exposes another to HIV during unprotected sex with the specific intent to infect is guilty of a felony.

10.5 ASSAULT WITH CAUSTIC CHEMICALS

Caustic Chemical Assault Defined—PC 244. Every person who willfully and maliciously places or throws, or causes to be placed or thrown, upon the person of another, any vitriol, corrosive acid, flammable substance, or caustic chemical of any nature, with the intent to injure the flesh or disfigure the body of such person, is punishable by imprisonment in state prison.

Specific intent to either injure the flesh or disfigure the body must be proven as an independent factor. If such intent is absent or the act is done with another intent, it is not a violation of this section. However, the perpetrator may very well be guilty of some other assault crime.

The offense is complete if any quantity of the substance described, however small in quantity or however weak in strength, is thrown or placed upon the person of another. This is providing, of course it is done willfully and maliciously with intent to injure the flesh or to disfigure to the slightest extent the body of another.

If the substance described in this section is thrown toward an intended victim but misses, it is not a violation of this section but could be prosecuted under PC 245.

10.6 POISONING FOOD—DRINK—WATER—MEDICINE

Poisoning Food, Drink—PC 347. Any person who willfully mingles any poison or harmful substance with any food, drink, or medicine, or who willfully places any poison or harmful substance in any public water supply, where the person knows or should have known that the same would be taken by any human being to his or her injury, is guilty of a felony punishable by imprisonment in the state prison.

Poisoning Alcoholic Beverages (PC 347b). It is a misdemeanor for any person, firm, or corporation to manufacture, sell, furnish, or give away, or offer to do so, any alcoholic solution of a potable (drinkable) nature containing any deleterious (harmful) or poisonous substance.

10.7 THROWING OBJECTS OR SHOOTING AT VEHICLES—DWELLINGS—AIRCRAFT

Throwing Substance at Vehicle—VC 23110. The Vehicle Code provides that: (a) Any person who throws any substance at a vehicle or any occupant thereof on a highway is guilty of a misdemeanor.

(b) Any person, who with intent to do great bodily injury, maliciously and willfully throws or projects any rock, brick, bottle, metal or other missile, or projects any other substance capable of doing serious bodily harm, is guilty of a felony.

Shooting at Aircraft—Motor Vehicles—PC 247. (a) Any person who willfully and maliciously discharges a firearm at an unoccupied aircraft, is guilty of a felony.

(b) Any person who discharges a firearm at an unoccupied motor vehicle is guilty of a public offense punishable as a felony (wobbler). ***Note:*** this section does not apply to shooting at abandoned vehicles.

Interference With Helicopter—PC 248. It is a misdemeanor to shine a light at a helicopter, of an intensity capable of impairing operation, with intent to interfere with the operation of the helicopter.

Wrecking Common Carriers (PC 219.1). Every person who throws, hurls, or projects any type of object at any common carrier (bus, etc.) or does any other unlawful act with intention of wrecking such vehicle or doing any bodily harm, and thus wrecks the same and causes bodily harm is guilty of a felony. A *specific intent* of wrecking the vehicle, or doing bodily harm must be proved.

Shooting at Common Carriers—PC 219.2. Any person who willfully shoots at or throws any hard object at a train, streetcar, bus, or watercraft used for carrying passengers or freight, is guilty of a felony (wobbler).

Shooting at Inhabited Places—PC 246. Any person who shall maliciously and willfully discharge a firearm at an inhabited dwelling house, occupied building, occupied motor vehicle, inhabited housecar (as defined in VC 362), or inhabited camper (as defined in VC 243), is guilty of a felony (wobbler).

Dangerous Discharge of Firearm—PC 246.3. Willfully discharging a firearm in a grossly negligent manner that could result in injury or death to a person is a felony (wobbler). Discharging a BB gun in such a manner is a misdemeanor.

Building Defined. A "building" is a structure that is regularly occupied, wholly or partially, as a habitation by human beings and includes any store, church, schoolhouse, railway station, or other place of assembly (Health & Safety Code 12171). "Building," also means any apartment house, hotel, or dwelling, either singly or in combination (Health & Safety Code 15006).

Inhabited Defined. As used in this section "inhabited" means currently being used for dwelling purposes, whether occupied or not (PC 246).

10.8 ASSAULT WITH INTENT TO COMMIT CERTAIN FELONIES

Assault to Commit Felony—PC 220. Every person who assaults another with intent to commit mayhem, rape, sodomy, oral copulation, or any violation of Section 264.1, 288 or 289, is punishable by imprisonment in the state prison.

Elements Defined:

1. Doing any direct, ineffectual act,
2. With *specific intent*, to
3. Commit mayhem, rape, sodomy, oral copulation or any violation of PC 264.1 (aiding in forcible rape), PC 288 (lewd act on child under 14), or PC 289 (forcible penetration of genital or anal opening by foreign object).

Discussion. There must exist in the mind of the assailant, at the time of the attack, the specific intent to commit one of the crimes specified. This intent must be proven as one of the elements of this crime.

Assault With Intent to Commit Rape. The crime is complete if at any moment during the assault the accused intends to have sex with the victim against her will and to use for that purpose whatever force may be required.

When evidence showed that the defendant had attacked the victim on a street at a place where there were no lights, had thrown her down, put his hands under her clothes, torn her underclothing, struck her when she screamed and left when people approached, a conviction was sustained.

Assault to Commit Sodomy. The offense is complete when the assault has been committed with specific intent to commit the act attempted.

Where accused was interrupted by the sudden and unexpected intrusion of a third person, and his attempt to commit a sodomy aborted, it did not prevent his conviction of an assault with intent to commit the crime (*People v. Dong Pok Yip*, 164 Cal. 143).

Assault With Intent to Commit Mayhem, Oral Copulation. PC 220, in effect, makes it a crime to assault another with intent to commit any of the crimes specified. This section, therefore, describes a type of attempt to commit the crimes enumerated. In many instances the perpetrator could be charged with either PC 220 or an attempt to commit the crime intended. PC 220 is usually charged, however, because it may be easier to prove and carries a greater penalty than an attempt. Attempts are punishable with one-half the sentence that would have been imposed if the crime was completed.

One can be found guilty of PC 220, even if the crime intended during the assault was not completed. To be guilty of assault to commit mayhem, for example, it is not necessary that the victim be disfigured (as defined in PC 203) or even seriously injured. If, however, the purpose or intent of the assault is actually accomplished, the perpetrator could be charged with committing the specific crime actually completed.

10.9 ADMINISTERING STUPEFYING DRUGS

Administering Drugs—PC 222. Every person guilty of administering to another any chloroform, ether, laudanum, or any controlled substance, anesthetic, or intoxicating agent, with intent thereby to enable or assist himself or herself or any other person to commit a felony, is guilty of a felony.

The term "intoxicating agent" includes any drug, substance or compound which, when introduced into the human system, produces a serious disturbance of the physical and mental equilibrium by causing sleep, stupor, unconsciousness, or semi-unconsciousness, together with impairment of the power of self-control.

10.10 TRAIN WRECKING

Train Wrecking Defined—PC 218. Every person who unlawfully throws out a switch, removes a rail, or places any obstruction or explosive material on or near any railroad with the intention of derailing any passenger, freight or other train, car, or engine is guilty of a felony. This section also makes it a felony to unlawfully set fire to any railroad bridge or trestle with intention of train wrecking.

Acts Resulting in Train Wrecking—PC 219. This section is worded the same as PC 218, above, with the exception that it requires a train, or a portion thereof, be blown up or derailed. Penalties in such cases are more severe.

Discussion—Train Wrecking. Both of the above sections require proof of a specific intent to wreck a train. Such being the case, these sections may not be applicable in cases involving acts by younger children. These two sections can be punishable with life imprisonment or death, depending on the extent of injuries caused.

Obstructing Railroad—PC 218.1. Any person who unlawfully and with gross negligence places or causes to be placed any obstruction upon or near the track of any railroad that proximately results in either the damaging or derailing of any train or injury to a passenger or employee is guilty of a felony ("wobbler").

10.11 MAYHEM

Mayhem Defined—PC 203. Every person who unlawfully and maliciously deprives a human being of a member of his body, or disables, disfigures, or renders it useless, or cuts or disables the tongue, or puts out an eye, or slits the nose, ear, or lip, is guilty of mayhem, a felony.

Aggravated Mayhem—PC 205. A person is guilty of aggravated mayhem when he or she unlawfully, under circumstances manifesting extreme indifference to the physical or psychological well-being of another person, intentionally causes permanent disability or disfigurement of another human being or deprives a human being of a limb, organ, or member of his or her body.

For purposes of this section, it is not necessary to prove an intent to kill. Aggravated mayhem is a felony punishable by imprisonment in the state prison for life.

Discussion. Mayhem is a general intent crime. It is not necessary to show a deliberate or premeditated intent to commit mayhem, although it would be proper to do so. The act committed must be done unlawfully and in a malicious state of mind. It is sufficient to prove only the commission of the act from which the law will presume that it was done unlawfully and maliciously unless done under circumstances of self-defense, within reason (*People v. Sears*, 62 Cal. App. 783). Assault is a lesser and included offense to mayhem (*People v. DeFoor*, 100 Cal. 150).

10.12 ABANDONMENT OF ASSAULT

Where the acts of a person have proceeded to the point of amounting in law to an assault, the abandonment by the perpetrator of his purpose before he has accomplished the object for which the assault was committed does not free him from the consequences of his acts.

A defendant is guilty of the assault whether he voluntarily ceases his attack, or whether he desisted because of the resistance of his intended victim, or because of the approach of other parties permitting his victim to escape (*People v. Jones*, 112 Cal. App. 68).

Where there is intent to commit a crime, coupled with an overt act, the abandonment of the criminal purpose is no defense to a charge of attempt to commit the crime (*People v. Carter*, 70 Cal. App. 495).

10.13 ASSAULTS—JUSTIFICATION AND EXCUSE

If the use of force, even though it involves an intent to commit physical injuries upon another, is lawful (such as self-defense) there is no assault.

Legal Justification for an Assault. The law allows a person to commit certain acts which would ordinarily be considered unlawful, but under certain conditions are not unlawful, either because of the law or public policy.

The use of force necessary to accomplish a lawful arrest, spanking a child (within lawful limits), etc., would not constitute assault, unless the application of force became excessive, and therefore, unlawful.

Physical injuries inflicted by accident and misfortune in the doing of a lawful act by lawful means and without negligence or criminal intent could not be the basis of a charge of assault.

10.14 DOMESTIC VIOLENCE

Inflicting Injury on Person With Whom Living—PC 273.5. (a) Any person who willfully inflicts upon his or her present or former spouse or cohabitant, or upon the person who is the mother or father of his or her child, corporal injury resulting in a traumatic condition, is guilty of a felony (wobbler). Upon conviction for a violation of this subsection, the sentencing judge "shall also consider" issuing a 10-year restraining order, prohibiting the defendant from any contact with the victim.

(b) Holding oneself out to be the husband or wife of the person with whom one is cohabiting is not necessary to constitute cohabitation as the term is used in this section.

(c) As used in this section, "traumatic condition" means a condition of the body, such as a wound or external injury, whether of a minor or serious nature, caused by physical force.

A domestic violence response report must show whether the officers noticed signs of drug or alcohol influence, determination of prior calls involving the same address and parties, and presence of firearms or other deadly weapons. Any firearm at the scene is subject to seizure, per PC 12028.5. (PC 13730.) Service of a protective order on a domestic violence suspect must be reported to the Department of Justice by CLETS transmission within one business day (Family Code 6380(d)). A DV victim can obtain new license plates from DMV immediately upon request, accompanied by a copy of a police report, protective order, or domestic violence agency certification (VC 4467).

Domestic Violence Victim Interview Rights—PC 679.05. Following the initial on-scene investigation to determine the commission of a crime of domestic violence, the victim must be advised orally or in writing of the right to the presence of a domestic violence advocate and a support person of the victim's choosing whenever the victim is to be interviewed by law enforcement or attorneys (unless authorities determine that the support person would be detrimental to the interview process).

Domestic Violence Protective Orders—Fam. Code 6275. Officers responding to domestic violence incidents must advise victims of the procedure for requesting an emergency protective order. If an officer believes the person is in immediate and present danger, the officer must request the order. A person served with an emergency protective order must, upon police request, immediately surrender to the officer any firearms in the person's possession (Fam. Code 6389).

Protective Order Violations—PC 273.6. Any intentional and knowing violation of a domestic violence protective order is a misdemeanor. A subsequent violation within seven years is a wobbler, if violence is used or threatened; a subsequent violation within one year is a wobbler, if physical injury occurs to the same victim.

When issuing a protective order, the court is required to order the subject of the order not to take any action to obtain the address or location of the victim or victim's family members, unless the court finds good cause not to include this order (Family Code 6252.5, 6322.7).

Destruction of Wireless Device—PC 591.5. It is a misdemeanor to maliciously remove or damage a wireless communication device to prevent a person from summoning assistance from a public safety agency.

Endangering Life or Health of Child—PC 273a. (1) Any person who, under circumstances or conditions likely to produce *great bodily harm or death*, willfully causes or permits any child to suffer, or inflicts thereon unjustifiable physical pain or mental suffering, or having the care or custody of any child, willfully causes or permits the person or health of such child to be injured, or willfully causes or permits such child to be placed in such situation that its person or health is endangered, is punishable by imprisonment in the county jail or in the state prison (felony wobbler).

(2) Any person who, under circumstances or conditions *other* than those likely to produce great bodily harm or death, willfully causes or permits any child to suffer, or inflicts thereon unjustifiable physical pain or mental suffering, or willfully causes or permits the person or health of such child to be

Domestic violence calls can be risky, volatile and unpredictable. *Photograph by Donna Ferrato, © 1991, courtesy of the Domestic Abuse Awareness Project*

injured, or willfully causes or permits such child to be placed in such situation that its person or health may be endangered, is guilty of a misdemeanor.

Causing Child's Death—PC 273ab. Any person in charge of child under age eight who assaults the child with force reasonably likely to produce great bodily injury, resulting in the child's death, is punishable by 25 years to life in prison, or may be prosecuted for murder or manslaughter (PC 273ab).

Cruel or Inhuman Punishment of a Child—PC 273d. Any person who willfully inflicts upon any child any cruel or inhuman corporal punishment or injury resulting in a traumatic condition is guilty of a felony (wobbler).

Discussion. A parent or other person standing in *loco parentis* (in place of parents), chastising his child, does not commit a criminal assault and battery if the punishment administered is reasonable. On the other hand, if a parent uses an instrument likely to cause serious injury, or inflicts punishment to an immoderate extent, either of which would indicate an intent to injure rather than to correct, such person is liable to prosecution for a criminal offense.

The *corpus delicti* of the offense of inflicting corporal injury upon a child was established when it was shown that such injury had been inflicted upon a child by the defendant, and circumstances and injuries to the child demonstrated that such injuries had been deliberately and intentionally inflicted upon her. These facts, having been established independently of the defendant's statement that he had hit the child, were admissible (*People v. Lawrence*, 141 Cal. App. 2d 630).

Child Abuse Reports Required—PC 11166. Health care practitioners, educators, peace officers and other designated persons who know or reasonably suspect that a child is the victim of physical or sexual abuse or neglect are mandated to make a report to law enforcement, as soon as is practicable by telephone, and then in writing. Failure to make a mandated report is a misdemeanor. Although not mandatory, reporters may also report suspected mental suffering and damage to a child's emotional well-being.

Notification of Parole—PC 3058.65. When a person convicted of violating 273a, 273ab, 273d or any sex offense against a minor is about to be paroled, the Department of Corrections must give 60 days' notice to immediate family members who have asked to be informed, and who have provided their current address to the department.

10.15 VICTIMS OF VIOLENT CRIME STATUTE

For many years the State of California has had a statute addressed to the aid of victims of violent crimes. However, less than one percent of victims have availed themselves of financial relief through the statute. For this reason the State Legislature enacted Government Code Sections 13959 and 13968(c).

Police Requirements. The above laws require law enforcement officers to provide victims or their families a sheet describing the victim program and where to obtain application forms. Because the field officer or investigator has other pressures on him or her at the time of contact with victims, the required form is now mailed out routinely from headquarters by most law enforcement agencies. A "notification of eligibility" card for victims, required to be made available by the Office of Criminal Justice Planning, may be provided to the victim by the investigating officer (PC 1191.21).

Victim's Responsibility. The Board of Control Form I-D, provides the essential information about the program. It is the responsibility of the victim to satisfy the Board of Control of the need for indemnification.

Required Information. When the Board convenes it will consider the following factors: Whether the victim was a resident of the State of California at the time of the incident; whether a financial loss was incurred which caused serious financial hardship; whether the victim substantially contributed by his or her actions to the injuries (if the incident was an automobile accident, this code does not apply except in hit and run or when caused by a person driving under the influence of alcohol or drugs); whether the victim has cooperated in promptly supplying all requested information and documents; and last, and most importantly, whether the victim cooperated with law enforcement agencies.

Maximum Damages. The Board of Control may award maximum reimbursement of up to $46,000 (Government Code 13965). Various amounts may be authorized to reimburse the victim and their family for medical or hospital expenses, psychological counselling, loss of wages or support, and job retraining and rehabilitation services.

Legal Fees and Personal Property Loss. The Board may also award funds for legal services rendered to the applicant which shall not exceed 10 percent of the amount of the award or $500, whichever is less.

Damage to or loss of personal property, as a result of a crime, will not be indemnified (covered) under this code. In all cases the amount of the reimbursement will be reduced by the amount of indemnification to the victim from any other source.

Intent of the Law. The intent of this code is to assist in reducing the financial pressure brought upon the victim as a result of the crime, and in no case is it intended that an improved financial situation shall result for the victim above that which existed prior to becoming a victim.

STUDENT REVIEW

TERMINOLOGY DEFINED—CHAPTER 10

Please see the Terminology Quiz at the end of this chapter.

1. Caustic: corrosive, capable of burning, acid.
2. Corporal injury: physical injury to the body.
3. Enjoin: to prohibit, to require (see Injunction).
4. Injunction: court order prohibiting or requiring some act.
5. *Loco parentis:* in place of parents.
6. Mayhem: crime of severing another's finger, ear, eye, etc.
7. *Modus operandi:* method of operation.
8. Moulage: casting used to preserve tire track, footprint.
9. *Nolo contendere:* no contest, a type of plea.
10. *Non compos mentis:* not of sound mind, insane.
11. Parole: conditional release of felon from prison.
12. Peace Officer: persons having police powers under PC 832.
13. Plaintiff: one who brings court action, civil or criminal.
14. Plea: accused's answer to charges against him in court.
15. Police power: right to restrict private acts for public welfare.
16. Present ability: actual possibility of accomplishment.
17. *Quasi:* similar to, e.g. quasi-military.
18. Simple assault: usually misdemeanor assault.
19. Traumatic injury: one caused by violence.
20. Violent injury: in assault, any unlawful use of force on another.

TRUE-FALSE QUIZ—CHAPTER 10

After reading this chapter you should be able to correctly answer the following items.

___ 1. An assault is an unlawful attempt, coupled with a present ability to commit a violent injury on the person of another.
___ 2. No actual touching of another is necessary to constitute assault.
___ 3. In the absence of "present ability" there can be no assault.
___ 4. The words "violent injury" as used in assault mean a serious injury.
___ 5. Assault against an on-duty police officer or firefighter is a felony.
___ 6. Pointing an unloaded gun at another in an angry, rude or threatening manner constitutes assault.
___ 7. Battery is the willful and unlawful use of force or violence on the person of another.
___ 8. Unlawfully spitting on another constitutes battery.
___ 9. There can be no assault without also committing battery.
___10. To be guilty of ADW, some instrument or weapon must be involved.
___11. In ADW, where no direct evidence as to the nature of the weapon is known, it may be established by circumstantial evidence.
___12. Specific intent to injure the flesh or cause disfigurement is necessary in assault with caustic chemicals.
___13. Any person who throws any substance at a vehicle or any occupant thereof on a highway is guilty of a felony.
___14. Assault to commit rape is a general intent crime.
___15. Assault is a lesser and included offense of mayhem.
___16. Accidently biting off a person's ear during an assault without specifically intending to do so constitutes the crime of mayhem.

___17. PC 273.5, inflicting corporal injury on cohabitant, applies to cohabitants of the same or opposite sex.

___18. Only parents and persons standing in *loco parentis* are subject to PC 273(d), inflicting cruel corporal punishment on a child.

___19. Government Code 13968(c) requires the police to provide victims of violent crimes or their families with information as to their rights to financial aid.

___20. A person would be guilty of aggravated mayhem, PC 205, for unlawfully and intentionally causing permanent disability or disfigurement.

ESSAY-DISCUSSION ITEMS—CHAPTER 10

After reading this chapter you should be able to correctly answer the following items.

1. What are the three elements of simple assault? Are certain assaults ever lawful?
2. Define battery and discuss the difference between simple assault and battery.
3. What are the elements of PC 417? Must the weapon be a firearm? If so, must it be loaded?
4. Discuss the elements of ADW (PC 245). Must actual injury be inflicted? Must injury be intended?
5. What are the five elements of PC 244, assault with caustic chemicals? What is the intent required?
6. What are the elements of PC 220, assault with intent to commit certain felonies? Discuss the type of intent required and how proven.
7. In PC 222, administering stupefying drugs, is specific intent of some type required? If so, what intent? Is administering of alcohol covered?
8. What are the elements of PC 203, mayhem? How does aggravated mayhem defined in PC 205, differ? What is the intent which must be proven in each?
9. What are the current police requirements for advising victims of violent crimes of their rights under Government Code 13968(c)?

TERMINOLOGY QUIZ—CHAPTER 10

Match terms and definitions by writing the number preceding the correct term in the appropriate brackets.

Terms	*Definitions*
1. Caustic	[ ] conditional release of felon from prison
2. Corporal injury	[ ] no contest, a type of plea
3. Enjoin	[ ] crime of severing another's finger, ear
4. Injunction	[ ] in assault, use of unlawful force on another
5. Loco parentis	[ ] similar to, somewhat like
6. Mayhem	[ ] an injury normally caused by violence
7. Modus operandi	[ ] corrosive, capable of burning
8. Moulage	[ ] one who brings a court action
9. Nolo contendere	[ ] in place of parents
10. Non compos mentis	[ ] not of sound mind
11. Parole	[ ] immediate possibility of accomplishment
12. Peace officer	[ ] accused's answer to charges in court
13. Plaintiff	[ ] court order prohibiting or requiring an act
14. Plea	[ ] method of operation
15. Police power	[ ] persons defined in PC 832
16. Present ability	
17. Quasi	
18. Simple assault	
19. Traumatic	
20. Violent injury	

CHAPTER 11

HOMICIDES

11.1 HOMICIDE DEFINED

The term "homicide" describes the killing of a human being or viable fetus by another human being. The killing may be either *justifiable* or *excusable*, in which case it is *not* unlawful. Or it may be *felonious*, in which event it is a crime. The word "homicide" is used to describe *all* taking of human life by human act or agency whether lawfully or unlawfully (PC 187-199).

The Killing. An unlawful homicide must be either the result of:

1. an affirmative act,
2. an omission to act, or
3. criminal negligence.

Although the act need not be the only cause of death, it must be a proximate (direct) cause. The death must occur within three years and one day after the cause of death is administered, or it will be rebuttably presumed that the death did not result from the act (PC 194).

Corpus Delicti. This term, meaning "body of the crime" is the essential elements of an offense, and does not necessarily refer to the body of a deceased person in a homicide case. This is especially true in California, since actually producing a dead body in a criminal homicide case is not an essential element of the crime of murder or manslaughter (*People v. Scott*, 176 Cal. App. 2d 458).

The *corpus delicti* of felonious (criminal) homicide consists of two basic elements:

1. death of a human being, and
2. an unlawful act, omission, or criminal agency causing such death.

It is not necessary that there be direct evidence as to the means used to accomplish the killing in attempting to prove the *corpus delicti* of homicide; such may be proven by circumstantial evidence (*People v. Wetzel*, 198 Cal. App. 2d 541).

Proximate Cause of Death. The cause of death must be directly, closely and immediately related to the perpetrator's criminal act or omission. If there is an intervening cause of death which is not the result of the defendant's act (so that death is not connected in a regular chain of causes and consequences), the defendant is not responsible. However, if a mortal wound was inflicted by an assailant and a second assailant inflicts another mortal wound, neither assailant is relieved of his or her responsibility for the death of the victim.

One who commits euthanasia (mercy killing), bears no ill will toward the victim and may even believe the act is morally justified. Nonetheless, he or she acts with malice if able to comprehend that society prohibits this act, regardless of personal beliefs (*People v. Conley*, 64 Cal. App. 2d 321). Also, a crime may be murder although the person killed is not the one whom the accused intended to kill (*People v. McAuliffe*, 154 Cal. App. 2d 332).

Proof of Death. Since in California both death and the criminal agency (act causing death) may be proven by circumstantial evidence, a physical body need not be produced. Evidence may be based on eye witnesses, parts of the body, or otherwise circumstantially. The fact that a person is merely missing is not sufficient evidence to support a *prima facie* (on its face) case of homicide. It should be noted, also, that one cannot be convicted on a confession alone.

Circumstantial evidence supported a first-degree murder conviction of a wife whose husband died as a result of chronic arsenic poisoning over a four-month period (*People v. Helwinkel*, 199 Cal. App. 2d 207).

Time Within Which Death Must Occur—PC 194. To make the killing either murder or manslaughter, the victim must die within three years and a day after the stroke received or the cause of death was administered, or a rebuttable presumption will arise that death did not result from this stroke. In the computation of such time, the whole of the day on which the act was done shall be reckoned the first.

11.2 MURDER DEFINED

Definition of Murder—PC 187. "(a) Murder is the unlawful killing of a human being, or a fetus, with malice aforethought.

(b) This section shall not apply to any person who commits an act which results in the death of a fetus if any of the following apply:

1. The act complied with the Therapeutic Abortion Act, Chapter 11 (commencing with Section 25950) of Division 20 of the Health and Safety Code.
2. The act was committed by a holder of a physician's and surgeon's certificate, as defined in the Business and Professions Code, in a case where, to a medical certainty, the result of childbirth would be death of the mother of the fetus, or where her death from childbirth, although not medically certain, would be substantially certain or more likely than not.
3. The act was solicited, aided, abetted, or consented to by the mother of the fetus.

(c) Subdivision (b) shall not be construed to prohibit the prosecution of any person under any other provision of law."

Murder—Burden of Proof—PC 189.5. "Upon a trial for murder, the commission of the homicide by the defendant being proven, the burden of proving circumstances of mitigation, or that justify or excuse it, devolves upon the defendant, unless the proof on the part of the prosecution tends to show that the crime committed only amounts to manslaughter, or that the defendant was justifiable or excusable."

Malice Defined—PC 188. "Such malice may be express or implied. It is express when there is manifested a deliberate intention unlawfully to take away the life of a fellow creature. It is implied when no considerable provocation appears, or when the circumstances attending the killing show an abandoned or malignant heart.

"When it is shown that the killing resulted from the intentional doing of an act with express or implied malice as defined above, no other mental state need be shown to establish the mental state of malice aforethought. Neither an awareness of the obligation to act within the general body of laws regulating society nor acting despite such awareness is included within the definition of malice."

Malice Aforethought Defined. Malice aforethought does not necessarily mean an actual intention to kill the deceased, nor does it necessarily imply deliberation. Rather, it indicates a purpose and design as contrasted with accident or mischance or misfortune. It is present when there is an intention to cause death or grievous bodily harm, or knowledge that one's acts will probably so result, when committed in the commission of a felony or other act which proves inherently dangerous to others. Malice does not necessarily mean hatred or personal ill will toward the person killed, nor an actual intent to take the victim's life, or anyone's life for that matter. Thus, if the killing was for the purpose of robbery, without any hatred or ill will against the person killed, it would be homicide. In this case, the crime would be first-degree murder.

Express Malice. As stated in PC 188: "Malice is express when there is manifested a deliberate intention unlawfully to take away the life of a fellow creature." Express malice must always be present in first-degree murder. It is considered to be present where the evidence shows a deliberate intention unlawfully to take the life of another human being, such as where one kills another with a deliberate and formed design.

Where homicide is committed by means of torture, the means used are conclusive evidence of express malice (*People v. Bitler*, 205 Cal. App. 2d 437).

The necessary malice required for murder in the first-degree is demonstrated when the evidence shows a deliberate intention to take the life of another human being (*People v. Keeling*, 152 Cal. App. 2d 4).

Implied Malice. As stated in PC 188: "Malice is implied, when no considerable provocation appears, or when the circumstances attending the killing show an abandoned and malignant heart." Implied malice has been defined as that which arises or may be inferred from the intentional doing of an unlawful or wrongful act with a wrongful purpose. Implied malice exists where the killing was done suddenly, without justification or excuse, and without provocation, or without provocation sufficient to reduce the homicide to manslaughter (*People v. Dugger*, 179 Cal. App. 2d 714).

Malice as an element of murder is implied where the defendant with antisocial motives and with utter disregard for human life engages in conduct involving high probability of resultant death (*Brooks v. Superior Court*, 239 Cal. App. 593). Where there is evidence of a lack of considerable provocation for a killing, and where the circumstances attending the killing showed an abandoned and malignant heart, malice for such killing may be implied (*People v. Hudgins*, 236 Cal. App. 2d 578).

The following Web Site covers several interesting related topics such as the motivation and personality of serial killers, short articles on the most notorious serial killers in U.S. history and the text of the infamous "Unabomber's" manifesto. Go to **http://www.talkjustice.com/browse.asp.** At this site, you will find a list of topics in alphabetical order. Scroll down your screen and click on *Homicide.*

11.3 DEGREES OF MURDER

Degrees of Murder—PC 189. "All murder which is perpetrated by means of a destructive device, explosive, a weapon of mass destruction, knowing use of ammunition designed primarily to penetrate metal or armor, poison, lying in wait, torture, or by any other kind of willful, deliberate, and premeditated killing, or which is committed in the perpetration of, or attempts to perpetrate, arson, rape, robbery, burglary, mayhem, kidnapping, trainwrecking, or any act punishable under Section 206 [torture], 286 [sodomy], 288 [child molest], 288a [oral copulation], or 289 [penetration by object], is murder in the first-degree, and all other kinds of murder are of the second degree.

"As used in this section, 'destructive device' shall mean any destructive device as defined in Section 12301 and 'explosive' shall mean any explosive as defined in Section 12000 of the Health and Safety Code.

"To prove the killing was 'deliberate and premeditated,' it shall not be necessary to prove the defendant maturely and meaningfully reflected upon the gravity of his or her act."

Discussion—First-Degree Murder. As stated in PC 189, all murder perpetrated by certain means specified in this section, become first-degree murder. These various means are discussed below.

Intentional drive-by murder by firearm is a "special circumstance" murder that is subject to the death penalty. *Courtesy of AP/Wide World Photos*

Using Armor Piercing Ammunition. The knowing use of armor piercing or metal piercing ammunition in a murder makes it first-degree. This provision was added by the legislature shortly after the police and many corporate executives began wearing bullet-proof vests. Except for police and military use, it is a felony to manufacture, import or possess metal or armor piercing ammunition (PC 12320, PC 12311 and PC 12322).

Destructive Device Defined—PC 12301. Murder becomes first-degree if either a destructive device or an explosive is used to cause death. A "destructive device" is defined as any of the following by PC 12301:

- Any projectile containing an explosive.
- Any bomb, grenade or explosive missile.
- Any weapon or fixed ammunition of arrestor than .60 caliber.
- Any rocket or rocket propelled projectile.
- Any breakable container of flammable liquid.

Explosive Defined—H&S Code 1200. As defined in the Health and Safety Code, an explosive is any highly volatile chemical, nitroglycerine, dynamite, or gunpowder.

Poison Defined. The word poison includes any substance which, when applied to the human body externally or internally, is capable of destroying life. Thus the deliberate introduction of poison into a person's system over a period of time which proximately results in the person's death is first-degree murder.

Lying in Wait Defined. The essence of "lying in wait" is that the perpetrator takes a position where he or she is waiting and watching with the intention of inflicting bodily injury likely to cause the death of another. Lying in wait may be likened to an "ambush."

Lying in wait is simply evidence which, if unexplained and unqualified by other evidence, would ordinarily establish that the perpetrator was guilty of willful, deliberate, and premeditated killing (*People v. Wolff,* 61 Cal. 2d 795).

Where defendant went to a cabin to await the arrival of the victim with a loaded rifle, the court held the defendant's actions to be within the scope of lying in wait (*People v. Tuthill*, 31 Cal. 2d 92).

Torture Defined. Kicking a helpless victim to death for a period of fifteen minutes before death actually resulted was held to be torture and thus first-degree murder (*People v. Gilliam*, 39 Cal. 2d 235). Where evidence disclosed that the victim was killed in an effort to get the combination to his safe, and that he was tortured for this purpose, the court held this to be first-degree murder (*People v. Cooley*, 211 Cal. App. 2d 173).

Deliberation and Premeditation Defined. The term "deliberate" means arrived at as a result of some thought and weighing of considerations. The term "premeditate" means to think on and resolve in the mind beforehand (*People v. Morris*, 174 Cal. App. 2d 93).

No set rule can be laid down as to the amount or type of deliberation necessary in every case of first-degree murder. The evidence must be sufficient to enable the jury to reasonably conclude that the defendant's action in connection with the homicide was actually premeditated (*People v. Nye*, 63 Cal. 2d 166).

Where a husband went to the home of his estranged wife and sought her out, and thereafter fired several shots into her body, evidence was sufficient to support an implied finding of the jury that the husband had a deliberate, thoughtful, and preconceived intent to kill his wife (*People v. Dement*, 48 Cal. 2d 600).

To establish the crime of first-degree murder, deliberation and premeditation may be inferred from proof of facts and circumstances, and direct evidence of a deliberate and premeditated purpose to kill is not required (*People v. Cartier*, 54 Cal. 2d 300).

Killing in Perpetration of a Felony. Where the killing is done in the perpetration or attempt to perpetrate arson, rape, robbery, burglary, carjacking, kidnapping, train wrecking or mayhem or any act punishable under PC 286, 288, 288(a) or 289, or during a "drive-by" shooting, the murder is, as a matter of law, murder in the first-degree and this is the law whether the killing was intentional or unintentional or even accidental.

Killing During Burglary. A killing, intentional or otherwise, committed during the course of a burglary constitutes first degree murder (*People v. Pollard*, 194 Cal. App. 2d 830).

Where in the perpetration of burglary and rape, the defendant inflicts injuries upon his victim which ultimately cause her death, he is guilty of first-degree murder even if he inflicts such injuries unintentionally (*People v. Cheary*, 48 Cal. 2d 301).

Where victim was inadvertently killed during a struggle with a shotgun which he was using in an attempt to thwart a burglary, such a killing is considered to have been done during the commission of a burglary and the crime is first-degree murder (*People v. Delaney*, 185 Cal. App. 2d 261).

Killing During Arson. A fatal fire and explosion deliberately caused by a defendant, wherein several persons lost their lives as a result, constitutes killing during the perpetration of arson (*People v. Chavez*, 50 Cal. 2d 778). Where two persons conspire to set fire to a cafe and one of the principals is accidently killed by the fire, the remaining co-conspirator is guilty of first-degree murder as the result of a killing during the perpetration of arson (*People v. Woodruff*, 237 Cal. App. 2d 749).

Killing During Rape. The majority of rape-murders must be proven by circumstantial evidence. Thus, where the woman was found beaten to death and physical evidence tended to show forced sexual intercourse shortly before death, a conviction of first-degree murder in the perpetration of rape was sustained (*People v. Quicke*, 61 Cal. 2d 155).

In proving a homicide which was perpetrated during the commission of rape, it is not necessary that it be shown that the rape itself had been completed (*People v. Subia*, 239 Cal. App. 262).

Killing During Robbery. A murder that is committed during the perpetration or attempt to perpetrate robbery is first-degree and continues to be so even after the robbery is consummated. Thus where a store was robbed and one of the employees attempted to follow the robbery suspects and was thereafter shot and killed by one of them, this was held to be first-degree murder under the felony-murder theory.

A killing, intentional or otherwise, committed during the perpetration of a robbery, whether it occurs during the process of robbing or immediately thereafter and during flight from the crime scene, is murder in the first-degree. Thus, one who commits robbery of a store and thereafter flees in a car which subsequently hits and kills a pedestrian is guilty of first-degree murder since the homicide resulted during flight from the robbery (*People v. Ketchel,* 59 Cal. 2d 503).

The required intent in first-degree murder is not merely to commit the act of discharging a firearm, but includes the intent to kill a human being as the objective or result of such act (*People v. Gorshen*, 51 Cal. 2d 716).

Killing During Mayhem. All murder which is committed in the perpetration of mayhem is murder of the first degree (*People v. Cartier*, 54 Cal. 2d 300).

Killing During Child Molestation. Any killing which occurs during the perpetration of acts denounced by PC 288 (crimes against children) is murder in the first degree. Since in the case of child molesting, the majority of victims are killed after having been molested or otherwise sexually violated, it makes no difference whether the homicide precedes or follows acts of molestation.

11.4 PENALTY FOR MURDER

First-Degree Murder—PC 190(a). Every person guilty of murder in the first-degree shall suffer death, confinement in state prison for life without possibility of parole, or confinement in state prison for a term of 25 years to life. If the victim was killed because of disability, gender or sexual orientation, punishment is imprisonment for life without parole (PC 190.03).

Second-Degree Murder—PC 190(a). Except as provided in subdivision (b) or (c), below, every person guilty of murder in the second degree is punishable in the state prison for a term of 15 years to life.

Killing of Peace Officer—PC 190(b). If the victim was a peace officer, every person guilty of murder in the second degree shall suffer confinement in the state prison for a term of 25 years to life. However, where the defendant reasonably should have known the victim was a peace officer performing official duty, second-degree murder is punishable by life (without parole), if there was proven a specific intent to kill or inflict great bodily injury, or if the defendant personally used a firearm or dangerous or deadly weapon (PC 190.26).

Drive-by Shooting—PC 190(d). Any second-degree drive-by murder is punishable by imprisonment for a term of 20 years to life.

First-Degree Murder With Special Circumstances—PC 190.2. The penalty for murder in the first-degree shall be death or confinement in the state prison for life without possibility of parole in any case in which one or more of the following *special circumstances* have been found to be true:

1. The murder was intentional and carried out for financial gain.
2. The defendant was previously convicted of murder in the first-degree or second-degree.
3. The defendant has in this proceeding been convicted of more than one offense of murder in the first- or second-degree.
4. The murder was committed by means of a destructive device, bomb, or explosive planted, hidden or concealed in any place.
5. The murder was committed for the purpose of avoiding or preventing a lawful arrest or for the purpose of attempting an escape from lawful custody.
6. The murder was committed by means of a destructive device, bomb, or explosive mailed or delivered.
7. The victim was a peace officer (as defined in the Penal Code) who, while engaged in performance of his or her official duties was intentionally killed, or was intentionally killed in retaliation for the performance of his or her official duties.
8. The victim was a federal law enforcement officer or agent, who, while engaged in the course of the performance of his or her duties was intentionally killed, or was intentionally killed in retaliation for the performance of his or her official duties.
9. The victim was a fireman as defined in Section 245.1, who while engaged in the course of the performance of his duties was intentionally killed, and such defendant knew or reasonably should have known that such victim was a fireman engaged in the performance of his duties.
10. The victim was a witness to a crime who was intentionally killed for the purpose of preventing his or her testimony in any criminal proceeding, and the killing was not committed during the commission, or attempted commission of the crime to which he was a witness; or the victim was a witness to a crime and was intentionally killed in retaliation for his testimony in any criminal proceeding.
11. The victim was a prosecutor or a former prosecutor of any local or state prosecutor's office in this state or any other state, or a federal prosecutor's office and the murder was carried out in retaliation for or to prevent the performance of the victim's official duties.
12. The victim was a judge or former judge of any court of record in the local, state or federal system in the State of California or in any other state of the United States and the murder was carried out in retaliation for or to prevent the performance of the victim's official duties.
13. The victim was an elected or appointed official or former official of the Federal Government, a local or State Government of California, or of any local or state government of any other state in the United States and the killing was intentionally carried out in retaliation for or to prevent the performance of the victim's official duties.
14. The murder was especially heinous, atrocious, or cruel, manifesting exceptional depravity. ***Note:*** this section is no longer applicable, having been struck down by the California Supreme Court. The Legislature has not yet changed the wording of the statute.
15. The defendant intentionally killed the victim while lying in wait.
16. The victim was intentionally killed because of his race, color, religion, nationality or country of origin.
17. The murder was committed while the defendant was engaged in or was an accomplice in the commission of, attempted commission of, or the immediate flight after committing or attempting to commit the following felonies:
    a. Robbery, PC 211.
    b. Kidnapping, PC 207 and 209.
    c. Rape, PC 261.
    d. Sodomy, PC 286.
    e. Lewd act upon child under the age of 14, PC 288.
    f. Oral copulation, PC 288a.
    g. Burglary in the first- or second-degree, PC 460.
    h. Arson, PC 451.
    i. Train wrecking, PC 219.
    j. Mayhem, PC 203.
    k. Rape by instrument, PC 289.
    l. Carjacking, PC 215.
18. The murder was intentional and involved the infliction of torture. For the purpose of this section torture requires proof of the infliction of extreme physical pain no matter how long its duration.
19. The defendant intentionally killed the victim by the administration of poison.
20. The victim was a targeted juror.

21. The murder was an intentional drive-by killing by firearm.

> **Note—Imposition of Death Penalty:** A participant in a robbery resulting in homicide may be found guilty of murder in the first-degree, even though his co-defendant fired the fatal shot. However, the United States Supreme Court held in *People v. Enmunds* (458 U.S. 782), that imposition of the death penalty on a "non-triggerman" accomplice requires evidence that such accomplice intended the killing to occur.

Death Penalty Perpetrator Under 18—PC 190.5. This section prohibits imposition of the death penalty on any person who was under the age of 18 years at the time the crime was committed.

Second-Degree Murder—PC 189. Murder of the second-degree may be simply defined as the unlawful killing of a human being with malice aforethought, but which is not done in any manner as previously described in the crime of first-degree murder.

The real difference between first- and second-degree murder is the element of "malice." Both first- and second degree murder require malice—*express* malice in first-degree murder and *implied* malice in second-degree murder. Thus, second-degree murder consists of an unlawful killing with malice aforethought but without premeditation or deliberation.

In second-degree murder there is no preconceived design to kill, yet, as previously mentioned, the element of malice is present and implied, under the existing circumstances. Thus, where one kills another as a result of a severe beating, an illegal abortion, during the course of stealing an automobile, or during the course of perpetrating any felony other than those defined in first-degree murder, or during the perpetration of a misdemeanor which is inherently dangerous to human life, the crime is murder in the second-degree.

Examples of Second-Degree Murder. An actual intent to kill is not a necessary element of second-degree murder. Malice may be implied from an assault with a dangerous weapon (*People v. Goodman*, 8 Cal. App. 3d 705).

An act which is dangerous to life need not be unlawful to make a resultant killing second-degree murder, if performed by one who knows that his conduct endangers the life of another (*People v. Phillips*, 64 Cal. 2d 574). Homicide that is the direct causal result of the commission of a felonious assault is murder in the second-degree (*People v. Montgomery*, 235 Cal. App. 2d 582). A homicide that directly results from the commission of a felony which is inherently dangerous to human life is second-degree murder (*People v. Nichols*, 3 Cal. 3d 150).

Death which results from the commission of a felony involving the administration of a narcotic substance, as denounced by the Health and Safety

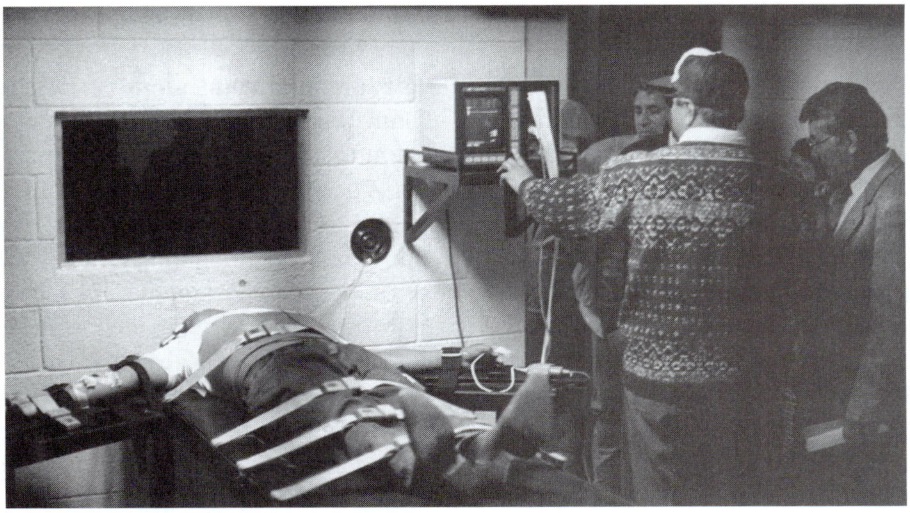

Most executions in California occur by lethal intravenous injection. *Courtesy of AP/Wide World Photos*

Code, constitutes murder in the second-degree (*People v. Taylor*, 11 Cal. App. 3d 57).

Where evidence is insufficient to show that a killing was done with premeditation, deliberation, or willfulness, or in the commission of the specified felonies by using poison, or lying in wait, or by torturing the victim, the crime will be murder in the second-degree (*People v. Granados*, 49 Cal. 2d 490).

11.5 PROXIMATE CAUSE—FELONY MURDER RULE

The felony murder rule, vicarious liability and proximate cause were discussed in Chapter 3. A brief review, however, will be helpful here. As previously indicated, murder liability is attributable to a suspect under the felony murder rule where he or his co-conspirator kills during the commission of a serious felony, in furtherance of the criminal conspiracy.

Also, each conspirator is liable for a murder committed by any of them in a case where all had agreed to kill, such as in a drive-by shooting or murder pact. And, under the proximate cause/provocative act doctrine, surviving accomplices can be convicted of murder where their conduct was the proximate cause of a lethal response by the victim or police, resulting in the death of one or more accomplices.

A good review of the three theories of attributed liability can be found in the opinion in the case of *In re Aurelio R.*, 157 Cal. App. 3d 52. Also see *Pizano v. Superior Court*, 21 Cal. 3d 128.

11.6 MANSLAUGHTER

Manslaughter Defined—PC 192. "Manslaughter is the unlawful killing of a human being, without malice. It is of three kinds:

(a) Voluntary—upon a sudden quarrel or heat of passion.

(b) Involuntary—in the commission of an unlawful act, not amounting to a felony; or in the commission of a lawful act which might produce death, in an unlawful manner, or without due caution and circumspection. This subdivision shall not apply to acts committed in the driving of a vehicle.

(c) Vehicular—(1) Except as provided in subdivision (a) of Section 191.5, driving a vehicle in the commission of an *unlawful* act, not amounting to a felony and *with gross negligence;* or driving a vehicle in the commission of a *lawful* act, which might produce death, in an unlawful manner, and *with gross negligence.*

(2) Driving a vehicle in the commission of an unlawful act, not amounting to felony, but without gross negligence; or driving a vehicle in the commission of a lawful act which might produce death, in an unlawful manner, but without gross negligence.

(3) Driving a vehicle in connection with a violation of paragraph (3) of subdivision (a) of section 550, where the vehicular collision or vehicular accident was knowingly caused for financial gain and proximately resulted in the death of any person. This provision shall not be construed to prevent prosecution of a defendant for the crime of murder.

"This section shall not be construed as making any homicide in the driving of a vehicle punishable which is not a proximate result of the commission of an unlawful act, not amounting to a felony, or of the commission of a lawful act which might produce death, in an unlawful manner.

'Gross negligence,' as used in this section, shall not be construed as prohibiting or precluding a charge of murder under Section 188 [malice defined] upon facts exhibiting wantonness and a conscious disregard for life to support a finding of implied malice, or upon facts showing malice, consistent with the holding of the California Supreme Court in *People v. Watson*, 30 Cal. 3d 290."

Negligence Defined—PC 7. "The words 'neglect,' 'negligence,' 'negligently' import a want of such attention to the nature or probable consequences of the act or omission as a prudent man ordinarily bestows in acting in his own concerns."

Murder and Manslaughter Distinguished. The distinction between murder and manslaughter is that murder requires malice and manslaughter does not. When the act causing the death, though unlawful, occurs in the heat of passion, or is caused by a sudden quarrel amounting to adequate provocation, the offense is manslaughter. In such a case, even if an intent to kill exists, malice, which is an essential element of murder, is absent.

To establish that a killing is murder and not manslaughter, the burden is on the state to prove beyond a reasonable doubt each of the elements of murder and that the act which caused the death was not done in the heat of passion or upon a sudden quarrel.

Note: Each type of manslaughter is discussed in more detail below. Please see Voluntary Manslaughter, 11.7; Involuntary Manslaughter, 11.8 and Vehicular Manslaughter, 11.9. Also, see the Homicide Chart later in this chapter, which shows the difference between manslaughter and justifiable and excusable homicide.

11.7 VOLUNTARY MANSLAUGHTER

Voluntary Manslaughter Defined—PC 192(a). Voluntary manslaughter is committed when a person *intentionally* but unlawfully kills in a sudden quarrel or heat of passion. It may also be committed when a person kills *unintentionally* in a sudden quarrel or heat of passion, where the killer acts with conscious disregard for life, knowing that the conduct endangers the life of another. (*People v. Lasko*, 23 Cal.4th 101.) In either kind of case, the crime is less than murder because of the absence of the element of *malice.* A person who is acting under the provocation of sudden emotion is not deemed as culpable as a person acting from a malicious motivation to kill.

Voluntary manslaughter may also be committed where a person kills another *intentionally*, in an unreasonable but good-faith belief in having to act in self-defense (sometimes called the "imperfect self-defense" doctrine). (*People v. Barton*, 12 Cal. 4th 186.) It may be also be committed when a person kills *unintentionally*, in an unreasonable but good faith belief in self-defense, where the killer acts with conscious disregard for life, knowing that the conduct endangers the life of another. (*People v. Blakely* Cal. 4th 82) Again, the self-defensive motivation, even though unreasonable, is deemed to make the killing less blameworthy than one committed with actual or implied malice.

Discussion. Heat of Passion—"Hot Blood." Although the "heat of passion" in manslaughter frequently means anger, it may be any of the other emotional outbursts which are referred to as passion, including sudden resentment, fear or jealousy, etc.

To be sufficient to reduce a killing to manslaughter, heat of passion must be such as would naturally be aroused in the minds of ordinary, reasonable persons of ordinary self-control under the given facts and circumstances (*People v. Lopez,* 205 Cal. App. 2d 807).

A homicide is voluntary manslaughter if the defendant's reason was, at the time of his act, disturbed or obscured by sufficient passion as would lead an ordinary man of average disposition to act rashly or without due deliberation (*People v. Dugger,* 179 Cal. App. 2d 714).

Adequate Provocation. Whether provocation is adequate to reduce the killing of a human being to manslaughter must be determined by considering whether the provocation would have created a similar reaction in the ordinary person under the same circumstances. If so, then it is adequate and will reduce the offense to manslaughter. If not, it is inadequate even though the degree of passion was indeed great (*People v. Webb*, 143 Cal. App. 2d 402).

Cooling Time. If provocation was originally sufficient to cause extreme emotion, but the perpetrator had calmed down previous to the homicide, the crime would then be murder. The test is: was there time between the provocation and the killing for the ordinarily reasonable man under the circumstances to have "cooled off?" (*People v. Taylor*, 197 Cal. App. 2d 372).

"Cooling time," in respect to the crime of manslaughter, is not the time it would take an ideal man to cool, but rather it is the time it would take the reasonable person, under like circumstances, to cool and collect his senses (*People v. Golsh*, 63 Cal. App. 609).

11.8 INVOLUNTARY MANSLAUGHTER

Every killing of a human being is involuntary manslaughter if it isn't murder, voluntary manslaughter, or excusable homicide under PC 195 or justifiable homicide under PC 196 or PC 197.

Involuntary Manslaughter—PC 192(b). Involuntary manslaughter is the unlawful killing of a human being *without* malice. This crime exists in two situations:

1. in the commission of an "unlawful" act, not amounting to a felony; or
2. in the commission of a "lawful" act which might produce death in an unlawful manner if done without due caution and circumspection.

Commission of an Unlawful Act Not Amounting to a Felony. The legislative intent of this section is to punish persons who violate laws designated to prevent injury to others. For example, where one violates a statute enacted under a police power provision, such as the reckless operation of a motor vehicle, or unintentionally killing a victim as the result of simple assault and battery, the crime is involuntary manslaughter. Similarly, where one exhibits a loaded gun in a rude, angry, or threatening manner (a misdemeanor under PC 417), and the gun discharges accidently, the crime is involuntary manslaughter. The important thing to remember about involuntary manslaughter is that it is a homicide *unintentionally* caused, and without malice, resulting from the commission of an unlawful act not amounting to a felony.

A person discharging a pistol with intent only to frighten and not to shoot the deceased is guilty of involuntary manslaughter should the victim die from such an act (*People v. McGee*, 31 Cal. 2d 229).

Commission of a Lawful Act Which Might Produce Death. If a person, in doing a lawful act which might produce death or serious bodily harm if done without due caution and circumspection, neglects to take such precautions as a reasonable man would take to prevent injury, he is guilty of involuntary manslaughter should the victim die. This may involve the failure to perform a legal duty. For example, a parent might leave a child in a closed car in the sun. The parent's legal duty is to protect the child and keep the child out of harm's way.

If the law requires a person to do an act and that person thereafter disregards this duty which proximately causes death by virtue of his negligence, misconduct, or refusal to act, he is guilty of involuntary manslaughter. A person who is under no legal duty to render care and attention to another, regardless of a possible moral duty, is not guilty of manslaughter if death is the result of his neglect.

Where a licensed pharmacist fills a prescription inaccurately while under the influence of a narcotic or intoxicant, and a death occurs as the result of such negligence and lack of due caution and circumspection, the defendant is guilty of involuntary manslaughter.

11.9 VEHICLE MANSLAUGHTER

Vehicle Manslaughter is defined in PC 192(c), subsections (1), (2) and (3) under 11.6 of your text. Each of these three subsections describes two types of acts involving the driving of a vehicle, any one of which constitutes vehicular manslaughter as follows:

PC 192(c)(1). Driving a vehicle,
- and commission of an *unlawful act*,
- not amounting to a felony,
- and *with* gross negligence; or
- commission of a *lawful* act
- which might produce death,
- done in an unlawful manner,
- and *with* gross negligence.

PC 192(c)(2). Driving a vehicle,
- and commission of an *unlawful act*,
- not amounting to a felony,
- but *without* gross negligence; or
- commission of a *lawful* act
- which might produce death,
- done in an *unlawful* manner,
- but *without* gross negligence.

PC 192(c)(3). While driving in violation of VC 23140, 23152 or 23153 (under the influence of drugs or alcohol, with/without injury),
- commission of an *unlawful* act,
- not amounting to a felony,
- and *with* gross negligence; or
- driving in violation of VC 23140, 23152 or 23153,
- commission of a *lawful* act,
- which might produce death,
- done in an *unlawful* manner,
- but *without* gross negligence.

The phrase "unlawful act, not amounting to a felony," used above, refers to either a misdemeanor or infraction.

PC 192(c)(4). Driver causing accident for insurance fraud,
- driving a vehicle,
- causing an accident,
- for financial gain,
- proximately causing a death.

A person can never be guilty of vehicular manslaughter unless the homicide was the proximate

Where death results from an unlawful act committed by a driver, the driver may be charged with vehicular manslaughter. *Photograph by Tony Freeman, courtesy of PhotoEdit*

result of the unlawful act, or of the lawful act which might produce death, committed in an unlawful manner. It is ultimately up to the trier of fact (judge or jury) to determine if an act was done with or without gross negligence.

Vehicular Manslaughter Examples. Driving at an excessive speed and hitting a person standing by the roadway near a parked car is manslaughter in the driving of a motor vehicle with gross negligence if death occurs (*People v. Markham*, 153 Cal. App. 2d 260).

Failure to stop at a traffic signal, all conditions being normal, which results in death to the other driver was sufficient to sustain a conviction for manslaughter for grossly negligent operation of an automobile (*People v. Pfeffer*, 224 Cal. App. 2d 578).

Death which results in a driver being blinded by approaching lights of another vehicle and where the driver, as a result of his visibility being impaired, strikes and kills a pedestrian in a crosswalk is manslaughter in the driving of a vehicle without gross negligence (*People v. Lett*, 77 Cal. App. 2d 917).

Gross Vehicle Manslaughter While Intoxicated—PC 191.5. This law makes unlawful the killing of a person *without malice aforethought,* in the driving of a vehicle while under the influence of drugs or alcohol or both (in violation of 23152 or 23153 of the Vehicle Code) and where the proximate cause of the death was either:

1. the commission of an *unlawful act,* not amounting to a felony, and *with gross negligence*, or
2. the commission of a *lawful act* which might produce death, in an unlawful manner, and *with gross negligence.* The crime is a felony.

Manslaughter While Operating Vessel—PC 191.5(b). Gross vehicular manslaughter while intoxicated also covers operating a vessel or boat (which includes water skis, aquaplanes, etc.) in violation of Section 655 of the Harbors and Navigation Code. The proximate cause of the death must be the same as in (1) and (2) in the paragraph above. This offense is a felony.

Punishment for Manslaughter—PC 193. Both voluntary and involuntary manslaughter are felonies, punishable by imprisonment in the state prison. Vehicular manslaughter is a felony (wobbler) except for PC 192(c)(2) which is a misdemeanor.

11.10 EXCUSABLE HOMICIDE

Excusable Homicide Defined—PC 195. "Homicide is excusable in the following cases:

1. When committed by accident and misfortune, or in doing any other lawful act by lawful means, with usual and ordinary caution, and without any unlawful intent.

2. When committed by accident and misfortune, in the heat of passion, upon any sudden and sufficient provocation, or upon a sudden combat, when no undue advantage is taken, nor any dangerous weapon used, and when the killing is not done in a cruel or unusual manner."

Discussion—Excusable Homicide. To excuse a homicide on the grounds of accident and misfortune, the accused must have been engaged in a lawful act and he must have been performing it with due care. If he was engaged in an unlawful act, or if the accident was the result of culpable (at fault) negligence, he is criminally liable for the consequence of his act.

The so-called "unwritten law" of avenging a wrong done to a female friend or member of one's family has no application in California and any homicide that results is criminal homicide (*People v. Young*, 70 Cal. App. 2d 28).

11.11 JUSTIFIABLE HOMICIDE BY PUBLIC OFFICERS

Justifiable Homicide by Public Officers—PC 196. "Homicide is justifiable when committed by public officers and those acting by their command in their aid and assistance, either:

1. In obedience to any judgment of a competent court; or
2. When necessarily committed in overcoming actual resistance to the execution of some legal process, or in the discharge of any other legal duty; or
3. When necessarily committed in retaking felons who have been rescued or have escaped, or when necessarily committed in arresting persons charged with felony, and who are fleeing from justice or resisting such arrest."

Discussion. The characteristic of a justifiable homicide, is that while the officer may have the intent to kill, and the action he takes is likely to result in death, the occasion is such that the law justifies the killing as a means of protecting and enforcing the rights of an individual, the community or the State.

To be considered a justifiable homicide, the killing in the overcoming of resistance to a legal process or in the discharge of any other legal duty must have, in fact, been necessary or have reasonably appeared to be necessary. If the duty could have been reasonably performed without the killing, it will not be a justifiable homicide.

Note: Officers must keep in mind that even though criminal action might not result, civil action could be filed under 42 United States Code, Section 1983, for violation of Fourth Amendment rights (see Chapter 7). The United States Supreme Court has ruled that deadly force can only be used on a fleeing felon when a suspect is dangerous and likely to harm the officer or others (*Garner v. Tennessee*, 471 U.S. 1).

In Obedience to a Judgment. The best example of this is the execution of persons in the state prison for crimes of which they have been found guilty in a competent court and for which they have been sentenced to death.

Overcoming Resistance to Legal Process. The resistance must be actual and life threatening to the officer in such instances. For example, when serving a felony warrant, the arrestee turns on the officer with a gun in his hand, forcing the officer to shoot in order to protect his own life.

Justifiable Homicide in Making an Arrest. The Penal Code is very specific as to the amount of force that can be used in making an arrest. It limits the use of force by a peace officer in making an arrest to what is reasonable to effect the arrest, prevent escape, or overcome resistance (*People v. Brite*, 9 Cal. 2d 666). Also, the officer does not lose the right of self-defense by the use of such reasonable force, if the arrestee physically resists or becomes combative (PC 835a).

Note that PC 196(3) refers only to *felons* who are fleeing or resisting arrest. The use of lethal force is not permissible in misdemeanor cases (*People v. Hughes*, 240 Cal. App. 681). It is the general policy of the law to allow a misdemeanant to escape or avoid recapture rather than to kill him.

As previously indicated, a police officer acting lawfully has at all times the right to self-defense, and if attacked by the person he is arresting, has the same rights as any citizen to defend himself. In such a situation the law of self-defense (PC 197) will apply rather than the laws governing arrests and recapture of persons fleeing from, or resisting arrest.

However, to justify a killing in self-defense, it must appear necessary to the officer (or private person), as a reasonable person, that he believes that he is in danger of receiving great bodily harm and he must also believe, as a reasonable person, that it is necessary for him to use in his own defense such force and means as might cause the death of his adversary to avoid this great bodily harm.

Justifiable Homicide in Preventing Escape and Recapturing Escaped Persons. In general, the same rules of law apply as in making arrests. Only that amount of force which is *necessary* and *reasonable* is allowed. Force that is likely to cause death can only be used if necessary to prevent serious injury to the officer or another person in preventing the escape or to effect the recapture of a felon. However, it should be noted here that neither a felon nor a misdemeanant who flees the physical custody of an officer is committing the crime of escape (*People v. Redmond*, 55 Cal. Rptr. 195).

11.12 JUSTIFIABLE HOMICIDE BY ANY PERSON

Justifiable Homicide by Private Persons—PC 197. This section justifies killings by private persons in self-defense or in the defense of others or in the defense of habitation. "Homicide is justifiable when committed by any person:

1. When resisting any attempt to murder any person, or to commit a felony, or to do some great bodily injury upon any person; or,
2. When committed in defense of habitation, property, or person, against one who manifestly intends or endeavors, by violence or surprise, to commit a felony, or against one who manifestly intends and endeavors, in a violent, riotous, or tumultuous manner, to enter the habitation of another for the purpose of offering violence to any person therein; or,
3. When committed in the lawful defense of such person, or of a wife or husband, parent, child, master, mistress, or servant of such person, when there is reasonable ground to apprehend a design to commit a felony or to do some great bodily injury, and imminent danger of such design being accomplished; but such person, or the person in whose behalf the defense was made, if he was the assailant or engaged in mutual combat, must really and in good faith have endeavored to decline any further struggle before the homicide was committed; or,
4. When necessarily committed in attempting, by lawful ways and means, to apprehend any person for any felony committed, or in lawfully suppressing any riot, or in lawfully keeping and preserving the peace."

Discussion. Under subsection 1, above, a killing must be reasonably necessary and justified on the basis that there is reason to believe that a serious and violent felony will be, or is being committed, and a homicide must be committed as a means to prevent the felony, there being no other immediate means of thwarting the act. Obviously an attempt to commit a felony involving no immediate injury to life, such as in forgery, etc., would not justify homicide.

Under subdivision 2, the defense of habitation, person or property, must be against one who intends or endeavors to use violence. Also see PC 198.5, below.

Under subdivision 3, there must be a reasonable ground to believe the perpetrator plans to commit a felony or to do some great bodily injury, and a real or apparent imminent danger must exist at the time of the killing (*People v. Ortiz*, 63 Cal. App. 662).

Under subdivision 4, one may use only that amount of force necessary to accomplish a lawful purpose. Generally, deadly force may be used only to prevent death or serious injury to the person (and others) who are acting lawfully to accomplish the purposes listed in this subdivision.

Justifiable Homicide in Protecting Home—PC 198.5. "Any person using force intended or likely to cause death or great bodily injury within his or her residence shall be *presumed* to have held a reasonable fear of imminent peril of death or great bodily injury to self, family, or a member of the household when that force is used against another person, not a member of the family or household, who unlawfully and forcibly entered the residence and the person using the force knew or had reason to believe that an unlawful and forcible entry had occurred [italics added for emphasis]."

Note: As used in this section, "great bodily injury" means a significant or substantial physical injury. This section creates a *presumption* of "fear of imminent peril of death or great bodily injury to self or family," from an assailant who unlawfully and forcibly enters one's home. This presumption can be overcome with evidence to the contrary, if the facts so indicate.

Bare Fear Will Not Justify Killing—PC 198. A "bare fear" will not justify a killing in defense of home. Circumstances must be sufficient to excite the fears of a "reasonable person," and the person using lethal force must have acted under the influence of such fears alone, to make such a killing justifiable.

Self-Defense. In applying the law of self-defense, a person must act as a reasonable and prudent individual would act under similar circumstances. The degree of force used to defend oneself must be proportionate to the injury threatened. One cannot kill a person, for example, who threatens to commit a simple assault or battery. The necessity for committing homicide must be founded upon a grave apprehension of receiving great bodily harm (*People v. Scroggins*, 37 Cal. 675).

If a person initiates a quarrel, and "gets more than he bargains for," he must honestly endeavor to retreat; and only thereafter can he stand his ground on the basis of self-defense.

Justifiable and Excusable Homicide—PC 199. Neither justifiable nor excusable homicide is a crime.

11.13 CAPITAL CRIMES

A defendant may be sentenced to death (if 18 years of age or older) if first degree murder is committed under any of the following circumstances:

1. Murder for financial gain (PC 190.2).
2. Explosive or destructive device, use of, (PC 189).
3. Poison, use of, (PC 189), during PC 187.
4. Torture, infliction of, (PC 189).
5. Arson, during commission of, (PC 451).
6. Rape, during commission of, (PC 261).
7. Robbery, during commission of, (PC 211).
8. Burglary, 1st or 2nd degree, (PC 460).
9. Mayhem, during commission of, (PC 203).
10. Peace officer, murder of in performance of duty (PC 190.2).
11. Perjury, causing execution of innocent person (PC 128).
12. Witness, murder to prevent testimony, (PC 190.2).
13. Kidnapping, murder during, (PC 209).
14. Child molesting, murder during, (PC 288).
15. Train wrecking causing death (219).
16. Murder by life convict (PC 4500).
17. Murder with prior conviction (PC 190.2).
18. Multiple murders (PC 190.2).
19. Sabotage, murder during (Military and Veterans Code 1670-72).
20. Conspiracy to commit capital crime. In the case of conspiracy to commit murder, the

Scott Peterson was convicted of murder with special circumstances for killing his pregnant wife. *Courtesy of Al Golub/Pool/The Modesto/Bee/UMA/Corbis Images*

Alejandro Avila was convicted of murder with special circumstances. Murder during kidnap, rape or child molestation is a capital offense. *Courtesy of Getty Images*

HOMICIDE CHART

(Not a Crime Itself—Descriptive of Several Acts)

MURDER—UNLAWFUL

FELONY		FELONY	
FIRST	SECOND	FIRST	SECOND
		B-Burglary	
E	I	A-Arson	O
X	M	R-Robbery	T
P	P	R-Rape	H
R	L	M-Mayhem	E
E	I	Carjacking	R
S	E	Child Molesting	
S	D	Drive-by Shooting	F
		Premeditation	E
		Explosives	L
		Torture	O
		Poison	N
		Lying in wait	I
		Kidnapping	E
		Sodomy	S
		Oral Copulation	
		Rape by object	
		Train wrecking	
		Race/religion, etc.	

DEATH

LAWFUL		UNLAWFUL	
JUSTIFIABLE HOMICIDE	EXCUSABLE HOMICIDE	VOLUNTARY MANSLAUGHTER	INVOLUNTARY MANSLAUGHTER
Judgment of court officer performing duties.	Accident or misfortune.	Without malice.	Without malice. Unlawful act causing death.
Self-Defense	Heat of passion sufficient provocation.	Sudden quarrel.	Unintentional killing.
		Intentional killing without provocation.	

IN DRIVING VEHICLE

Unlawful act, not a felony.

Lawful act, unlawful manner, with or without gross negligence.

Definition of Malice: Two types—express and implied (PC 188)

Express: Manifested by a deliberate intent to take the life of another willfully.

Implied: Exists where no considerable provocation appears or when the circumstances attending the killing show an abandoned and malignant heart.

The difference between first- and second-degree murder is malice—express is first and implied is second.

Premeditation must be proven to establish murder. Premeditation means to think of the act beforehand. Premeditation may take only seconds. Deliberation is simply prolonged premeditation.

punishment shall be that prescribed for murder in the first-degree, (PC 182).

21. Murder committed for the purpose of preventing a lawful arrest or during or attempting an escape from lawful custody (PC 190.2).
22. Firefighter, murder of, while engaged in performance of duty, and defendant knows or should know victim performing duties (PC 190.2).
23. Prosecutor, murder of, and carried out in retaliation for or to prevent performance of official duties (PC 190.2).
24. Judge, murder of, carried out in retaliation for or to prevent performance of official duties (PC 190.2).
25. Elected or appointed official, murder of, carried out in retaliation for or to prevent performance of official duties (PC 190.2).
26. Murder by defendant lying in wait (PC 190.2).
27. Victim was intentionally killed because of race, color, religion, nationality, or country of origin (PC 190.2).
28. Sodomy, murder committed during commission of PC 286 (PC 190.2).
29. Oral copulation, murder committed during PC 288a (PC 190.2(17)(vi)).
30. Murder especially atrocious, cruel or pitiless (PC 190.2(14)).
31. Murder during rape by object, juror retaliation, drive-by shooting, or car jacking.

Mental Retardation Determination—PC 1376. The U.S. Supreme Court ruled that a mentally retarded murderer cannot be executed. This section sets out the procedure for determining whether a murderer fits the definition of "mentally retarded," meaning "of significantly subaverage intellectual functioning existing concurrently with deficits in adaptive behavior and manifested before the age of 18."

STUDENT REVIEW

TERMINOLOGY DEFINED—CHAPTER 11

Please see the Terminology Quiz at the end of this chapter.

1. Arson: an intentional unlawful setting on fire.
2. Dying declaration: dying person's statement on cause of impending death.
3. Excusable homicide: unintentional killing by accident or misfortune.
4. Express malice: deliberate intention to unlawfully take a life.
5. Euthanasia: "mercy killing" of one believed incurably ill.
6. Gross negligence: great negligence, extremely careless of consequences.
7. Heat of passion: in anger, under emotional stress.
8. Implied malice: malice inferred from intentionally doing wrongful act.
9. Judicial notice: court's acknowledgment of fact unnecessary to prove.
10. Justifiable homicide: legally necessary killing although intentional.
11. Legal insanity: inability to tell right from wrong.
12. Manslaughter: unlawful killing without malice by negligence or in anger.
13. Murder: unlawful killing of a human being with malice aforethought.
14. Mutual provocation: joint consent such as agreement to fight.
15. Nighttime: legally hours between sunset and sunrise.
16. Prosecution: court proceedings for convicting a criminal.
17. Psychotic: a person having serious mental disorders.
18. Real evidence: physical things as opposed to verbal testimony.
19. The intentional killing of another in heat of passion but without justification and without malice is voluntary manslaughter.
20. Remand: to send back into custody, to commit to jail.

TRUE-FALSE QUIZ—CHAPTER 11

After reading this chapter you should be able to correctly answer the following items.

___ 1. The term "homicide" refers to the killing of a human being which may not necessarily be a crime.

___ 2. To convict one of murder in California a physical body need not necessarily be produced or even found.

___ 3. The way someone is killed may be proven entirely by circumstantial evidence even if a weapon is not used or if used, is not found.

___ 4. To convict someone of murder, the victim's death must occur within one year and a day from the date injury is inflicted.

___ 5. Generally one who commits euthanasia is not guilty of criminal homicide.

___ 6. One can be guilty of felonious homicide by omitting an act which proximately causes the victim's death.

___ 7. Manslaughter is the unlawful killing of a human being or fetus with malice aforethought.

___ 8. Malice in murder may be either expressed or implied.

___ 9. Malice aforethought does not necessarily mean actual intention to kill the deceased.

___10. Malice aforethought is a necessary element of both first- and second-degree murder.

___11. Murder which is committed in the perpetration of any felony is murder of the first-degree.

___12. Any murder which is not willful, deliberate, and premeditated is of the second-degree.

___13. Any unintentional killing during a robbery would be murder of the second-degree.

___14. Under the felony-murder theory, the killing of a witness who attempted to follow the suspect after a robbery was committed is still first-degree.

___15. Every person who commits first-degree murder is subject to the death penalty in all cases as a matter of law.

___16. Under no circumstances may the death penalty be imposed upon any person who was under 18 when the crime was committed.

___17. If a jury finds the defendant guilty of "murder for hire" the mandatory death penalty is applicable.

___18. Express malice must be proven to constitute first-degree murder.

___19. The intentional killing of another in heat of passion but without justification and without malice is voluntary manslaughter.

___20. Motive is a legally required element of any first-degree murder.

ESSAY-DISCUSSION ITEMS—CHAPTER 11

After reading this chapter you should be able to correctly answer the following items.

1. Briefly define the term "homicide."
2. Within what period of time must the victim die to constitute either murder or manslaughter?
3. What is the definition of murder as given in PC 187?
4. What is the difference between express and implied malice?
5. A killing committed during the perpetration of what crimes is first-degree murder?
6. Under what four circumstances is a homicide by private persons justifiable under PC 197?
7. Under what two circumstances is a homicide excusable under PC 195?
8. Define manslaughter and list the three kinds described in PC 192.
9. Under what three circumstances is a homicide by public officers justified under PC 196?
10. Briefly define "proximate cause" and describe its importance in a homicide case.
11. Discuss: According to the U.S. Supreme Court, the Eighth Amendment forbids executing murderers who are "mentally retarded." What is the test of retardation, and how does this differ from insanity?

TERMINOLOGY QUIZ—CHAPTER 11

Match terms and definitions by writing the number preceding the correct term in the appropriate brackets.

Terms	*Definitions*
1. Arson	[ ] unintentional killing by accident or misfortune
2. Dying declaration	[ ] to commit to jail
3. Excusable homicide	[ ] inability to tell right from wrong
4. Euthanasia	[ ] killing without malice through negligence or anger
5. Express malice	[ ] pertinent, related to case at hand
6. Gross negligence	[ ] physical things as opposed to testimony
7. Heat of passion	[ ] deliberate malicious intent to unlawfully take a life
8. Implied malice	[ ] mercy killing
9. Judicial notice	[ ] in anger, under emotional stress
10. Justifiable homicide	[ ] a person having serious mental disorders
11. Legal insanity	[ ] malice inferred from intentionally doing wrongful act
12. Manslaughter	
13. Murder	[ ] court proceedings for convicting a criminal
14. Mutual provocation	[ ] court's acknowledgment of fact without proof
15. Nighttime aforethought	[ ] legally necessary killing although intentional
	[ ] unlawfully killing a human being without malice
16. Prosecution	
17. Psychotic	
18. Real evidence	
19. Relevant	
20. Remand	

CHAPTER 12

FALSE IMPRISONMENT—RESTRAINT CRIMES—KIDNAPPING—CHILD ABDUCTION—RAPE—UNLAWFUL SEXUAL INTERCOURSE

12.1 FALSE IMPRISONMENT

False Imprisonment Defined—PC 236. "False imprisonment is the unlawful violation of the personal liberty of another."

Punishment—PC 237. In general, false imprisonment is a misdemeanor punishable by a fine or by imprisonment in the county jail or by both fine and imprisonment. If the false imprisonment is accomplished by violence, menace, fraud, or deceit, it is a felony punishable by imprisonment in the state prison. [PC 237(a); and PC 237(b), PC 368(f)—elder victims].

Discussion—PC 236. False imprisonment is any unlawful restraint of a person's liberty and is committed whenever a person detains another, by force, actual or constructive, and without his or her consent and without legal cause. Two essential elements are necessary to the accomplishment of this crime:

1. There must be a restraint of the victim's liberty, and
2. The restraint (imprisonment) must be unlawful.

Significant problems could arise in the area of law enforcement should an officer falsely imprison someone as a result of an illegal arrest. The taking of a person into custody without probable cause amounts to a violation of this section.

The courts do not distinguish clearly between a "false arrest" and "false imprisonment" because an unlawful arrest is regarded as a wrongful confinement on which an action for false imprisonment may be based (*Wilson v. Lousatalot*, 193 Cal. 2d 127). In order to bring an action against an officer for false imprisonment, it is only necessary to allege sufficient facts to show a confinement or restraint resulting from an arrest without a warrant (*Monk v. Ehret*, 219 Cal. 2d 452). It then becomes the responsibility of the officer to show authorization that will justify the restraint upon the individual under PC 836 (arrest without warrant).

Restraint Required. False imprisonment requires direct restraint of the person for some length of time, compelling him or her to stay or go somewhere against his or her will. A false arrest is one way to commit false imprisonment; i.e., since the arrest involves detention or restraint, it always involves an imprisonment. False arrest and false imprisonment are therefore not separate wrongs.

Confinement Defined. The confinement necessary to constitute imprisonment may consist of confinement in the broadest sense of that term; e.g., detention of an individual in a room, building, street or vehicle; or compelling by force, or threat of force, to go from one place to another. Any exercise of force, or express or implied threat of force, by which in fact the other person is deprived of his or her liberty or is compelled to remain where he or she does not wish to remain, or to go where he or she does not wish to go, is an imprisonment.

The restraint may be committed by acts, words, or both, and by merely operating upon the will of the individual, or by personal violence, or both. The restraint is sufficient where an individual voluntarily submits to a show of authority by an officer threatening an arrest (*People v. Agnew*, 107 Cal. 2d 601). Of course, if the detention or arrest is legal, there is no false arrest or imprisonment.

The Internet is highly effective in keeping you informed on the latest crime news. Go to **http://news.findlaw.com/legalnews/crime/.** Click on the headline to read about current or prominent cases.

Private Person Arrests. Officers are completely protected against false arrest and imprisonment charges by PC 847(c), when they aid in a private persons arrest. The reason is that PC 142 makes it a felony for an officer to refuse to accept a person arrested by a private person. Therefore, the officer does not have a true choice whether to accept the prisoner of a "questionable" arrest. However, it is perfectly legal for the officer to immediately release the prisoner on his or her written promise to appear (citation) where appropriate.

A private person who assists in the making of an arrest pursuant to request or persuasion of an officer is not liable for false imprisonment. However, an officer who persuades a private person to make an unlawful arrest may be held liable for the false imprisonment. (***Note:*** For an additional discussion of the laws of arrest, see text Chapter 7.)

Taking Hostages—PC 210.5. An act of false imprisonment to prevent arrest which causes an increased risk of harm, or to use the person as a shield, is a felony.

12.2 CRIMES OF RESTRAINT

Abduction of Women—PC 265. "Every person who takes any woman unlawfully, against her will, and by force, menace, or duress, and compels her to marry him, or to marry any other person, or to be defiled, is punishable by imprisonment in the state prison."

Discussion. This section requires that the female be abducted against her will, but also be forced to marry someone whom she does not want to marry, or to be "defiled." Defiled, as used here, refers to sex acts of any type to which she does not consent willingly and without duress.

Seduction for Prostitution—PC 266. Every person who inveigles or entices any unmarried female, of previous chaste character, under the age of 18 years, into any house of ill fame for the purpose of prostitution or to have illicit carnal connection (sex acts) with any man; and every person who aids or assists in the enticement; and every person who by false pretenses, or any fraudulent means procures any female to have illicit carnal connection with any man, is guilty of a felony (wobbler).

Discussion. The purpose of this section is to punish those who take advantage of young women, such as runaways, etc. It should be noted the female must be under the age of 18, unmarried and of previous "chaste" character. It is not necessary in all cases that the female be enticed into a house of prostitution, only that she have sex relations with any man.

Abduction for Prostitution—PC 266a. Every person who, takes any person against his or her will and without his or her consent, or with his or her consent procured by fraudulent inducement or misrepresentation, for the purpose of prostitution, as defined in PC 647, is guilty of a felony.

Discussion. This law is for the purpose of preventing young men and women from being taken for purposes of prostitution against their will or by false representations (offer of a job, modeling career, movie contract, etc.). Note that the law is equally applicable to male and female victims. Note, also, the law does not refer to age, marital status or previous moral character of the victim.

Abduction for Cohabitation—PC 266b. Every person who takes any other person unlawfully, and against his or her will, and by force, menace or duress, compels him or her to live with such person in an illicit relation, against his or her consent, or to so live with any other person, is punishable by imprisonment in the state prison.

Discussion. This section is similar to PC 266a, except that the element of prostitution (sex for money) is not involved. As in the previous section, the victim's sex is not a factor. This section would punish anyone who kept another prisoner for purposes of illicit sex.

Selling Person for Immoral Purposes—PC 266f. Every person who sells any person or receives any money or other valuable thing for placing in custody, for immoral purposes, any person whether with or without his or her consent, is guilty of a felony.

Human Trafficking—PC 236.1. It is a felony to deprive another of his or her liberty with the intent to obtain forced labor, services or sexual activity, accomplished by means of duress, fraud, deceit, coercion, violence, menace or threat.

Placing Wife in House of Prostitution—PC 266g. This section makes it a felony punishable by imprisonment in the state prison for a man to force, intimidate, persuade or by any means place his wife in a house of prostitution or consent to or permit her to remain there. In such cases, a wife is a competent witness against her husband.

Abduction of Juvenile for Prostitution—PC 267. Any person who takes away any other person under the age of 18 years from the father, mother, guardian, or other person having the legal charge of the other person, without their consent, for the purpose of prostitution, is punishable by imprisonment in the state prison and a fine not exceeding $2,000.

Stalking or Threatening Violence—PC 646.9. Any person who willfully, maliciously, and repeatedly follows or harasses another person and who makes a credible threat with the intent to place that person in reasonable fear of death or great bodily injury is guilty of the crime of stalking, punishable as a misdemeanor. A second conviction or stalking in violation of a restraining order is a felony (wobbler). Note: A peace officer may obtain, serve and enforce an emergency protective order, as outlined in PC 646.91. The Department of Corrections must give 45 days' notice to the sheriff or police chief of the impending release of an imprisoned stalker (PC 3058.61). A person subject to a protective order cannot own, possess, purchase or receive a firearm while the order is in effect.

12.3 KIDNAPPING

Kidnapping Defined—PC 207(a). "Every person who forcibly, or by any other means of instilling fear, steals or takes, or holds, detains, or arrests any person in this state and carries the person into another country, state, or county, or into another part of the same county, is guilty of kidnapping."

> **Discussion.** Kidnapping under PC 207(a) is a *general intent* crime. No specific reason or purpose (intent) for the kidnapping need be proved in order for the perpetrator to be found guilty of kidnapping under this section.

Kidnapping Child Under 14—PC 207(b). "Every person, who for the purpose of committing any act defined in Section 288 (child molesting), hires, persuades, entices, decoys, or seduces by false promises, misrepresentations, or the like, any child under the age of 14 years to go out of this country, state, or county, or into another part of the same county, is guilty of kidnapping."

> **Discussion.** Kidnapping under PC 207(b) is a *specific intent* crime. It must be proved that the perpetrator kidnapped the victim with the *specific intent* and purpose of committing lewd or lascivious (obscene, lustful) acts, as defined in PC 288, with or upon the kidnapped child.

Amber Alert Activation—Government Code 8594. A law enforcement agency investigating a reported abduction of a child under 18 or a disabled victim shall, absent extenuating investigative needs, request that the California Highway Patrol activate the Emergency Alert System. This requirement applies where it is determined that the victim is in imminent danger of serious bodily injury or death, and there is information available that could help recover the victim if disseminated to the general public. It does not apply in non-threatening custody disputes. Upon request, the Highway Patrol shall activate the system.

Kidnapping for Involuntary Servitude—PC 207(c). "Every person who forcibly, or by any other means of instilling fear, takes or holds, detains, or arrests any person with design to take the person out of this state, without having established a claim, according to the laws of the United States, or of this state, or who hires, persuades, entices, decoys, or seduces by false promises, misrepresentations, or the like, any person to go out of this state, or to be taken or removed therefrom, for the purpose and with the intent to sell that person into slavery or involuntary servitude, or otherwise to employ that person for his or her own use, or to the use of another, without the free will and consent of that persuaded person, is guilty of kidnapping."

> **Discussion.** Kidnapping under PC 207(c) is a *specific intent* crime. The kidnapping must be done for the purpose and intent of "involuntary servitude" as described in PC 207(c), above.

Kidnapping—Bringing Victim Into State—PC 207(d). "Every person who, being out of this state, abducts or takes by force or fraud any person contrary to the law of the place where that act is committed, and brings, sends, or conveys that person within the limits of this state, and is afterwards found within the limits thereof, is guilty of kidnapping."

> **Discussion.** Kidnapping at common law amounted to the forcible abduction of a person from his own country and sending him to another. Current laws refer to the crime as a false imprisonment aggravated by forcibly conveying a person to another place in the same county or to another county, state or country. Compelling a driver to convey one to a certain location is kidnapping. This section would also cover, for example, a case where a police officer from another state, in fresh pursuit of a felon from that state, takes the suspect into custody in California, but fails to arraign him or her before the nearest magistrate, taking the suspect instead back to the other state. Such an act is kidnapping in California.

Additional acts punishable under this section include the enticing or seducing of one by false promises, misrepresentation, etc., to exploit the person for various reasons or purposes (usually something such as involuntary servitude). Such acts may include, but are not limited to, prostitution, selling magazine subscriptions, or becoming involved in other activity which the victim did not contemplate at the time due to the pretense or falsehoods on the part of the perpetrator. In order to satisfy or establish the elements of kidnapping in this type of case, the victim must be taken out of the state and must have relied upon the misrepresentations made by the perpetrator.

PC 207(d) pertains to bringing into California a person from another state, by force or fraud, or in any other manner contrary to the law of the *other* state. Under these circumstances, the crime is completed and punishable in California. PC 207(d) requires only *general intent*.

Forcible Taking Defined. In kidnapping, the taking is "forcible" within the meaning of the statute if it is accomplished through the giving of orders which the victim feels compelled to obey because he or she fears harm or injury from the kidnapper, providing the victim's apprehension is reasonable under the circumstances (*People v. Dagampat*, 167 Cal. App. 2d 492).

Where a victim of a kidnapping has at first willingly accompanied the accused, a subsequent restraining of the victim's liberties by force and compelling the victim to accompany the accused, after the victim no longer wants to do so, is sufficient to constitute the crime of kidnapping (*People v. Gallagher*, 164 Cal. App. 2d 414).

Forcible Taking—Infant or Child. When the victim of a kidnap is an unresisting infant or child, the amount of force that will satisfy the element of a forcible taking "is simply the amount of physical force required to take and carry the child away a substantial distance for an illegal purpose or with an illegal intent" (*In re Michele D.*; PC 207(e)).

Asportation—Movement Required. The asportation (movement) element of simple kidnapping under PC 207 requires *substantial* movement. *People v. Stanworth*, 11 C3d 588. No specific distance will necessarily meet this requirement, but movement of 90 feet was held inadequate in *People v. Green*, 27 C3d 1. Asportation of one-half block was ruled substantial in *People v. Scott* 221 C3d 1243.

Multiple Offenses—PC 654. Where a victim was dragged into a truck by two individuals, who later stopped to purchase some beer, and then drove for some twenty minutes before raping the victim, the codefendants were convicted of both simple kidnapping and rape (*People v. Fields*, 190 Cal. App. 2d 515). However, where a kidnapping, though complete before the crime of rape was committed, was incidental to and a means of accomplishing the rape, a defendant, under the multiple punishment rule of PC 654, can be punished only for the most serious crime that of rape, in this case (*People v. Nelson*, 233 Cal. App. 2d 440).

Punishment for Kidnapping—PC 208. Kidnapping is a felony punishable by imprisonment in the state prison. If the person kidnapped is under the age of 14 at the time of the crime, the state prison penalty is greater, as is the penalty for kidnapping for ransom.

12.4 KIDNAPPING FOR RANSOM—EXTORTION—ROBBERY—RAPE

Kidnapping for Ransom—Extortion—PC 209(a). "Every person who seizes, confines, inveigles, entices, decoys, abducts, conceals, kidnaps, or carries away any individual by any means whatsoever, with intent to hold or detain, or who holds or detains such individual for ransom, reward, or to commit extortion or to exact from another person any money or valuable thing, or any person who aids or abets any such act is guilty of a felony and upon conviction thereof shall be punished by imprisonment in the state prison for life without possibility of parole in cases in which any person subjected to any such act suffers death or bodily harm, or is intentionally confined in a manner which exposes that person to a substantial likelihood of death, or shall be punished by imprisonment in the state prison for life with possibility of parole in cases where no such person suffers death or bodily harm."

Kidnap for Robbery or Sex Crime—PC 209(b). Any person who kidnaps or carries away any individual to commit robbery, rape, spousal rape, oral copulation, sodomy, or sexual penetration in violation of Section 289, shall be punished by imprisonment in the state prison for life with possibility of parole. This subdivision shall apply only if the movement of the victim is beyond that merely incidental to the commission of, and increases the risk of harm to the victim over and above that necessarily in, the intended underlying offense.

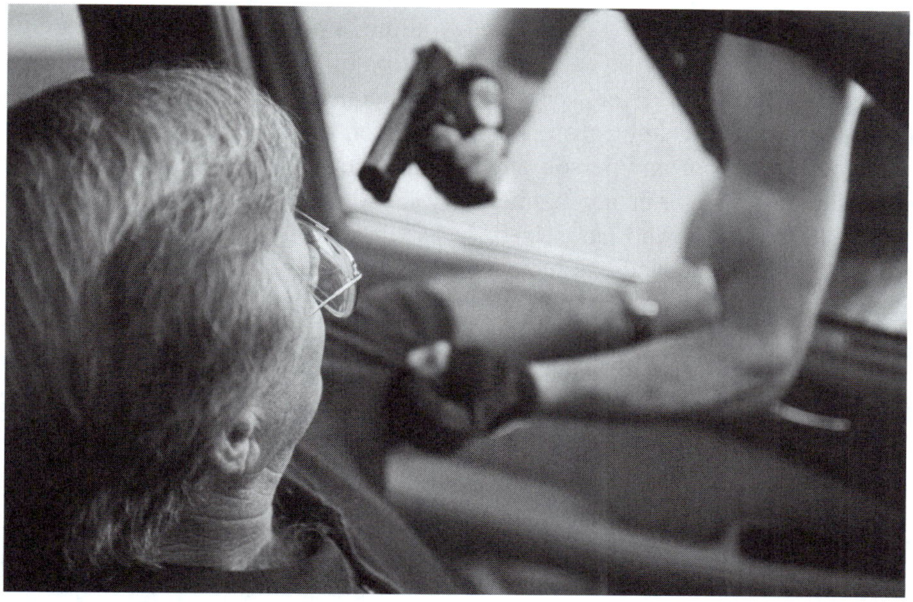

Kidnapping during a carjacking is punishable by imprisonment for life. *Courtesy of Tony Stone Images*

Discussion—Risk of Harm. The term "risk of harm" refers to an increase in the odds that the victim may suffer greater physical injuries (due to forced movement) over and above those to which a victim of a robbery is normally exposed (*People v. Timmons*, 4 Cal. 3d 411). The "risk of harm" test was satisfied when a person was forced to travel over five miles under a threat of imminent injury by a deadly weapon (*People v. Janford*, 63 Cal. App. 3d 952). It was held that movement by car for 10 to 13 blocks was substantial and not merely incidental to the commission of the robbery (*In re Earley*, 14 Cal. 3d 122).

Discussion. Under this section the robbery and kidnapping need not relate to the same person as long as the defendant's purpose was that of accomplishing a robbery. Thus, where one robs a store and thereafter commandeers the driver of a vehicle to effect an escape, the crime is kidnapping for the purpose of robbery. It is sufficient if any of this activity takes place during the course of the kidnapping.

Where the defendant, after robbing a man and his female companion, later forced the woman to submit to an act of oral copulation some distance from where the robbery took place, both acts were held to be within the scope of this statute (*People v. Chessman*, 38 Cal. 2d 494).

Movement From Public to Private Area. Movement of the victim even a short distance from a place open to public view to a secluded area in order to rob or rape is sufficient to constitute the crime of kidnap for robbery or rape. (*People v. Dominguez*)

Bodily Harm Defined. Trivial injuries sustained by the victims held by a robbery suspect in the course of escape were not sufficient to constitute "bodily harm" within the meaning of PC 209 (*People v. Gilbert*, 63 Cal. 2d 690).

"Bodily harm" within the meaning of PC 209 was not intended to include the self-inflicted injuries sustained by the victim in making an escape from custody. However, in a case where a female victim jumped from a moving car being driven by her kidnapper, when he threatened to rape her, the court held that her injuries constituted "bodily harm" under PC 209 (*People v. Monk*, 56 Cal. 2d 288).

Kidnap for Carjacking—PC 209.5. Kidnapping in the commission of carjacking is punishable by life imprisonment with parole. Movement of the victim must be more than incidental to the carjacking, must be a "substantial distance", and must subject the victim to increased risk of harm.

12.5 EXTORTION BY POSING AS KIDNAPPER

Posing as Kidnapper—PC 210. "Every person who for the purpose of obtaining any ransom or reward, or to extort or exact from any person any money or thing of value, poses as, or in any manner represents himself to be a person who has seized, confined, inveigled, enticed, decoyed, abducted, concealed, kidnapped or carried away any person, or who poses as, or in any manner represents himself to be a person who holds or detains such person, or who poses as, or in any manner represents himself to be a person who has aided or abetted any such act, or who poses as or in any manner represents himself to be a person who has the influence, power, or ability to obtain the release of such person so seized, confined, inveigled, enticed, decoyed, abducted, concealed, kidnapped or carried away, is guilty of a felony and upon conviction thereof shall be punished by imprisonment [in the state prison]."

Discussion. This statute is obviously applicable to those who pose as the real kidnappers in a case, and indicate the ability to obtain release of the victim for some consideration, usually money. Any person who, though not connected with the actual kidnapping, makes some false pretense that he or she in fact was connected with the crime and, as such, has the ability to release the kidnapped person for some consideration is punishable under this section. PC 210 requires proof that the perpetrator was posing as a kidnapper with *specific intent* of extorting something of value.

This section does not prohibit someone who, in good faith, and who has had no part or connection with a kidnapping, from offering to rescue or obtain the release of a kidnap victim for financial consideration.

12.6 CHILD ABDUCTION

Child Stealing—PC 278. Every person, *not* having a right of custody, who maliciously takes, entices away, detains, or conceals any minor child with intent to detain or conceal such child from a parent, guardian, or public agency having lawful charge of such child is guilty of a felony (wobbler).

Violation of Custody—PC 278.5. This section makes it a felony (wobbler) to violate the custody or visitation provisions of a court custody order by taking or concealing a child with intent to deprive another person of his or her rights to physical custody or visitation.

Protective Custody—PC 279.6. This section allows a peace officer investigating a report of violation of PC 278 or 278.5, to take a minor child into protective custody if it reasonably appears to the officer that any person unlawfully will flee the jurisdiction with the minor child.

A child who has been detained or concealed shall be returned to the person or agency having lawful charge of the child, or to the court or probation department in the county in which the victim resides.

Any expenses incurred in returning the child shall be reimbursed as provided in Section 3234 of the Family Code. Such costs shall be assessed against any defendant convicted of a violation of any of these sections.

Discussion. The legislative intent of PC 278 or 278.5 is to protect either parent against worry and grief which necessarily follow decoying away and retaining of their children—often by the other parent. The essence of the offense of child stealing consists of the taking and enticing away of a minor child with the *specific intent* to detain or conceal such child from the person having legal charge of it, thus depriving them of their custody rights (*People v. Black*, 147 Cal. 426).

The crime of child abduction is complete the moment that one transports a child from the environs of its own home with the intent to detain and conceal it from its parents or legal guardians (*People v. Wisecarver*, 67 Cal. App. 2d 203).

Concealment of Child Pursuant to Adoption Proceeding—PC 280. Every person who willfully causes or permits the removal or concealment of any child in violation of Section 8713, 8803 or 8910 of the Family Code (adoption procedures) is guilty of a misdemeanor if the child is concealed elsewhere in the state. The offense is a felony (wobbler) if the child is taken outside the state.

Discussion. Cases of this type usually occur as a result of disputes between the Welfare Department and foster parents or among relatives. Children of unwed mothers are frequently subject to the purview of this section.

Adoption Brokerage—PC 273. It is a misdemeanor for any person or agency to pay, offer to pay, or receive, a fee for arranging an adoption (other than through an attorney, licensed adoption service, or social services department), or for a parent to accept financial aid for maternity expenses under fraudulent pretenses.

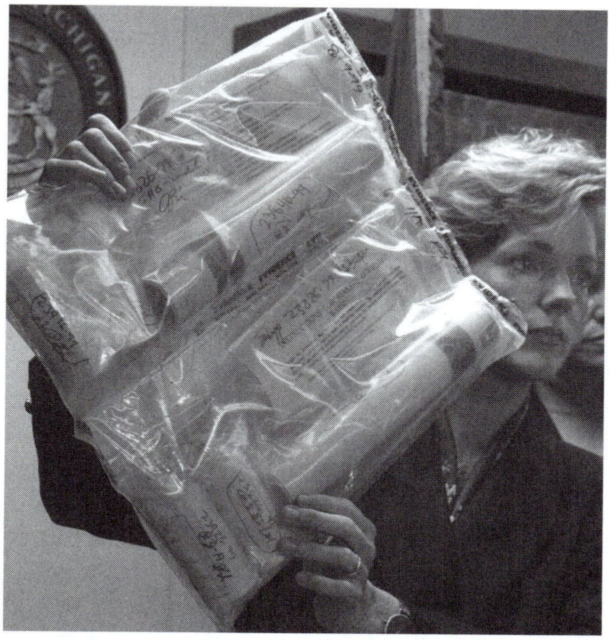

The use of so-called "date rape" drugs to overcome resistance does not change the criminal nature of nonconsensual sex. (Shown: courtroom exhibition of kits used for manufacturing "date rape" drugs). *Photograph by Paul Warner, courtesy of AP/Wide World Photos*

Child Enticement. An adult stranger over 21 years of age who contacts or communicates with a minor 12 years of age or younger and reasonably known to be so, for the purpose of luring the minor away from the parents' or guardians' custody or other known whereabouts, without express parental consent and with intent to avoid consent, is guilty of an infraction or a misdemeanor (PC 272(b)(1)).

12.7 RAPE

Rape Defined—PC 261. (a) Rape is an act of sexual intercourse accomplished with a person *not* the spouse of the perpetrator, under any of the following circumstances:

1. Where a person is incapable, because of a mental disorder or developmental or physical disability, of giving legal consent, and this is known or reasonably should be known to the person committing the act.
2. Where it is accomplished against a person's will by means of force, violence, duress, menace, or fear of immediate and unlawful bodily injury on the person or another.

   As used here "duress" means a direct or implied threat of force, violence, danger, hardship, or retribution sufficient to coerce a reasonable person of ordinary susceptibilities to perform an act which otherwise would not have been performed, or acquiesce (comply) in an act to which one otherwise would not have submitted. "Menace" means any threat, declaration or act which shows an intention to inflict an injury upon another.
3. Where the person is prevented from resisting by any intoxicating or anesthetic substance, or any controlled substance, and this condition was known, or reasonably should have been known by the accused.
4. Where a person is at the time unconscious of the nature of the act, and this is known to the accused.

   As used here, "unconscious of the nature of the act" means incapable of resisting because the victim meets one of the following conditions:
   a. Was unconscious or asleep.
   b. Was not aware, knowing, perceiving or cognizant that the act occurred.
   c. Was not aware, knowing, perceiving, or cognizant of the essential characteristics of the act due to the perpetrator's fraud in fact.
   d. Was unaware of the essential characteristics of the act because of the perpetrator's fraudulent misrepresentation of a professional purpose for the act of intercourse.
5. Where a person submits under the belief that the person committing the act is the victim's spouse, and this belief is induced by any artifice, pretense, or concealment practiced by the accused, with intent to induce this belief.
6. Where the act is accomplished against the victim's will by threatening to retaliate in the future against the victim or any other person, and there is a reasonable possibility that the perpetrator will execute the threat.

   As used here, "threatening to retaliate" means a threat to kidnap or falsely imprison, or to inflict extreme pain, serious bodily injury, or death.
7. Where the act is accomplished against the victim's will by threatening to use the authority of a public official to incarcerate, arrest, or deport the victim or another, and the victim has a reasonable belief that the perpetrator is a public official.

As used here, "public official" means a person employed by a governmental agency who has the authority, as part of that position, to arrest or deport another. The perpetrator does not actually have to be a public official.

Penetration Sufficient to Complete Crime—PC 263. The essential guilt of rape consists in the outrage to the person and feelings of the victim. Any sexual penetration, however slight, is sufficient to complete the crime. The law does not require that the penetration be of the *victim's* body. Therefore, it would be rape, for example, for a female to arouse a male and force penetration of her own body against his will. Even if a person initially consents, if the act forcibly continues after consent is withdrawn during intercourse, rape is committed (In re John Z., 29 Cal.4th 756).

No Corroboration Required. A conviction for rape may be had upon the uncorroborated testimony of the victim. PC 1111 (which requires corroboration of an accomplice's testimony) does not apply in rape cases since the person attacked is not an accomplice but a victim. PC 1108 also does not apply since that section has to do with corroborating a victim's testimony in cases of abortion and seduction for purposes of prostitution (*People v. Frye*, 117 Cal. App. 2d 101).

Discussion. Many think of rape primarily as a "sex crime." Rape is much more aptly described as a hostile personal assault against a victim by an assailant who is giving vent to deep-seated hostility and hatred, often of women. Many rapes have few aspects having anything to do with sexual attraction. Many female victims, for example, are extremely elderly and physically infirm; offering little in the way of "sex appeal" as we normally think of the term. Other victims are so very young and undeveloped physically, the same could be said of them relative to psychologically mature sex appeal.

In many cases, the assailant beats, mutilates, abuses and even murders the victim. None of these acts has any relationship to sex, *per se.* One occasionally reads of rapes where the victim is the assailant's mother; again demonstrating what current psychologists tell us: that rape is not a crime involving sexual satisfaction on the part of the rapist in the traditional sense. Interviews with convicted rapists further substantiate the fact that their greatest "thrill" came from stalking and demeaning their victim.

Many rapists admit that they do not experience sexual gratification or satisfaction in any traditional sense. A domination and demeaning of the victim for the purpose of releasing latent deep-seated feelings of hatred of and hostility toward women is the real purpose of attack in forcible rape crimes.

Victim of Unsound Mind—PC 261(a)(1). This subdivision provides that the act of intercourse is rape where the person is incapable of consenting by reason of an unsound mind, and the assailant knows or should know this. Under this subsection, even though the victim submits or assents to the act, but is unable to comprehend its true meaning, or the moral significance and probable consequences of the acts it is no defense (*People v. Perry*, 26 Cal. App. 143).

Where a twenty-two year old female with the mentality of one twelve years of age gave a childish explanation for consenting to an act of sexual relations with the defendant, his conviction under this section was upheld (*People v. Boggs*, 107 Cal. App. 492).

Forcible Rape—PC 261(a)(2). The key element here is that the victim's resistance is overcome by the perpetrator. The California courts no longer follow the rule that the victim must resist to the utmost as it was at common law. It is now sufficient merely to show nonconsent by the victim to the sexual act.

"Force," for purposes of the rape statute, does not require proof that it be "substantially different or greater than that necessary to accomplish the act itself." It need merely be shown that the act of intercourse was against the will of the victim (*People v. Griffin,* 33 Cal.4th 1015).

Consent to intercourse induced by fear is no consent at all, and when a victim reasonably determines that he or she cannot resist without peril to his or her life, or the safety of others, no further resistance is demanded by the law (*People v. Hinton*, 166 Cal. App. 846).

Threats of Bodily Harm. Threats made to the victim in an effort to cause the victim to submit to an act of sexual intercourse need not be accompanied by the use of a weapon, but must be such as would indicate to the victim the immediate possibility of making good the threats made.

A conviction for rape by threat was sustained where the defendant held a knife to the victim's throat and threatened to kill her child, and where the victim offered no resistance and was given permission to use a contraceptive to avoid possible pregnancy (*People v. Blankenship*, 171 Cal. App. 2d 66).

Resistance. Under PC 261(a)(2), forcible rape, the extent to which the victim must resist is a determination for the victim to make under the existing circumstances, and she is required to go no further than is necessary to make clear her unwillingness to yield to the perpetrator (*People v. Blankenship*, above). The victim's request that the defendant use a condom is not sufficient to constitute consent to rape or other forcible sex acts (PC 261.7).

Rape by Intoxicants—Anesthetics—Drugs—PC 261(a)(3). Relative to the victim's resistance being overcome by an intoxicant, anesthetic, or any controlled substance, the key phrase in this subsection is "administered by or with the 'privity' of the accused." The term "privity" as used here means "without joint knowledge," or "without the awareness of one of the parties." If the victim, for example, is *voluntarily* so drunk that she is unconscious of the nature of the act, this subsection does not apply, but PC 261(a)(4), below, does.

Evidence was sufficient to sustain a conviction of rape by use of drugs given by a doctor during a medical examination (*People v. Wojahn*, 169 Cal. App. 2d 135).

Victim Unconscious of Nature of Act—PC 261(a)(4). This section punishes one who knowingly takes advantage of a victim who, for whatever reason, is unconscious of the nature of the act. Such a state may be voluntary or involuntarily induced by ingestion of intoxicants or drugs. Such cases may be likened somewhat to PC 261(a)(2) (victim of unsound mind), in that no consent can be given by the victim because in her state of mind she does not possess the power of informed, voluntary consent.

Rape by Fraud—PC 261(a)(5). The leading case in California relative to this section is *People v. McCoy*, (58 Cal. App. 534). In this case, the female was the victim of a "mock marriage" arranged by the male and entered into in good faith by the female. All subsequent acts of sexual relations would constitute a violation of this section up to a six-year period, which is the statute of limitations on rape. Thus, this section provides that where fraud is perpetrated, such a fraud precludes the existence of consent as a matter of law.

Threatened Retaliation—PC 261(a)(6). This subdivision is similar to PC 261(a)(2), except that the victim's resistance is overcome by fear for her safety, or that of another, in the *future* if she does not cooperate. A threat to injure the victim's child at a later date would suffice. Consent to sexual relations induced by threats to retaliate for resisting is not legal consent in any sense of the word. It must appear to the victim that there is a reasonable possibility that the perpetrator will execute his threat.

Threatening to Arrest—Deport—PC 261(a)(7). This subdivision describes a rape where the victim's resistance is overcome by threatening to use the authority of a "public official" to have her (or another) arrested or deported. The assailant may be a governmental employee, but such is not necessary, if the victim has reasonable belief that he is a public official who has the authority to arrest or deport.

Punishment for Rape—PC 264. Rape, as defined in PC 261 is a felony punishable by imprisonment in the state prison.

Aiding and Abetting Rape—PC 264.1. In any case in which the defendant, voluntarily acting in concert with another person, by force or violence and against the will of the victim, committed an act described in PC 261 (rape) or PC 289 (penetration of genital or anal opening by foreign object), either personally or by aiding and abetting the other person, the defendant is punishable by imprisonment in state prison.

Rape by Instrument—PC 289. Forcible, nonconsensual penetration of a person's anal or genital opening by foreign object, for the purpose of sexual arousal, gratification or abuse, is a felony. The foreign object could be a part of the body, except a sexual organ (PC 289(l)).

Penetration of a Cadaver—H&S 7052. It is a felony to commit an act of sexual penetration of the mouth, vagina or anus or to orally copulate the genitals of a dead body, for arousal, gratification or abuse.

12.8 RAPE OF SPOUSE

Spousal Rape—PC 262. Rape of a person who is the spouse of a perpetrator is an act of sexual intercourse accomplished under any of the following circumstances:

1. Where it is accomplished against a person's will by means of force, violence, menace, or fear of immediate and unlawful bodily injury on the person or another.

   As used here, means a direct or implied threat of force, violence, danger, or retribution sufficient to coerce a reasonable person of ordinary susceptibilities to perform an act which otherwise would not have been performed, or acquiesce (comply) in an act to which one otherwise would not have submitted. "Menace" means any threat, declaration, or act that show an intention to inflict an injury upon another. ***Note:*** The total circumstances, including the age of the victim, and his or her relationship to the defendant, are factors to consider in apprising the existence of .
2. Where a person is prevented from resisting by any intoxicating or anesthetic substance, or any controlled substance, administered by or with the knowledge of the accused.
3. Where the person is at the time unconscious of the nature of the act, and this is known to the accused. As used here, "unconscious of the nature of the act" means incapable of resisting because the victim meets one of the following conditions:
   a. Was unconscious or asleep.
   b. Was not aware, knowing, perceiving, or cognizant that the act occurred.
   c. Was not aware, knowing perceiving, or cognizant of the essential characteristics of the act due to the perpetrator's fraud in fact.

4. Where the act is accomplished against the victim's will by threatening to retaliate in the future against the victim or any other person, and there is a reasonable possibility that the perpetrator will execute the threat.

   As used here, "threatening to retaliate" means a threat to kidnap or falsely imprison, or to inflict extreme pain, serious bodily injury, or death.
5. Where the act is accomplished against the victim's will by threatening to use the authority of a public official to incarcerate, arrest, or deport the victim or another, and the victim has a reasonable belief that the perpetrator is a public official.

   As used here, "public official" means a person employed by a governmental agency who has the authority, as part of that position, to arrest or deport another. The perpetrator does not actually have to be a public official.

Penetration Sufficient to Complete Crime—PC 263. Any sexual penetration, however slight, is sufficient to complete the crime.

Punishment for Spousal Rape—PC 264. Rape as defined in PC 262 is a felony punishable by imprisonment in the state prison. ***Note:*** If probation is granted, the condition of probation may include, in lieu of a fine, one or both of the following requirements:

1. That defendant pay up to $1,000 to a battered women's shelter and
2. reimburse the victim for reasonable cost of counseling and other reasonable expenses that the court finds are the direct result of the defendant's offense (PC 262(e).

Victim's Marital Status and Gender. Formerly a wife could not be raped by her husband, nor could a man be the victim of rape. With the addition of PC 262 (rape of spouse) and the rewording of PC 261 (rape of a *person*), the law has changed. Either a male or female may be the victim of rape and the crime can be committed by either spouse against the other spouse or any other person.

12.9 UNLAWFUL SEXUAL INTERCOURSE

Unlawful Sexual Intercourse Defined—PC 261.5. Unlawful sexual intercourse is an act of sexual intercourse accomplished with a person not the spouse of the perpetrator, where the victim is under the age of eighteen years.

Penetration Sufficient to Complete Crime—PC 263. Any sexual penetration, however slight, is sufficient to complete the crime.

Discussion. PC 261.5 defines what is sometimes known as "statutory rape" and is distinguished from other forms of rape in that the consent and willing participation of the victim is neither an excuse nor a defense. The law makes it legally impossible for a person under eighteen years of age to consent to an act of sexual intercourse, except with a spouse. Sexual intercourse with a person under the age of 18 who is *not* the spouse of the perpetrator, is "unlawful sexual intercourse" and a violation of PC 261.5, even if the victim consents. If the victim does *not* consent, but his or her resistance is overcome by any of the means or conditions described in PC 261 (subsections 1-7), the crime is rape regardless of the victim's age.

Apparent Age of Victim a Defense. In the landmark case of *People v. Hernandez*, (61 Cal. 2d 537), a good faith belief that the victim was eighteen years of age or over, based on the way she dressed, her obvious physical maturity, coupled with the fact that the victim lied about her age was ruled a defense to this crime.

If a jury finds that the defendant in an unlawful sexual intercourse case did not really believe that the consenting victim was over the statutory age of consent, or that if the defendant believed that the victim was over eighteen years, defendant was not acting as a reasonable person in view of the circumstances, there may be a conviction for PC 261.5 (*People v. Winters*, 242 Cal. App. 880).

Sexual intercourse with a female who was under age eighteen and who was not the defendant's wife, constituted the crime of unlawful sexual intercourse, even though the female was a married woman (*People v. Courtney*, 180 Cal. App. 2d 61).

The fact that a previously married female under eighteen years of age may enter into a second marriage without parental consent, does not mean that she can consent to an illicit act of sexual intercourse, and she is a legitimate victim of "statutory rape" (*Courtney*, above).

Fornication. Fornication is sexual intercourse between an unmarried male and female, both of whom are 18 years of age or over. There is no statute (law) in California which makes fornication, as described, a crime. The same is true of any other sex act, providing both parties are 18 or over and both knowingly consent to the act. As soon as the element of fraud, force, or any of the factors given in PC 261 are present, the act becomes a crime. However, see "Incest," Section 13.6 of your text.

Punishment 264. Unlawful sexual intercourse, as defined in PC 261.5, is punishable as a felony (wobbler). The offense is a misdemeanor where the age difference is three years or less. If the victim is under 16 and the offender is 21 or older, the crime is a felony, punishable by two, three or four years in prison [PC 261.5(d)]. Civil penalties ranging from $2,000 to $25,000 may also be imposed.

Advocate at Sexual Assault Interview—PC 679.04. A victim of a sexual assault or spousal rape has the right to have a counselor and a friend, relative or other support person of the victim's choice present at any evidentiary, medical or physical examination by law enforcement authorities or defense attorneys.

Victims' DNA Bill of Rights—PC 680. Upon the request of a sexual assault victim, the investigating law enforcement agency may inform the victim of the existence, testing and match of DNA evidence, and shall give written notice before rape kit DNA evidence is destroyed, if the statute of limitation has not expired.

STUDENT REVIEW

TERMINOLOGY DEFINED—CHAPTER 12

Please see the Terminology Quiz at the end of this chapter.

1. Abduct: to kidnap, to wrongfully carry away.
2. Accost: to approach, to solicit, to confront or attack.
3. Artifice: a ruse, deception, trickery.
4. Carnal knowledge: sexual intercourse, sexual contact with another.
5. Carry away: kidnapping, moving victim any distance whatever.
6. Castration: removal of testicles.
7. Coroner: official with duty to determine cause of unusual deaths.
8. Grand Jury: body sworn to investigate crime and county government.
9. Indictment: formal accusation of crime by Grand Jury.
10. Kidnapping: carrying away another unlawfully; usually for ransom.
11. Libel: malicious publication injurious to reputation.
12. Maiming: to mutilate, cripple, to render imperfect.
13. Personal property: money, goods, animals, clothing, vehicles.
14. Privileged communication: conversation with spouse, attorney, doctor.
15. Probation: conditional release in lieu of sentencing.
16. Repudiate: refuse to accept, to deny or reject.
17. Robbery: taking personal property by force or fear.
18. Shanghaiing: slang for type of kidnapping, usually for servitude.
19. Trespass: entry upon another's land without permission.
20. Surreptitious: secretive, clandestine, stealth.

TRUE-FALSE QUIZ—CHAPTER 12

After reading this chapter you should be able to correctly answer the following items.

___ 1. The crime of kidnapping is applicable to both persons and property.
___ 2. Premeditation is a necessary element which must be proven in kidnapping.
___ 3. A police officer who is in "fresh pursuit" of a felon from another state is guilty of kidnapping if he catches the suspect in California and returns him without first arraigning him in California.
___ 4. Not all movement of a victim from one place to another constitutes kidnapping.
___ 5. The taking or imprisonment of the victim must be against the victim's will to constitute child stealing under PC 278.
___ 6. Overcoming a woman's resistance to having sex by threatening to use the authority of a public official to deport her constitutes rape.
___ 7. Compelling a cab driver against his will to take someone to another part of town constitutes kidnapping.
___ 8. Enticing one by false promises for purposes of keeping them for prostitution or involuntary servitude constitutes kidnapping.
___ 9. The crime of kidnapping is complete where one willingly accompanied the accused but was subsequently restrained from leaving by force.
___10. It is the fact of movement, not the distance of forcible removal, which constitutes kidnapping under the *Daniels* rule.
___11. Kidnapping is no longer applicable to robberies in which the movement of the victim is merely incidental to the robbery.

____12. If the victim does not suffer bodily harm, the penalty for kidnapping is life imprisonment without possibility of parole.
____13. False imprisonment is the unlawful violation of the personal liberty of another.
____14. The police are protected against false arrest and imprisonment charges when the officer accepts a private person's arrestee.
____15. Generally, a man cannot be found guilty of committing rape on his own wife.
____16. The element of force or fear is required in the crime of unlawful sexual intercourse.
____17. Both men and women can be the victims of rape.
____18. It is legally possible for a female to be found guilty of the rape of another female.
____19. It is a crime (unlawful sexual intercourse) for a man to have sex with a consenting 17 year old female who is married to another.
____20. A conviction for rape may *not* legally be had on the uncorroborated testimony of the victim.

ESSAY-DISCUSSION ITEMS—CHAPTER 12

After reading this chapter you should be able to correctly answer the following items.

1. Does kidnapping (PC 207) require general or specific intent? Must the victim be moved? If so, how far?
2. What activities come under the purview of PC 210 (posing as kidnapper)? Is the crime a felony or misdemeanor?
3. What are the elements of child abduction (PC 278)? What effect does consent of the child have?
4. What is the difference in elements between felony and misdemeanor false imprisonment under PC 236–237?
5. Briefly explain the minimum restraint and confinement necessary to constitute false imprisonment.
6. What is "constructive force" as it applies in rape cases?
7. Discuss the legal effect in unlawful sexual intercourse cases when the suspect believes the victim is eighteen or over even though she is not.
8. What degree of force is necessary to constitute "forcible rape" under PC 261(a)(2)? What degree of resistance is required of the female?
9. Discuss whether or not a subject can be guilty of raping another by use of alcoholic beverages. Must alcohol be given to her involuntarily? Must the victim be passed out to constitute a crime?
10. Under what circumstances, if any, may a female be found guilty of rapes?
11. Discuss: The California Supreme Court has ruled that even if an act of sexual intercourse begins consensually, it becomes rape at the point where one person withdraws consent and tells the other person to stop. What problems would investigation and prosecution of such cases involve?

TERMINOLOGY QUIZ—CHAPTER 12

Match terms and definitions by writing the number preceding the correct term in the appropriate brackets.

Terms	*Definitions*
1. Abduct	[ ] formal accusation of crime by Grand Jury
2. Accost	[ ] mutilate, cripple, to render imperfect
3. Artifice	[ ] conditional release in lieu of sentencing
4. Carnal knowledge	[ ] taking a person prisoner for ransom
5. Carry away	[ ] to kidnap, to wrongfully carry away
6. Castration	[ ] entry upon another's lands without permission
7. Coroner	[ ] malicious publication injurious to reputation

8. Grand Jury
9. Indictment
10. Kidnapping
11. Libel
12. Maiming
13. Personal property
14. Privileged communication
15. Probation
16. Repudiate
17. Robbery
18. Shanghaiing
19. Trespass
20. Surreptitious

[ ] to approach, to solicit, to confront
[ ] refuse to accept, to deny or reject
[ ] a ruse, deception or trickery
[ ] sexual intercourse with another
[ ] slang for type of kidnapping
[ ] taking personal property by force or fear
[ ] secretive, clandestine, stealth
[ ] money, goods, animals, clothing, vehicles

CHAPTER 13

PUBLIC SAFETY AND MORALS

13.1 OBSCENE MATTER

Definitions—PC 311. As used in this chapter, the following definitions shall control the meaning of the respective terms: (a) *'Obscene matter'* means matter, taken as a whole, which to the average person, applying contemporary statewide standards, appeals to the prurient [lewd] interest, and is matter which, taken as a whole, depicts or describes in a patently offensive way sexual conduct; and which taken as a whole lacks serious literary, artistic, political, or scientific value.

(1) When it appears from the nature of the matter or the circumstances of its dissemination, distribution or exhibition that it is designed for clearly defined deviant sexual groups, the appeal of the matter shall be judged with reference to its intended recipient group.

(2) In prosecutions under this chapter, where circumstances of production, presentation, sale, dissemination, distribution, or publicity indicate that matter is being commercially exploited by the defendant for the sake of its prurient appeal, such evidence is probative [tending to prove] with respect to the nature of the matter and can justify the conclusion; that the matter lacks significant literary, artistic, political, or scientific value.

(3) In determining whether the matter taken as a whole lacks serious literary, artistic, political, or scientific value in description or representation of such matters, the fact that the defendant knew that the matter depicts persons under the age of 16 years engaged in sexual conduct, as defined in subdivision (c) of Section 311.4, is a factor which can be considered in making that determination.

(b) 'Matter' means any book, magazine, newspaper, or other printed or written material or any picture, drawing, photograph, motion picture, or other pictorial representation or any statue or other figure, or any recording transcription or mechanical, chemical, or electrical reproduction or any other articles, equipment, machines, or material. 'Matter' also means live or recorded telephone messages when transmitted, disseminated, or distributed as part of a commercial transaction.

(c) 'Person' means any individual, partnership, firm, association, corporation, or other legal entity.

(d) 'Distribute' means to transfer possession of, whether with or without consideration.

(e) 'Knowing' means being aware of the character of the matter or live conduct.

(f) 'Exhibit' means to show.

(g) 'Obscene live conduct' means any physical human body activity, whether performed or engaged in alone or with other persons, including but not limited to singing, speaking, dancing, acting, simulating, or pantomiming, taken as a whole, which to the average person, applying contemporary statewide standards is to the prurient interest, and is conduct which taken as a whole depicts or describes in a patently offensive way sexual conduct and which taken as a whole, lacks serious literary, artistic, political, or scientific value.

(1) When it appears from the nature of the conduct or the circumstances of its production, presentation or exhibition that it is designed for clearly defined deviant sexual groups, the appeal of the conduct shall be judged with reference to its intended recipient group.

(2) In prosecutions under this chapter, where circumstances of production, presentation, advertising, or exhibition indicate that live conduct is being commercially exploited by the defendant for the sake of its prurient appeal, such evidence is probative with respect to the nature of the conduct and can justify the conclusion that the conduct lacks serious literary, artistic, political, or scientific value.

(3) In determining whether the live conduct taken as a whole lacks serious literary, artistic, political or scientific value in description or presentation

of such matters the fact that the defendant knew that the live conduct depicts persons under the age of 16 years engaged in sexual conduct, as defined in PC 311.4(c) is a factor which can be considered in making that determination [section summarized].

Discussion—PC 311. "Obscene matter" means that which when judged by the average person, and applying current statewide standards, appeals predominantly to a shameful or morbid (deviant) interest in sex, nudity, or body excrement. It is also matter which goes considerably beyond our customary limits of candor and frankness. Obscene matter must be judged on the whole and must lack serious literary, artistic, political, or scientific value. It must also portray sexual conduct in an offensive way, as judged by the average person applying contemporary statewide standards. All of the judgements, discussed above, are decisions for the trier of fact [judge or jury] to make.

Child Pornography. Knowingly possessing producing or distributing obscene matter depicting unemancipated children under 18, simulating or engaging in sexual conduct, is a wobbler.

Sale or Distribution of Obscene Matter—PC 311.2. "(a) Every person who knowingly sends or causes to be sent, or brings or causes to be brought, into this state for sale or distribution, or in this state possesses, prepares, publishes, or prints, with intent to distribute or to exhibit to others, or who offers to distribute, distributes, or exhibits to others, any obscene matter is for a first offense, guilty of a misdemeanor." (Subsequent violations may be punished by fines up to $50,000, and by jail.)

(b) This subdivision is very similar to PC 311.2(a), above. There are, however, three differences. PC 311.2(b) applies: (1) to *commercial* preparation, sale, possession, etc., of obscene matter, (2) which the accused knows, depicts a person *under the age of 18* years personally engaging in, or personally simulating sexual conduct, as defined in Section 311.4, and (3) it is a felony on the first offense.

(c) This subdivision is similar to PC 311.2(b), except that it applies to obscene matter depicting a person *under the age of 17*, which the perpetrator intends to distribute, etc., to persons *18 or over.* Violation is a felony (wobbler).

(d) This subdivision is similar to (b) and (c), above, except that it applies to obscene matter which the accused intends to *distribute to* or exchange with persons *under 18* years of age. To be guilty of this subdivision, the perpetrator must know the matter depicts a person under the age of 17 years personally engaging in or personally simulating sexual conduct as defined in PC 311.4(d). Violation of this subsection is a felony. It is not necessary to prove commercial consideration or that the matter is obscene in order to establish a violation of this subsection.

Crime and Trial News on the Internet. For current news articles go to: **http://news.findlaw.com/legalnews/crime/.** To find specific articles not listed, enter key words in the "Search News" box on your screen. For example, enter "child porn" to read about a Washington teacher convicted in a child pornography case.

Exceptions—PC 311.2(e). Subdivisions (a) to (d), inclusive, do not apply to law enforcement and prosecuting agencies in the investigation and prosecution of criminal offenses. They, also, are not applicable to legitimate medical, scientific, or educational activities, or to lawful conduct between spouses.

Exceptions—PC 311.2(f). PC 311.2 does not apply to matter which depicts a child under the age of 18, if the child is *legally emancipated* (free of parental control), or lawful conduct between spouses when one or both are under the age of 18.

Sexual Exploitation of Child—PC 311.3. A person is guilty of sexual exploitation of a child when he or she knowingly develops, duplicates, prints, or exchanges any film, photograph, video tape, negative, or slide, etc., in which a person under the age of 14 years is engaged in an act of sexual conduct.

As used in this section, "sexual conduct" means any of the acts described in PC 311.4(d), below. A first conviction of this offense is a misdemeanor. The crime is a felony if the person has been previously convicted of any section of Penal Code Chapter 7.5 (Obscene Matter).

Employing Minor to Perform Prohibited Acts—PC 311.4. (a) Every person who, with knowledge that a person is a minor, [person under 18] or who, while in possession of any facts on the basis of which he should reasonably know that the person is a minor, hires, employs, or uses such minor to do or assist in doing any of the acts described in Section 311.2, is guilty of a felony (wobbler). A fine not exceeding $50,000 can be added for a second conviction of this section.

(b) Every person who, with knowledge that a person is a minor *under the age of 17 years,* or who, while in possession of such facts that he should reasonably know that such person is a minor under the age of 17 years, knowingly promotes, employs, uses, persuades, induces, or coerces a minor under the age of 17 years, or any parent or guardian of a minor under the age of 17 years under his or her control who knowingly permits such minor, to engage in or assist others to engage in either posing or modeling alone or with others for purposes of preparing a film, photograph, negative, slide, etc., or live performance involving *sexual conduct* by a minor under the age of 17 years alone or with other persons or animals, for *commercial* purposes, is guilty of a felony and shall be punished by imprisonment in the state prison.

(c) This subdivision is the same as PC 311.4(b), above, except that it is not necessary to prove commercial purposes in order to establish a violation. It, also, is a felony.

Sexual Conduct Defined—PC 311.4(d). As used in subdivision (b) and (c), above, "sexual conduct" means any of the following, whether actual or simulated: sexual intercourse, oral copulation, anal intercourse, anal oral copulation, masturbation, bestiality, sexual sadism, sexual masochism, penetration of the vagina or rectum by any object in a lewd or lascivious manner, exhibition of the genitals, pubic or rectal area for the purpose of sexual stimulation of the viewer, any lewd or lascivious sexual act as defined in PC 288, or excretory functions performed in a lewd or lascivious manner, whether or not any of the above conduct is performed alone or between members of the same or opposite sex or between humans and animals.

Simulated Sex Act Defined—PC 311.4(d). "An act is simulated when it gives the appearance of being sexual conduct."

Advertising or Sale of Matter Represented to be Obscene—PC 311.5. "Every person who writes, creates, or solicits the publication or distribution of advertising or other promotional material, or who in any manner promotes the sale, distribution, or exhibition of matter represented or held out by him to be obscene, is guilty of a misdemeanor."

Advertising Known Obscene Matter—PC 311.10. "(a) Any person who advertises for sale or distribution any obscene matter knowing that it depicts a person under the age of 18 years personally engaging in or personally simulating sexual conduct, as defined in Section 311.4, is guilty of a felony and is punishable by imprisonment in the state prison . . .

(b) Subdivision (a) shall not apply to the activities of law enforcement and prosecution agencies in the investigation and prosecution of criminal offenses."

Obscene Live Conduct in Public Prohibited—PC 311.6. "Every person who knowingly engages or participates in, manages, produces, sponsors, presents, or exhibits obscene live conduct to or before an assembly or audience consisting of at least one person or spectator in any public place or in any place exposed to public view, or in any place open to the public or to a segment thereof, whether or not an admission is charged, or whether or not attendance is conditioned upon the presentation of a membership card or other token, is guilty of a misdemeanor."

Defense to Obscene Matter Charge—PC 311.8(a). "It shall be a defense in any prosecution for a violation of this chapter that the act charged was committed in aid of legitimate scientific or educational purposes."

Possession of "Kiddie Porn"—PC 311.11. It is a felony (wobbler) to knowingly possess any matter depicting children younger then eighteen in actual or simulated sexual conduct.

Destruction of Matter—PC 312. This section authorizes the court to order destruction of any obscene matter in possession of the court, district attorney or law enforcement agency, upon conviction of the accused.

Public Urination—PC 370. Urination in public has been held to constitute a public nuisance, in violation of PC 370 (misdemeanor). (*People v. McDonald*)

13.2 HARMFUL MATTER—MINORS

Harmful Matter Defined—PC 313. This section is almost identical to PC 311 (above) except that PC 313 substitutes the words "harmful matter" for "obscene matter" as used in PC 311. "Harmful matter" means matter, taken as a whole, which to the average person, applying contemporary statewide standards, appeals to the prurient interest, and is matter which, taken as a whole, lacks serious literary, artistic, political, or scientific value for minors. A minor is any person under 18 years.

Distribution of Harmful Matter to Minors—PC 313.1. (a) Every person who, with knowledge that a person is a minor, or who fails to exercise reasonable care in ascertaining the true age of a minor, knowingly sells, rents, distributes, sends, causes to be sent, exhibits, or offers to distribute or exhibit by any means, including, but not limited to, live or recorded telephone messages, any harmful matter to the minor shall be punished as specified in Section 313.4 [See pg. 142].

(b) Every person who misrepresents himself to be the parent or guardian of a minor and thereby causes the minor to be admitted to an exhibition of any harmful matter shall be punished as specified in Section 313.4.

(c) Any person who knowingly displays, sells, or offers to sell in any vending machine which is located in a public place, other than a place from which minors are excluded, any harmful matter displaying to the public view photographs or pictorial representations of the commission of any of the following acts shall be punished as specified in Section 313.4: sodomy, oral copulation, sexual intercourse, masturbation, bestiality, or a photograph of an exposed penis in an erect and turgid state.

Exemption of Parent or Guardian—PC 313.2. This section does not prohibit a parent or guardian from distributing "harmful matter" to his child or ward or permitting his child or ward to attend an exhibition of any harmful matter if the child or ward is accompanied by the parent or guardian.

Also, PC 311.2(b) provides that a person is not prohibited from exhibiting any harmful matter to a minor who is accompanied by an adult who represents himself to be the parent or guardian of the minor and who the person by exercise of reasonable care, does not have reason to know is not the parent of guardian of the minor.

Evidence in Prosecution—PC 312.1. "In any prosecution for violation of the provisions of this chapter or of Chapter 7.6 (commencing with Section 313), neither the prosecution nor the defense shall be required to introduce expert witness testimony concerning the obscene or harmful character of the matter or live conduct which is the subject of any such prosecution. Any evidence which tends to establish contemporary community standards of appeal to prurient interest or, of customary limits of candor in the description or representation of nudity, sex, or excretion, or which bears upon the question of significant literary, artistic, political, educational, or scientific value shall, subject to the provisions of the Evidence Code, be admissible when offered by either the prosecution or by the defense."

Scientific or Educational Purposes a Defense—PC 313.3. "It shall be a defense in any prosecution for a violation of this chapter that the act charged was committed in aid of legitimate scientific or educational purposes."

Penalty—PC 313.4. Every person who violates PC 313.1, above, is punishable by a fine or by imprisonment in the county jail, or by both such fine and imprisonment. If a person has been previously convicted of a violation of Section 313.1 or any section of Chapter 7.5 (commencing with Section 311) of Title 9 of Part I of this code, he is punishable by imprisonment in the state prison.

Internet Obscenity—PC 288.2(b). Sending harmful matter to minors via electronic mail or computer online service, for purposes of sexual arousal or gratification, is a felony (wobbler) on first offense, and a straight felony on subsequent convictions.

For interesting supplemental information on this subject, see Web Site: **http://www.talkjustice.com/browse.asp.** At this site, click on *Missing and Abused Children* and *Victims and Victimology.*

13.3 CONTRIBUTING TO DELINQUENCY OF MINOR

Contributing Defined—PC 272. "Every person who commits any act or omits the performance of any duty, which act or omission causes or tends to cause or encourage any person under the age of 18 years to come within the provisions of Sections 300, 601, or 602 of the Welfare and Institutions Code or which act or omission, contributes thereto, or any person who, by any act or omission, or by threats, commands, or persuasion, induces or endeavors to induce any person under the age of 18 years or any ward or dependent child of the juvenile court to fail or refuse to conform to a lawful order of the juvenile court, or to do or to perform any act or to follow any course of conduct or to so live as would cause, or manifestly tend to cause, any such person to become or to remain a person within the provisions of Sections 300, 601, or 602 of the Welfare and Institutions Code, is guilty of a misdemeanor and upon conviction thereof shall be punished by a fine . . . or by imprisonment in a county jail . . . or by both such fine and imprisonment . . . or may be released on probation for a period not exceeding five years."

An adult stranger 21 or older who communicates with a minor under 14 to lure the minor away with intent to avoid parental consent is guilty of an infraction or misdemeanor (PC 272(b)(1)).

Discussion—PC 272. This section makes it a crime to do any act which encourages any minor to do any act or commit any crime which would make them a delinquent under the Welfare and Institutions Code. Such acts could range from encouraging or assisting a minor to run away from home to more serious offenses.

Child Neglect or Abandonment—PC 270. A parent who wilfully and without legal excuse neglects the provision of food, shelter, clothing or medical care is guilty of a misdemeanor. Abandonment or desertion of the child is prima facie proof of violation. However, there is no violation if the parent voluntarily surrenders the child to a hospital within the first 72 hours after birth. (PC 271.5.) A county board of supervisors may designate additional drop-off sites (H&S 1255.7).

Unattended Children in Vehicle—Vehicle Code 15620. A parent, guardian, or other responsible adult who leaves a child 6 or younger inside an unattended vehicle without supervision of someone at least 12 years old commits an infraction ($100 fine) if conditions present a significant risk to health and safety, if the engine is left running, or the keys are left in the ignition.

Smoking with Minor Passenger—HS 118948. It is an infraction (up to $100 fine) for a person to smoke a cigarette, pipe or cigar in a vehicle when occupied by a person under the age of 18. Police may not stop a vehicle solely to determine whether the driver is in violation of this law (HS 118949).

Body Piercing or Tattooing Minors—PC 652, 653. It is an infraction to perform or offer to perform any body piercing on an unemancipated minor under 18, except in the presence of or with the written, notarized consent of the parent or guardian (PC 652). It is a misdemeanor to tattoo or offer to tattoo a person under 18 (PC 653).

13.4 CRIMES AGAINST CHILDREN

Aggravated Sexual Assault of a Child. A person who is ten or more years older than a victim under the age of fourteen who commits a forcible rape, sodomy or oral copulation is guilty of a felony, punishable by 15 years to life in prison (PC 269).

Lewd Acts Against Children—PC 288(a). "Any person who shall willfully and lewdly commit any lewd or lascivious [immoral, indecent] act including any of the acts constituting other crimes provided for in Part I of this code upon or with the body, or any part or member thereof, of a child under the age of 14 years, with the intent of arousing, appealing to, or gratifying the lust or passions or sexual desires of such person or of such child, shall be guilty of a felony and shall be imprisoned in the state prison. . . ."

Use of Force or Fear—PC 288(b). "Any person who commits an act described in subdivision (a), by use of force, violence, duress, menace, or fear of immediate and unlawful bodily injury on the victim or another person, shall be guilty of a felony and shall be imprisoned in the state prison. . . ."

Ten Years Older—PC 288(c). Where the victim of a violation of 288(a) is 14 or 15 and the defendant is

Pop star Michael Jackson was acquitted of lewd acts against a child. Celebrity cases often present special challenges to the justice system. *Courtesy of Robert Galbraith/Reuters/ Corbis Images*

at least ten years older than the child, the offense is a felony (wobbler).

Preventing Psychological Harm—PC 288(d). In any arrest or prosecution under this section, the peace officer, the district attorney, and the court shall consider the needs of the child victim and shall do whatever is necessary and constitutionally permissible to prevent psychological harm to the child victim.

Added Penalty—Witness Assistance Fund. PC 288(e) provides that upon conviction of a person for violating subdivisions (a) or (b), above, the court may, in addition to any other penalty, order the defendant to pay an additional fine not to exceed $5,000.

In setting the amount of this fine, the court will consider the gravity of the offense, and whether the defendant derived any economic gain or the victim suffered economic loss. Any fines collected under this enhancement are deposited in the Witness Assistance Fund to be available to fund child abuse counseling centers.

Added Penalty—Sex With Minor for Money—PC 675. A person who is convicted of specified sex crimes against minors (including some acts of unlawful sexual intercourse, sodomy, lewd acts and oral copulation), where the act was committed for money or other consideration, is punishable by an additional year of imprisonment.

Suspension of Sentence—PC 288.1. Any person convicted of committing any lewd or lascivious act with or upon the body of a child under the age of 14 years, shall not have his sentence suspended until the court obtains proof from a reputable psychiatrist as to the mental condition of such person.

Contacting Minor With Lewd Intent—PC 288.4. A person who communicates in any manner with a person reasonably known to be a minor, for the purpose of engaging in specified sex acts or production of pornography involving the minor, is punishable by the sentence specified for an attempt to commit the target crime.

Immoral Practices or Drunkenness in Child's Presence—PC 273g. "Any person who in the presence of any child indulges in any degrading, lewd, immoral or vicious habits or practices, or who is *habitually drunk* in the presence of any child in his care, custody or control, is guilty of a misdemeanor."

Note that an isolated incident of drunkenness is not sufficient for a violation of this section. The drunkenness must be frequent or habitual.

Discussion—Child Molesting—PC 288. This offense, often referred to as "child molesting," consists of committing lewd and lascivious acts upon any part of the body of a child under 14 years with the intent of arousing, appealing to or gratifying the lust or passions or sexual desires of *either* the victim or the perpetrator. In analyzing the statute, it is well to remember the following three things:

1. The sex of the child is immaterial as long as he or she is under 14 (not to be misinterpreted as 14 or under).
2. That portion of the statute which refers to "upon or with the body" indicates that some physical touching is necessary but such touching is not restricted to the private parts.
3. The intent is specific, i.e., to arouse, appeal to, etc., either the victim or the suspect, however, it is not necessary that either actually be aroused as long as the intent is present.

The crime of child molesting may be proven by either direct or circumstantial evidence. Thus, where the physical condition of the child is such as to indicate an obvious physical trauma to the genitals, the *corpus delicti* is sufficiently established *(People v. Smith,* 100 Cal. App. 2d 166).

In crimes against children, punishable under this section, the child is a victim, not an accomplice, since the offense can *only* be perpetrated against one *under* the age of fourteen years and the child's willing consent to such an act is immaterial *(People v. Wilder,* 151 Cal. App. 2d 698).

Proof of the commission of the crime of child molestation may be made circumstantially, and it is not necessary to show that there was any actual arousal of either the passions of the accused or the victim. The specific intent (to arouse) required for a violation of PC 288, may be inferred from the circumstances of the case *(People v. Mansell,* 227 Cal. App. 2d 842). Corroboration of victim's testimony is not necessary in proving acts of a lewd and lascivious nature with a child under the age of 14 years *(People v. Pilgrani,* 215 Cal. App. 2d 374).

Mandatory Reporting—PC 152.3. Any person who reasonably believes that he or she has observed a murder, rape or forcible lewd act where the victim is under the age of 14 is required to make a report to a peace officer. (Misdemeanor.) This provision does not apply to specified close relatives of the victim or offender, or where a reasonable mistake of fact or fear for personal or family safety exists.

In addition, mandated reporters (includes health care providers, school officials, peace officers and firefighters, social workers and others) who knows or reasonably suspects that a child is being abused or neglected must make an immediate report to a designated law enforcement agency or welfare department. Failure to make a mandated report is a misdemeanor (PC 11166(b)).

13.5 SODOMY AND ORAL COPULATION

Sodomy Defined—PC 286. "(a) Sodomy is sexual conduct consisting of contact between the penis of one person and the anus of another person."

Participant under 18—PC 286(b)(1). "Except as provided in PC 288, any person who participates in an act of sodomy with another person who is under 18 years of age shall be punished by imprisonment in the state prison or in a county jail . . . [felony wobbler]."

Participant Under 16—PC 286(b)(2). "Except as provided in PC 288, any person over the age of 21 who participates in an act of sodomy with another person who is under 16 years of age shall be guilty of a felony."

Victim under 14—Force or Fear—PC 286(c). "Any person who participates in an act of sodomy with another person who is under 14 years of age and more than 10 years younger than he or she, or when the act is accomplished against the victim's will by means of force, violence, duress, menace, or fear of immediate and unlawful bodily injury on the victim or another person, or where the act is accomplished against the victim's will by threatening to retaliate in the future against the victim or any other person, and there is a reasonable possibility that the perpetrator will execute the threat shall be punished by imprisonment in the state prison. . . ."

Sex With Child Aged 10 or Younger—PC 288.7. A person aged 18 or older who engages in sexual intercourse or sodomy with a child who is 10 years of age or younger is punishable by a prison term of 25 years to life. A person 18 or older who engages in oral copulation or penetration of the anus or vagina with a foreign object against a child 10 or younger is punishable by imprisonment for 15 years to life.

Aiding and Abetting—Force or Fear—PC 286(d). "Any person who, while voluntarily acting in concert with another person, either personally or by aiding and abetting such other person, commits an act of sodomy when the act is accomplished against the victim's will by means of force or fear of immediate and unlawful bodily injury on the victim or another person, or where the act is accomplished against the victim's will by threatening to retaliate in the future against the victim or any other person, and there is a reasonable possibility that the perpetrator will execute the threat shall be punished by imprisonment in the state prison. . . ."

Participants in State Prison—PC 286(e). "Any person who participates in an act of sodomy with any person of any age while confined in any state prison, as defined in Section 4504, or in any local detention facility, as defined in Section 6031.4, shall be punished by imprisonment in the state prison . . . or in a county jail . . . [felony wobbler]."

Victim Unconscious—PC 286(f). "Any person who commits an act of sodomy and whose victim is at the time unconscious of the nature of the act, and this is known to the person committing the act, shall be punished by imprisonment in the state prison. . . ." The victim may be unconscious of the nature of the act because of sleep or other lack of perception of what is happening, or because of the perpetrator's fraudulent misrepresentations of a professional purpose for the act of sodomy.

Mental or Physical Disability—PC 286(g). "Except as provided in subdivision (h), a person who commits an act of sodomy, and the victim is at the time incapable, because of mental disorder or developmental or physical disability, of giving legal consent, and this is known or reasonably should be known to the person committing the act, shall be punished by imprisonment in the state prison. . . ."

Mental Patients—PC 286(h). This subsection is identical to (g), above, except that it applies when both the victim and the perpetrator are at the time confined in a state hospital for the care and treatment of the mentally disordered. The offense is a felony (wobbler).

Victim Intoxicated or Drugged—PC 286(i). "Any person who commits an act of sodomy, where the victim is prevented from resisting by an intoxicating or anesthetic substance, or any controlled substance, and this condition was known, or reasonably should have been known by the accused, shall be punished by imprisonment in the state prison. . . ."

Victim Believes Perpetrator is Spouse—PC 286(j). "Any person who commits an act of sodomy, where the victim submits under the belief that the person committing the act is the victim's spouse, and this belief is induced by any . . . pretense or concealment practiced by the accused, with intent to induce the belief, shall be punished by imprisonment in the state prison. . . ."

Victim Fears Arrest—PC 286(k). "Any person who commits an act of sodomy, where the act is accomplished against the victim's will by threatening to use the authority of a public official to incarcerate, arrest, or deport the victim or another and the victim has a reasonable belief that the perpetrator is a public official, shall be punished by imprisonment in the state prison. . . ."

Threat to Retaliate Defined—PC 286(1). "As used in subdivisions (c) and (d) [above] 'threatening to retaliate' means a threat to kidnap or falsely imprison, or inflict extreme pain, serious bodily injury, or death."

Penetration Defined—PC 286(a). "Any sexual penetration, however slight, is sufficient to complete the crime of sodomy."

Oral Copulation Defined—PC 288a. "(a) Oral copulation is the act of copulating the mouth of one person with the sexual organ or anus of another person."

Penal Code Section 288a (oral copulation) reads identically to PC 286 (sodomy) except, of course, for the term "oral copulation" used in PC 288a and "sodomy" used in PC 286. Except for the specific act, all the other elements of both crimes are the same. A violation of any of the following subsections is a felony.

Participant Under 18—PC 288a(b)(1). Any person who participates in an act of oral copulation with another person who is under 18 years of age is guilty of a felony (wobbler).

Participant Under 16—PC 288a(b)(2). Except as provided in PC 288 (child molesting), any person over the age of 21 years who participates in an act of oral copulation with another person who is under 16 years of age shall be guilty of felony (briefed).

Victim Under 14—PC 288a(c). Any person who participates in an act of oral copulation with another person who is under 14 years of age and more than 10 years younger than he or she, or when the act is accomplished against the victim's will by means of force, or fear of immediate bodily injury, or threat of retaliation on the victim or another person, is guilty of a felony (briefed).

Aiding and Abetting—Force or Fear—PC 288a(d). Any person who, while voluntarily acting in concert with another person, either personally or by aiding and abetting such other person commits an act of oral copulation (1) when the act is accomplished against the victim's will by means of force or fear of immediate and unlawful bodily injury on the victim or another person, or (2) where the act is accomplished against the victim's will by threatening to retaliate in the future against the victim or another and there is a reasonable possibility that the perpetrator will execute the threat, or (3) where the victim is at the time incapable because of a mental disorder or developmental disability of giving legal consent and this is known to the perpetrator, shall be punished by imprisonment in the state prison.

Prison Inmates—PC 288a(e). Any person who participates in an act of oral copulation while confined in any state prison, as defined in Section 4504, or in any local detention facility, as defined in Section 6031.4, shall be punished by imprisonment in the state prison, or in a county jail (briefed).

Victim Unconscious—PC 288a(f). Any person who commits an act of oral copulation and whose victim is at the time unconscious of the nature of the act, and this is known to the person committing the act, shall be punished by imprisonment in the state prison (briefed). The victim may be unconscious of the nature of the act because of sleep or other lack of perception of what is happening, or because of the perpetrator's fraudulent misrepresentations of a professional purpose for the act of oral copulation.

Victim With Mental Disorder—PC 288a(g). Any person who commits an act of oral copulation, and the victim is at the time incapable, through mental disorder of developmental disability, of giving legal consent and this is known of the person committing the act, shall be punished by imprisonment in the state prison (briefed).

Mental Hospital Patients—PC 288a(h). This section is the same as (g), above, except that it applies when both victim and defendant are confined in a state mental hospital. The offense is a felony (wobbler).

Victim Intoxicated or Drugged—PC 288a(i). This subsection applies where the victim is prevented from resisting by any intoxicant, anesthetic or drug and this condition was known, or reasonably should have been known by the accused. The offense is a felony.

Victim Believes Perpetrator is Spouse—PC 288a(j). This subsection applies where the victim submits under the fraudulently induced belief that the accused is the victim's spouse. The offense is a felony.

Victim Fears Arrest—PC 288a(k). This subsection covers cases where oral copulation is accomplished against the victim's will by threatening to use the authority of a public official to arrest or deport the victim. The offense is a felony.

Threatened Retaliation Defined—PC 288a(l). As used in 288a(c) and (d), above, "threatening to retaliate" means a threat to kidnap or falsely imprison, or to inflict extreme pain, serious bodily injury, or death.

Genital or Anal Penetration by Foreign Object—PC 289. "(a) Every person who causes the penetration, however slight, of the genital or anal opening of another person for the purpose of sexual arousal, gratification, or abuse by any foreign object, substance, instrument, or device when the act is accomplished against the victim's will by means of force, violence, duress, menace, or fear of immediate and unlawful bodily injury on the victim or another person or where the act is accomplished against the victim's will by threatening to retaliate in the future against the victim or any other person, and there is a reasonable possibility that the perpetrator will execute that threat, shall be punished by imprisonment in the state prison. . . ."

Like PC 286 (sodomy), and 288a (oral copulation), PC 289 includes several subsections. Each subsection defines as a crime the act prohibited when accomplished against the victim's will under a variety of circumstances and conditions similar to PC 286 and PC 288a (above).

Custodial Sex—PC 289.6. Any officer or employee of a detention facility who engages in sexual activity with a consenting adult inmate is guilty of a misdemeanor (first offense) or a felony (subsequent convictions).

Foreign Object Defined—PC 289. As used throughout PC 289, "foreign object, substance, instrument, or device," includes any part of the body, except a sexual organ. When it cannot be determined whether penetration was by a penis or other object, the act is punishable by state prison, as specified in PC 289.5.

Assaulting Animals Sexually—PC 286.5. "Any person who sexually assaults any animal protected by Section 597f for the purpose of arousing or gratifying the sexual desire of the person is guilty of a misdemeanor."

13.6 INCEST

Incest Defined—PC 285. "Persons being within the degrees of consanguinity [blood relationship] within which marriages are declared by law to be incestuous and void, who intermarry with each other, or who, being 14 years of age or older, commit fornication or adultery with each other, are punishable by imprisonment in the state prison."

Degrees of Consanguinity Defined. Section 59 of the California Civil Code declares incestuous and void all marriages between parent and child, ancestors and descendants, brothers and sisters of the half or whole blood, uncles and nieces and aunts and nephews, whether the relationship is legitimate or illegitimate. First cousins, therefore, may legally marry in the state of California.

Discussion—Incest. Incest was not a common law crime, but is so declared by statute today. It is simply defined as illicit sexual intercourse between persons who are related within the degrees of consanguinity or affinity wherein marriage is prohibited by law. Prior to 1650, incest was an offense punished by the ecclesiastical (church) courts. In that year it was made a capital offense.

In California, the crime of incest is punished as a felony whenever sexual intercourse is had by a man and a woman who are so nearly related that the law prohibits them from marrying, as in the case of father and daughter, mother and son, or brother and sister, niece and uncle or nephew and aunt. One act of intercourse is enough to constitute the crime. If there is mutual consent, then both parties are guilty and may be prosecuted.

No distinction is made by the law in the crime of incest between relatives of half blood or whole blood. A man who has sexual intercourse with the daughter of his half-sister is guilty of incest *(People v. Wonlack,* 167 Cal. App. 2d 130).

13.7 INDECENT EXPOSURE

Indecent Exposure Defined—PC 314. "Every person who willfully and lewdly, either:

1. Exposes his person, or the private parts thereof in any public place, or in any place where there are present other persons to be offended or annoyed thereby; or,
2. Procures, counsels, or assists any person so to expose himself or take any part in any model artist exhibition, or to make any other exhibition of himself to public view, or the view of any number of persons, such as is offensive to decency, or is adapted to excite to vicious or lewd thoughts, or acts, is guilty of a misdemeanor.

Every person who violates subdivision 1 of PC 314 [above] after having entered, without consent, an inhabited dwelling house or trailer coach as defined in VC 635, or the inhabited portion of any other building, is punishable by imprisonment in the state prison, or in the county jail not exceeding one year.

Upon the second and each subsequent conviction under subdivision 1 of this section, or upon a first conviction under subdivision 1 of this section after previous conviction under Section 288 of this code [lewd acts against children], every person so convicted is guilty of a felony and is punishable by imprisonment in the state prison."

Discussion—Indecent Exposure. Note that indecent exposure is elevated from a misdemeanor to a felony (wobbler) if the perpetrator commits the offense after having entered an inhabited house or trailer coach without consent.

A conviction of PC 314(1), requires proof that the actor not only meant to expose himself, but intended by such conduct to direct public attention to his genitals for the purposes of sexual arousal, gratification, or affront *(In re Birch,* 10 Cal. 3d 314).

Indecent exposure is punishable as a misdemeanor except with a prior conviction, or prior conviction of PC 288 (crimes against children). Both willfulness and lewdness are requisites of this offense. Although no movement or manipulation of the body or body parts is necessary to establish a *prima facie* case, the private parts must be exposed at the time.

Revocation of Teaching Credentials. Education Code, Section 13207, requires a mandatory revocation of a teaching credential for cases involving convictions under this section, PC 647.6 (below), and PC 272 (contributing) (39 *Opinions Attorney General 304).*

13.8 ANNOYING OR MOLESTING CHILDREN

Annoying or Molesting Children—PC 647.6. "Every person who annoys or molests any child under the age of eighteen is punishable by a fine . . . or by imprisonment in the county jail . . . or by both fine and imprisonment.

Every person who violates this section after having entered, without consent, an inhabited dwelling house, or trailer coach as defined in Section 635 of the Vehicle Code, or the inhabited portion of any other building, is punishable by imprisonment in the state prison, or in the county jail . . . " [Section briefed.]

It is also a misdemeanor under this section for an adult to commit such acts on another adult believed to be a child, where motivated by an unnatural sexual interest in children.

Discussion—PC 647.6. The legislative intent of this section is to discourage abnormal sex motivation and conduct on the part of a potential perpetrator. The words "annoy" and "molest" as used within this section have an abnormal and sexual connotation *(People v. Moore,* 137 Cal. App. 2d 197).

The terms "annoy" and "molest" as used here also mean to disturb or irritate, and imply a continued or repeated activity. The terms also have reference to injury, injustice, damage, or some other physical hurt.

Although there is no indication that physical contact is necessary to sustain a conviction for this offense, such acts as physical touching wherein sexual gratification is apparent, would be conducive to a *prima facie* case.

This section prohibiting annoying or molesting any child does not require a physical act as contrasted to an utterance *(People v. Carskaddon,* 170 Cal. App. 2d 45). In order to justify a conviction of this section, it is not necessary to show that the defendant touched the body of the child *(People v. Thompson,* 167 Cal. App. 2d 727). The child, in cases prosecuted under this section, is a victim and not an accomplice and thus his or her testimony need not be corroborated.

It is the objectionable acts of the accused that constitute this offense. Acts characterized as being so lewd or obscene that the normal person would undoubtedly be irritated by them constitute a violation of this section *(People v. Fernandez,* 196 Cal. App. 2d 265).

Harassing Employee's Child—PC 11414. It is a misdemeanor to intentionally harass the child or ward of a person because of that person's employment. "Harassment" means knowing and willful conduct directed at a specific child that seriously alarms, annoys, torments, or terrorizes the child, and that serves no legitimate purpose. The conduct must be such as would cause a reasonable child to suffer substantial emotional distress, and actually cause the victim to suffer substantial emotional distress. Subsequent convictions require specified minimum jail terms.

13.9 LOITERING NEAR SCHOOLS—PUBLIC PLACES

Loitering About Public Places Attended by Children—PC 653b. Every person who loiters about any school or public place at or near which children attend or normally congregate, and who remains at any school or public place at or near which children so attend or congregate or who reenters or returns to such place within 72 hours, after having been asked to leave by the chief administrative official (or his designee) of that school, or by a member of the security patrol of the school district (who has been given authorization in writing), or any peace officer, is a vagrant, and is punishable by a fine or by imprisonment in the county jail, or by both such fine and imprisonment (section briefed).

> **Discussion—Loitering Defined.** The Appellate Court stated that persons who merely sit on park benches, pause in the vicinity of schools, or linger in the many public areas frequented by children cannot reasonably be considered as loitering within the meaning and purpose of the statute. It is only when the loitering is of such a nature that from the totality of the person's actions, and in the light of prevailing circumstances, it may be reasonably concluded that it is being engaged in "for the purpose of committing a crime as opportunity may be discovered" that such conduct falls within the statute. *(People* v. *Huddleson,* 229 Cal. App. 2d 618).

13.10 SEX OFFENDER REGISTRATION

Required Registration—PC 290. This section requires that every person convicted in any state of: (1) assault to commit, (2) actual commission of, or (3) attempt to commit any of the offenses listed below, must register as a sex offender. They must register with the chief of police or sheriff within 5 days of coming into the city or county. Also, they must register with the chief of campus police if domiciled on a University of California or State University campus or its facilities.

Registration consists of fingerprinting and photographing of the person. This section applies to both Adult Authority and Youth Authority parolees, as well as persons coming here from out of state. Registrants are also required to notify the law enforcement agency where they registered of any change of address within 5 days. Failure to register or notify the authorities of an address change, as required, is a misdemeanor, if the prior conviction was for a misdemeanor offense, or a felony, if the prior sex act resulted in a felony conviction. Subsequent violations are felonies. It also subjects the offender to revocation of parole or probation. Conviction of some specific offenses requiring the perpetrator to register are as follows:

1. Assault to commit rape or sodomy (220)
2. Rape (261)
3. Aiding or abetting rape (264.1)
4. Enticing for prostitution (266)
5. Abduction for prostitution (267)
6. Incest (285)
7. Sodomy (286)
8. Lewd acts against children under 14 (288)
9. Oral copulation (288a)
10. Penetration of genital/anal opening by foreign object (289)
11. Molesting children under 18 (647.6)
12. Possessing/importing child pornography (311.1)
13. Indecent exposure (314)
14. Lewd acts with minor (272)
15. Mentally disordered sex offender (W&I Code 6300)

Interstate Flight in 290 Cases—PC 289.5. It is a misdemeanor for a person charged or convicted of a registrable sex offense to flee into California to avoid prosecution or confinement.

Chemical Treatment—PC 645. A person convicted of a violation of section 286(k) or (d), 288(b)(1), 288a(b) or (d), or 289(a) or (j), upon a victim under thirteen years of age, may be ordered to undergo chemical treatment to reduce the sexual urge. Such treatment begins upon release on parole, subject to discretion of the court (PC 645(a)).

Any person guilty of a second or subsequent violation as specified above *must* be ordered to undergo chemical treatment upon parole (PC 645(b)).

Arrest of School Employee—PC 291. This section requires the chief of police or the sheriff, to notify school authorities (public and private) upon the arrest of any school employee for any of the offenses listed in PC 290 (above).

Disclosure of Status—PC 290.95. A 290-registrant must disclose this fact when becoming an employee or a volunteer where working in unaccompanied contact with minor children. A registrant whose crime was against a child under 16 cannot work unaccompanied with minor children. Those required to register under section 290 must also disclose their status when applying for work that involves touching minors (PC 290.95), must register with the administrator and receive permission to gain access to school grounds (PC 626.81), and must register with the administrator of an elder care establishment if previously convicted of sexual abuse of an elder or dependent adult (PC 653c).Violation is a misdemeanor.

Sexual Predator Release Notification—WI 6609. Modeled after New Jersey's "Megan's Law," California statutes provide that whenever the Department of Mental Health or a court orders the release of a sexually violent predator, the sheriff, police chief and district attorney must be notified-both where the crime occurred, and where the predator will be residing (WI 6609.1). These officials in turn *may* notify "any person designated by the sheriff or chief of police as an appropriate recipient of the notice" (WI 6609.2), and *must* notify the victims, witnesses and family members involved in the predator's case who have requested notice (WI 6609.3). ***Note:*** The word "may" makes notification optional. The word "must" means required notification.

AIDS Testing of Sex Offenders—PC 1202.1. Within 180 days of conviction of specified sex offenses (including rape, oral copulation, sodomy, penetration with a foreign object, and sexual abuse of a child), the convict must submit to testing of his blood or saliva for AIDS antibodies. The local health officer has responsibility for disclosing the test results to the crime victim.

DNA Sample Required—PC 298.1. Specified sex offenders, serious felony arrestees, and anyone convicted or sentenced for any felony crime (including juveniles) must submit to a buccal swab (inside the cheek) for DNA testing, as well as a right thumbprint and both palm prints. Refusal to provide specimens is a misdemeanor.

STUDENT REVIEW

TERMINOLOGY DEFINED—CHAPTER 13

Please see the Terminology Quiz at the end of this chapter.

1. Bestiality: sexual intercourse with animals.
2. Brothel: house of prostitution.
3. Buggery: common term for anal intercourse, sodomy.
4. Consanguinity: related by blood.
5. Cunnilingus: oral copulation of female sex organ.
6. Ecclesiastical law: religious doctrine, canon law.
7. Fellatio: oral stimulation of the penis.
8. Fetus: unborn or less than full-term human child.
9. Fornication: sexual intercourse between unmarried persons.
10. Harmful matter: lacks literary value, etc., for minors.
11. Indecent exposure: public exposure of one's private parts.
12. Miscarriage: premature delivery of a fetus.
13. Nuisance: a health, safety or property rights hazard.
14. Obscene: appealing primarily to prurient interest.
15. Panderer: one who derives income from pimping.
16. Pimping: common term for selling services of prostitute.
17. Prurient: lewd, lustful, impure, shameful, morbid.
18. Seduction: sexual intercourse induced by marriage promise.
19. Slander: spoken words injurious to another's reputation.
20. Sodomy: legal term for anal intercourse.

TRUE-FALSE QUIZ—CHAPTER 13

After reading this chapter you should be able to correctly answer the following items.

___ 1. Obscene matter, as defined in PC 311, means any matter which offends the individual.
___ 2. It is a misdemeanor to bring obscene matter into California for personal use.
___ 3. Providing entry is by membership card only, a show involving live sex acts is legal.
___ 4. It is a defense to PC 311 that the act charged was committed in aid of legitimate scientific or educational purposes.
___ 5. Under present law, even if convicted, all obscene material must be returned to the defendant as his personal property at the end of the trial.
___ 6. Harmful matter, as defined under PC 313, is that which appeals primarily to prurient interest and lacks significant literary, artistic, political, or scientific value for minors.
___ 7. There is nothing in the law to prohibit a parent or guardian from providing a minor child with pornographic material.
___ 8. To be guilty of selling hard core pornographic material it must be proven the defendant was aware of the character of the material.
___ 9. It is not against the law for one to possess pornographic movies for private showing in his or her own home.
___10. Encouraging a minor to leave home against the parent's wishes constitutes "contributing" under PC 272.
___11. To constitute "child molesting" under PC 288, the accused must have touched the child's private parts.
___12. To constitute child molesting, the victim must be the opposite sex of the accused.
___13. Voluntary oral copulation between persons of the opposite sex is not a crime if both are 18.

___14. Voluntary oral copulation between two 18 year old persons of the same sex is a crime.

___15. It is a crime for the one who is more than 10 years older to participate in a voluntary act of sodomy with an 18 year old person.

___16. Sodomy and oral copulation are felonies if one of the participants uses duress or if the other person is 14 years of age and 10 years younger than the perpetrator.

___17. A marriage or sexual relations between first cousins is incestuous and unlawful in California.

___18. Other persons must be present in a public place before the exposure of one's private parts constitutes indecent exposure under PC 314.

___19. The courts have ruled that to be guilty of "loitering about a school" (PC 653g), the loitering must appear to be for the purpose of committing a crime as opportunity may provide.

___20. A person required to register under PC 290 for having committed sex crimes against a victim under age 16 may not be permitted to work directly with minor children in an unaccompanied setting.

ESSAY-DISCUSSION ITEMS—CHAPTER 13

After reading this chapter you should be able to correctly answer the following items.

1. What is the legal definition of the word "obscene" for the purpose of PC 311 (obscene matter)?
2. What is meant by "distribute" as the word is used in obscene matter, PC 311?
3. What is the age limit given in "contributing" (PC 272), and what results must the suspect's acts cause or tend to cause in the victim or the accused?
4. What are the elements of PC 273g (immoral acts in the presence of children)?
5. List by name any five of the several crimes, conviction of which requires the perpetrator to register as a sex offender (PC 290).
6. List the elements making oral copulation or sodomy a crime.
7. Are an uncle and his niece who have sexual intercourse with each other guilty of incest? Would it be legal for them to marry each other?
8. Can a person commit the crime of indecent exposure (PC 314), in his or her own home? If so, under what circumstances to make it a crime?
9. Briefly, what is the difference between PC 288, crimes against children, and PC 647.6, annoying or molesting children?
10. What are the elements of "loitering" under PC 653g (loitering about schools)?

TERMINOLOGY QUIZ-CHAPTER 13

Match terms and definitions by writing the number preceding the correct term in the appropriate brackets.

Terms	*Definitions*
1. Bestiality	[ ] common term for anal intercourse
2. Brothel	[ ] lewd, lustful, impure, shameful, morbid
3. Buggery	[ ] unborn child, less than full term
4. Consanguinity	[ ] sexual intercourse between unmarried persons
5. Cunnilingus	[ ] sexual intercourse with animals
6. Ecclesiastical	[ ] house of prostitution
7. Fellatio	[ ] sexual intercourse induced by marriage promise
8. Fetus	[ ] anal intercourse with humans or animals
9. Fornication	[ ] related by blood

10. Harmful matter	[ ]	premature delivery of fetus
11. Indecent exposure	[ ]	oral copulation of female sex organ
12. Miscarriage	[ ]	church or religious doctrine
13. Nuisance	[ ]	one who derives income from pimping
14. Obscene	[ ]	oral stimulation of the penis
15. Panderer	[ ]	appealing primarily to prurient interest
16. Pimping		
17. Prurient		
18. Seduction		
19. Slander		
20. Sodomy		

CHAPTER 14

BURGLARY

14.1 BURGLARY DEFINED

Burglary Defined—PC 459. "Every person who enters any house, room, apartment, tenement, shop, warehouse, store, mill, barn, stable, outhouse or other building, tent, vessel, as defined in Section 21 of the Harbors and Navigation Code, floating home, etc., railroad car, locked or sealed cargo container, whether or not mounted on a vehicle, trailer coach as defined in Section 635 of the Vehicle Code, any house car as defined in Section 362 of the Vehicle Code, inhabited camper as defined in Section 243 of the Vehicle Code, vehicle as defined by the Vehicle Code when the doors are locked, aircraft as defined by Section 21012 of the Public Utilities Code, mine, or any underground portion thereof, with intent to commit grand or petit larceny or any felony is guilty of burglary. As used in this chapter, 'inhabited' means currently being used for dwelling purposes, whether occupied or not. A house, trailer, vessel designed for habitation, or portion of a building is currently being used for dwelling purposes if, at the time of the burglary, it was not occupied solely because a natural or other disaster caused the occupants to leave the premises."

Elements of Burglary.

1. Entry (actual or constructive).
2. Of a building or structure (as defined in PC 459).
3. Or a vessel, as defined in the Harbors & Navigation Code.
4. Or a vehicle (when the doors are locked), trailer coach, house car or inhabited camper, each as defined in the Vehicle Code.
5. Or an aircraft, as defined in the Public Utilities Code.
6. With *specific intent* to commit (a) grand or petty theft or (b) any felony.

Discussion. At common law, burglary was a felony and was formerly punishable by death. The crime under the old common law consisted of breaking in, either actually or constructively, and entering the dwelling house of another in the nighttime—both the breaking and the subsequent entry being for the purpose of committing a felony inside.

Current Statutory Provisions. As indicated in PC 459, California law requires only entry, whether forced or not, as long as the perpetrator had the requisite intent (i.e., to commit grand or petty theft, or any felony), at the time he or she entered one of the numerous structures, places or vehicles listed in PC 459. It is not necessary that the crime of burglary be committed at nighttime, as was the provision at common law. See degrees of burglary PC 460.

The following WWW site provides highly interesting information on burglary rates, identity theft, burglary facts and home and business burglary prevention tips. See: **http://www.talkjustice.com/browse.asp.**

14.2 THE ACT OF ENTRY IN BURGLARY

As previously indicated, in order to constitute a burglary, there must be an entry, no matter how slight, of one of the various structures or places listed in the statute. While at common law the entry had to be accomplished by a "breaking and entering," in California no particular degree of breaking is necessary.

The act necessary to the completion of the crime of burglary need not amount to the taking, or asportation (moving) of an article of value, nor is it necessary that some felony actually be consummated within one of the designated structures. The offense is complete the moment that entry is made, even though after the entry the burglar abandons his purpose (*People v. Steward*, 113 Cal. App. 2d 687).

The insertion of a stolen bank card into an exterior ATM is not considered an "entry" within the meaning of the burglary statute. Doing so, however, is still petty or grand theft depending on the amount stolen. *Courtesy of PhotoDisc, Inc.*

When Entry Not Applicable to Burglary. One who enters his own residence, even if he or she does so with the intent to commit a theft or some felony, does not commit burglary. This is based on an absolute right to enter the building (*People v. Pendleton*, 25 Cal. 3d 371). Under the same theory, there would be no "illegal" entry for burglary purposes where one entered a building which he was leasing and stole some of the landlord's fixtures (*People v. Gauze*, 15 Cal. 3d 709). Even though in these two examples, the perpetrator would not be guilty of burglary, he or she would be guilty of any crimes committed after they entered the building.

Examples of Nonforced Entry in Burglary. If a person enters a store with the intention of stealing goods therein, it would be a burglary even though he or she enters the building during the day with a crowd of customers (*People v. Ferns*, 27 Cal. App. 285).

A person invited in when he asked to use the telephone, and who subsequently steals property within the structure, may be guilty of burglary if it can be shown he entered with the intent to steal or commit a felony (*People v. Talbot*, 64 Cal. 2d).

A person who enters a public coin operated laundry with the intent to commit a theft therein, commits a crime of burglary, even though the laundromat was a public place and the entrance was made during business hours (*People v. Hildreth*, 202 Cal. App. 2d 468).

Where one conspires with a salesman and enters a retail store to obtain merchandise below cost, the salesman pocketing the money given him by the knowing buyer, the offense is burglary on the part of the buyer on the theory that he knowingly entered the store (a structure as defined by the burglary statute) and participated in a theft. Though it is apparent that the salesman in this case was guilty of embezzlement, the court held him guilty of the more serious offense of burglary, since he was a principal to the crime (*People v. Sparks*, 44 Cal. App. 2d 748).

Entry is complete as soon as there is penetration of the outer plane of the structure. Thus, where a burglar removed the outer window screen but was unable to force the window open with a screwdriver, he was properly convicted of burglary (*People v. Valencia,* 28 Cal.4th 1).

Constructive Entry Defined. Entry of a structure for the purpose of burglary need not be made by the physical person of the defendant. Entry may be made by another person on the defendant's behalf, or by means of an animal, tool or instrument under the defendant's control. In both such cases, the entry is said to be "constructive" on the part of the perpetrator.

Constructive Entry Examples. A suspect committed "constructive entry" by inserting a small three-pronged garden fork into the return slot of a video rental store. He hooked several tapes and pulled them up to the return slot for removal. The perpetrator is guilty of burglary.

Inserting a stolen automatic teller machine (ATM) card into a bank panel to withdraw funds is not sufficient to constitute "entry" for second degree burglary. (*People v. Davis*, 18 Cal. 4th 712).

14.3 THE INTENT IN BURGLARY

In all cases of burglary, there must be a *specific intent to* commit a theft, either grand or petty, or a felony within the structure burglarized. No other intent, however strong it may be, will suffice. The perpetrator's intent may be inferred, in most cases from the facts and circumstances surrounding the commission of the crime. Thus, an entry into a structure with the intent to commit an act denounced by PC 288a (forced oral copulation) constitutes the crime of burglary if it can be inferred that the defendant's conduct was such as to enter with the specific intent to consummate this sex crime (*People v. Bias*, 170 Cal. App. 2d 502).

Similarly, a *prima facie* case of burglary is established when a defendant enters a dwelling in the nighttime and seizes a female who is asleep and then runs away after the victim screams. In this case it may be inferred from the facts and circumstances present that the accused entered with the intent to commit rape (*People v. Nanez*, 84 Cal. App. 2d 778). Although the burden is on the prosecution to prove a specific intent to commit a felony within a structure, in the above two cases such intent might reasonably be inferred from the unlawful entry alone.

Since the gist of the offense of burglary is the defendant's intent to commit theft or a felony at the time he or she enters the building, the proof of the intent at the time of the burglary does not depend on the subsequent commission of a felony or theft, or even an attempt to commit such acts (*People v. Robles*, 207 Cal. App. 2d 891).

Even an entry with intent to consume something of only slight value will suffice for a burglary conviction. For example, where a defendant broke into the victim's home and fixed himself a meal, intending to take a shower and use the victim's water and shampoo, he was properly convicted of burglary (*People v. Martinez*).

Consummation of Intent. A burglarious intent can reasonably be inferred from the unlawful entry alone of a structure, even if no crime was committed after entry. Thus, where one goes into a store to "boost" articles within the store, by using any number of contrivances to accomplish this purpose (e.g., "booster box", coat with large inside pockets, shopping bag, bloomers, etc.), the crime is complete the moment that the perpetrator enters the structure. ***Note:*** a "booster box" is a package appearing to be completely sealed or tied. However, an end or side panel is designed with a hinged spring so that articles can be quickly shoved inside. The panel automatically snaps back into place.

No overt act need be made toward the commission of theft. The acquiring of dominion over articles of property within the store is not necessary, nor is the element of asportation, which is necessary to the crime of theft. It is enough that entry is made with the intent to commit grand or petty theft, or any felony.

When a person enters a store, removes an article, and thereafter takes the article to a sales person stating that he lost his receipt and would like a refund, not only is he perpetrating a fraud (theft), but the crime is burglary if, prior to entering the store, his purpose (specific intent) was to accomplish this act.

Proof of specific intent to commit a theft at the time of entering a building may be established by the facts and circumstances surrounding the burglary (*People v. Huber*, 225 Cal. App. 2d 536).

Existence of Intent. The specific intent to commit burglary must exist at the time of entry. If a person enters a structure without either the intent to steal or to commit a felony, but, after the entry has been made, decides to steal or commit a felony, his intent is said to have been formed within the building and thus the crime of burglary is not committed (*People v. Lowen*, 109 Cal. 381).

Again, it is the facts and circumstances surrounding the case on which a basis for proof of the crime is founded. As indicated in the cases cited relative to entry and intent, it will be noted that a *prima facie* case may be established by such things as articles used to make entry, *modus operandi,* constructive entry, and implements with which to commit theft or felony, to name but a few facts from which inferences may be drawn.

14.4 STRUCTURES SUBJECT TO BURGLARY

Numerous structures and places may be burglarized as indicated in the burglary statute. Those specifically mentioned in PC 459 are defined as follows:

Aircraft. An "aircraft" includes any contrivance used or designed for flying except a parachute or other device used primarily for safety (Public Utilities Code Section 21012).

Camper. A "camper" is a structure designed to be mounted upon a motor vehicle and to provide facilities for human habitation or camping purposes (VC 243).

Cargo Container. A "cargo container," for purposes of the burglary statute, means a permanent, reusable receptacle having a cubic displacement of 1,000 cubic feet or more and designed for carrying goods on one mode of transport or another.

House Car. A "house car" (motor home) is a motor vehicle originally designed or permanently altered, and equipped for human habitation, or to which a camper has been permanently attached. A motor vehicle equipped with a camper having an axle that is designed to support a portion of the weight of the camper unit, shall be considered a three-axle house car regardless of the method of attachment or manner of registration (VC 362).

Trailer Coach. A "trailer coach" (house trailer) is a vehicle, other than a motor vehicle, designed for human habitation, or human occupancy for industrial, professional, or commercial purposes, for carrying property on its own structure, and for being drawn by a motor vehicle (VC 635).

Vehicle. A "vehicle" is a device by which any person or property may be propelled, moved, or drawn upon a highway, excepting a device moved by human power or used exclusively on stationary rails or tracks (VC 670).

Vessel. The word "vessel" includes ships of all kinds, steamboats, canal boats, barges and every structure adapted to be navigated from place to place for the transportation of merchandise or persons (Harbors and Navigation Code Section 21).

Discussion—Structure/Building Defined. A necessary and essential element of the crime of burglary is the entry of a house, room, apartment, tenement, shop, warehouse, etc., as listed in the burglary statute. Occasionally a structure will be entered which, in itself, is not descriptive of one of those listed in the statute. In such instances, one may look to case decisions for the answer.

The leading case in California which defines a building or structure for purposes of the burglary statute is *People v. Stickman* (34 Cal. 242). In this case, the court held that a building which may be the subject of a burglary, notwithstanding the legal definitions of a mine, vehicle, trailer house, cargo container, or aircraft, etc., is a structure which has *walls on all sides and is covered with a roof.* The walls can take various forms and need not reach the roof, but they must act as a significant barrier to entrance without cutting or breaking (*In re Amber S.* 33 Cal. App. 4th 185).

In another case, the California Appellate Court held in *People v. Nunez* (7 Cal. App. 3d 655), that a telephone booth with three walls, a door, roof, and floor was a "building" within the meaning of PC 459. As such, a telephone booth could be the subject of a burglary and anyone who enters same with intent to steal (even if there is no forced entry) could be found guilty of burglary.

An old passenger bus, stationary on cement blocks and with the wheels removed, and which had a door, windows, and a roof, and which was used as an office by a firm, was a "building" within the meaning of the burglary statute (*People v. McLaughlin*, 156 Cal. App. 291).

A roofed garage having walls on three sides, the fourth side being a door, is a building within the law of burglary, even though at the time of entry the door was open (*People v. Picaroni*, 131 Cal. App. 2d 612).

Residential burglary can be committed as to any structure which is "attached and integral to" the residence proper. This includes an attached garage (*People v. Moreno*, 158 Cal. App. 3d 109), a carport (*In re Christopher J*, 102 Cal. App. 3d 76), an enclosed patio (*People v. Cook*, 135 Cal. App. 3d 785), and a storeroom (*People v. Conton*, 171 Cal. App. 3d 192).

Even if a person lawfully enters a residence, additional entry into an interior room while harboring the requisite intent constitutes burglary. For example, a door-to-door salesman who obtained consent entry into a residence in order to sell magazines, but who thereafter entered the woman's bedroom with the intent to rape her, was properly convicted of both the rape and residential burglary (*People v. Sparks,* 28 Cal.4th 71).

Houses Under Construction. Questions often arise as to the possibility of burglarizing a house or building under construction. The test is usually the *Stickman* case, previously discussed. It is assumed that if the structure has a roof and walls on all sides, whether either is permanently covered, a burglary could be committed, especially if the building could be secured. However, a building which consists of only framing, without some covering, insecure and impermanent as it may be, would ordinarily not be the subject of a burglary.

Motor Vehicles. The statute defining burglary specifically states that a vehicle may be the subject of burglary only when it is a vehicle as defined by the Vehicle Code and when the doors are locked. The courts have held that a vehicle is locked where one of its widows was rolled down about three inches *(In re James B.,* 109 Cal.App.4th 862). However, in *People v. Malcolm* (47 Cal. App. 3d 217), the court held that a vehicle was "locked," where the doors were locked, all the windows were rolled up, but the wind-wing window lock was broken.

The term "door" includes the trunk lid of an automobile. When the trunk and all other doors were locked, entry constituted burglary (*People v. Toomes*, 148 Cal. App. 2d 465). However, if the closed trunk of an unlocked vehicle is opened by pulling a latch in the passenger compartment, no burglary occurs. (*People v. Allen,* 86 Cal.App.4th 909.) Stealing from an unlocked vehicle would only amount to theft, especially where there is no evidence to indicate the locking or securing of the vehicle (*People v. Burns*, 114 Cal. App. 2d 566).

Trailers. Entry into a sealed semitrailer, which was a separate enclosed part of the tractor-trailer combination, and which could not be entered from the passenger or cab part of the tractor, is burglary even though the doors on the cab part of the tractor were not locked. The court held the vehicle to be "locked" within the meaning of the burglary stat-ute (*People v. Massie*, 241 Cal. App. 1023).

Inhabited Camper. A camper is defined above. It should be noted here that to constitute burglary of a camper, the camper must be inhabited. Theft from an uninhabited camper would be petty or grand theft depending on the value of the property stolen.

Automobile Trunk Burglary. Where the victim reported that he had left his vehicle parked and locked, forcible entry of the trunk by prying it open, in order to steal from within, constituted an automobile burglary, notwithstanding that the passenger compartment may not have been entered. *(People v. Toomey*, 148 Cal. App. 2d 465.)

In a similar case the defendant appealed his conviction of burglary of an automobile trunk on the theory that the prosecution failed to show the doors of the vehicle were locked, and that in order to constitute burglary of an auto trunk, all the doors *and* the trunk had to be locked. The Court of Appeal sustained the conviction, noting:

1. It would be ridiculous to make the existence of burglary turn on the locked or unlocked state of an area not involved in the entry. If the entry is made by unlocking or forcing open the trunk lid, it is immaterial that some other door leading to some other space was unlocked.
2. The forced entry of a locked trunk of an automobile for the purpose of theft is burglary as defined in PC 459.
3. The corpus delicti of burglary, i.e., the entry by someone into the victim's automobile trunk, when that trunk was locked, with intent to commit theft, was more than amply met (*People v. Trimble*, 16 Cal. App. 4th 1255).

14.5 DEGREES OF BURGLARY

Degrees of Burglary Defined—PC 460.

1. "Every burglary of an inhabited dwelling house, vessel, as defined in the Harbors and Navigation Code, which is inhabited and designed for habitation, floating home or trailer coach as defined in the Vehicle Code, or the inhabited portion of any other building, is burglary of the first degree.
2. All other kinds of burglary are of the second degree.
3. This section shall not be construed to supersede or affect Section 464 [safe burglary] of the Penal Code."

Discussion—Degrees of Burglary. There is no distinction between day and night burglaries relative to degree. All burglary of an "inhabited dwelling, vessel designed for habitation, trailer coach," etc., whether committed during the day or at night, is first degree burglary (See below for 1st and 2nd degree penalty).

Discussion—Inhabited Dwelling. The word "inhabited" as used in PC 460 includes both a "dwelling house" and a "building." Inhabited means that persons must actually reside in the building which is customarily used as a dwelling house, although the occupants may be temporarily absent as long as they intend to return.

Note: For burglary of a vessel or boat to be first degree burglary it must be "designed for habitation," that is, it must be equipped with at least basic sleeping and living quarters. Also, it must be "inhabited" at the time, even if the occupants are on vacation or otherwise are temporarily absent.

Any unoccupied dwelling, not scheduled for immediate occupancy, is not considered an inhabited dwelling, and, therefore, is not subject to first-degree burglary (*People v. Valdez,* 203 Cal. App. 2d 559).

14.6 PUNISHMENT FOR BURGLARY

Punishment—PC 461. Burglary is punishable as follows:

1. Burglary in the first degree: by imprisonment in the state prison.
2. Burglary in the second degree: by imprisonment in the county jail or in the state prison.

Probation—PC 462(a). "Except in unusual cases where the interests of justice would best be served if the person is granted probation, probation shall not be granted to any person who is convicted of a burglary of an inhabited dwelling house or trailer coach . . . or the inhabited portion of any other building."

14.7 BURGLARY WITH EXPLOSIVES OR ACETYLENE TORCH

Burning Device or Explosive—PC 464. "Any person who, with intent to commit crime, enters, either by day or by night, any building, whether inhabited or not, and opens or attempts to open any vault, safe or other secure place by use of acetylene torch or electric arc, burning bar thermal lance, oxygen lance, or any other similar device capable of burning through steel, concrete, or any other solid substance, or by use of nitroglycerine, dynamite, gunpowder, or any other explosive, is guilty of a felony and upon conviction shall be punished by imprisonment in the state prison. . . ."

Discussion. A "secure place" is one designed primarily for the purpose of storing valuables and includes a fire safe. This is considered a more serious type of burglary and carries an increased penalty. In a prosecution resulting in a conviction for burglary and willfully and maliciously placing an explosive in a building, testimony of a police officer as to his findings at the scene of the crime and as to the conduct of the accused were ample to sustain a conviction for this offense (*People v. Robinson*, 149 Cal. App. 2d 342). Evidence showing that the defendants entered a safe by the use of an oxy-acetylene torch was sufficient to sustain a conviction under this section (*People v. Wilson*, 46 Cal. App. 2d 218).

14.8 POSSESSION OF BURGLARY TOOLS —UNAUTHORIZED KEYS—DEVICES

Possession of Burglary Tools—PC 466. "Every person having upon him or her or in his or her possession a picklock, crow, keybit, crowbar, screwdriver, vice grip pliers, water-pump pliers, slidehammer, slim jim, tension bar, lock pick gun tubular lock pick, floor-safe door puller, master key, ceramic or porcelain spark plug chips or pieces, or other instrument or tool with intent feloniously to break or enter into any building, railroad car, aircraft or vessel, trailer coach, or vehicle as defined in the Vehicle Code, or who shall knowingly make or alter, or shall attempt to make or alter, any key or other instrument above named so that the same will fit or open the lock of a building, railroad car, aircraft or vessel, trailer coach, or vehicle as defined in the Vehicle Code, without being requested so to do by some person having the right to open the same, or who shall make, alter, or repair any instrument or thing, knowing or having reason to believe that it is intended to be used in committing a misdemeanor or felony, is guilty of a misdemeanor. Any of the structures mentioned in Section 459 of this code shall be deemed to be a building within the meaning of this section."

Possession of Means to Enter Coin-Operated Machine—PC 466.3. "(a) Whoever possesses a key, tool, instrument, explosive, or device, or a drawing, print or mold of a key, tool, instrument, explosive, or device designed to open, break into, tamper with, or damage a coin-operated machine as defined in subdivision (b) with intent to commit a theft from such machine, is punishable by imprisonment in the county jail . . . or by fine . . . or by both.

(b) As used in this section, the term 'coin-operated machine' shall include any automatic vending machine or any part thereof, parking meter, coin telephone, coin laundry machine, coin dry cleaning machine, amusement machine, music machine, vending machine dispensing goods or service, or money changers."

Possession or Use of Motor Vehicle Master Key—PC 466.5. "(a) Every person who, with the intent to use it in the commission of an unlawful act, possesses a motor vehicle master key is guilty of a misdemeanor.

(b) Every person who, with the intent to use it in the commission of an unlawful act, uses a motor vehicle master key to open a lock or operate the ignition switch of any motor vehicle is guilty of a misdemeanor.

(c) Every person who knowingly manufactures for sale, advertises for sale, offers for sale, or sells a motor vehicle master key or a motor vehicle wheel master key, except to persons who use such keys in their lawful occupations or businesses, is guilty of a misdemeanor.

(d) As used in this section: (1) 'Motor vehicle master key' means a key which will operate all the locks or ignition switches, or both the locks and ignition switches, in a given group of motor vehicle locks or motor vehicle ignition switches, or both motor vehicle ignition switches, each of which can be operated by a key which will not operate one or more of the other locks or ignition switches in such group.

(2) 'Motor vehicle wheel lock' means a device attached to a motor vehicle for theft protection purposes which can be removed only by a key unit unique to the wheel lock attached to a particular motor vehicle.

(3) 'Motor vehicle wheel lock master key' means a key unit which will operate all the wheel locks in a given group of motor vehicle wheel locks, each of which can be operated by a key unit which will not operate any of the other wheel locks in the group."

Motor Vehicle Keys: Unlawful Possession—PC 466.7. "Every person who, with the intent to use it in the commission of an unlawful act, possesses a motor vehicle key with knowledge that such key was made without the consent of either the registered or legal owner of the motor vehicle or of a person who is in lawful possession of the motor vehicle, is guilty of a misdemeanor."

Possession of Code Grabber—PC 466.9. It is a misdemeanor to possess an auto security alarm system "code grabbing device," with intent to use it unlawfully.

Unauthorized Duplication or Possession of Keys—PC 469. "Any person who knowingly makes duplicates, causes to be duplicated, or uses or attempts to make, duplicates, cause to be duplicated, or use, or has in his possession any key to a building or other area owned, operated or controlled by the State of California, any state agency, board, or commission, a county, city, or any public school or community college district without authorization from the person in charge of such building or area or his designated representative and with knowledge of the lack of such authorization is guilty of a misdemeanor."

14.9 UNLAWFUL FORCED ENTRY

Forcible Entry and Destruction of Property—PC 603. "Every person other than a peace officer engaged in the performance of his duties as such who forcibly and without consent of the owner, representative of the owner, lessee or representative of the lessee thereof, enters a dwelling house, cabin, or other building occupied or constructed for occupation by humans, and who damages, injures, or destroys any property of value in, around or appertaining to such dwelling house, cabin or other building, is guilty of a misdemeanor."

Discussion. PC 603 is an appropriate section to use in "non-burglaries" where the specific intent of entering to commit theft or a felony is absent or cannot be proved. The building entered must be a dwelling house and the entry must be forced. One should also note that the culprit must cause some damage to the building or its contents.

Generally the damage caused by the forced entry is sufficient to satisfy this element of the offense. Consumption of food in the house would constitute "destruction of property" as used in this section, as would a malicious mischief or defacing of property in the house.

STUDENT REVIEW

TERMINOLOGY DEFINED—CHAPTER 14

Please see the Terminology Quiz at the end of this chapter.

1. Abandonment: surrendering property rights, giving up attempted crime.
2. Abate: to end, nullify, e.g., abatement proceedings.
3. Abscond: to leave secretly, fleeing to avoid legal proceedings.
4. Abstract: a summary of essential points.
5. Boost: slang term for theft, especially with special device.
6. Building: any structure with walls on all sides and a roof.
7. Burglary: entering a building with intent to commit theft or a felony.
8. Burglary tools: any tool used or designed for unlawful entry.
9. Constructive entry: removing items without physically entering.
10. Dwelling house: a residence, apartment, etc.
11. Entering: any physical intrusion or by reaching in.
12. Forced entry: physically breaking in, prying door, window or lock.
13. Inhabited building: occupied as a residence, even if absent at time.
14. Larcenous intent: with intent to steal, to commit theft.
15. Larceny: theft, to permanently deprive owner of property.
16. Lockpick: a device for opening locks without a key.
17. Master key: key which will open all locks of a given type.
18. Tenant: a renter, one who holds a lease on property.
19. Trailer coach: house trailer, designed for habitation.
20. True bill: indictment by Grand Jury.

TRUE-FALSE QUIZ—CHAPTER 14

After reading this chapter you should be able to correctly answer the following items.

___ 1. In order to constitute burglary, there must be a physical breaking and entering of a building as defined in the Penal Code.

___ 2. One can commit burglary and still not physically enter a building.

___ 3. Burglary is a specific intent crime.

___ 4. A building for purposes of burglary may be any structure with walls on all sides and a roof.

___ 5. One may commit burglary by entering a building for the purpose of committing rape.

___ 6. Walking into a super market during business hours for the purpose of stealing a loaf of bread constitutes burglary.

___ 7. One would not be guilty of burglary even though he entered a building with intent to burglarize it, if he abandoned his purpose once inside and left without taking anything.

___ 8. "Constructive entry" is sufficient to constitute burglary if the other elements are present.

___ 9. Unauthorized breaking into a building for the purpose of retrieving one's own property is not burglary.

___10. Asportation is an essential element of burglary.

___11. One is guilty of burglary if after entering a building on legitimate business he subsequently steals something.

___12. One cannot be found guilty of burglary unless he enters one of the structures specifically named in PC 459.

___13. To constitute burglary of a vehicle it must be defined as such in the Vehicle Code and the doors must be locked.

___14. If a building under construction meets the *Stickman* test, it may be the subject of a burglary.
___15. One is guilty of first degree burglary if one enters a locked office building in the nighttime.
___16. Burglary of an inhabited residence during the afternoon hours is first degree burglary.
___17. A burglar who steals a loaded firearm as part of his loot is considered to have armed himself and, therefore, is guilty of first degree burglary.
___18. It is a misdemeanor to possess any type of lockpick or altered key for the purpose of un-lawfully entering any building or opening any coin operated machine.
___19. Unauthorized and knowing possession of a key to any State, city, county or school building is a misdemeanor.
___20. To be guilty of unauthorized forced entry under PC 603, the building entered must be a dwelling.

ESSAY-DISCUSSION ITEMS—CHAPTER 14

After reading this chapter you should be able to correctly answer the following items.

1. What are the elements of burglary?
2. Discuss and give an example of how a person might "constructively" enter a building in the crime of burglary. How might one nonforcibly enter a building and still be guilty of burglary?
3. May a person be guilty of burglarizing his own home? If so, how?
4. Define a building as it is used in PC 459 and cite the prevailing case which so defines it.
5. List five types of structures, places, or vehicles as defined in PC 459 which are not residences but which can be burglarized.
6. What are the elements of burglary of a motor vehicle?
7. What are the elements which differentiate first and second degree burglary?
8. Define the term "inhabited dwelling" as it applies to burglary.
9. What intent is required to make possession of a "picklock" a violation of PC 466 (possession of burglary tools)? Is the intent general or specific?
10. Discuss whether or not a drunk who broke a window of an inhabited dwelling and entered for the purpose of "sleeping it off" would be guilty of burglary, PC 459.
11. Can a person be arrested for burglary for inserting a stolen ATM card into a machine mounted in the wall of the bank building? For removing the window screen of a home? What are the significant differences between these two situations?

TERMINOLOGY QUIZ—CHAPTER 14

Match terms and definitions by writing the number preceding the correct term in the appropriate brackets.

Terms	*Definitions*
1. Abandonment	[ ] a residence, apartment, etc.
2. Abate	[ ] any physical intrusion or reaching in
3. Abscond	[ ] house trailer, designed for habitation
4. Abstract	[ ] indictment by Grand Jury
5. Boost	[ ] a device for opening locks without a key
6. Building	[ ] with intent to steal, to commit theft
7. Burglary	[ ] slang term for theft, to steal
8. Burglary tools	[ ] occupied residence, even if absent at time
9. Constructive entry	[ ] any structure with walls on all sides and a roof
10. Dwelling house	[ ] physically breaking in; prying door, lock

11. Entering
12. Forced entry
13. Inhabited building
14. Larcenous intent
15. Larceny
16. Lockpick
17. Master key
18. Tenant
19. Trailer coach
20. True bill

[ ] entering a building intending to steal or commit a felony
[ ] removing items without personally entering building
[ ] any tool designed or used for unlawful entry
[ ] to leave secretly, flight to avoid prosecution
[ ] to end, nullify, e.g., abatement proceedings

CHAPTER 15

ROBBERY AND EXTORTION

15.1 ROBBERY DEFINED

Robbery Defined—PC 211. "Robbery is the felonious taking of personal property in the possession of another, from his person or immediate presence, and against his will, accomplished by means of force or fear."

Discussion. At common law, robbery was a felony crime against both the person and the property of another. Then, as it is today, robbery amounted to the taking of the personal property of another, from the victim's person or immediate presence, by violence or intimidation, and against victim's will.

Robbery is distinguished from theft in that theft (larceny) is an offense against property. Robbery is classified as a crime against persons in the Penal Code, because of the grave danger to which a robbery victim is subjected. In robbery it is necessary that the taking be with force or fear, against the victim's will, and from the person or immediate presence of the victim (*People v. Jones*, 53 Cal. 2d 58).

The vast majority of robberies are committed by armed perpetrators between the ages of sixteen and twenty-five years, many of whom are drug users.

15.2 ELEMENTS OF ROBBERY

Robbery includes, as a necessary element, the specific intent to *permanently* deprive the owner of his or her property, and the crime must include asportation (*People v. Jones*, above). The perpetrator must have actually taken or acquired dominion (control) over the property of the victim before the crime is complete. In other words, a theft must have occurred.

The *corpus delicti* of robbery may be proven by circumstantial evidence. Thus, where the victim is assaulted and rendered unconscious and awakes with his property missing, it may be properly inferred that the elements of robbery have been established (*People v. Hubler*, 102 Cal. App. 2d 689).

The essential elements (*corpus delicti*) of robbery include:

1. Taking (theft) of personal property of some value in the possession of another (asportation).
2. From the person or immediate presence of the victim.
3. Against victim's will (without consent).
4. Accomplished by means of force or fear (violence or threatened violence).

Asportation. Taking of personal property (asportation) includes the taking and carrying away of the property of another. This must be accomplished by the use of force or by intimidation or the "putting in fear" of the victim. Therefore, without asportation the crime is not complete but may amount to an attempt under PC 664.

The courts have held that forcing the victim to throw a wallet on the ground is asportation even though the perpetrator failed to pick it up (*People v. Quinn*, 77 Cal. App. 2d 734).

To support a conviction of robbery there must be a taking of personal property which is in the possession of another from his person or immediate presence, and although some asportation is required, the distance the property is taken may be very short. The fact that the defendant and his partner refused the wallet taken from the victim did not preclude a finding that the victim had actually been robbed (*People v. Salcido*, 186 Cal. App. 2d 684).

From the Person—Immediate Presence. The taking in order to constitute robbery must be either from the owner's person or in his immediate presence. It is sometimes difficult to draw a line between "from his person" or "immediate presence." However, such is not actually necessary in most cases, because either is sufficient to complete the crime. For example, forcibly binding the owner in one room of a home and extorting information as to money or valuables in another room

Using force or fear to obtain property from the person of another is robbery. *Courtesy of AP/Wide World Photos*

is considered "from the person." Also, tying an owner of a theater in one room and taking money from a safe in another is accomplishing the act "in the immediate presence" of the victim.

Where the robbery is committed within the hearing or perception of the victim who is restrained nearby, the defendant cannot contend that the robbery was not in his victim's "immediate presence" (*People v. Lavender*, 137 Cal. App. 582).

Against the Victim's Will. The element of consent is lacking in the crime of robbery and thus distinguishes it from the crime of extortion, which is defined as "obtaining property from another with his consent." Generally, in the crime of extortion there is also the element of choice, but such is not the case in robbery (see Extortion, Section 15.6, this chapter).

A person may be unconscious and devoid of will, as from a blow on the head administered by the suspect, accompanied by the actual taking of his property. The crime in such cases is robbery. In cases where absence of will is brought on by the victim, such as voluntary intoxication, where the victim is being "rolled" and is unconscious of any activity, the crime is not robbery but grand theft.

Fear as a Means of Robbery—PC 212. The "fear" mentioned in Section 211, is further defined in PC 212. It may be either:

1. The fear of an unlawful injury to the person or property of the person robbed, or of any relative or member of his or her family; or
2. The fear of an immediate and unlawful injury to the person or property of any one in the company of the person robbed at the time of the robbery.

Force or Fear. Some violence, fear or intimidation must be used in the taking of property by robbery, or the crime is merely theft. Thus, while pocket picking and purse snatching are grand theft, being thefts from the person, such are generally not robbery unless sufficient force or fear is added and can be proven.

Whenever there is a struggle by the victim to keep his or her property, or if it is detached by force as, for instance, a purse strap broken in a purse snatching ("strong arm" robbery), there is sufficient force to constitute robbery.

Intimidation, or putting in fear, will supply the requisite fear in the commission of robbery. It must be remembered, however, that the crime does not require both force and fear, but force or fear. Thus, one element may operate independently of the other.

It has also been held that the threat of violence must be such as to create a reasonable apprehension of danger or it is not sufficient to make the taking robbery. Such fear need not be of a personal nature; it may be instilling fear of burning one's home or office.

The fear in robbery may be directed to another person who is present at the time of the commission of the robbery. Thus, where the victim, a relative, or another person in his company is threatened should the victim fail to comply in giving up his property, this is robbery.

The crime of robbery is complete when money and property are taken from the person or immediate presence accomplished by force or fear, and the crime does not become incomplete by the intervention of police officers as long as the essential elements of the crime are satisfied (*People v. Johnson*, 219 Cal. App. 2d 631).

Either force or intimidation is the essence of the crime of robbery (*People v. Calliham*, 81 Cal. App. 2d 928), and the force or violence necessary to the crime of robbery distinguishes it from the crime of larceny.

The snatching of property from the owner's person or the taking by threats or menaces of great bodily harm creating grave apprehension on the part of the victim is sufficient "force or fear" necessary to the commission of robbery (*People v. Jefferson*, 31 Cal. App. 2d 562).

If a person forcibly takes property under a good-faith claim of right (even though mistaken), this belief can be a defense to a robbery charge, even if force or fear was used (*People v. Butler*, 65 Cal.2d 569). However, this defense does not apply where property is taken in a good-faith belief that the taking is appropriate to satisfy a debt or other obligation; rather, it applies only where the item "recovered" is claimed in good faith to be the property of the person who takes it from another (*People v. Tufunga*, 21 Cal.4th 935).

Return of Property. Once the act of asportation has occurred the crime is complete and it is no defense that the property was returned, not even if the restitution occurred directly after the taking (*People v. Tipton*, 96 Cal. App. 2d 840).

Degrees of Robbery—PC 212.5. (a) Every robbery of any person who is performing his or her duties as an operator of any bus, taxicab, cable car, streetcar, trackless trolley, or other vehicle, including a vehicle operated on stationary rails or on a track or rail suspended in the air, and used for the transportation of persons for hire, every robbery of any passenger which is perpetrated on any of these vehicles, and every robbery which is perpetrated in an inhabited dwelling house, a vessel as defined in Section 21 of the Harbors and Navigation Code, an inhabited floating home, or trailer coach as defined in the Vehicle Code, which is inhabited, or the inhabited portion of any other building, is a robbery of the first degree.

(b) Every robbery of any person while using an automated teller machine or immediately after the person has used an automated teller machine and is in the vicinity of the automated teller machine is robbery of the first degree.

(c) All kinds of robbery other than those listed in subdivisions (a) and (b) are of the second degree.

Attempted Robbery. Where the intent to commit robbery is evident and the robber has taken an act toward "commencement of consummation" of the crime, he or she can be convicted of attempted robbery. For example, where defendant, wearing a poncho that only partially concealed his rifle, approached the entrance to a liquor store but turned away without making entry when a customer approached him, this was held to be a sufficient act toward the accomplishment of robbery to constitute the crime of attempted robbery (*People v. Vizcarra,* 110 Cal. App. 3d 858).

15.3 OWNERSHIP AND VALUE OF PROPERTY

In robbery, the amount and value of an item of personal property taken by the perpetrator is immaterial. If all other elements of the crime are present, the offense is complete though the value of the property be slight (*People v. Simmons*, 28 Cal. 2d 699). However, as in the crime of theft, the property itself must have some legal value.

Where defendants took money from a theater during the manager's absence, the court concluded that when force or fear is instilled in other employees in an effort to obtain the theater property, the crime is robbery (*People v. Dean*, 66 Cal. App. 459). Thus, a security guard or night watchman could be placed in a similar position since he is in a "quasi-fiduciary" position to the owner of the goods and property which he is guarding. For example, when a Standard Oil Company service station is held up by robbery suspects, both Standard Oil and the attendant are victims. The person being robbed doesn't have to be the owner of the property to be a victim of robbery.

Multiple Victims, Multiple Counts. When robbers confront several employees during the robbery of a business, a separate count of robbery can be charged for each victim who was present, even though only one of the victims may have actually had physical possession of the money or other property taken by the robbers *(People v. Gilbeaux,* 111 Cal. App. 4th 515).

15.4 MISCELLANEOUS ASPECTS—INCREASED PENALTY

Train Robbery—PC 214. This section of the Penal Code makes it a felony to board any railroad train with intention of robbing any person.

Carjacking—PC215. Taking a motor vehicle, from a person's possession or immediate presence, against his will, intending permanent or temporary deprivation, by force or fear, is a felony punishable by three, five or nine years in prison.

Inflicting Great Bodily Injury—PC 12022.7. Torture is sometimes used in the commission of the crime of robbery, often to compel the victim to disclose the location of money or property. Obviously torture would constitute "force" as used in PC 211. There are cases, however, where the victim is subjected to severe physical abuse such as choking, kicking, or vicious assault with fists or some instrument, during or after consummation of the robbery.

In such instances PC 12022.7 provides for punishment of an additional term of three years for inflicting "great bodily injury" on the victim. "Great bodily injury" means a significant or substantial physical injury.

Armed With Firearm or Deadly Weapon—PC 12022. If any person committing a felony is armed with a firearm, every principal is subject to an additional sentence "enhancement" (one additional year for most firearms, three years for assault weapons or machine guns).

Every person who personally uses a deadly or dangerous weapon to commit a felony is subject to a one-year enhancement (unless such use is an element of the underlying felony).

Additional terms of three to five years are added for personal arming with a firearm in specified narcotics offenses (see PC 12022(a)(1)(c)).

Use of Firearm—PC 12022.53. Personal use of a firearm during a robbery (or during other specified felonies) adds a mandatory, consecutive term of ten years of imprisonment; personal discharge of a firearm during the robbery requires a consecutive twenty year term; and if great bodily injury results (other than to an accomplice), an enhancement of twenty-five years to life applies.

15.5 PUNISHMENT FOR ROBBERY

Punishment For Robbery—PC 213. Robbery is punishable as follows:

1. Robbery of the first degree: by imprisonment in the state prison for three, four, or six years. However, if the robbery is committed by three or more persons in concert, punishment is three, six or nine years in prison.
2. Robbery of the second degree: by imprisonment in the state prison for two, three, or five years.

Notwithstanding PC 664 [punishment for attempts], attempted robbery is punishable by imprisonment in the state prison.

15.6 EXTORTION DEFINED

Extortion Defined—PC 518. "Extortion is the obtaining of property from another, with his consent, or the obtaining of an official act of a public officer, induced by a wrongful use of force or fear, or under color of official right."

Discussion. The crime of extortion, which is frequently called "blackmail," is closely akin to robbery in many respects (see Comparison of Elements Chart which follows). The essence of the offense of extortion is that it results in unlawfully obtaining something of value by wrongfully using force or fear. This statute covers the crime of obtaining money or property from another, with *the victim's consent.* The victim's "consent," of course, is obtained by using force or fear.

The origin of the term "blackmail," has an interesting history. Wealthy knights of old wore gilded armor with fancy chain mail. Poor knights wore black armor with plain mail. It was the custom that any knight knocked off his horse in a tourney lost his horse to his opponent. A few especially crafty jousters donned black armor, unhorsed the richest knights and sold the prize horses back to the knights who lost them. The "scam" became so common it was given a name only later to mean something else: Blackmail.

The differentiation between robbery and extortion is slight and amounts to the element of "consent" on the part of the victim. Consent, as previously pointed out, is given in response to the perpetrator's threat—usually to expose the victim to something he or she doesn't want known.

15.7 CONSENT—FORCE—FEAR—THREATS

The Element of Consent. Consent in extortion is more in the nature of a choice. Thus, while the victim of extortion does not wish to voluntarily part with his property, he generally has the choice to do so or suffer the consequences of being subjected to accusations, unlawful injury, or the exposing of some criminal offense. It doesn't matter if the information the perpetrator threatens to reveal is true or not.

The Elements of Force or Fear. The elements of force or fear required in the crime of extortion may be accomplished by one of the threats listed below, either to the individual threatened, or to a third party.

Threats Constituting Extortion. PC 519 states that "Fear, such as will constitute extortion, may be induced by a threat, either:

1. To do an unlawful injury to the person or property of the individual threatened or of a third person; or
2. To accuse the individual threatened, or any relative of his or member of his family, of any crime; or
3. To expose, or impute to him or them any deformity or disgrace, or crime; or
4. To expose any secret affecting him or them."

To constitute extortion, the victim must consent unwillingly, and with obvious coercion, to surrender his property. The wrongful use of force or fear must be the operating or controlling cause compelling such consent by the victim (*People v. Goodman*, 159 Cal. App. 2d 54).

One who threatens to "blast" his victims in a magazine for a failure to advertise in the defendant's publication is guilty of extortion if the threats made amount to those listed in PC 519 (*People v. Terantino*, 45 Cal. 2d 590).

15.8 THREAT OF UNLAWFUL INJURY

A threat to do bodily harm to others, or to inflict property damage is a threat to do an unlawful injury within the meaning of PC 519. Thus, when one threatens to burn down the factory of a wealthy industrialist if money or property is not paid, the crime is extortion if the victim consents to part with his property because of the unlawful threat. By comparison, the intimidation in the crime of robbery is so extreme as to overcome the will of the victim and cause him to part with his money or property *without* actual consent.

The Threat of Exposure. The "badger game" is a type of an extortion trick, usually in the form of enticing a man into a compromising position with a woman whose real or pretended husband comes upon the scene and demands payment under the threat of prosecution or exposure. Such a threat is sufficient under this section to constitute the crime of extortion within the meaning of PC 519.

15.9 ATTEMPTED EXTORTION

Attempt Extortion—PC 524. Every person who attempts, by means of any threat, such as is specified in PC 519, to extort money or other property from another is guilty of a felony (wobbler).

Discussion. One is guilty of the crime of attempted extortion when his or her acts are ineffectual in bringing about the contemplated results of extorting money or property from his victim. Thus, if a victim feigns the amount of fear necessary to the commission of the crime, leading his extortioner to believe that he will consent to giving up his property, but does so only to detect and prosecute the extortioner, the crime is attempted extortion. This is on the theory that the requisite element of force or fear was not actual and the crime of extortion itself is, therefore, not consummated.

To commit the offense of attempted extortion, there must be a specific intent to commit the crime and a direct ineffectual act done toward its commission (*People v. Franquelin*, 109 Cal. App. 525).

15.10 OBTAINING SIGNATURE BY THREAT

Obtaining Signature—PC 522. "Every person who, by an extortionate means, obtains from another his signature to any paper or instrument, whereby, if such signature were freely given, any property would be transferred, or any debt, demand, charge, or right of action created, is punishable in the same manner as if the actual delivery of such debt, demand, charge, or right of action were obtained."

15.11 SENDING THREATENING LETTERS

Sending Letters With Intent to Extort—PC 523. "Every person who, with intent to extort any money or other property from another, sends or delivers to any person any letter or other writing, whether signed or not, expressing or implying, or adapted to imply, any threat such as is specified in PC 519, is punishable in the same manner as if such money or property were actually obtained by means of such threat."

Discussion. Note in the above section, that merely sending or delivering a threatening letter, containing the threats listed in PC 519, with intent to extort money or property, is punishable as extortion even if no money or property is actually obtained.

Threatening Letters—When Crime Complete—PC 660. In the various cases in which the sending of a letter is made criminal by this code, the offense is deemed complete at the time when such letter is deposited in any post office or any other place, or delivered to any person, with intent that it shall be forwarded.

Discussion. Where the defendant sent a letter to a person in which he indicated that he would expose the person to some derogatory information if the latter did not withdraw an appeal in a civil case, it was held that this was sufficient threat under PC 523 and PC 519 (*People v. Cadman*, 57 Cal. 2d 562).

Letters sent to a judge by a defendant fined and jailed by the jurist, which demanded return of the fine paid, and also inquired as to whether the judge's windows were insured was held to be not a simple inquiry but rather an implied threat under PC 523 and PC 519 (*People v. Oppenheimer*, 209 Cal. App. 2d 413).

15.12 PENALTY FOR EXTORTION

Punishment For Extortion—PC 520. Every person who extorts any money or property from another, under circumstances not amounting to robbery, by means of force, or any threat such as is mentioned in PC 518, is punishable by imprisonment in the state prison.

Public Officials—Penalty—PC 521. "Every person who commits any extortion under color of official right, in cases for which a different punishment is not prescribed in this Code, is guilty of a misdemeanor."

Attempt Extortion—Penalty—PC 524. Every person who attempts, by means of any threat, such as is specified in PC 519, to extort money or other property from another is guilty of a felony (wobbler).

COMPARISON OF ELEMENTS: ROBBERY AND EXTORTION	
ROBBERY (PC 211)	**EXTORTION (PC 518)**
1. Felonious taking (asportation) 2. Personal property of another 3. From victim's person or immediate presence 4. Against victim's will 5. By means of force or fear	1. Obtaining (need not actually take) 2. Personal property of another or an official act by a public officer 3. With victim's consent (Note difference between robbery and extortion) 4. Induced by wrongful use of force or fear
FEAR IN ROBBERY	**FEAR IN EXTORTION**
1. Threat of immediate unlawful injury to: a. Victim's person b. Victim's property c. Victim's relative 2. Immediate and unlawful injury to: a. Victim's person b. Victim's property c. Anyone accompanying victim at time of robbery	1. Threat of future unlawful injury to: a. Victim's person b. Victim's property c. Victim's relatives d. Any third person 2. Fear of accusation or exposure of: a. Any crime (victim or relative) b. Deformity, disgrace or crime c. Any secret

STUDENT REVIEW

TERMINOLOGY DEFINED—CHAPTER 15

Please see the Terminology Quiz at the end of this chapter.

1. Against will: absence of voluntary consent.
2. Appurtenant: pertaining or belonging to, an attachment.
3. Asportation: physical control or movement of property.
4. Badger Game: extortion fraud based on accusation of adultery.
5. Blackmail: another term for extortion.
6. Dangerous weapon: article capable of causing injury.
7. Deadly weapon: an article capable of causing death.
8. Extortion: taking property by illegal threats or fear.
9. Fear: intimidation based on realistic threats.
10. Fence: a receiver of stolen property.
11. Force: physically striking, abusing.
12. Immediate presence: within hearing or perception range, nearby.
13. Impute: to accuse or attribute, to ascribe.
14. Intimidation: putting one in fear.
15. Market value: reasonable current value of any property.
16. Misprision: to conceal a felony, to interfere with justice.
17. Nullify: make void, abrogate, enjoin, cancel.
18. *Obiter dictim:* An opinion of a judge, may be informal.
19. Quasi-fiduciary: similar to position of trust.
20. Torture: intentional infliction of pain or anguish on another.

TRUE-FALSE QUIZ—CHAPTER 15

After reading this chapter you should be able to correctly answer the following items.

___ 1. Robbery is the felonious taking of personal property from another with or without his knowledge or consent.
___ 2. The element of asportation is essential for the crime of robbery to be complete.
___ 3. The *corpus delicti* of robbery may be proven entirely by circumstantial evidence.
___ 4. If all other elements are present, forcing a victim to throw his wallet on the ground constitutes asportation and the robbery is complete even though the suspect does not pick it up.
___ 5. If a victim is bound and gagged in another room, it is still considered "immediate presence" for purposes of robbery.
___ 6. The "fear" mentioned in PC 211 is limited to fear of unlawful injury to the victim personally.
___ 7. Some violence or intimidation must be used in the taking of property by robbery or the crime is merely theft.
___ 8. Immediate restitution of the stolen property in robbery would nullify the crime by eliminating the element of theft.
___ 9. In robbery, the amount and value of the property taken is immaterial.
___10. The taking of property by robbery from one who is not the true owner is merely theft.
___11. Robbery of an off-duty bus driver is a misdemeanor.
___12. Robbery while "armed" with a toy gun is a felony.
___13. Any instrument, depending on how it was used, could make one guilty of using force in robbery.
___14. If only one of two suspects is armed with a loaded gun during a robbery, both are guilty of armed robbery.

____15. To be guilty of robbery involving a gun, the weapon must have been displayed, if only for a moment.
____16. If one uses a loaded gun for the purpose of committing rape, he may be charged with both robbery and rape.
____17. The key difference between robbery and extortion is the element of consent.
____18. Threatening to have someone arrested for failing to pay a legal debt constitutes extortion.
____19. Threatening to publicly accuse a city official of being gay or a lesbian unless he or she issues a needed permit is extortion even though no money or property is involved.
____20. The "Badger Game" is an example of a type of extortion.

ESSAY-DISCUSSION ITEMS—CHAPTER 15

After reading this chapter you should be able to correctly answer the following items.

1. What are the elements of extortion (PC 518)? By what common name is the crime sometimes known?
2. Discuss the element of "consent" as it applies to extortion.
3. Discuss the force or fear requisite to the crime of extortion. What are the four ways in which fear, such as will constitute extortion, may be induced?
4. What are the elements of PC 523 relative to sending threatening letters? Must this be done for purposes of extortion to constitute a crime under this section?
5. Under PC 523, if a threatening letter is sent with intent to extort, what is the effect if money or property is not actually obtained as a result of sending the letter? What is the effect if money or property *is* obtained?
6. Define the elements of robbery and discuss the following factors: (1) asportation, (2) immediate presence, (3) force or fear.
7. What effect does ownership and value of the property taken in robbery have on the *corpus delicti*?
8. How does armed robbery differ in its *corpus delicti* from extortion?
9. Discuss the meaning of "dangerous" or "deadly" weapon as it applies to robbery.
10. As indicated in PC 660, when is the crime of sending threatening letters as defined under PC 523 complete?

TERMINOLOGY QUIZ—CHAPTER 15

Match terms and definitions by writing the number preceding the correct term in the appropriate brackets.

Terms	*Definitions*
1. Against will	[ ] an article capable of causing death
2. Appurtenant	[ ] to accuse or attribute to, ascribe to
3. Asportation	[ ] article capable of causing injury
4. Badger Game	[ ] intimidation based on realistic threats
5. Blackmail	[ ] make void, abrogate, enjoin, cancel
6. Dangerous weapon	[ ] absence of voluntary consent
7. Deadly weapon	[ ] physical control or movement or property
8. Extortion	[ ] to conceal a felony, to interfere with justice
9. Fear	[ ] extortion based on accusation of adultery
10. Fence	[ ] putting one in fear
11. Force	[ ] another term for extortion

12. Immediate presence
13. Impute
14. Intimidation
15. Market value
16. Misprision
17. Nullify
18. Obiter dictim
19. Quasi-fiduciary
20. Torture

[ ] a receiver of stolen property
[ ] physically striking, abusing
[ ] within hearing or perception, nearby
[ ] taking property by illegal threats or fear

CHAPTER 16

THEFT AND EMBEZZLEMENT

16.1 THEFT DEFINED

Theft Defined—PC 484. "(a) Every person who shall feloniously steal, take, carry, lead or drive away the personal property of another, or who shall fraudulently appropriate property which has been entrusted to him, or who shall knowingly and designedly, by any false or fraudulent representation or pretense, defraud any other person of money, labor, or real or personal property, or who causes or procures others to report falsely of his wealth or mercantile [business] character and by thus imposing upon any person, obtains credit and thereby fraudulently gets or obtains the labor or service of another, is guilty of theft."

Various Acts Constituting Theft. As will be noted by reading the above, the section defining theft covers several acts, any one or combination of which can constitute theft. Following is a list of four acts, each of which is considered theft under PC 484.

1. It is theft to:
   a. Feloniously (unlawfully) steal, take, carry, lead or drive away,
   b. The personal property of another.
2. It is theft (embezzlement) to:
   a. Fraudulently appropriate property,
   b. By the person to whom it was entrusted.
3. It is theft (false pretenses) to:
   a. Defraud another,
   b. By false or fraudulent pretense,
   c. Of money, labor, or real or personal property.
4. It is theft when one:
   a. Causes or procures another to falsely report one's wealth,
   b. For purpose of obtaining credit, and thus,
   c. Fraudulently obtains money, property, or services of another.

Determining Value of Property—PC 484. "(a) In determining the value of the property obtained, for purposes of this section, the reasonable and fair market value shall be the test, and in determining the value of services received, the contract price shall be the test. If there be no contract price, the reasonable and going wage for the service rendered shall govern. For the purposes of this section, any false or fraudulent representation or pretense made shall be treated as continuing, so as to cover any money, property or service received as a result thereof, and the complaint, information, or indictment may charge that the crime was committed on any date during the particular period in question. The hiring of any additional employee or employees without advising each of them of every labor claim due and unpaid and every judgment that the employer has been unable to meet shall be *prima facie* evidence of intent to defraud.

(b) Except as provided in Section 10855 of the Vehicle Code [failure to return leased vehicle], intent to commit theft by fraud is presumed if one who has leased or rented the personal property of another pursuant to a written contract fails to return the personal property to its owner within 20 days after the owner has made written demand by certified or registered mail following the expiration of the lease or rental agreement for return of the property so leased or rented.

(c) Notwithstanding the provisions of subdivision (b), if one presents, with criminal intent, identification which bears a false or fictitious name or address for the purposes of obtaining the lease or rental of the personal property of another, the presumption created herein shall apply upon the failure of the lessee to return the rental property at the expiration of the lease or rental agreement, and no written demand for the return of the leased or rented property shall be required.

(d) The presumptions created by subdivisions (b) and (c) are presumptions affecting the burden of producing evidence.

(e) Within 30 days after the lease or rental agreement has expired, the owner shall make written demand for return of the property so leased or rented. Notice addressed and mailed to the lessee or renter at the address given at the time of the making of the lease or rental agreement and to any other known address shall constitute proper demand. Where the owner fails to make such written demand the presumption created by subdivision (b) shall not apply."

Diversion of Money Received for Labor or Materials—PC 484b. "Any person who receives money for the purpose of obtaining or paying for services, labor, materials, or equipment and willfully fails to apply such money for such purpose by either willfully failing to complete the improvements for which funds were provided or willfully failing to pay for services, labor, materials or equipment provided incident to such construction, and wrongfully diverts the funds to a use other than that for which the funds were received, shall be guilty of a public offense [felony wobbler]."

Note: If the amount diverted is less than one thousand dollars ($1,000), the person is guilty of a misdemeanor. This type of funds diversion is typical of some unethical contractors who are given money to pay for building materials, etc., but instead put the funds to their own use.

"Theft" Substituted for Other Terms—PC 490(a). Prior to 1927 the Penal Code made a technical distinction between (1) larceny (theft), (2) embezzlement, and (3) obtaining money under false pretenses. Due to the difficulty in determining which crime had been committed, Section 490(a) was added, which reads:

"Whenever any law or statute of this state refers to or mentions larceny, embezzlement, or stealing, said law or statute shall hereafter be read and interpreted as if the word 'theft' were substituted therefor."

Value of Property Taken. To determine the value of the property taken, the reasonable and fair market value is the test. In determining the value of services received, the contract price shall be the test. If there is no contract price, the reasonable and going wage for the service rendered shall govern.

Property Subject of Theft. In order for property to be capable of being stolen, it must have some genuine market value, whether intrinsic or extrinsic. Thus it has been held that the theft of a lottery ticket has an initial market value of its cost. If, however, it is a winning ticket, it has a market value equal to the prize which it represents (*People v. Gonzales*, 62 Cal. App. 3d 274).

Real property (land and buildings) as well as personal property may be the subject of theft. Thus where a fixture, which is part of a building is removed and stolen, it is theft.

Dogs are legally considered personal property under PC 491 and may be the subject of theft. However, cats are generally not placed within this category unless some legal value (such as a pedigreed show animal) can be established, the theory being that cats are not personal property since no license fees are paid on them.

Certain types of thefts are made crimes by separate statute. Thus, passenger tickets may be stolen (PC 493), as well as water and electricity (PC 498). Also, if the thing stolen consists of any evidence of debt or other written instrument, the amount of money due thereon, or which might be collected thereon, or the value of the property the title to which is shown thereby, is the value of the thing stolen (PC 492).

16.2 THE ACT OF TAKING IN THEFT

Asportation Defined. The act of taking in theft consists in taking *and* carrying away the property of another, not taking *or* carrying away. Such a taking and carrying away is called "asportation" and is an essential element of every crime of theft. In addition, the taking requires a violation of another's possession; there must be a trespass. Consequently, if the defendant was already in possession of the goods, there could be no taking (although there could still be theft by embezzlement).

Where the accused endeavored to steal an overcoat hung on a clothing dummy standing in front of a store and had unbuttoned the coat and removed it from the dummy, but was prevented from carrying it away because of a chain which passed through the sleeve and was fastened to the dummy, there was not sufficient asportation to constitute larceny (*People v. Meyer*, 75 Cal. 838). The perpetrator could, however, be charged with attempted theft.

To constitute the necessary asportation, the thief must move the property so that in some degree

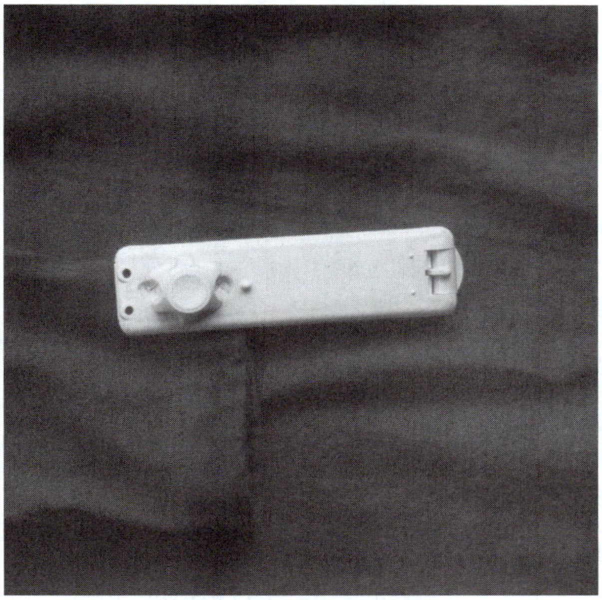

To fight shoplifting losses, retailers use a variety of sensor devices. *Photograph by M. Antman, courtesy of The Image Works*

it occupies a different position than it previously occupied and the conditions must be such that the thief secures such dominion over the property as to be able to carry it away (*People v. Wilcoxin*, 69 Cal. App. 2d 267).

Where a shoplifter removes merchandise from a store display and presents it at the check stand for a "refund," the crime of theft of the property has been committed (*People v. Davis*, 19 Cal. 4th 301). If a "refund" is actually given to the thief, theft of the refunded amount has been committed (*Davis*). If a "refund" is refused by the merchant and the thief leaves with the merchandise, a theft of the merchandise has occurred (*People v. McLemore*, 27 Cal. App. 4th 601).

Asportation need not be by the use of any personal force. An animal may be stolen by being enticed away by food; or tapping a pipe and taking gas or water from it will constitute the necessary asportation to commit the crime of theft.

Elements of Theft. The four elements necessary to constitute theft are:

1. The taking of a thing of value from the owner (or any other person in possession of the property);
2. Without consent of the owner or person then in possession of the property;
3. With intent to permanently deprive the owner of the use or title of the property, or of a major portion of its value or enjoyment, and
4. Asportation (movement) of the property. One cannot commit theft by looking at, longing for, or even wanting to steal property (*People v. Johnson*, 136 Cal. App. 2d 665).

16.3 THE INTENT IN THEFT

One of the essential elements of the crime of theft is an intent to steal. The intent in theft must be to permanently deprive the owner (or person in possession) of the use of or title to the property. This element is satisfied if the one who takes property keeps it "for so extended a period as to deprive the owner of a major portion of its value or enjoyment," as for example, when the property taken is dated or perishable, or is useful only for seasonal use, or is abandoned by the taker under circumstances making it unlikely the owner will recover it (*People v. Avery, 27* Cal.4th 49).

Since specific intent must exist at the time of the taking of the property of another, the taking of an automobile belonging to another in his absence and without his consent, but without any intention of permanently depriving the owner of his property, while it might constitute a violation of Section 10851 of the Vehicle Code (unlawful driving), would not constitute theft (*People v. Tucker*, 104 Cal. 440).

Similarly, the taking of property which is rented on a time basis, and failing to return it at a specified time, is not necessarily theft, unless the person renting the property intended to steal it at the time of negotiating the rental. If one in good faith takes the property of another, thinking it to be his own, and assuming that he has a legal right to it, it is not theft due to the absence of a specific intent to deprive the owner of his property.

However, where a person takes a car which does not belong to him, and without the owner's consent, and thereafter trades the spare tire for a tank of gasoline, such has been held sufficient to establish the required specific intent to commit theft (*People v. Crawford*, 115 Cal. App. 2d 838).

Theft is ordinarily the felonious taking of property of another without his consent with the intent to deprive him thereof, and includes larceny, embezzlement, obtaining money by false pretenses, and theft by trick or device (*People v. Goodman*, 159 Cal. App. 2d 54).

Possession of Stolen Property. A suspect who is in possession of stolen property has a duty to explain his possession in order to remove the effect of possession as a circumstance, taken with other suspicious facts, indicating theft (*People v. Arriola*, 164 Cal. App. 2d 430).

Where the perpetrator of a theft takes the personal property of another and is subsequently found in possession of same, such evidence is admissible for two purposes: (1) it tends to show the identity of the perpetrator, and (2) it tends to connect the defendant with the offense. However, there must be, in addition to proof of the possession of stolen property, other evidence tending to show the commission of the offense by the accused.

Where recently stolen property is found in knowing possession of a defendant who, upon being questioned by police, gives an erroneous and false explanation regarding his possession or remains silent under circumstances indicative of guilt, an inference of guilt is permissible and is a question for the jury to resolve (*Rollins v. Superior Court*, Cal. App. 2d 219).

A defendant who is in possession of stolen property has a duty to explain his possession in order to remove the effect of possession as a circumstance, taken with other suspicious facts, of guilt (*People v. Wells*, 187 Cal. App. 2d 324).

Possession of stolen goods is not of itself sufficient to justify a conviction of theft, although it is a circumstance to be considered in connection with other proven facts (*People v. Edwards*, 159 Cal. App. 2d 208).

Evidence of possession of stolen property by the defendant, coupled with his attempt to dispose of the property at far less than its market value, together with inconsistent and misleading statements as to its procurement, justified a finding that the property was stolen and a conviction for grand theft was sustained even though there was no direct testimony or admission of the theft by the accused (*People v. Phelps*, 192 Cal. App. 2d 12).

16.4 ANALYSIS OF TYPES OF THEFT

There are four general categories of theft:

1. theft (larceny) in general,
2. obtaining property by false pretenses,
3. obtaining property by trick or device, and
4. theft by embezzlement.

As previously indicated, whenever any law or statute of this state refers to or mentions larceny, embezzlement, or stealing, the law or statute should be read and interpreted as if the word "theft" were substituted (PC 490a).

Thus the former crimes of larceny, embezzlement, and obtaining property by false pretenses are merged into the one crime of theft. The punishment for the commission of these offenses will either be grand or petit (petty) theft, depending on the circumstances of the case and the value of the property.

16.5 THEFT IN GENERAL

Theft in general consists of a wrongful or fraudulent taking and carrying away, by any person, of the personal goods of another, from any place, without any color of right for the act, with the intention to deprive the owner, not temporarily, but permanently of his property.

The intent of the owner or person in possession is that he never intends that the taker shall take or keep his property, and title remains with the owner at all times. Possession of the property taken remains "constructively" with the owner, while the wrongdoer obtains custody. No corroboration is necessary to prove a general theft, which is simply the stealing of another's property.

16.6 THEFT BY FALSE PRETENSES

Theft by False Pretenses—PC 532. The crime of obtaining property by false pretenses is included in PC 484 defining theft, but is more specifically defined in PC 532, which states, "Every person who knowingly and designedly, by any false or fraudulent representation or pretense, defrauds any other person of money, labor, or property, whether real or personal, or who causes or procures others to report falsely of his wealth or mercantile character, and by thus imposing upon any person obtains credit, and thereby fraudulently gets possession of money or property, or obtains the labor or service of another, is punishable in the same manner and to the same extent as for larceny of the money or property so obtained."

The Act in Theft by False Pretenses. The act consists in the perpetrator gaining control over the property of another in an illegal manner. Such property may be tangible or in the form of credit or services rendered. The intent of the taker is to defraud by making false representations of a present or past existing fact and not opinions, future promises, or so-called "puffing of wares."

The owner in this case voluntarily gives his property to the wrongdoer in reliance on the false representations and deceit, without any reservations. Both title and possession of the property pass into the hands of the wrongdoer because the owner intends to part with his property in reliance on the fraud. Corroboration is required (PC 1110) to sustain a conviction for theft perpetrated under these circumstances.

A conviction of grand theft by false pretenses can rest either on a fraudulent statement of a factual character or on a promise made without intent to perform it (*People v. Carlin*, 178 Cal. App. 2d 705). And, a promise made without intention to perform is a misrepresentation of a state of mind and hence a misrepresentation of existing facts and is a false pretense within the meaning of this section (*People v. DeCasaus*, 194 Cal. App. 2d 666).

Where a party offers to sell an interest in a business which has not been established and paints a rosy picture of the future based on false statements which the prospective purchaser believes to be true, the fraud is complete (*People v. Carlin*, 178 Cal. App. 2d 705).

Theft by Impersonation—PC 530.5. Willfully obtaining and using, without authorization, any personal identifying information (such as names and numbers) in order to obtain credit, goods or services in another's name is a misdemeanor, punishable by $1000 fine and one year in jail, or less.

16.7 THEFT BY TRICK OR DEVICE

This type of theft, often referred to as "bunco theft" or the perpetration of a "confidence" game, is similar to theft by false pretenses. The act of this type consists in the perpetrator gaining control over the property of another by some trick, fraud, or false representation. The intent of the taker is to feloniously steal, which means to permanently deprive the owner of his property at the time the possession is acquired. While corroboration is necessary to prove a theft by false pretenses, corroboration is not necessary in proving a theft by trick or device (*People v. Reinschreiber*, 141 Cal. App. 2d 688).

The intent of the owner in a theft by trick and device is to voluntarily give his property to the wrongdoer in reliance on some scheme, device, trick or artifice, but only for some agreed-upon special use, and generally for a specified period of time. Title of the property taken remains with the owner because the owner never actually intends to give up title.

Possession, on the other hand, passes to the wrongdoer, but again, only for a special purpose. Corroboration is unnecessary in sustaining a conviction for this type of theft.

Examples of this type of theft include false and fraudulent spiritual manifestations, obtaining money to bet on an allegedly "fixed" horse race, or buying property for the victim and then "jacking" up the price in an effort to pocket the proceeds therefrom.

Inherent in the crime of larceny by trick and device is the employment of fraud and trickery in obtaining possession of property by one who has a preconceived design to appropriate it to his own use. Thus, where one perpetrates a short-change trick, the crime of theft by trick and device is committed and the amount of money taken in the exchange will determine the degree of theft (*People v. Stone*, 155 Cal. App. 2d 259).

The gist of the offense of larceny by trick and device is the appropriation of property, the possession of which was fraudulently acquired, and if a person, with a preconceived design to appropriate property to his own use, obtains possession of it by means of fraud or trickery, the taking is unquestionably theft (*People v. Robertson*, 167 Cal. App. 2d 571).

Difference Between Trick and Device and False Pretenses. Theft by "trick and device" and theft by "false pretenses" are distinguished in that theft by trick and device is the appropriation of property, the possession of which was fraudulently acquired, and requires no corroboration to sustain a conviction. Theft by false pretenses is the fraudulent or deceitful acquisition of both title and possession, and requires corroboration to sustain a conviction (*People v. Hodges*, 153 Cal. App. 2d 788).

16.8 THEFT BY EMBEZZLEMENT

Embezzlement Defined—PC 503. "Embezzlement is the fraudulent appropriation of property by a person to whom it has been entrusted."

Embezzlement by Clerk—PC 508. "Every clerk, agent, or servant of any person who fraudulently appropriates to his own use, or secretes with a fraudulent intent to appropriate to his own use, any property of another which has come into his control or care by virtue of his employment as such clerk, agent or servant, is guilty of embezzlement."

Distinct Act of Taking—PC 509. "A distinct act of taking is not necessary to constitute embezzlement."

Restoring Property as Defense—PC 512. "The fact that the accused intended to restore the property embezzled, is no ground of defense or mitigation of punishment, if it has not been restored before an information has been laid before a magistrate, or an indictment found by a grand jury, charging the commission of the offense."

Note: If the embezzler does replace or restore the embezzled money or property before charges are filed (as per PC 512, above) it is no defense to the crime, but the court may mitigate punishment at its discretion (PC 513).

Discussion. The act of embezzlement does not require a distinct act of taking because the gist of the offense is the wrongful use of property entrusted to a servant, employee, agent, bailee, trustee, or public servant. The perpetrator is said to enjoy a "fiduciary relationship" (one involving trust) with the owner of the property, and he thus comes into possession of the property legally. For example, a store manager gives possession of a specific number of dollars in cash to a clerk at the beginning of a day to make change. If the clerk thereafter appropriates this cash to his own use, which he has legal possession of at the time, he is then surreptitiously claiming ownership and title of the property which he is not entitled to do.

The intent in embezzlement is to feloniously steal, but only after possession is acquired. This is called "appropriation with fraudulent intent." The intent of the owner is that he never intends to part with title or ownership of the property, but stipulates that the "trustee" shall use the property only for a specified purpose agreed upon. As previously indicated, title remains with the owner at all times, but possession passes to the wrongdoer only for a special purpose of trust. No corroboration is necessary to sustain a conviction for embezzlement.

The property which may be the subject of embezzlement may be money, goods, chattels, things in action, or evidence of debt (*People v. Hart*, 28 Cal. App. 335).

Possession of property in some kind of fiduciary capacity is an essential element of embezzlement. Where a trustee of a union welfare fund withdrew excessive amounts of money from a fund in the form of a cashier's check which he did not endorse or cash but which check was still outstanding, there was a completed embezzlement, regardless of his alleged intention to return the check to the trust fund (*People v. Williams*, 145 Cal. App. 2d 163).

Where an official of a union had control of union-owned real estate, and directed the sale of it, thereafter appropriating to his own use part of the proceeds of the sale, he was guilty of embezzlement (*People v. Swanson*, 174 Cal. App. 2d 453).

The essential elements of embezzlement are a fiduciary relationship arising where one entrusts property to another, and fraudulent appropriation of that property by the latter (*People v. Darling*, 230 Cal. App. 2d 615).

Punishment For Embezzlement—PC 514. Every person guilty of embezzlement is punishable in the manner prescribed for theft of property of the value or kind embezzled. If the embezzlement is of public funds, the offense is a felony punishable by imprisonment in the state prison; and the person so convicted is ineligible thereafter to hold any office of honor, trust, or profit in this state (briefed).

16.9 THEFT OF ACCESS CARDS

Definitions—PC 484d. As used in this section and Sections 484e to 484j, inclusive:

1. "Cardholder" means any person to whom an access card is issued or any person who has agreed with the card issuer to pay obligations arising from the issuance of an access card to another person.
2. "Access card" means any card, plate, code, account number, or other means of account access that can be used, alone or in conjunction with another access card, to obtain money, goods, services, or any other thing of value, or that can be used to initiate transfer of funds, other than a transfer originated solely by a paper instrument.
3. "Expired access card" means an access card which shows on its face it has elapsed.
4. "Card issuer" means any person who issues an access card or the agent of such person with respect to such card.
5. "Retailer" means every person who is authorized by an issuer to furnish goods, money, services or anything else of value upon presentation of an access card by a cardholder.
6. An access card is "incomplete" if part of the matter other than the signature of the cardholder which an issuer requires to appear on the card before it can be used by a cardholder has not been stamped, embossed, imprinted, or written on it.

High-tech forgery of credit cards causes huge losses each year. *Photo by Michael Newman, courtesy of PhotoEdit*

7. "Revoked access card" means an access card which is no longer authorized for use by the issuer, such authorization having been suspended or terminated and written notice thereof having been given the cardholder.
8. "Counterfeit access card" means any access card that is counterfeit, fictitious, altered, or forged, or any false representation or depiction of an access card or component thereof.
9. "Traffic" means to transfer or otherwise dispose of property to another, or to obtain control of property with intent to transfer or dispose of it to another.
10. "Card making equipment" means any equipment, machine, plate, mechanism, impression, or other device designed, used, or intended to be used to produce an access card.

Theft of Access Card—PC 484e. "(a) Every person who acquires an access card from another without the cardholder's or issuer's consent or who, with knowledge that it has been so acquired, acquires the access card, with intent to use it or to sell or transfer it to a person other than the issuer or the cardholder, is guilty of petty theft.

(b) Every person who acquires an access card that he or she knows to have been lost, mislaid, or delivered under a mistake as to the identity or address of the cardholder, and who retains possession with intent to use it or to sell it or to transfer it to a person other than the issuer or the cardholder is guilty of petty theft.

(c) Every person who sells, transfers, conveys, or receives an access card with the intent to defraud, or who acquires an access card with the intent to use it fraudulently, is guilty of petty theft.

(d) Every person other than the issuer, who within any consecutive twelve-month period, acquires access cards issued in the names of four or more persons which he has reason to know were taken or retained under circumstances which constitute a violation of subdivisions (a), (b), or (c) of this section is guilty of grand theft.

(e) Every person who acquires access card account information with respect to an access card validly issued to another person, without the cardholder's or issuer's consent, with the intent to use it fraudulently is guilty of grand theft."

Forgery of Access Card—PC 484f. Every person who, with intent to defraud, designs makes, alters, or embosses a counterfeit access card or utters or otherwise attempts to use a counterfeit access card is guilty of forgery.

A person other than the cardholder or a person authorized by him or her who, with intent to defraud, signs the name of another or of a fictitious person to an access card, sales slip, sales draft, or instrument for the payment of money which evidences an access card transaction, or who makes any alteration to an access card that causes false billing, is guilty of forgery.

Use of Forged Access Card—PC 484g. "Every person, who with intent to defraud,

(a) uses for the purpose of obtaining money, goods, services, or anything else of value an access card obtained or retained in violation of Section 484e or 484f or an access card which he or she knows is forged, expired, or revoked, or

(b) obtains money, goods, services or anything else of value by representing, without the consent of the cardholder, that he or she is the holder of an access card or by representing that he or she is the holder of an access card and the card has not in fact been issued, is guilty of theft.

If the value of all money, goods, services, and other things of value obtained in violation of this section exceeds four hundred dollars ($400) in any consecutive six-month period, then the same shall constitute grand theft."

Furnishing Goods or Services on Forged Access Card—PC 484h. "Every retailer or other person who, with intent to defraud:

(a) Furnishes money, goods, services or anything else of value upon presentation of an access card obtained or retained in violation of Section 484e or an access card which he or she knows is a counterfeit access card or is forged, expired, or revoked, and who receives any payment therefor, is guilty of theft.

If the payment received by the merchant for all money, goods, services, and other things of value furnished in violation of this section exceeds four hundred dollars ($400) in any consecutive six-month period, then the same shall constitute grand theft.

(b) Presents for payment a sales slip or other evidence of an access card transaction, and receives payment therefor, without furnishing in the transaction money, goods services, or anything else of value that is equal in value to the amount of the sales slip or other evidence of an access card transaction, is guilty of theft."

Counterfeiting Access Card—PC 484i. Possession of a partial counterfeit with intent to complete is a misdemeanor. Other counterfeiting and possession of cards or equipment is a wobbler. Unauthorized publishing of account numbers with intent to defraud is a misdemeanor (PC 484j).

Misuse of Scanning Devices and Encoders—PC 502.6. It is a misdemeanor to possess or use a scanning device to read magnetic strips on payment cards, or an encoding device for placing encoded information on a magnetic strip, with fraudulent intent.

16.10 THEFT OF LOST PROPERTY

Appropriation of Lost Property—PC 485. "One who finds lost property, under circumstances which give him knowledge of or means of inquiry as to the true owner, and who appropriates such property to his own use or to the use of another person not entitled thereto, without first making reasonable and just efforts to find the owner and restore the property to him, is guilty of theft."

Discussion. This section applies only to cases in which the property was first lost and then found by one who took it, not as a thief, but as a finder of lost property. In such a case the finder is guilty of this offense if, having the means of inquiry as to the true owner, he or she appropriates the property to his or her own use without making reasonable efforts to find the owner and restore the property to the true owner. ***Note:*** also see Section 16.14 Receiving or Concealing Stolen Property.

Finder of Lost Property. The Civil Code provides the manner in which one who has found lost property should pursue a legal course of action in attempting to restore such property to its rightful owner.

Duty of Finder—Civil Code 2080. "Any person who finds a thing lost is not bound to take charge of it, but if he does so he is thenceforward a depository for the owner, with the rights and obligations of a depository for hire. Any person who finds and takes possession of any money, goods, things of action, or other personal property, or saves any domestic animal from drowning or starvation shall, within a reasonable time, inform the owner, if known, and make restitution without compensation, except a reasonable charge for saving and taking care of the property."

Unknown Owner—Civil Code 2080.1. "If the owner is unknown or has not claimed the property, the person saving or finding the property shall, if the property is of the value of one hundred dollars ($100) or more, within a reasonable time, turn the property over to the police department of the city, if found therein, or the sheriffs department if found outside the city limits, and shall make an affidavit stating when and where he or she found or saved the property, particularly describing it. If the property was saved, the affidavit shall state:

1. From what and how it was saved.
2. Whether the owner of the property is known to the affiant.
3. That the affiant has not secreted, withheld, or disposed of any part of the property.

(b) The police department or the sheriffs department shall notify the owner, if his or her identity is reasonably ascertainable, that it possesses the property and where it may be claimed. The police department or sheriffs department may require payment by the owner of a reasonable charge to defray costs of storage and care of the property."

Claiming Property—Civil Code 2080.2. If the owner appears within ninety days and proves his ownership and pays all reasonable charges, the police department or sheriffs department shall restore the property to him."

Finder Gets Title—Civil Code 2080.3. If no owner of the property valued at $250 or more appears within ninety days, the police or sheriffs department shall publish at least once in a newspaper notice of the found or saved property. If after seven days following the notice, no owner appears and proves ownership, then title shall vest in the person who found or saved the property. If the property was found by an employee of any public agency, the property shall be sold at public auction. Title to unclaimed property valued below $250 vests in the finder after 90 days, without publication.

16.11 DEGREES OF THEFT

Degrees of Theft—PC 486. "Theft is divided into two degrees, the first of which is termed grand theft; the second, petty theft."

Grand Theft Defined—PC 487. "Grand theft is theft committed in any of the following cases:"

1. **Money, Labor, Personal Property.** When the money, labor, or real or personal property taken is of value *greater* than four hundred dollars ($400), or theft is committed in any of the following cases, it is grand theft.
2. **Fowls, Farm Products.** When domestic fowls, avocados, olives, citrus or other fruits, vegetables, nuts, artichokes, or other farm crops are taken of a value greater than one hundred dollars ($100) it is grand theft. *Note:* To establish that the value of avocados or citrus fruit *exceeds* $100, the wholesale price on the day of the theft is used.
3. **Aquaculture Products** (grown in water). When fish, shellfish, mollusks, crustaceans, kelp, algae or other aquaculture products are taken from a commercial operation *exceeding* $100 in value, it is grand theft.
4. **Theft by Employee, etc.** Where money, labor, or real property (real estate) or personal property is taken by a servant, agent, or employee of the victim, and totals $400 or more *in any 12 consecutive month period*, it is grand theft.
5. **Grand Theft From Person—Value of Property.** Property taken from the person of another constitutes grand theft. This is true regardless of what is taken as long as it has any value whatever. Theft of an empty wallet by a pickpocket would be grand theft on the theory that the wallet itself would have some value, even if small. Theft of a bus token worth but a few cents, if taken from the person, would also be grand theft.

From the Person Defined. To constitute taking "from the person," the property must be taken:

1. from a receptacle (purse, etc.) being carried at the time,
2. from the victim's clothing being worn at the time,
3. from his or her hands while carrying the item stolen or
4. while attached to his or her person physically in some way, such as a locket hanging around the neck.

If the victim lays the property down, even for a moment, at which time it is stolen, the theft is not "from the person." Property placed under one's pillow while sleeping, for example, is not considered to be on the person, thus, theft of such property would not automatically constitute grand theft unless the amount stolen *exceeded* four hundred dollars or is a firearm.

In summary, to constitute theft "from the person," the property must be either held, in a pocket of clothing being worn, or secured to or attached in some way to the victim's physical person at the time it is stolen. Otherwise the theft is petty or grand depending solely on the type of property stolen and its value.

6. **Automobile, Firearm, Animals.** It is grand theft when the property taken is an automobile, firearm, horse, make gelding, any bovine (cattle) animal, any caprine (goat) animal, mule, jenny, jack, (female/male jackass) sheep, lamb, hog, sow, gilt (young sow), barrow (castrated male hog) or pig. The $100 or $400 value applicable in other grand thefts is not an element in the above.

Stealing Livestock Carcass—PC 487a. "(a) Every person who shall feloniously steal, take, transport, or carry the carcass of any bovine [cattle], caprine [goat], equine [horse], ovine [sheep], or suine [pig] animal or of any mule, jack, or jenny, which is the personal property of another, or who shall fraudulently appropriate such property which has been entrusted to him, is guilty of grand theft.

(b) Every person who shall feloniously steal, take, transport, or carry any portion of the carcass of any bovine, caprine, equine, ovine or suine animal or of any mule, jack or jenny, which has been killed without the consent of the owner thereof, is guilty of grand theft."

Grand Theft Real Estate—PC 487b. "Every person who converts real estate of the value of one hundred ($100) or more into personal property by severance from the realty of another, and with felonious intent to do so, steals, takes, and carries away such property is guilty of grand theft and is punishable by imprisonment in the state prison."

Petty Theft Real Estate—PC 487c. "Every person who converts real estate of the value of less than one hundred dollars ($100) into personal property by severance from the realty of another, and with felonious intent to do so, steals, takes, and carries away such property is guilty of petit theft and is punishable by imprisonment in the county jail . . . or by a fine . . . or by both fine and imprisonment."

Grand Theft at Mine—PC 487d. "Every person who feloniously steals, takes, and carries away, or attempts to take, steal, and carry from any mining claim, tunnel, sluice, undercurrent, riffle box, or sulfurate machine another's gold dust, amalgam, or quicksilver is guilty of grand theft and is punishable by imprisonment in the state prison."

Dog Stealing Grand Theft—PC 487e. "Every person who feloniously steals, takes, or carries away a dog of another which is of a value exceeding four hundred dollars ($400) is guilty of grand theft."

Dog Stealing Petty Theft—PC 487f. "Every person who feloniously steals, takes, or carries away a dog of another which is of a value *not* exceeding four hundred dollars ($400) is guilty of petty theft."

Dog Stealing for Medical Research—PC 487g. Every person who feloniously steals, takes, or carries away a dog of another for purposes of sale, medical research, slaughter, or other commercial uses, is guilty of grand theft.

Grand Theft of Cargo—PC 487h. The theft of cargo valued at more than $400 is grand theft. "Cargo" means any goods, wares, products, or manufactured merchandise that has been loaded into a trailer, railcar, or cargo container, awaiting or in transit.

Petty Theft Defined—PC 488. This section defines the crime of petty theft and reads simply: "Theft in other cases is petty theft." This means that theft in California must be either "petty" or "grand." If the theft does not meet the criteria for grand theft (see PC 487) because of the amount of money or property stolen or the manner in which the theft was committed, it is deemed to be petty theft. In other words, if it's not grand theft, it's petty theft.

Discussion. The offense of "theft" includes larceny, embezzlement, larceny by trick and device, and obtaining property by false pretenses (*People v. Schwenker*, 191 Cal. App. 2d 46).

The elements of the crime of theft remain the same except that the difference between grand and petty theft is in (1) the type of articles stolen, (2) if the articles were taken from the person of another, and (3) in the fair market value of the property stolen (*Gomez v. Superior Court*, 50 Cal. 2d 640).

Elements of Theft. The essential elements of theft consist of:

1. taking the personal property of another, of some value,
2. without the owner's or possessor's consent,
3. asportation of the goods stolen, and
4. intent to deprive the owner of his property wholly and permanently (*People v. Torres*, 201 Cal. App. 2d 290).

Value of Property Taken. The market value of property for determining petty or grand theft, is the "fair market value" at the time and place where the property was stolen (*People v. Simpson*, 26 Cal. App. 2d 223).

16.12 PUNISHMENT FOR THEFT

Grand Theft Punishment—PC 489. "Grand theft is punishable as follows:

(a) When the grand theft involves the theft of a firearm, by imprisonment in the state prison for 16 months, 2, or 3 years.

(b) In all other cases, by imprisonment in a county jail not exceeding one year or in the state prison."

Petty Theft Punishment—PC 490. "Petty theft is punishable by a fine not exceeding one thousand ($1,000) dollars, or by imprisonment in the county jail not exceeding six months, or both."

Embezzlement of Public Funds Punishment—PC 514. If the embezzlement is of public funds of the United States, or of this state, or any county or municipality within this state, the offense is a felony, and is punishable by imprisonment in the state prison; and the person so convicted is ineligible thereafter to hold any office of honor, trust, or profit in this state.

16.13 PETTY THEFT PRIOR CONVICTIONS

Petty Theft Second Offenses—PC 666. "Every person who having been convicted of petit theft [PC 488], grand theft [PC 487], auto theft under Section 10851 of the Vehicle Code, burglary [PC 459], carjacking [PC 215], robbery [PC 211], or a felony violation of Section 496 and having served a term therefor in any penal institution, or having been imprisoned therein as a condition of probation for such offense, is subsequently convicted of petit theft, then the person convicted of such subsequent offense is punishable by imprisonment in the county jail not exceeding one year, or in the state prison."

Foreign Conviction of Former Offense—PC 668. "Every person who has been convicted in any other state, government, country or jurisdiction of an offense for which, if committed within this state, such person could have been punished under the laws of this state by imprisonment in a state prison, is punishable for any subsequent crime committed within this state in the manner prescribed by law, and to the same extent as if such prior conviction had taken place in a court of this state."

Discussion. The object in charging prior felony convictions is not necessarily for a determination of the career criminal status of the person charged, but is for the information of the court in determining the punishment to be imposed in case of conviction.

In order to subject the defendant to an increased penalty on conviction for petty theft because of a prior felony conviction, it is not necessary for the prosecution to allege and prove that the defendant had been imprisoned for the full term of his sentence. It is not necessary that the defendant shall have served the full term of imprisonment for his prior offense; service of a portion thereof is sufficient (*People v. James*, 155 Cal. App. 2d 604).

16.14 SEPARATE MULTIPLE THEFTS

When the property of several victims is stolen at the same time, and under the same circumstances, they are considered to be but one theft, however many victims there may be. For example, if three surfboards are taken from atop a vehicle while the three owners are absent from the vehicle, there is but a single theft committed with three victims of the theft. Assuming that the surf boards are worth $ 150 each, the offense would be grand theft, a felony.

However, where the taking is from different persons at different places and under different circumstances, or where property is taken *from the person* of different individuals at the same time (such as a robbery) or from different individuals by the same trick and device, each transaction is a separate theft (*People v. Sichofsky*, 58 Cal. App. 257).

Where it is the intent of a person to steal an entire lot of merchandise, it makes no difference whether asportation (the taking) is complete in one time period or is extended over a period of time to facilitate the carrying away of property, as long as there is one common purpose, intent, and design to remove the lot of property.

For example, if one intends to steal $450 worth of property which will take three successive nights to haul away, he is committing one act of grand theft rather than three separate and distinct acts of petty theft wherein the value of the property taken on each occasion is less than $400. However, the intent of the perpetrator in these cases must be in furtherance of but one intention, one general impulse, and one plan, even though there is a series of transactions (*People v. Bailey*, 55 Cal. 2d 514).

A defendant may be properly convicted upon separate counts charging grand theft from the same person if the evidence shows that the offenses are separate and distinct, and were not committed pursuant to one intention, general impulse, or course of action (*People v. Stanford*, 16 Cal. 2d 247).

Thus where a person embezzles, on various occasions, with but a single purpose on each occasion, and

THEFT ANALYSIS CHART

Theft Includes	Larceny (Theft)	Obtaining Property By False Pretenses	Obtaining Property By Trick And Device	Embezzlement (Trust Relationship)
The Act	Must be a taking and carrying away of personal property (known as asportation). Original taking is a trespass.	Control over the property is illegally obtained. Property may be tangible or is in the form of credit or services rendered.	Control over the property is obtained by some trick, fraud, or false representation. Usually referred to as a "bunco game."	Distinct act of taking is not required because gist of offense is a wrongful use of property entrusted to servant, employee, agent, bailee, trustee or public servant.
The Intent of the Taker	Intent is to "feloniously" steal, at the time of the taking, which means to intend to deprive the owner permanently of his property, not in jest, claim of right, or temporarily.	Intent is to defraud by making false representations of a present or past fact — not opinions, future promises or "puffing" of wares.	Intent to "feloniously" steal, which means to intend to deprive the owner permanently of his property, by false schemes or trickery.	Intent is to "feloniously" steal, but only *after* possession is acquired. This is called "appropriation with fraudulent intent."
The Intent of the Owner	Owner never intends that the taker shall take or keep his property.	Owner voluntarily gives his property to the wrongdoer in reliance on these false representations and deceit, without any reservation.	Owner voluntarily gives his property in reliance on the scheme of the wrongdoer, but only for some agreed special use.	Owner never intends that the "trustee" shall use the property for any purpose other than specified or agreed upon.
Title	Remains with the owner at all times.	Passes to the wrongdoer because the owner so intends.	Remains with the owner because owner never intends to give up title.	Remains with the owner at all times.
Custody or Possession	Remains "constructively" with owner — the wrongdoer obtains custody, unlawfully.	Passes to the wrongdoer with consent of owner because of the fraud.	Passes to wrongdoer but only for a special purpose or use.	Passes to wrongdoer but only for a special purpose of trust.
Proof	Corroboration not necessary.	Corroboration necessary.	Corroboration not necessary.	Corroboration not necessary.

there was no evidence of a common purpose, intent, design, or general impulse in taking the money entrusted to him in a fiduciary capacity, each taking constituted a separate intent and thus resulted in a separate crime of embezzlement (*People v. Hill*, 32 Cal. App. 554).

A different situation arises when a clerk, in pursuance of one design and purpose, takes merchandise of his employer and converts it to his own use by selling it to "personal customers" and thereafter pockets the proceeds made on the transaction. This is clearly but one theft (embezzlement), since there was but one general intent on the part of the perpetrator (*People v. Howes*, 99 Cal. App. 2d 808).

16.15 RECEIVING OR CONCEALING STOLEN PROPERTY

Receiving or Concealing Stolen Property—PC 496. "(a) Every person who buys or receives any property that has been stolen or that has been obtained in any manner constituting theft or extortion, knowing the property to be so stolen or obtained, or who conceals, sells, withholds or aids in concealing or withholding any such property from the owner, knowing the property to be so stolen or obtained, is punishable by imprisonment in a state prison, or in a county jail. . . ." (felony wobbler).

(b) This subsection of PC 496 requires every swap meet vendor, as defined in Section 21661 of the Business and Professions Code, and every person whose principal business is dealing in or collecting used or second-hand merchandise or personal property, to make a reasonable inquiry as to the ownership of the property by the seller. If the buyer does not make such inquiry when circumstances indicate he should, he is guilty of a wobbler or misdemeanor, depending on the value of the property ($400 or more, or less).

(c) Any person who has been injured by a violation of paragraph 1 of this section may bring an action for three times the amount of actual damages, if any, sustained by the plaintiff, plus costs of suit and reasonable attorney's fees.

(d) Notwithstanding Section 664, attempts to violate this section may be punished as a misdemeanor or felony.

Discussion. The essence of the offense of receiving or concealing stolen property is that purchase or receipt be with the knowledge that the property was stolen (*People v. Salazar*, 210 Cal. App. 2d 89). ***Note:*** PC 496 is the proper charging section for what is commonly called "possession of stolen property," providing the suspect knew the property was stolen.

Even though a person is not aware the property is stolen when he or she first comes into possession of it, if he or she subsequently learns of its stolen nature and then conceals or withholds it from the true owner, he or she is guilty of receipt of stolen property (*People v. Scaggs*, 153 Cal. App. 2d 339).

A person cannot be convicted of both stealing and receiving the same property, unless in completely separate transactions—e.g., the thief sells the stolen property and later buys some of it back (*People v. Strong*, 30 Cal. App. 4th 366).

Elements of Receiving Stolen Property. The elements of receiving stolen property are: (1) that property found in possession of defendant was acquired by acts constituting theft or extortion; (2) that defendant received, concealed, or withheld property from the owner; and (3) that the defendant knew that the property was stolen (*People v. Azevedo*, 218 Cal. App. 483).

Possession of stolen property, accompanied by no explanation, or an unsatisfactory explanation of the possession, or by suspicious circumstances, will justify an inference that the goods were received with the knowledge that they had been stolen (*People v. Barnes*, 210 Cal. App. 2d 740).

Among the elements from which knowledge as to stolen property may be inferred by the defendant is the fact that the property was obtained from a person of questionable character, that it was purchased at a ridiculously low price and failure of the defendant to satisfactorily explain his possession (*People v. Boinus*, 153 Cal. App. 2d 618).

Receiving Stolen Property in Another State—PC 789. The jurisdiction for receiving stolen property in another state and bringing it into this state is in any competent court into or through which the property has been brought.

16.16 RELATED THEFTS

Taking Excess Complimentary Papers—PC 490.7. Taking more than 25 copies of a complimentary newspaper to sell, recycle or withhold from readers is an infraction (can be a misdemeanor on subsequent convictions).

Purchase of Metal by Junk Dealers—PC 496a. This section punishes second-hand dealers who do not use due diligence in ascertaining the right of persons who attempt to sell solder, iron, brass, wire, cable, copper, lead, etc.

Receiving Stolen Books—PC 496b. This statute relates to book dealers and collectors and prohibits them from buying or receiving books, manuscripts, and other literature bearing a mark indicating ownership by a public library or institution without ascertaining by diligent inquiry the seller's right to dispose of such property.

Bringing Stolen Property Into State—PC 497. A person who receives stolen property in another state or country and brings it into this state may be convicted and punished in this state for receiving stolen property.

Evasion of Utility Payments—PC 498. Any person who with intent to obtain for himself or herself utility services without paying the full lawful charge therefor, or with intent to enable another person to do so, is guilty of a misdemeanor.

"Utility" means any electrical, gas, or water corporation as those terms are defined in the Public Utilities Code.

Temporarily Taking Vessel or Bicycle—PC 499b. "Any person who shall, without the permission of the owner thereof, take any bicycle or motorboat or vessel, for the purpose of temporarily using or operating the same shall be deemed guilty of a misdemeanor. . . ."

Taking of Aircraft—PC 499d. "Any person who operates or takes an aircraft not his own, without the consent of the owner thereof, and with intent to either permanently or temporarily deprive the owner thereof of his title or possession of such vehicle, whether with or without intent to steal the same, or any person who is a party or accessory to or an accomplice in any operation or unauthorized taking or stealing is guilty of a felony [wobbler]. . . ."

Fraudulently Obtaining Telephone Services—PC 502.7. This section makes it a criminal offense to use any device, code, mechanism, access card or technique whatever, to make local or long distance telephone calls without paying for same. If the total value of the phone service fraudulently received is over $400, the crime is a felony (wobbler). A second conviction under this section is a felony. If the stolen service totals $400 or under, the crime is a misdemeanor.

Unauthorized Cable Television Connection—PC 591. This section makes it a felony (wobbler) to remove or sever any cable TV lines or to remove or sever any telephone or telegraph lines. PC 593(d) contains a comprehensive scheme for penalizing unauthorized interception of cable TV programming.

Possession or Sale of Pirated Recordings—PC 653w. Any person who trafficks in pirated audio or video recordings that do not show the identity of the maker of the unauthorized copy is guilty of a misdemeanor (first offense) or felony wobbler (subsequent offenses or any offense involving 100 or more articles).

Recording Motion Picture—PC 653z. It is a misdemeanor (one year/$2500 fine) to make an unauthorized recording of a motion picture in a theater.

Internet Piracy—PC 653aa. It is a misdemeanor for an adult to disseminate by electronic means any copyrighted recording or audiovisual work to more than 10 other people without disclosing the title of the work and the sender's email address. A minor's first and second offenses are infractions; third and subsequent offenses by a minor are misdemeanors.

16.17 DISPOSAL OF STOLEN PROPERTY BY OFFICIALS

The following sections pertain to the manner in which stolen or embezzled property shall be disposed of by authorities.

PC 1407. When property, alleged to have been stolen or embezzled, comes into the custody of a peace officer, he must hold it subject to the order of the magistrate authorized by the next section to direct the disposal thereof.

PC 1408. Order for its delivery to owner. This section provides that the magistrate before whom the complaint is laid must order stolen or embezzled property returned to the owner.

PC 1411. If the property is not claimed before six months (three months in the case of bicycles) from the conviction of the thief, the officer must deliver it to the city or county treasurer for sale.

PC 1412. The officer must give a receipt when taking money or property from the defendant and deliver one copy of the receipt to the defendant and keep one copy with the property.

PC 1413. Duties of persons having charge of property. The police clerk must attach a number to each article and enter the description and number of each article into a suitable book.

16.18 DEFRAUDING AN INNKEEPER

PC 537. This section makes it a crime for any person to obtain any food or accommodations at any hotel, inn, restaurant, boarding house, lodging house, apartment house, bungalow court, motel, or auto camp, ski area, or public or private camp ground, without paying therefor, with intent to defraud the proprietor or manager thereof.

If the value of the credit, food, or accommodations is four hundred dollars ($400) or less, the crime is a misdemeanor. If over $400, the crime is a felony (wobbler).

16.19 ARTICLES WITH SERIAL NUMBERS REMOVED, ALTERED

PC 537e—Transfer or Possession of Articles. Any person who knowingly buys, sells, receives, disposes of, conceals, or has in his or her possession any "personal property" from which the manufacturer's serial number or any other distinguishing number or identification mark has been removed, defaced, covered, altered or destroyed, is guilty of a misdemeanor.

If the article's value is $400 or more or the property is an integrated computer chip or panel, the crime is punishable as a felony (wobbler).

For purposes of this section, "personal property" includes, but is not limited to, any television, radio, recorder, telephone, typewriter, any musical instrument, any household appliance, or exercise equipment.

STUDENT REVIEW

TERMINOLOGY DEFINED—CHAPTER 16

Please see the Terminology Quiz at the end of the chapter.

1. Chattels: any personal or real property, possessions.
2. Contingency: an event possible, uncertain or unforeseen.
3. Corroboration: additional proof or substantiation.
4. Diversion: personal use of funds intended for another purpose.
5. Embezzlement: theft by a person entrusted with property.
6. Fiduciary capacity: position of trust, employer-employee.
7. Fraud: theft by false pretense or promises.
8. Gaming: gambling with dice, cards or other devices.
9. Intrinsic: inherent value, basic, internal.
10. Joy riding: taking car without permission, not a theft.
11. Kleptomaniac: one with abnormal impulse to steal.
12. Misappropriate: misuse, divert from intended purpose.
13. Ownership: legal title or right to possession of property.
14. Possession: under one's care, direction, or control.
15. Presumption: assumed true until proven otherwise.
16. Real value: the fair market value, the going price.
17. Reliance: dependence upon, trusting in, confidence in.
18. Steal: taking with intent to permanently deprive owner of property, or its major use or enjoyment.
19. Trial: court action to determine guilt or innocence.
20. Trustee: one entrusted with fiduciary obligations.

TRUE-FALSE QUIZ—CHAPTER 16

After reading this chapter you should be able to correctly answer the following items.

___ 1. One is not guilty of theft unless he takes something of value intending to permanently deprive the owner of the use or title of the property, or to interfere with a major portion of its value or enjoyment.

___ 2. The terms "theft" and "larceny" are synonymous.

___ 3. To constitute asportation in theft, the thief must move or otherwise attain some dominion over the property stolen.

___ 4. To determine the value of property taken in a theft, the value placed on it by the owner shall be the ultimate test.

___ 5. In order for property to be stolen it must have some real value.

___ 6. Asportation is an essential element of theft.

___ 7. Taking an automobile without the owner's consent, using it for two days, and returning it is not auto theft.

___ 8. Selling parts from a car which was taken without the owner's permission would be evidence of grand theft auto.

___ 9. Possession of stolen property is of itself sufficient to justify a conviction of theft.

___10. Once stolen property is sold to an innocent third person, the owner legally loses his title to the property.

___11. In theft by false pretenses, PC 532, both title and possession of the property pass to the wrongdoer.

___12. The crime of embezzlement requires a distinct act of taking the same as other types of theft.

___13. Some kind of fiduciary relationship between the victim and the wrongdoer is essential to the crime of embezzlement.
___14. If a trustee diverts funds for some unauthorized purpose, even if he does not personally gain from the diversion, he is still guilty of embezzlement.
___15. Theft of an access card, because it has no intrinsic value, is not a crime until it has been fraudulently used.
___16. Theft of $400 from one's employer within a twelve consecutive month period constitutes grand theft.
___17. Theft of $100 worth of avocados constitutes grand theft.
___18. Theft of money from under a pillow where the victim was sleeping constitutes grand theft from the person.
___19. Theft of money from a purse lying immediately next to the owner is grand theft from person.
___20. Theft of any amount of money by picking a pocket is grand theft.

ESSAY-DISCUSSION ITEMS—CHAPTER 16

After reading this chapter you should be able to correctly answer the following items.

1. What is the basis or test for determining the value of stolen property?
2. What are the four basic elements of theft?
3. May real property as well as personal property be the subject of theft? Are farm animals considered personal property? What about dogs and cats?
4. What are the four general categories or types of theft?
5. Of what does the "act" in theft consist? What is meant by asportation in theft?
6. Is theft a general or specific intent crime? What factors make it one or the other?
7. Is possession of stolen property of itself sufficient to justify conviction of theft? Does the possessor have any legal duty to explain his possession?
8. What are the elements of embezzlement?
9. What constitutes "from the person" in theft under PC 487, Section 2? Is this a felony or misdemeanor?
10. What are the three elements of receiving stolen property under PC 496?

TERMINOLOGY QUIZ—CHAPTER 16

Match terms and definitions by writing the number preceding the correct term in the appropriate brackets.

Terms	*Definitions*
1. Chattels	[ ] assumed to be true until proven otherwise
2. Contingency	[ ] one with abnormal impulse to steal
3. Corroboration	[ ] under one's care, direction, or control
4. Diversion	[ ] inherent, basic, internal, inherent value
5. Embezzlement	[ ] taking with intent to permanently deprive
6. Fiduciary capacity	[ ] any real or personal property
7. Fraud	[ ] an event possible, uncertain, unforeseen
8. Gaming	[ ] dependence upon, trusting or confidence in
9. Intrinsic	[ ] use of funds intended for other purposes
10. Joy riding	[ ] theft by a person entrusted with property
11. Kleptomaniac	[ ] legal title or right to property
12. Misappropriate	[ ] one entrusted with fiduciary obligations

13. Ownership	[ ] theft by false pretense or promises
14. Possession	[ ] position of trust, employer-employee
15. Presumption	[ ] misuse, divert from intended purpose
16. Real value	
17. Reliance	
18. Steal	
19. Trial	
20. Trustee	

CHAPTER 17

CONTROLLED SUBSTANCE AND ALCOHOL ABUSE CRIMES

17.1 CONTROLLED SUBSTANCES ACT

Most drug crimes are found in Division 10 of the Health and Safety (H&S) Code (beginning with Section 11000), which is entitled the *Uniform Controlled Substances Act.* This act covers such offenses as possession, sale, transportation, manufacture, furnishing, administering, possession of paraphernalia, under the influence, cultivation, etc., of controlled substances. A few drug and alcohol related laws are also found in the Penal Code, Vehicle Code and the Business and Professions (B&P) Code.

The Uniform Controlled Substances Act covers the legal as well as the unlawful use of controlled substances. For example, treatment of addicts, prescription requirements, offenses and penalties, are all described in this Act.

17.2 DEFINITIONS

Drug—H&S 11014. "Drug" means (a) substances recognized as drugs in the official United State Pharmacopoeia, official Homeopathic Pharmacopoeia of the United States, or official National Formulary, or any supplement to them; (b) substances intended for the use in the diagnosis, cure, mitigation, treatment, or prevention of disease in man or animals; (c) substances (other than food) intended to affect the structure or any function of the body of man or animals; and (d) substances intended for use as a component of any article specified in subdivision (a), (b), or (c) of this section.

Dangerous Drug—B&P 4211. The Business and Professions Code defines "dangerous drug" as any drug unsafe for self-medication, except veterinary drugs which are labeled as such.

Marijuana—H&S 11018. "Marijuana" means all parts of the plant *Cannabis sativa L.*, whether growing or not, and every derivative of the plant.

Concentrated Cannabis—H&S 11006.5. "Concentrated cannabis" means the separated resin obtained from marijuana.

Dispense—H&S 11010. "Dispense" means to deliver a controlled substance to an ultimate user.

Narcotics—H&S 11032. Whenever the term "narcotics" is used, it shall mean controlled substances classified in Schedules I and II.

Narcotic Drug—H&S 11019. "Narcotic drug" means any of the following, whether produced directly or indirectly...or by extraction or synthesis.

- Opium or any derivative thereof.
- Opium poppy and poppy straw.
- Coca leaves or any derivative thereof.
- Cocaine, whether natural or synthetic.
- Ecgonine and its derivatives.
- Acetylfentanyl and its derivatives.

Opiate—H&S 11020. "Opiate" means any substance having an addiction-forming quality similar to morphine.

Opium Poppy—H&S 11021. "Opium poppy" means the plant of the species *Papaver somniferum L.,* except its seeds.

Poppy Straw—H&S 11025. "Poppy straw" means all parts, except the seed, of the opium poppy, after mowing.

Tolerance. A state in which the body's tissue cells adjust to the presence of a drug. The term "tolerance" refers to a state in which the body becomes used to the presence of a drug in given amounts and eventually fails to respond to ordinarily effective dosages. Hence, increasingly larger doses are necessary to produce desired effects.

Habituation (psychological dependence). The result of repeated consumption of a drug which produces psychological but no physical dependence. The psychological dependence produces a desire (not a compulsion) to continue taking drugs for the sense of improved well-being.

Physiological Dependence (addiction). This occurs when a person cannot function normally without the repeated use of a drug. If the drug is withdrawn, the person has severe physical and psychic disturbance.

17.3 OPIATES—PSYCHEDELICS—STIMULANTS—DEPRESSANTS

Controlled Substance Schedules. Schedules I through V (Health and Safety Code Sections 11054 through 11058) list controlled substances formerly identified as "Narcotics" or "Restricted Dangerous Drugs." The most dangerous substances (highest potential for abuse) are listed in Schedule I and II. The slightly less dangerous substances (milder or less addictive) are listed in Schedules III through V Some drugs are listed in more than one schedule, depending on the amount of opiates they contain.

1. Substances such as heroin, LSD, and marijuana are listed under Schedule I.
2. Cocaine, amphetamine, and other stimulants are listed under Schedule II.
3. The depressants such as the barbiturates and tranquilizers are listed under Schedules III and IV.
4. Compounds containing milder opiates, narcotic and non-narcotic medicinal ingredients are listed in Schedule V. Please see Schedules I through V, below. (Also, see *Table of Controlled Substances*, this chapter).

Schedule I Substances—H&S 11054. The more commonly known controlled substances listed under Schedule I are:

- Cocaine base
- Hallucinogens (not included elsewhere)
- Heroin
- LSD (lysergic acid diethylamide)
- Marijuana
- Mescaline
- Methaqualone
- Opiates (not included elsewhere)
- Peyote
- Gamma-hydroxybutyrate (GHB), precursors and salts (no FDA approval)

Schedule II Substances—H&S 11055. The more commonly known controlled substances listed under Schedule II are:

- Amphetamine
- Cocaine (not included elsewhere)
- Codeine
- Demoral
- Methadone
- Morphine
- Opium (various forms)
- Pentobarbital
- Percodon
- Secobarbital

Schedule III Substances—H&S 11056. The more commonly known controlled substances listed under Schedule III are:

- Anabolic steroids (muscle builders)
- Barbiturates
- Depressants (not included elsewhere)
- PCP (phencyclidine)
- Stimulants (not included elsewhere)
- Testosterone (male hormone)
- Gamma-hydroxybutyrate (GHB), precursors and salts (FDA approved)

Schedule IV Substances—H&S 11057. The depressants such as the barbiturates and tranquilizers are listed under Schedule IV.

Schedule V Substances—H&S 11058. Compounds containing narcotic and non-narcotic medicinal ingredients are covered in Schedule V.

17.4 CONTROLLED SUBSTANCE POSSESSION

One may not legally possess any controlled substance unless it was obtained by a written prescription from a physician, dentist, podiatrist or veterinarian licensed to practice in California. Illegal possession is a felony or felony wobbler, depending on the substance possessed. The substance possessed must be

A patient or caregiver may possess up to 8 ounces of dried marijuana, and no more than 6 mature or 12 immature plants. *Courtesy of PhotoDisc, Inc.*

in a usable amount to constitute a crime. Except for those with certain prior convictions and those who use firearms or commit other crimes, defendants convicted of simple possession must be sentenced to probation and treatment, and cannot be generally incarcerated (PC 1210.1).

Narcotic Possession—H&S 11350. This section makes unlawful possession of any of the following a felony. ***Note:*** heroin, cocaine and peyote cannot be legally prescribed.

- Cocaine (Coke)
- Codeine (pure)
- Demerol
- Dilaudid
- Heroin
- Mescaline
- Methadone
- Methaqualone ("Ludes")
- Morphine
- Opium
- Peyote
- THC

Marijuana Possession—H&S 11357(b). This section makes illegal possession of not more than 28.5 grams (1 ounce) of marijuana a misdemeanor. Possession of concentrated cannabis is a felony (wobbler).

Release on Citation. In any case in which a person is arrested for a violation of this subdivision and does not demand to be taken before a magistrate, such person shall be released by the arresting officer upon presentation of satisfactory evidence of identity and giving his written promise to appear in court, as provided in Section 853.6 of the Penal Code, and shall not be subjected to booking.

Marijuana Planting, Processing—H&S 11358. Every person who plants, cultivates, harvests, dries, or processes any marijuana or any part thereof, except as otherwise provided by law, shall be punished by imprisonment in the state prison.

"Medicinal Marijuana"—H&S 11362.5. Section 11357 (possession) and 11358 (cultivation of marijuana) "shall not apply" to a patient or primary caregiver who cultivates or possess marijuana for medical purposes, on the written or oral recommendation or approval of a physician. A "primary caregiver" is an individual who has consistently assumed responsibility for the housing, health or safety of the patient.

The county health department must issue photo identification cards to patients and primary caregivers upon satisfactory proof that the patient has a physician's prescription for medicinal marijuana, and law enforcement officers must accept such cards, unless they are believed to be fraudulently possessed (H&S 11362.7-11362.81).

Marijuana Possession for Sale—H&S 11359. Every person who possesses for sale any marijuana, except as otherwise provided by law, shall be punished by imprisonment in the state prison.

Controlled Substance Possession—H&S 11377. This section makes the unlawful possession of any controlled substance which is listed in Schedule III, IV or V, and which is not a narcotic drug, without a prescription a felony (wobbler). This section includes such drugs as:

- Amphetamines (speed)
- Barbiturates
- Lysergic Acid (LSD)
- Methamphetamines

- Methaqualone
- Phencyclidine (PCP)
- Psilocybin (mushrooms)
- Ritalin

Possession of ketamine is a misdemeanor (H&S 11377(b))2)).

17.5 ELEMENTS OF POSSESSION

In order to prove the commission of the crime of possession under the Health and Safety Code, each of the following four elements must be proved:

1. That a person exercised control over, or had the right to exercise control over a certain controlled substance.
2. That such person had knowledge of the presence of the controlled substance.
3. That such person had knowledge of its nature as a controlled substance.
4. That the substance was in an amount sufficient to be used as a controlled substance.

Two Types of Possession. The law recognizes two kinds of possession: (1) actual possession and (2) constructive possession.

1. **Actual possession:** A person who knowingly has direct physical control over a thing is then in actual possession of it.
2. **Constructive possession:** A person who, although not in actual possession, knowingly has the right of control over a thing, either directly or through another person or persons, is then in constructive possession of it.

The law recognizes that one person may have possession alone, or that two or more persons jointly may share actual or constructive possession (*People v. Piper*, 19 Cal. App. 3d 248).

17.6 UNDER THE INFLUENCE

Under the Influence Defined. If a controlled substance is appreciably affecting the nervous system, brain, muscles, or other parts of a person's body, or is creating in this person any perceptible or abnormal mental or physical condition, such a person is under the influence of a controlled substance.

Under Influence of Controlled Substances—H&S 11550. It is a misdemeanor to use or be under the influence of the many drugs listed in the schedules above, except as authorized by a physician. Some of the more commonly abused drugs covered by this section are:

- Amphetamines
- Cocaine
- Codeine
- Demerol
- Heroin
- Mescaline
- Methadone
- Methamphetamine
- Methaqualone
- Opium
- Peyote
- PCP

This section puts the burden of proof on the defendant to prove that his or her being under the influence was within the law, i.e., "administered by or under the direction of a person licensed by the state to dispense, prescribe or administer controlled substances."

Toluene Ingestion—PC 381. This section makes it a misdemeanor to be under the influence or possess toluene (glue, paint, etc.) or similar substances for purposes of inhaling the fumes ("glue sniffing").

Under the Influence of Drugs—PC 647(f). This section makes it a misdemeanor to be under the influence of any drug, toluene, controlled substance, intoxicating liquor or combination of drugs and alcohol in a public place. The person must be unable to care for his or her own safety or the safety of others.

17.7 TRANSPORTATION—SALE—MANUFACTURE

Unlawful Possession For Sale—H&S 11351. This section makes it a felony to possess for sale or to purchase for sale any narcotic drug or certain controlled substances specified in H&S 11054.

Unlawful Transportation, Sale—H&S 11352. It is a felony to transport, import into California, sell, furnish, administer or give away any narcotic drug. This section covers heroin, mescaline, peyote, THC, Opium, cocaine, methaqualone, etc.

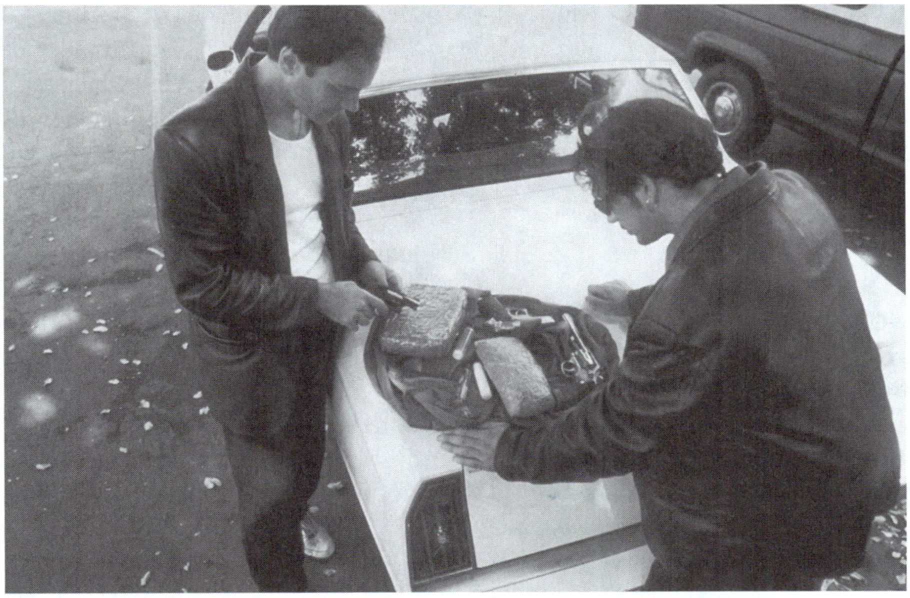

In some neighborhoods, drug dealers brazenly "set up shop" at street corners and other open places frequented by users. *Photograph by Michael Newman, courtesy of PhotoEdit*

Elements: Possession for Sale. In order to prove the commission of the offense "possession for sale" of a controlled substance, each of the following elements must be proved:

1. That a person unlawfully exercised control or had the right to exercise control over a certain controlled substance.
2. That such person had knowledge of its presence.
3. That such person had knowledge of its nature as a controlled substance.
4. That the substance was in an amount sufficient to be used for sale or consumption as a controlled substance.
5. That such person possessed the controlled substance with the specific intent to sell same.

Unlawful Manufacture—H&S 11379.6. This section makes it a felony to unlawfully manufacture any controlled substance specified in H&S Code Section 11054, 11055, 11056, 11067 or 11058.

Unlawful Possession of Precursors—H&S 11383.5. It is a felony to possess the precursor substances with the intent to manufacture methamphetamine or its analogs. It is also a felony to possess precursor substances with the intent to sell them with knowledge they will be used to manufacture methamphetamine, PCP or analogs (H&S 11383.6, 11383.7).

Adult Involving Minor—H&S 11353. It is a felony for any person 18 years of age or over to solicit a minor to violate any of the provisions relating to controlled substances. This includes providing, administering, using a minor to sell or transport, etc.

Minor Involving Minor—H&S 11354. It is also a felony for any person under the age of 18 years to in any manner induce a minor to violate any provisions of the controlled substance chapter.

Adult Sale on School Grounds—H&S 11353.5. It is a felony for any person 18 years of age or older to unlawfully sell or give a controlled substance to a minor, on any kindergarten through grade 12 school grounds, while school is in session or open for school related programs. This section also applies to any public playground during the time in which school related programs for minors are being held.

Loitering for Drug Activities—H&S 11532(a). It is a misdemeanor to loiter in any public place in a manner and under circumstances manifesting the purpose and with the intent to commit specified drug offenses (including most possession and distribution crimes). Relevant circumstances indicating criminal intent include (1) acting as a look-out, (2) transferring items, (3) attempts at concealment,

(4) use of signals, (5) repeated contacts with vehicles and passersby, (6) possessing or being under the influence of drugs, (7) prior convictions, (8) probation or parole restrictions, (9) prior conduct within six months, (10) known drug area, and any other pertinent facts.

17.8 IMITATION CONTROLLED SUBSTANCE

Selling Imitation Drugs—H&S 11355. It is a felony (wobbler) to sell any substance in place of a controlled substance, leading the buyer to believe that he or she is buying a controlled substance.

This section obviously gives the police a weapon to control incidents involving fake drug sales. The perpetrator cannot escape punishment by claiming that when they sell talcum powder for heroin, for example, they are not violating any law.

Manufacture, Possession Imitation Drugs—H&S 11680. It is a misdemeanor for any person to knowingly manufacture, distribute or possess with intent to distribute, any imitation controlled substance.

This section is similar to the one immediately above, except that it may permit an arrest of a perpetrator prior to their actually selling a fake controlled substance.

17.9 DRUG PARAPHERNALIA

Possession of Needles or Syringes—B&P 4149. This Business and Professions Code section makes it a misdemeanor to unlawfully possess any professional hypodermic needles or syringes. Persons, such as diabetics, with a doctor's prescription, are exempt from this section. If authorized by the city or county, a pharmacist may dispense up to 10 hypodermic needles and syringes to a person 18 or older without a prescription (B&P 4145), and the person may lawfully possess 10 or fewer needles and syringes for personal use (H&S 11364(c)).

Possession of Paraphernalia—H&S 11364.7. This law makes it a misdemeanor to possess or manufacture any drug paraphernalia with the intent to deliver, furnish, or transfer it under circumstances where the perpetrator should reasonably know that the paraphernalia will be used in connection with a controlled substance. The purpose of this section is to allow for control of so-called "head shops."

Drug Paraphernalia Defined—H&S 11014.5. "Drug paraphernalia" means all equipment, products and materials of any kind which are designed for use, or marketed for use, in planting, propagating, cultivating, growing, harvesting, manufacture, compounding, . . . injecting, ingesting, inhaling or otherwise introducing a controlled substance into the human body in violation of this division. It includes, but is not limited to: (a) hypodermic syringes and needles, (b) cocaine spoons, (c) "roach" clips, (d) controlled substance testing equipment, (e) objects designed for use in ingesting, inhaling or otherwise introducing marijuana, cocaine, or hashish into the human body, and (f) container designed for use in storing or concealing controlled substances.

17.10 PLACE DRUGS SOLD OR USED

Visiting Where Drugs Used—H&S 11365. It is a misdemeanor to knowingly visit or be present in any room or place where specified controlled substances are being unlawfully smoked or used. It includes such drugs as heroin, mescaline, peyote, opium and cocaine. It does *not* cover marijuana.

Maintaining Place For Using Drugs—H&S 11366. It is a felony (wobbler) to open or maintain a place for unlawfully selling, giving away, or using any of the controlled substances specified. Controlled substances covered under this section include cocaine, heroin, opium, marijuana, peyote, THC, and mescaline. This section prohibits so-called "crash pads" or "shooting galleries."

False Compartments for Smuggling—H&S 11366.8. It is a felony to design or install a false compartment in a vehicle with intent to facilitate drug smuggling. It is a wobbler to use, possess or control such a false compartment with similar intent.

17.11 PERSONS REQUIRED TO REGISTER

Drug Offenders Must Register—H&S 11590. Any person convicted of specified narcotics offenses, or any person who is discharged or paroled from a penal institution where he or she was confined because of the commission of any such offense, or any person convicted in any other state of any offense which, if committed or attempted in this state, would have been punishable as one or more of the above-mentioned offenses,

TABLE OF CONTROLLED SUBSTANCES AND RELATED HEALTH AND SAFETY CODE SECTIONS

CONTROLLED SUBSTANCES

	Drugs	Calif. Sched.	Often Prescribed Brand Names	Health & Safety Code Sec.			Adult
				Possession	Possession For Sale	Sale	Use Of Minor
NARCOTICS	OPIUM	II	Dovers powder, Paregoric	11350	11351	11352	11353
NARCOTICS	MORPHINE	II	Morphine	11350	11351	11352	11353
NARCOTICS	CODEINE	II	Codeine	11350	11351	11352	11353
NARCOTICS	HEROIN	I	None	11350	11351	11352	11353
NARCOTICS	MEPERIDINE (pethidine)	II	Demerol, Pethadol	11350	11351	11352	11353
NARCOTICS	METHADONE	II	Dolophine, Methadone Amidone	11350	11351	11352	11353
NARCOTICS	OTHER NARCOTICS	II	Dilaudid, Percodan Numorphan, Leritine	11350	11351	11352	11353
DEPRESSANTS	CHLORAL HYDRATE	IV	Noctec, Somnos	11377	11378	11379	11380
DEPRESSANTS	BARBITURATES	III	Amytal, Nembutal, Tuinal Seconal	11377	11378	11379	11380
DEPRESSANTS	OTHER BARBITURATES	IV	Veronal (Barbital) Luminal (Phenobarbital)	11377	11378	11379	11380
DEPRESSANTS	METHAQUALONE	III	Quaalud, Sopor, Parest	11377	11378	11379	11380
DEPRESSANTS	TRANQUILIZERS	IV	Miltown (Meprobromate) Equanil	11377	11378	11379	11380
DEPRESSANTS	OTHER DEPRESSANTS	IV	Placidyl (Ethchlorvynol) Valmid (Ethinamate)	11377	11378	11379	11380
STIMULANTS	COCAINE	II	Cocaine	11350	11351	11352	11353
STIMULANTS	AMPHETAMINES	II	Benzedrine, Biphetamine Desoxyn, Dexedrine, Obetrol, Obedrin	11377	11378	11379	11380
STIMULANTS	PHENMETRAZINE	II	Preludin	11377	11378	11379	11380
STIMULANTS	METHYLPHENIDATE	II	Ritalin	11377	11378	11379	11380
STIMULANTS	OTHER STIMULANTS	II		11377	11378	11379	11380
HALLUCINOGENS	LSD	I	None	11377	11378	11379	11380
HALLUCINOGENS	MESCALINE	I	None	11377	11378	11379	11380
HALLUCINOGENS	PHENCYCLIDINE (PCP)	III	Sernylan	11377	11378.5	11379.5	11380
HALLUCINOGENS	OTHER HALLUCINOGENS		None	11377	11378	11379	11380
CANNABIS	MARIJUANA HASHISH HASHISH OIL	I	None None None	11357a,b,c 11357a 11357a	11359 11359 11359	11360 11360 11360	11361 11361 11361

This table names each controlled substance, lists its H & S Code Schedule, indicates medical brand names, and identifies the proper booking section for a violation of possession, possession for sale, sale, or use of a minor by an adult for any of these violations.

shall within 30 days of his or her coming into any county or city, in which he or she resides or is temporarily domiciled for such length of time, must register with the chief of police of the city in which he or she resides or the sheriff of the county if he or she resides in an unincorporated area.

17.12 DRIVING OFFENSES—ALCOHOL OR DRUGS

Under Influence—Alcohol or Drugs—VC 23152. The Vehicle code defines any one of the following three acts as a misdemeanor offense:

1. Driving a vehicle under the influence of an alcoholic beverage or any drug, or under the combined influence of both.
2. It is also unlawful for any person who has .08 percent or more, by weight, of alcohol in his or her blood to drive a vehicle.
3. It is unlawful for any person who is addicted to the use of any drug to drive a vehicle. ***Note:*** this latter offense does not apply to a person who is participating in a methadone treatment program, as provided by law.
4. It is unlawful for a person with a BAC of .04% or more to drive a commercial vehicle.

DUI-DWI Defense Web Site: http://www.duicenter.com. Every criminal justice student, especially police officers, should browse this unique Web Site. Click on any underlined heading for details. Don't overlook "The 20 Most Frequently Asked Drunk Driving Questions" and "The Driver's Guide to DUI."

Alcohol to Minor Driver—B&P 25658.2. It is a misdemeanor for a parent to allow a minor child to drink at home to the point of a BAC level of .05% or higher and then to drive, if the minor then causes a traffic collision.

Alcohol or Drugs—Causing Injury—VC 23153. This Vehicle Code Section defines felony drunk driving. It is similar to VC 23152, above, except that VC 23153 involves injury to persons other than the driver. The offense consists of:

1. driving a vehicle under the influence of drugs or alcohol or both,
2. or, driving a vehicle with a blood-alcohol count of .08 percent or more,
3. and while driving, doing, or failing to do, any act forbidden or required by law (e.g., speeding, running red light),
4. which act or neglect proximately causes bodily injury to any person other than the driver.

Subsequent Offenses. A person convicted of DUI with three or more prior convictions for DUI or "wet reckless" (VC 23103.5, essentially a reduced charge in a DUI case), within the previous ten years, is guilty of a felony (wobbler) (VC 23566).

Where the defendant has a prior felony DUI or alcohol-related vehicular manslaughter within 10 years, a subsequent DUI is a felony (wobbler) (VC 23566).

A DUI with injury within 10 years of a previous conviction for DUI or "wet reckless" is a felony (wobbler) which carries increased penalties (VC 23185). A DUI with injury with two or more priors within 10 years is a straight felony (VC 23566).

Implied Malice Advisory—VC 23593. When a person is sentenced for DUI or "wet reckless," the court must give a warning about the dangers of driving under the influence, and must advise the person that if he or she continues to drive under the influence and causes a death, murder charges can result. (This advisory may assist the prosecution in proving implied malice in a second-degree murder case arising from a fatal DUI crash where the errant driver has a prior DUI conviction.)

Implied Consent Law—VC 23612. This Vehicle Code Section provides that any person who drives a motor vehicle is deemed to have given his or her consent to chemical testing of his or her blood or breath to determine alcoholic content, or blood or urine to determine the drug content. If neither of the specified tests is available, the remaining test may be given.

Failure or refusal to submit to one of the above tests can result in a fine and/or suspension of one's driving privilege for one year, even if not convicted of driving under the influence. The penalty is more severe if the driver refuses the test and is also convicted of VC 23152, 23153 or has been convicted of reckless driving within five years of the refusal.

Administrative License Suspension—VC 23612 (e)-(g), VC 23158.5. These two sections specify that peace officers, acting on behalf of the Department of Motor Vehicles (DMV), shall seize the driver's license and issue a temporary forty-five (45) day operating permit to any DUI arrestee who:

(1) refuses to submit to chemical testing,
(2) fails to complete a chosen test,
(3) tests above .08% on a breath test, or
(4) insists on taking only a blood or urine test.

Smoking In or Near Public Buildings—GC 7597. It is an infraction for any person to smoke inside a public building, or within 20 feet of a window or the main entrance or exit of such building, or inside a state-owned vehicle.

STUDENT REVIEW

TERMINOLOGY DEFINED—CHAPTER 17

Please see the Terminology Quiz at the end of this chapter.

1. Controlled substance: drugs listed in Schedule I-V, H&S Code.
2. Heroin: an opium derivative.
3. Tolerance: body's adjustment to presence of drugs.
4. Addiction: physical craving, physiological dependence.
5. Implied consent: legally imposed testing of suspected drunk drivers.
6. LSD: lysergic acid, an illegal psychedelic.
7. PCP: phencyclidine, a psychedelic.
8. Marijuana possession: crime defined in H&S Code 11357.
9. Marijuana sale: crime defined in H&S Code 11360.
10. Narcotics possession: crime defined in H&S Code 11350.
11. Felony DUI: drunk driving causing injury to another.
12. Constructive possession: having a right of control.
13. Actual possession: direct physical control.
14. Marijuana's botanical name: *cannabis sativa L.*
15. Hashish oil: a derivative of marijuana.

TRUE-FALSE QUIZ—CHAPTER 17

After reading this chapter you should be able to correctly answer the following items.

___ 1. One may legally possess a controlled substance if it was obtained with a physician's written prescription.
___ 2. Most narcotics laws are found in the Welfare and Institutions Code.
___ 3. H&S Code Schedules I-V identify all currently controlled substances.
___ 4. Heroin is a derivative of opium.
___ 5. LSD and PCP are both psychedelics.
___ 6. Cocaine is an opium derivative.
___ 7. Possession of no more than 28.5 grams of marijuana is an infraction.
___ 8. Criminal "possession" requires knowledge the substance is a narcotic.
___ 9. One can be guilty of felony drunk driving without causing injury.
___10. It is a crime to refuse a chemical test for suspected drunk driving.

ESSAY-DISCUSSION ITEMS—CHAPTER 17

After reading this chapter you should be able to correctly answer the following items.

1. What are the differences in elements between misdemeanor and felony drunk driving?
2. What four elements must be proved in the crime of "possession?"
3. How many kinds of "possession" are there, and how are they different as explained in your text?
4. What constitutes "constructive possession" of drugs as explained in the text?
5. Is it (1) no crime, (2) a felony, (3) a misdemeanor or (4) an infraction to plant or cultivate marijuana?
6. Discuss: How has the advent of legalized medicinal marijuana complicated enforcement of marijuana laws? How can officers evaluate claims by those who possess or cultivate marijuana that they are legally entitled to do so?

TERMINOLOGY QUIZ—CHAPTER 17

Matching terms and definitions by writing the number preceding the correct term in the appropriate brackets.

Terms	*Definitions*
1. Actual possession	[ ] Cannabis sativa L.
2. Addiction	[ ] Physical craving, physiological dependence
3. Constructive possession	[ ] Drugs listed in H&S Code Schedules I-V
4. Controlled substance	[ ] Having right of control
5. Felony DUI	[ ] Drunk driving, causing injury
6. Hashish oil	[ ] Legally imposed testing of DUI suspects
7. Heroin	[ ] Phencyclidine, a psychedelic
8. Implied consent	[ ] Crime defined under H&S Code 11350
9. LSD	[ ] Crime defined under H&S Code 11357
10. Marijuana's name	[ ] a derivative of marijuana
11. Marijuana possession	
12. Marijuana sale	
13. Narcotics possession	
14. PCP	
15. Tolerance	

CHAPTER 18

MISCELLANEOUS OFFENSES

18.1 FORGERY DEFINED

Forgery of Legal Documents—PC 470. Every person who with intent to defraud, signs the name of another person or of a fictitious person, knowing that he or she has no authority so to do, or falsely makes, alters, forges, or counterfeits any . . . lottery ticket, deed, . . . check, draft, . . . contract, promissory note, due bill for the payment of money or property, receipt for money or property, or counterfeits or forges the handwriting of another, or utters, publishes, passes or attempts to pass, as true and genuine, any of the above-named false, altered, forged, or counterfeit matters, knowing the same to be false, altered, forged, or counterfeited, with intent to prejudice, damage, or defraud any person . . . is guilty of forgery. (briefed)

Discussion. There are many kinds of forgery defined under PC 470 through PC 483. Generally, forgery is the false making or material alteration of writing with intent to defraud. The crime consists of either the making or altering of a document described under one of the forgery sections, without authority, or uttering (cashing) such document with intent to defraud.

Note: PC 470 does *not* apply to a crime such as selling a fake Picasso painting which the art world would call a "forgery." In this type of case the crime would be theft by false pretense and would either be petty or grand theft depending on the amount of money so defrauded (see text Sections 16.1, 16.4 and 16.6).

Material Alteration. One may make a "material alteration" of a document merely by changing a word, a letter, or perhaps even a decimal point. "Writing," as used in forgery, is not limited solely to handwriting but includes any kind of written or printed reproduction.

Making—Uttering Defined. The term "making," as used in forgery also includes any alteration, however slight. "Uttering" is merely giving, offering, cashing or passing or attempting to do so.

18.2 INTENT TO DEFRAUD

The specific intent to defraud is an essential element of this crime. However, it is not necessary to prove that any person was actually defrauded or lost money or property as a result of the forgery. It is sufficient to show that either a specific individual, a business or members of the public would have been injured or defrauded as a result of the defendant's act.

It is not necessary to show that the defendant benefited in any way as the result of his or her act, nor is it important, in the case of a check, that it was ever presented to the bank.

It is important to remember that forgery consists of either of two types of acts, either of which is a crime:

1. writing, signing, making, or altering any of the documents described in the section, and
2. passing, attempting to pass, uttering, or giving a false instrument as a genuine one. As mentioned previously, the intent to defraud must be present in each case.

18.3 TYPES OF FORGERY AND FICTITIOUS CHECKS

Discussion—PC 470. This section includes any document, check, personal note, will, or writing on which the perpetrator makes some alteration. It also includes documents which he or she might prepare in whole or part. Raising the amount of a check, or making out personal or payroll checks or stolen money orders, would be an example.

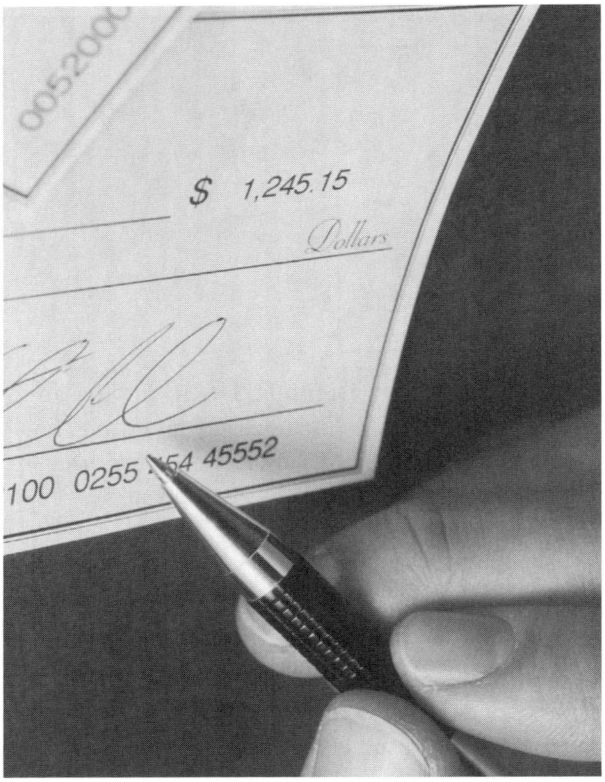

"NSF" checks are prosecuted under Penal Code § 476a, or may be diverted to a collection program under the direction of the prosecutor. *Courtesy of PhotoDisc, Inc.*

Forgery of Endorsement—PC 470. Forgery of endorsement on a check with intent to defraud is also covered by PC 470. If a person gives another permission to sign his name, it is not a crime. It is not a crime for an employee to sign his employer's name, or a wife to endorse her husband's check, providing there is express or implied permission to do so. Permission to sign another's name need not be in writing. Intent to defraud is the key element of forgery.

PC 470 also prohibits falsifying a notary acknowledgment, as well as knowingly false acknowledgments by a notary (PC 470(d)).

Fictitious Name Forgeries—PC 476. This section would be applicable where there is no real person of the name used on the check. It is necessary, under this section, to prove that the telephone and perhaps other directories have been checked and no such person exists. If such person does exist, it would be necessary to subpoena him or her to court to testify that he or she did not write the check and did not give the defendant permission to do so. Knowledge of the fictitious nature of the document and intent to defraud are both essential elements of PC 476.

Mere Possession—PC 476. This section also makes it a crime (felony wobbler) to have in one's possession, with intention to cash it, any fictitious or forged check or other instrument in writing for the payment of money.

Fraudulent Possession of Completed Check—PC 475a. This section makes it a felony (wobbler) to possess any completed check, money order, traveler's check or county warrant, whether real or fictitious, with intention to utter of pass the same, or to permit, cause, or procure the same to be uttered or passed, to defraud any person.

Issuing Check With Intent to Defraud—PC 476a. This section is used to prosecute insufficient funds checks, account-closed checks, and no-account checks; the latter being those cases where the defendant uses his or her true name, but does not have an account in the bank upon which the check was drawn.

When one willfully, and with intent to defraud, writes, draws or delivers a check, draft, or money order upon any bank for the payment of money, knowing at the time that he or she does not have sufficient funds on deposit or credit with the bank, or an account with the bank in question, he or she is in violation of PC 476a.

Post-dated Checks—PC 476a. A check dated in the future (bearing a date later than the date issued), may also be prosecuted under PC 476a. If, however, the person issuing the post-dated check can prove that he or she informed the person who accepted the check that it was post-dated, then there is no deception or intent to defraud and the check becomes a promissory note.

The mere fact that the perpetrator fails to keep his or her promise and deposit funds in the bank to cover the check on the due date, does not constitute a crime. In such cases the payee (person to whom check is payable) would have to take civil action to recover the money or property given for the post-dated check.

Credit (Access) Card Forgery—PC 484f. Every person who, with intent to defraud, designs, makes, alters, or embosses a counterfeit access card or utters [uses] or otherwise attempts to use a counterfeit access card is guilty of forgery.

Every person other than the card holder or a person authorized by him or her who, with intent to defraud, signs the name of another or a fictitious person to an access card, sales slip, sales draft, or instrument for the payment of money which evidences an access card transaction, or who makes any alteration to an access card that causes false billings, is guilty of forgery.

18.4 PENALTIES—FORGERY AND FICTITIOUS CHECKS

Punishment for Forgery—PC 473. Forgery is a felony (wobbler) punishable by imprisonment in the state prison, or by imprisonment in the county jail.

Fictitious Checks—PC 476. Violations are punishable by imprisonment in the county jail for not more than one year, or in the state prison.

Insufficient Funds—PC 476a. Violations are punishable by imprisonment in the county jail, or in the state prison.

Exception—PC 476(b). If the total amount of all checks that the defendant is convicted of making or uttering does not exceed two hundred dollars ($200), the offense is punishable only by imprisonment in the county jail. If the defendant has been previously convicted in this or any other state of PC 470, 475, 476, or petty theft, then the penalty given under PC 476a is applicable.

18.5 ARSON

Definitions—PC 450. In the arson statutes the following terms have the following meanings:

a. "Structure" means any building, or commercial or public tent, bridge, tunnel, or power plant.
b. "Forest land" means any brush-covered land, cut-over land, forest, grasslands, or woods.
c. "Property" means real property or personal property, other than a structure or forest land.
d. "Inhabited" means currently being used for dwelling purposes whether occupied or not. "Inhabited structure" and "inhabited property" do not include the real property (land) on which an inhabited structure or an inhabited property is located.
e. "Maliciously" imports a wish to vex, defraud, annoy, or injure another person, or an intent to do a wrongful act, established either by proof or presumption of law.
f. "Recklessly" means a person is aware of and consciously disregards a substantial and unjustifiable risk that his or her act will set fire to, burn, or cause to burn a structure, forest land, or property. The risk shall be of such nature and degree that disregard thereof constitutes a gross deviation from the standard of conduct that a reasonable person would observe in the situation. A person who creates such a risk but is unaware thereof

Arson is often used as a means to attack others, to destroy business competitors, or to collect insurance on a failing business. *Photograph by David Young-Wolff, courtesy of PhotoEdit*

solely by reason of voluntary intoxication also acts recklessly with respect thereto.

Punishment for Arson—PC 451. A person is guilty of arson and punishable by imprisonment in the state prison when he or she willfully and maliciously sets fire to or burns or causes to be burned or who aids, counsels or procures the burning of, any structure, forest land or property. Additional terms of imprisonment are imposed for prior convictions, injuries to safety personnel, multiple structures, multiple injuries, and use of accelerants or timers (PC 451.1).

Punishment of 10 years to life is the term for aggravated arson, based on intent to injure, with specified prior convictions or damages to five or more inhabited structures or losses exceeding five million dollars (PC 451.5).

For purposes of this section, arson of property does not include burning or causing to be burned one's own personal property unless there is intent to defraud or there is injury to another person or another person's structure, forest land, or property.

Discussion. It is not necessary that the property burned actually be destroyed; it is sufficient if there is but a slight degree of burning with respect to the property damage. However, the offense is complete if the burning is willful and malicious, and is of an intentional or incendiary origin, and proof of the *corpus delicti* of the crime may be proven circumstantially (*People v. Nagy*, 199 Cal. 235).

All that is needed to establish the *corpus delicti* in a prosecution for arson, in addition to the actual burning, is that the fire was intentional or of an incendiary origin, and this is generally established by circumstantial evidence, such as finding separate and distinct fires on the premises (*People v. Clagg*, 197 Cal. App. 2d 209).

Attempt to Burn—PC 455. "Any person who willfully and maliciously attempts to set fire to or attempts to burn or to aid, counsel, or procure the burning of any structure, forest land, or property, or who commits any act preliminary thereto, or in furtherance thereof, is punishable by imprisonment in the state prison. . . .

"The placing or distributing of any inflammable, explosive, or combustible material or substance, or any device in or about any structure, forest land, or property in an arrangement or preparation with intent to eventually willfully and maliciously set fire to or burn same, or to procure the setting fire to or burning of same shall, for the purposes of this act constitute an attempt to burn such structure, forest land, or property."

Discussion. This section is designed to make "attempt arson" a crime. It would be a violation of PC 455 to place a "firebomb" (see PC 453) or any incendiary device for the purpose of subsequently causing a fire. This section would also cover instances where one arranges with or procures another to burn a structure for insurance fraud purposes. In the latter case, a violation of PC 182 (conspiracy) might also exist.

Duty to Register—PC 457.1. In addition to any other punishment, a person convicted of arson or attempted arson must register with the sheriff or police chief within 14 days of residency. Failure to register is a misdemeanor.

18.6 UNLAWFULLY CAUSING FIRE

Definition and Punishment—PC 452. A person is guilty of unlawfully causing a fire when he or she recklessly sets fire to or burns or causes to be burned, any structure, forest land or property. Unlawfully causing a fire that burns any structure or forest land is punishable as a felony (wobbler). Unlawfully causing a fire which burns property, only, is a misdemeanor.

For purposes of this section, unlawfully causing a fire of property does not include one burning or causing to be burned one's own personal property unless there is injury to another person or to another person's structure, forest land, or property.

Discussion. PC 452 differs from PC 451 in several respects. In PC 451, the burning must be "willful and malicious," such as burning with intent to defraud an insurance company. In PC 452, it is necessary only that the burning be done unlawfully and recklessly (with negligence) to sustain a conviction.

Note that PC 452 does not make it a crime to burn one's own property unless there is injury to other persons or their structures (buildings), or to forest land or property. In the latter instances, a violation of PC 452, even if one burns one's own property, is a felony or misdemeanor depending on the damage or injury caused.

18.7 POSSESSION OF FLAMMABLES AND EXPLOSIVES

Possession With Intent to Burn—PC 453. (a) Every person who possesses, manufactures or disposes of any flammable or combustible material or substance, or any incendiary device, with intent to willfully and maliciously use this material, substance or device to set fire to or burn any structure, forest land or property, is punishable by imprisonment in the state prison, or in the county jail.

18.8 CRIMES AGAINST INSURED PROPERTY

Defrauding Insurer—PC 548. "Every person who willfully injures, destroys, secretes, abandons, or disposes of any property, which at the time is insured against loss of damage by theft or embezzlement, or any casualty with intent to defraud or prejudice the insurer, whether the same be the property or in the possession of such person or any other person, is punishable by imprisonment in the state prison. . . . For purposes of this section, 'casualty' does not include fire."

Discussion. This section applies strictly to the destruction, secreting, or disposing of personal property with intent to defraud the insurance carrier. It should be noted the specific intent to defraud or prejudice the insurer is a necessary element of this offense. Where the property is destroyed or injured by burning, the act usually involves the crime of arson or unlawful burning (PC 451 or 452). Since this offense and arson are two distinct crimes, they may be jointly charged and tried.

18.9 ABANDONED APPLIANCES

Abandoned Appliances—PC 402b. Any person who discards or abandons or leaves in any place accessible to children, any refrigerator, icebox, deep freeze locker, clothes dryer, washing machine or other appliance having a capacity of one and one-half cubic feet or more, which is no longer in use, and which has not had the door removed or the hinges and such portion of the latch mechanism removed to prevent latching or locking of the door, is guilty of a misdemeanor.

Any owner, lessee, or manager who knowingly permits such appliances to remain on premises under his or her control without having the door removed or the hinges and such portion of the latch mechanism removed to prevent latching or locking of the door, is guilty of a misdemeanor (briefed).

18.10 DEPOSITING OBJECTS ON PUBLIC HIGHWAYS

Throwing Glass, Etc. On Highway—PC 588a. "Any person who throws or deposits any oil, glass bottle, glass, nails, tacks, hoops, wire, cans, or any other substance likely to injure any person, animal, or vehicle upon any public highway in the State of California shall be guilty of a misdemeanor; provided however, that any person who willfully deposits any such substance upon any public highway in the State of California with the intent to cause great bodily injury to other persons using the highway shall be guilty of a felony."

18.11 DESTROYING SIGN BARRIERS

Destroying or Removing Authorized Sign—PC 588b. "Any person who willfully breaks down, removes, injures, or destroys any barrier or obstruction erected or placed in or upon any road or highway by the authorities in charge thereof, or by any authorized contractor engaged in the construction or maintenance thereof, or who tears down, defaces, removes, or destroys any warnings, notices, or directional signs erected, placed or posted in, upon, or adjacent to any road or highway or who extinguishes, removes, injures, or destroys any warning light or lantern or reflectorized warning or directional sign, erected, placed, or maintained by any such road or highway, shall be guilty of a misdemeanor."

18.12 DESTRUCTION OF LANDMARKS—TREES—SIGNS

Removing, Defacing Landmarks—PC 605. "Every person who either:

1. Maliciously removes any monument erected for the purpose of designating any point in the boundary of any lot or tract of land, or a place where a subaqueous [underwater] telegraph cable lies; or
2. Maliciously defaces or alters the marks upon any such monument; or
3. Maliciously cuts down or removes any tree upon which any such marks have been made for such purpose, with intent to destroy such marks, is guilty of a misdemeanor."

18.13 INJURING WORKS OF ART

Injuring Improvements—PC 622. "Every person, not the owner thereof, who willfully injures, disfigures, or destroys any monument, work of art, or useful or ornamental improvement within the limits of any village, town, or city, or any shade tree or ornamental plant growing therein, whether situated upon private ground or on any street, sidewalk, or public park or place is guilty of a misdemeanor."

18.14 INJURING OR TAMPERING WITH AIRCRAFT

Tampering With Aircraft—PC 625b. Every person who willfully injures or tampers with any aircraft or the contents or parts thereof, or removes any part of or from any aircraft without the consent of the owner, and every person who, with intent to commit any malicious mischief, injury, or other crime, climbs into or upon an aircraft or attempts to manipulate any of the controls, starting mechanisms, brakes, or other mechanism or device of an aircraft while it is at rest and unattended or who sets in motion any aircraft while it is at rest and unattended, is guilty of a misdemeanor (briefed).

Anyone who willfully and maliciously damages any aircraft in such a manner as to make it unsafe for flight, is guilty of a felony (wobbler).

18.15 INJURY TO JAIL

Destroying Jail—PC 4600. "Every person who willfully and intentionally breaks down, pulls down, or otherwise destroys or injures any jail or prison, is [guilty of a felony wobbler], except that where the damage or injury to any city, city and county or county jail property is determined to be four hundred dollars ($400) or less, such person is guilty of a misdemeanor."

Unauthorized Possession in Jail—PC 4575. It is a misdemeanor, punishable by $1000 fine, for an inmate of a local correctional facility to possess a cell phone, pager or wireless internet device without authorization. Unauthorized possession of tobacco in designated facilities is a $20 infraction.

18.16 INVASION OF PRIVACY

Wiretapping—PC 631. It is a felony (wobbler) to make an unauthorized connection to a wire or cable system and learn, without the consent of all parties, the contents of any intercepted communication. Evidence obtained via unauthorized wiretap is inadmissible in any proceeding, except against the one who made it.

Eavesdropping on or Recording Confidential Communications—PC 632. It is a felony (wobbler) to use any electronic amplifying or recording device to hear or record any confidential communication between parties, without their consent. A "confidential communication" is one made under circumstances indicating that any of the parties might reasonably have expected it to be confined to themselves. For example, where an employer or coworker surreptitiously records private conversations, this offense may be committed (*Coulter v. Bank of America*, 28 Cal. App.4th 923).

Intercepting Cellular or Cordless Communication—PC 632.5-632.7. Additional wobbler offenses are committed by the unauthorized interception or recording of confidential communications, without consent of all the parties, where those communications are carried on by means of combinations of cell phones, cordless phones, and landline phones, faxes, etc.

Intercepting Public Safety Communications—PC 636.5. It is a misdemeanor for an unauthorized person to intercept or divulge any public safety communications (via police scanner, for example), to assist in committing or avoiding apprehension for any crime.

Electronic Tracking—PC 637.7. It is a misdemeanor to use an electronic tracking device (transponder), attached to a vehicle or other movable thing, to track the movements or location of a person, without consent. This section does not prohibit lawful tracking by enforcement officers.

Law Enforcement Exemption—PC 633. Specified law enforcement officers have a limited exemption from the prohibitions of sections 631, 632, 632.5, 632.6 and 632.7, allowing the interception and recording of communications where permitted by federal law and the Constitution. For example, officers may record conversations by two or more arrestees in a police car (*People v. Lucero*, 190 Cal. App.3d 1065), and may record a prisoner's jailhouse call to an accomplice or victim (*People v. Guilmette*, 1 Cal. App.4th 1534) with the consent of one party, or where there is no reasonable expectation of privacy (signs or notices may be posted). However, it is a felony to intercept or record a prisoner's confidential communications with an attorney, physician or spiritual advisor (PC 636).

Evidentiary Recording—PC 633.5. Once party may record a confidential communication to obtain evidence of extortion, kidnapping, bribery, violent felony against the person, or obscene or annoying phone calls. Also, the victim of a domestic violence restraining order may be authorized by the judge to record any prohibited communication from the perpetrator (PC 633.6).

18.17 OTHER OFFENSES

Occupied Locked Vehicles—VC 22516. This Vehicle Code section provides that no person shall leave standing a locked vehicle in which there is any person who cannot readily escape therefrom.

Discussion. This section is applicable to thoughtless or careless persons who leave a helpless child, or elderly infirm person in a locked vehicle from which they could not readily escape. The obvious intent of the legislature is to prevent injury and death in the case of emergency or overheating of the interior of the vehicle.

Ticket Scalping—PC 346. This section makes it a misdemeanor to sell a ticket (1) at a price higher than that printed on the ticket, (2) on the grounds where the event is to be held or where tickets are being sold, (3) without the written permission of the owner or operator of the property where the event is being held, (4) providing the ticket was originally purchased for the purpose of resale. If any one of the above elements is missing, the resale is not a crime.

Poisoning Food, Medicine, Water—PC 347. This section makes it a felony to add any harmful substance to any food, water supply, etc., with the intent that such will be taken by any human being to his injury.

False Telephone, Telegraph Messages—PC 474. Knowingly and willfully sending a false telephone or telegraph message or knowingly delivering such message is a felony (wobbler).

False Name to Newspaper—PC 538a. It is a misdemeanor to sign and send a letter to a newspaper using a name other than one's own, with intent to cause the newspaper to believe that letter was written by the person whose name was signed.

Vandalism Defined—PC 594. Every person who maliciously: (1) defaces with graffiti or other inscribed material (2) damages, or (3) destroys any real or personal property not his own, is guilty of vandalism.

If the amount of defacement, etc., is less than $400, the offense is a misdemeanor. If the defacement, damage or destruction is $400 or more, the crime is a felony wobbler.

Aerosol Paint Cans—PC 594.1. This section makes it a misdemeanor:

1. for any person (other than legal guardian) to sell or give any person under 18 years of age, any aerosol can (containing more than 6 ounces of paint or etching cream) that is capable of defacing property, without first obtaining evidence of age and identity; or
2. for anyone under age 18 to purchase an aerosol can or etching cream as described; or
3. for any person to carry in plain view an aerosol can or etching cream as described, in any posted public facility, park, etc.; or
4. for anyone under age 18 to possess an aerosol container of paint (net contents larger than 6 ounces) or etching cream for the purpose of defacing property while in any public place.

Possession of Graffiti Tools—PC 594.2. It is a misdemeanor to possess paint, markers or cutting tools with intent to commit vandalism.

Poisoning Animals—PC 596. Every person who, without the consent of the owner, willfully administers poison to any animal, the property of another, or exposes any poisonous substance, with the intent to poison any such animal, is guilty of a misdemeanor. [Briefed.]

Note: There are exceptions to this law which exempt placing poison out for control of predatory animals or livestock-killing dogs.

Cruelty to Animals—PC 597. (a) Except as provided in subdivision (c), every person who maliciously and intentionally maims, wounds, tortures, or mutilates a living animal which is the property of another, or maliciously and intentionally kills an animal which is the property of another, is guilty of [a felony wobbler].

(b) Except as otherwise provided in subdivision (a) or (c), every person who overdrives, overloads, . . . overworks tortures, torments, deprives of necessary sustenance, drink or shelter, cruelly beats, mutilates or cruelly kills any animal . . . is guilty of a misdemeanor.

(c) Every person who maliciously and intentionally maims, mutilates, or tortures any mammal, bird, reptile, amphibian, or fish . . . is guilty of an offense . . . [punishable as a felony wobbler]. [Briefed.]

Unlawful Sale of Puppies—PC 597z. Except for animal shelters and specified organizations, it is an infraction or misdemeanor to sell a dog under the age of 8 weeks without written authorization from a veterinarian.

Fighting Dogs—PC 597.5. Any person who owns, trains, permits or causes any dog to engage in exhibition fighting for amusement or gain, is guilty of a felony (wobbler). It is a misdemeanor for a person to knowingly be present at a place where animal fighting is taking place, or where preparations are made for such fights (PC 597c).

Unlawful Restraint of Animals—PC 597.7, H&S 122335. It is an infraction (first offense with no injury) or a misdemeanor (where injury results, or subsequent offenses) to leave an animal unattended in a vehicle under conditions where it is exposed to risks of heat, cold, or lack of food and water, and might suffer great bodily injury (PC 597.7). It is an infraction or misdemeanor (subsequent offenses) to tether a dog to a tree, fence, doghouse or other fixed object, except to perform a brief task (H&S 122335).

Gaming Offenses—PC 337. Various acts of cheating or manipulating games of chance at gambling establishments are prohibited misdemeanors, punishable by a maximum of one year in jail and fines ranging from $5000 (first offense) to $15,000 (subsequent offenses). These include fraudulently altering or misrepresenting the odds (PC 337u), using any device to track the cards played or to analyze probabilities in order to enhance play (PC 337v), using counterfeit chips or any device to cheat at a game or steal receipts (PC 337w), cheating in any game at a gambling establishment (PC 337x), and manufacturing cheating devices or training another in how to cheat (PC 337 y).

Fighting Birds or Animals—PC 597b. Any person who, for amusement or gain, causes any bull, bear, cock, or other animal (not including dogs) to fight with any kind of animal or a human being, is guilty of a misdemeanor. Second and subsequent offenses are punishable as felonies (wobblers). Fines may range up to $25,000.

Employment Surveillance—Labor Code 435. It is an infraction for any employer to make audio or video recordings of employees in restrooms, locker rooms or changing rooms, except with a court order.

Soliciting Inmate Bail Business—PC 160. It is a misdemeanor for a bail bondsman to pay a jail inmate to solicit other inmates for bail referrals.

Solicitation/Sale of Official Information—PC 146g. It is a misdemeanor punishable by $1000 fine for public officials to sell, or for anyone to solicit the sale of, information from criminal investigation files, or photographs or videos of inmates within a secure facility.

STUDENT REVIEW

TERMINOLOGY DEFINED—CHAPTER 18

Please see the Terminology Quiz at the end of this chapter.

1. Arson: maliciously setting fire to any structure or forest lands.
2. Conveyance: instrument for transferring title to property.
3. Counterfeit: any unlawful duplication of writing with intent to defraud.
4. Debenture: written security for a loan, a type of bond.
5. Defamation: written or spoken words injurious to another.
6. Defraud: breach of legal duty injurious to another.
7. Draft: a check, an order in writing for payment of money.
8. Due process: according to rules for protection of one's rights.
9. Forgery: falsely altering or signing another name with fraudulent intent.
10. Career criminal: third conviction of one twice convicted before.
11. Incendiary: a fire intentionally set, a device for setting fire, arson.
12. Malicious mischief: injuring or destroying real or personal property.
13. Material alteration: any alteration which changes a document's meaning.
14. Payee: one to whom a check or money is to be paid or is payable.
15. Post-dated: dated in the future, after date issued.
16. Promissory note: an acknowledgment of debt, not a check.
17. Uttering: giving, offering, passing, or presenting.
18. Warrant: type of government check order for payment of money.
19. Will: declaration in writing for distribution of property after death.
20. Writing: in forgery, any duplication or reproduction of words.

TRUE-FALSE QUIZ—CHAPTER 18

After reading this chapter you should be able to correctly answer the following items.

___ 1. One can commit forgery merely by changing a word on a document without signing another's name.
___ 2. Specific intent to defraud is an essential element of forgery.
___ 3. One cannot be guilty of check forgery unless it is presented to a bank for payment.
___ 4. Uttering a false instrument in writing constitutes forgery.
___ 5. Fraudulently raising the amount of a check constitutes forgery.
___ 6. Cashing an insufficient funds check is a crime regardless of one's intent.
___ 7. If the payee is not aware of it, it is a crime to cash a post-dated check with him.
___ 8. One cannot be guilty of forgery (PC 470), if one in fact signs the name of a non-existent person.
___ 9. Specific intent to defraud is an essential element of writing a check on a closed account under PC 476a.
___10. Forgery is punishable by a sentence in either county jail or state prison.
___11. If in fact no one was defrauded, one cannot be guilty of forgery regardless of initial intent.
___12. Even if one does not intend to defraud an insurance company, willful and malicious burning of a building constitutes the crime of arson.
___13. One is guilty of arson if one accidentally but with gross negligence sets fire to another person's home.
___14. One cannot be guilty of arson for willfully burning one's own property.
___15. It is a felony to remove one's own property following a fire for the purpose of defrauding the insurance carrier.

___16. It is a misdemeanor to abandon a refrigerator one and one-half cubic feet or larger without first removing the lock, hinges, or door.

___17. Any person who deposits material of any kind on a public highway is guilty of a misdemeanor under PC 588a.

___18. A "confidential communication" is one made where any of the parties might reasonably have expected it to be confined to themselves.

___19. One party may legally record a confidential communication without the other's knowledge to obtain evidence of extortion against the other person.

___20. If one willfully damages jail property, the crime is a felony or misdemeanor depending on the charge for which one is serving time.

ESSAY-DISCUSSION ITEMS—CHAPTER 18

After reading this chapter you should be able to correctly answer the following items.

1. What are the elements of forgery under PC 470?
2. Briefly define the terms (1) "material alteration" and (2) "uttering," as they apply to forgery.
3. Briefly, what is a post-dated check? Under what circumstances is issuing one a crime and when not?
4. What are the elements of arson under PC 451?
5. What does the word "maliciously" mean as it applies to arson? Is specific or general intent required for arson?
6. Discuss whether or not one may be guilty of arson for burning his own property. What effect would the insurance factor have?
7. What size of abandoned refrigerator comes under the purview of PC 402(b)? What must the owner do to avoid a violation of this section?
8. What is the difference, in elements, between a misdemeanor and felony violation of PC 588a (depositing materials on a public highway)?
9. What must the suspect do to constitute "tampering" under PC 625b (injuring or tampering with an aircraft)?
10. What differentiates between misdemeanor and felony injury to prison or jail under PC 4600?

TERMINOLOGY QUIZ—CHAPTER 18

Match terms and definitions by writing the number preceding the correct term in the appropriate brackets.

Terms

1. Arson
2. Conveyance
3. Counterfeit
4. Debenture
5. Defamation
6. Defraud
7. Draft
8. Due process
9. Forgery
10. Career criminal
11. Incendiary
12. Malicious mischief
13. Material alteration

Definitions

[ ] one to whom a check is payable
[ ] a check or order in writing for payment of money
[ ] fire intentionally set, a fire-setting device
[ ] injuring or destroying another's property
[ ] any unlawful duplication of writing, fraudulent
[ ] instrument for transferring title to property
[ ] written document for distribution of property after death
[ ] type of government check, order for payment of money
[ ] written or spoken words injurious to another
[ ] written security for a loan, type of bond
[ ] any alteration which changes a document's meaning

14. Payee	[ ] to give, offer, pass, or present for cashing
15. Post-dated	[ ] dated in the future, after date cashed
16. Promissory note	[ ] an acknowledgment of debt, not a check
17. Uttering	[ ] breach of legal duty injurious to another
18. Warrant	
19. Will	
20. Writing	

APPENDIX A

CRIME ELEMENTS CHART

Elements of Selected Penal Code Sections
(In Alphabetical Order by Offense)

CRIME - PENALTY	ELEMENTS
Abduction For Marriage or Defilement **265 PC** *Felony*	1. Takes woman unlawfully; 2. Against her will; 3. By force, menace, or duress; 4. Compels her to marry him or another, or to be defiled.
Abduction For Prostitution **266a PC** *Misdemeanor*	1. Takes any person; 2. Against his or her will and without his or her consent, or with his or her consent, produced by fraud, inducement or misrepresentation; 3. For the purpose of prostitution.
Abduction For Illicit Relations **266b PC** *Felony*	1. Takes any person; 2. Unlawfully and against his or her will; 3. By force, menace, or duress; 4. Compels him or her to live with another against his or her consent; 5. In an illicit relationship.
Abduction of Female Under 18 **267 PC** *Felony*	1. Takes female under 18; 2. From parents, guardian, or another having legal custody; 3. Without their consent; 4. For purpose of prostitution.
Abortion **274 PC** *Felony*	1. Provides, administers, employs; 2. Any means whatever; 3. With intent to procure miscarriage; 4. Except as provided in H & S Code 25950.
Arson **451 PC** *Felony*	1. Willfully and maliciously; 2. Sets fire to or burns or causes to be burned; 3. Any structure, forest land or property.
Assault (Simple) **240 PC** *Misdemeanor*	1. Unlawful attempt; 2. Present ability; 3. To commit violent injury.
Assaulting Peace Officer, Firefighter, Paramedic, Nurse, Doctor **241(b) PC** *Misdemeanor*	1. Assault on peace officer, firefighter, (etc.); 2. Engaged in performance of duties, or; 3. Doctor, nurse giving emergency field care; 4. Assailant knows or should know victim's status.

CRIME - PENALTY	ELEMENTS
Assault With Deadly Weapon (ADW) **245 (a) (1) PC** **245 (a) (2) PC** *Felony (Wobbler)**	1. Assaults person of another; 2. With deadly weapon or instrument (a)(1) or; 3. Any force likely to produce great bodily injury or; 4. With a firearm (a) (2).

* *Note:* A felony (wobbler) is punishable by imprisonment either in the county jail or a fine or both; or by imprisonment in the state prison.

CRIME - PENALTY	ELEMENTS
Assault (ADW) Peace Officer, Firefighter **245 (c) PC** **245 (d) PC** *Felony*	1. Assault with deadly weapon or instrument (c) or; 2. A firearm (d); 3. Person of peace officer or firefighter; 4. Engaged in performance of duty; 5. Assailant knows or should know police/fire and on-duty status.
Assault With Caustic Chemical **244 PC** *Felony*	1. Willfully and maliciously; 2. Places or throws upon another; 3. Caustic chemical of any nature; 4. Intent to injure or disfigure.
Assault With Intent to Commit Certain Crimes **220 PC** *Felony*	1. Assault with; 2. Intent to commit rape, sodomy or mayhem, oral copulation, or any violation of PC 264.1, PC 288 or PC 289.
Battery **242 PC** *Misdemeanor*	1. Willful and unlawful; 2. Use of force or violence on person of another. 3. (With serious bodily injury: Felony Wobbler.)
Battery, Peace Officer, Firefighter, (etc.) **243 (c) PC** *Felony (Wobbler)*	1. Battery resulting in injury; 2. Against peace officer, firefighter, paramedic, (etc.); 3. Engaged in performance of duty; 4. Assailant knows or should know victim's status.
Battery (Sexual) **243.4 PC** *Felony (Wobbler)*	1. Touching intimate part of another; 2. Against their will; 3. While restrained by accused or accomplice; 4. For purpose of sexual arousal or gratification.
Battery of Spouse, Cohabitant **273.5 PC** *Felony (Wobbler)*	1. Willfully inflicts corporal injury; 2. On spouse or cohabitant; 3. Resulting in traumatic condition.
Battery, Transportation Personnel **243.3 PC** *Felony (Wobbler)*	1. Battery inflicted against; 2. Operator of bus, taxi, streetcar, motor vehicle; 3. Or on ticket or station agent; 4. While victim engaged in duty; 5. Assailant knows or should know victim on duty. (If injury, penalty increased)
Breaking and Entering **603 PC** *Misdemeanor*	1. Forcibly enters dwelling house, cabin, building; 2. Intended for human occupancy; 3. Without permission of owner, lessee; 4. Destroys property of value in, around building.

CRIME - PENALTY	ELEMENTS
Bribing Officer **67 PC** *Felony*	1. Gives, offers any bribe; 2. To any executive officer; 3. With intent to influence in respect to; 4. Any act, vote, official decision.
Burglary **459 PC** *Felony* *First degree —inhabited* *Second degree —all others.*	1. Entry of; (need not be forced) 2. Building or place listed in statute; 3. With intent to commit grand or petty theft or any felony.
Burglary With Explosives **464 PC** *Felony*	1. Enters any building; 2. With intent to commit crime; 3. Opens or attempts to open any vault or safe; 4. By use of explosives, torch, burning bar.
Burglary Tools (Possession) **466 PC** *Misdemeanor*	1. Possession of picklock, or tool; 2. With intent to feloniously enter; 3. Any building, etc., described in section; 4. Or knowingly alter any key to unlock a building; 5. Without permission of owner, lessee.
Child Abuse **273a PC** *Felony (Wobbler)*	1. Any person having care or custody of a child; 2. Willfully permits child to suffer; 3. Or inflicts physical pain or mental suffering; 4. Under conditions likely to produce great bodily injury or death. (If conditions not likely to cause great bodily injury: Misdemeanor)
Child Concealing **280 PC** *Felony—Misdemeanor*	1. Willfully causes or permits; 2. Removal or concealment of child; 3. In violation of Civil Code 226.10. (If taken out of state —Felony)
Child Molesting **(Under 14)** **288 PC** *Felony*	1. Willfully and lewdly; 2. Commits any lewd or lascivious act upon any part of the body; 3. Of a child under 14; 4. With intent of arousing, appealing to, or gratifying lust passions or sexual desires; 5. Of child or perpetrator.
Child Molesting **(Under 18)** **647.6 PC** *Misdemeanor*	1. Annoys or molests; 2. Any child under 18. Second conviction or prior conviction of 288 PC (Felony) Violation of this section after having entered inhabited dwelling without consent (Felony, Wobbler).
Child Neglect **270 PC** *Misdemeanor*	1. Parent willfully omits; 2. Without lawful excuse; 3. To furnish food, clothes, shelter, etc.; 4. Of minor child. (If court has adjudicated matter, penalty: Felony (Wobbler).)
Child Stealing **278 PC** *Felony (Wobbler)*	1. Not having right of custody; 2. Maliciously takes, entices away, detains, or conceals; 3. Any minor child; 4. With intent to detain and conceal; 5. From parent or guardian, or other person having lawful charge.

CRIME - PENALTY	ELEMENTS
Conspiracy **182 PC** *Felony*	1. Two or more persons conspire; 2. To commit any crime; 3. And do an overt act in furtherance or preparation; 4. To falsely indict, charge, or cause arrest; 5. To cheat any person of any property; 6. To commit any act injurious to public health; 7. To commit any acts injurious to public officials listed; 8. To falsely bring any suit or action; 9. To obtain money or property by false pretenses.
Contributing to Minor's Delinquency **272 PC** *Misdemeanor*	1. Commits any act or omits any duty; 2. Causing a person under 18; 3. To come under the provisions of W & I Code 300, 601, or 602 (delinquency).
Copulation **288a PC** *Felony—Felony (Wobbler)*	1. Copulates the mouth with sexual organs or anus of another who is under 18, or; 2. Copulation by force or threats; 3. Copulation while in jail or prison; 4. When 10 years difference in age, and youngest party is under 14, or; 5. When one is participating under threat of immediate bodily harm, force, violence, duress or menace; 6. In concert with another by force or violence and against the will; 7. Copulation by person over 21 with another under 16.
Defrauding Hotel/Restaurant **537 PC** *Misdemeanor (Under $400)* *Felony (Wobbler) (Over $400)*	1. Obtaining food, credit or accommodations; 2. At any hotel, restaurant, boarding house, ski lodge, campground, etc.; 3. Without paying and with intent to defraud; 4. By use of any false pretense, or; 5. Surreptitiously absconds with intent not to pay.
Defrauding Insurer **548 PC** *Felony (Wobbler)*	1. Willfully injures, secretes, disposes of; 2. Any insured property; 3. With intent to injure or defraud insurer.
Discharging Firearm at Building **246 PC** *Felony (Wobbler)*	1. Maliciously and willfully; 2. Discharges a firearm; 3. At inhabited dwelling, housecar, or camper or occupied building or occupied motor vehicle.
Disorderly Conduct **647 PC** *Misdemeanor*	1. Solicits or engages in lewd conduct in public place, or; 2. Solicits or engages in act of prostitution, or; 3. Begging in a public place, or; 4. Loiters about public toilets for purpose of lewd acts, or; 5. Loiters on public streets and refuses to identify self andaccount for presence to a peace officer, or; 6. Is under influence of liquor or drugs in a public place.
Disturbing Public Meeting **403 PC** *Misdemeanor*	1. Willfully and illegally; 2. Disturbs any lawful meeting.
Disturbing the Peace **415 PC** *Misdemeanor*	1. Unlawfully fighting in a public place; 2. Or challenging another person in a public place to fight, or; 3. Maliciously and willfully disturbs another person by loud and unreasonable noise; 4. Or using offensive words in a public place which are inherently likely to produce an immediate violent reaction.

CRIME - PENALTY	ELEMENTS
Drawing or Exhibiting Firearm or Deadly Weapon **417 PC** *Misdemeanor*	1. Not in self-defense; 2. Draws or exhibits firearm; 3. Or other deadly weapon, loaded or unloaded; 4. In rude, angry, or threatening manner; 5. Or in any manner uses same in quarrel. 6. In presence of peace officer: *Felony (Wobbler)*
Embezzlement (Includes theft) **503 PC** *Felony—Misdemeanor*	1. Fraudulent appropriation of property; 2. By person to whom it has been entrusted. (Penalty same as for theft of like amount.) (If public funds embezzled: Felony.)
Enticing Female Under 18 For Prostitution **266 PC** *Felony (Wobbler)*	1. Any person who inveigles or entices; 2. Any unmarried female; 3. Of previous chaste character; 4. Under the age of 18; 5. For prostitution or to have illicit carnal relations with any man; **OR** 1. Any person who by false pretenses, etc.; 2. Procures any female; 3. To have illicit carnal relations with any man.
Extortion (Blackmail) **518 PC** *Felony*	1. Obtaining property from another; 2. With victim's consent, or; 3. Obtaining official act by public officer; 4. By wrongful use of force or fear, or; 5. Under color of official right.
False Bomb Report **148.1 PC** *Felony (Wobbler)*	1. Reports to police, airline, newspapers, etc.; 2. That bomb has been or will be placed; 3. Knowing same to be false, or; 4. Maliciously informs another that a bomb has been or will be placed, or; 5. Maliciously sends false bomb to any person.
False Crime Report **148.5 PC** *Misdemeanor*	1. Reports to any peace officer during performance of duty; 2. That any crime has been committed; 3. Knowing report is false.
False Imprisonment **236 PC** *Misdemeanor—Felony (Wobbler)*	1. Unlawful violation of; 2. Personal liberty of another. (If by means of violence, fraud: Felony)
Failure to Disperse (on lawful command) **416 PC** *Misdemeanor*	1. Assembly by two or more persons; 2. With intent to disturb the peace or commit unlawful act; 3. Fail to disperse on lawful command of public officer
Fictitious Check **476a PC** *Misdemeanor—Felony*	1. Willfully, with intent to defraud; 2. Writes or delivers; (Depends on amount of check) 3. Any check; 4. Knowing at time there are insufficient funds or credit in bank for payment in full.
Forgery **470 PC** Felony (Wobbler)	1. Signs name of real or fictitious person; 2. Or alters any document listed in section; 3. Or attempts to pass as genuine; 4. Knowing has no authority to do so; 5. With intent to defraud.

CRIME - PENALTY	ELEMENTS
Grand Theft **487 PC** *Felony (Wobbler)*	1. Takes money, labor, real or personal property of value over $400, or; 2. Domestic fowls, avocados, olives, citrus, or deciduous fruits, fruits, nuts, and artichokes, valued over $100 or; 3. From person of another, or; 4. Where money, labor, or property is taken by a servant, agent, or employee from principal or employer and aggregates $400 or more in any 12 consecutive months, or; 5. An automobile, horse, mare, firearm, lamb, gelding, cow, pig, mule, dog, etc., regardless of the value; 6. With intent to permanently deprive.
Gratuity, Unauthorized Acceptance **70 PC** *Misdemeanor*	1. Executive, ministerial officer, employee or appointee; 2. Of city, county or state; 3. Knowingly asks for or receives; 4. Gratuity, reward or promise of same; 5. For doing an official act; 6. Except as authorized by law.
Incest **285 PC** *Felony*	1. Persons more closely related by blood than first cousins; 2. Who marry, or; 3. Commit fornication or adultery.
Inciting Riot **404.5 PC** *Misdemeanor*	1. Commits an act which urges a riot, or; 2. Urges other to acts of force or violence; 3. With intent to cause riot; 4. Under conditions producing immediate danger.
Indecent Exposure (Lewd conduct) **314 PC** *Misdemeanor*	1. Willfully and lewdly either; 2. Exposes his person or private parts; 3. In any public place, or in any place where there are other persons to be offended thereby, or; 4. Procures another to so exhibit themselves to public view; 5. Such as is offensive to decency, or; 6. Excites lewd thoughts or acts.
Kidnapping **207 PC** *Felony*	1. Forcibly steals, takes, or arrests any person in this state; 2. And takes to another location in this state or county; **OR** 1. Forcibly persuades by false promises; 2. Any child under 14; 3. For purposes of PC 288; 4. To go to another place in or out of the county; **OR** 1. Hires, persuades, entices, decoys, or seduces; 2. By false promises, misrepresentation, or the like; 3. Any person to go out of the state; 4. With intent to sell him into slavery or involuntary servitude, or otherwise employ him to his own use; **OR** 1. Abducts or brings; 2. Any person into this state from another state; 3. By force or fraud; 4. Contrary to the law of the place where the act is committed.

CRIME - PENALTY	ELEMENTS
Kidnapping for Extortion, or Ransom **209 PC** *Felony*	1. Conceals, confines, inveigles, entices, kidnaps, or decoys, or carries away; 2. Any person by any means; 3. With intent to hold or detain; 4. For ransom, reward, or extortion. **OR** 1. Kidnaps or carries away; 2. To commit robbery, or; 3. Aids or abets such act.
Kidnapper, Posing as: (Attempt to Profit by Kidnapping) **210 PC** *Felony*	1. Fraudulently; 2. Represents to be in a position to obtain release of victim; 3. For the purpose of obtaining any ransom, or reward, or money or thing of value.
Lynching **405-405b PC** *Felony*	1. Taking any person; 2. From lawful custody of peace officer; 3. By means of a riot.
Malicious Mischief (Vandalism) **594 PC** *Misdemeanor—Felony (Wobbler)* *Penalty depends on amount of damage.*	1. Maliciously defaces with paint; or 2. Injures or destroys; 3. Any real or personal property; 4. Not his own.
Manslaughter (Voluntary) **192(1) PC** *Felony*	1. Unlawfully, kills a human being; 2. Upon sudden quarrel or heat of passion; 3. Without malice.
Manslaughter (Involuntary) **192(2) PC** *Felony*	1. Unlawfully, kills a human being; 2. In commission of unlawful act, not amounting to a felony, or lawful act in an unlawful manner or without due caution or circumspection which might produce death; 3. Without malice.
Manslaughter (Felony in driving vehicle—involuntary) **192(3)(a) PC** *Felony (Wobbler)*	1. Driving a vehicle; 2. Kills a human being; 3. Unlawful act, not amounting to felony, or a lawful act which might produce death in an unlawful manner; 4. **With** gross negligence. 5. Act must be proximate cause of death; 6. Without malice.
Manslaughter (Misdemeanor in driving vehicle—involuntary) **192(3)(b) PC** *Misdemeanor*	1. Same elements as above except **without** gross negligence.
Mayhem **203 PC** *Felony*	1. Unlawfully and maliciously; 2. Amputates, disables, disfigures or renders useless; 3. A member of another's body, or; 4. Slits the tongue, nose, ear, or lip, or; 5. Puts out an eye.

CRIME - PENALTY	ELEMENTS
Murder (first degree) **187-189 PC** *Felony—Possible Death Penalty*	1. Unlawful killing; 2. Of human being or fetus; 3. With malice aforethought; 4. Willful, deliberate or premeditated, or; 5. By poison, lying in wait, torture, or in commission of burglary, arson, robbery, rape, or mayhem, or 288 PC, or; 6. With knowing use of explosives, or; 7. Armor piercing ammunition.
Murder (second degree) **187-189 PC** *Felony*	1. Unlawful killing; 2. Of human being or fetus; 3. With malice aforethought.
Pandering **266i PC** *Felony*	1. Procures another for purposes of prostitution, or; 2. By promises, threats, violence causes another; 3. To become a prostitute, or; 4. By threats, promises, violence, causes another; 5. To remain in prostitution, or; 6. By abuse of any position of authority; 7. Procures another for prostitution, or; 8. Receives anything of value for procuring another for prostitution.
Petty Theft **484 - 488 PC** *Misdemeanor*	1. Takes money or property; 2. Valued at $400 or less, not listed in 487 PC; 3. With intent to permanently deprive.
Pimping **266h PC** *Felony*	1. Knowing another is a prostitute; 2. Derives support, lives; 3. From earnings of a prostitute.
Poisoning Animals **596 PC** *Misdemeanor*	1. Without consent of the owner; 2. Willfully administers poison; 3. To any animal; 4. The property of another; 5. Or exposes poison with intent that it shall be taken by an animal.
Poisoning Food, Water Supply, Medicine **347 PC** *Felony*	1. Willfully mingles any harmful substance; 2. With any food, drink, medicine, water supply; 3. With intent it be taken by humans to their injury.
Rape (Victim of unsound mind) **261(1) PC** *Felony*	1. Act of sexual intercourse; 2. Victim not spouse of perpetrator; 3. Victim incapable of giving legal consent due to unsound mind.
Rape (By force) **261(2) PC** *Felony*	1. Act of sexual intercourse; 2. Victim not spouse of perpetrator; 3. Against victim's will; 4. Accomplished by force or fear; of immediate unlawful bodily injury to victim, or of another.
Rape (By drugs) **261(3) PC** *Felony*	1. Act of sexual intercourse; 2. Victim not spouse of perpetrator; 3. Prevented from resisting by any intoxicating narcotic or anesthetic substance; 4. Administered by or with knowledge of the accused.

CRIME - PENALTY	ELEMENTS
Rape (Victim unconscious of nature of act) **261(4) PC** *Felony*	1. Act of sexual intercourse; 2. Victim not spouse of perpetrator; 3. Victim is unconscious of the nature of the act; 4. This fact is known to perpetrator.
Rape (Victim believes perpetrator to be spouse) **261(5) PC** *Felony*	1. Act of sexual intercourse; 2. Victim not spouse of perpetrator; 3. Victim believes perpetrator to be his or her spouse; 4. This belief induced by artifice, pretense or concealment by perpetrator; 5. With intent to induce such belief.
Rape of Spouse **262 PC** *Felony (Wobbler)*	1. Act of sexual intercourse; 2. Accomplished against the will of the spouse; 3. By force or fear of immediate unlawful bodily injury; 4. On the spouse or another, or; 5. When accomplished by threat of future retaliation; 6. Against the victim or another, and; 7. There is reasonable possibility of execution.
Receiving Stolen Property **496 PC** *Felony—Misdemeanor* *(Penalty according to value, same as theft)*	1. Buying or accepting stolen property; 2. Knowing property is stolen, or; 3. Concealing, selling stolen property; 4. Knowing property is stolen.
Rescuing Prisoner **4550 PC** *Felony—Misdemeanor* *(Penalty depends on rescued prisoner's sentence)*	1. Rescues, attempts, or aids; 2. Prisoner from prison, road camp jail; 3. Or any peace officer having lawful custody.
Riot **404 PC** *Misdemeanor*	1. Any use of force or violence, or; disturbance of peace, or threat to use such force if accompanied by immediate power of execution; 2. By two or more persons acting together; 3. Without authority of law.
Riot (Remaining at riot after command to disperse) **409 PC** *Misdemeanor*	1. Remains present; 2. At riot, rout, or unlawful assembly; 3. After lawful command to disperse.
Robbery **211 PC** *Felony*	1. Felonious taking of personal property; 2. In possession of another; 3. From person or immediate presence; 4. Against his will; 5. By means of force or fear. (Robbery of public vehicle operator, 211a PC.)
Rout **406 - 408 PC** *Misdemeanor*	1. Two or more persons acting together; 2. Attempt or advance toward an act; 3. If committed would be a riot.
Seduction **268 PC** *Felony*	1. By promising marriage; 2. Seduces and has sexual relation with; 3. An unmarried female; 4. Of previous chaste character.

CRIME - PENALTY	ELEMENTS
Schools (Loitering about adult schools) **647b PC** *Misdemeanor*	1. Loitering; 2. About any school in which adults attend; 3. And who annoys or molests any person in attendance.
Shooting From Highway **374c PC** *Misdemeanor*	1. Shooting any firearm; 2. From or upon a public road or highway.
Shooting at Dwelling **246 PC** *Felony (Wobbler)*	1. Maliciously and willfully discharges a firearm; 2. At an inhabited dwelling or occupied building, motor vehicle, camper. (***Note:*** "Inhabited" means currently used for dwelling, whether occupied or not.)
Sodomy **286 PC** *Felony*	1. Contact between the penis of one and anus of another under 18, or; 2. By one over 21 with another under 16, or; 3. With one who is under 14 and more than 10 years younger, or; 4. When accomplished by force, violence, fear, and against will of the other, or; 5. When acting with another is accomplished against victim's will by force or fear of immediate bodily injury on victim or another, or; 6. By anyone in jail or prison, or; 7. When victim is unconscious of the act, and; 8. This is known to assailant, or; 9. Victim is incapable of giving consent due to temporary or permanent unsoundness of mind; 10. And this fact is known to assailant.
Theft—False Pretenses **532 PC** *Felony—Misdemeanor* *(Depending on value, as in theft)*	1. Knowingly and by false pretense or fraud; 2. Defrauds another of money, labor, property; 3. Or falsely obtains credit, thereby; 4. Fraudulently obtains money, labor, property of another.
Theft—Gas, Water, Electricity **498 PC** *Misdemeanor*	1. Willfully, with intent to defraud; 2. Connects any pipe (or wire); 3. With any service pipe (or wire); 4. For the purpose of taking (gas) (water) (electricity); 5. Without payment.
Theft—Phone Calls **502.7 PC** *Misdemeanor*	1. Knowingly, willfully, and with intent to defraud; 2. Avoids or aids or attempts or assists another; 3. Or who uses a code, prearranged scheme; 4. To avoid any lawful charges for service.
Ticket "Scalping" **346 PC** *Misdemeanor*	1. Without written permission of owner/operator; 2. Sells tickets to any event; 3. Which were obtained for resale; 4. At any price in excess of that on ticket; 5. While on grounds or place where event is held.
Train Wrecking **219 PC** *Felony*	1. Unlawfully throws a switch, removes a rail, places explosive or obstruction on or near the track of any railroad; 2. With intention to wreck train; 3. And wrecks, derails, or blows up train. (When any person suffers death) Penalty: Death

CRIME - PENALTY	ELEMENTS
Train Wrecking (Intention of wrecking train; Attempt) **218 PC** *Felony*	1. Unlawfully throws a switch, removes a rail, places explosives or obstruction on or near; 2. The track of any railroad; 3. Or sets fire to any structure or track over which a train must pass; 4. With intention to wreck train.
Unlawful Assembly **407 - 408 PC** *Misdemeanor*	1. Two or more persons assembled; 2. With intent to do unlawful act or lawful act in a violent boisterous or tumultuous manner.
Unlawfully Causing Fire **452 PC** *Felony (Wobbler)*	1. Recklessly sets fire to any structure or forest land; 2. Unlawfully causing great bodily injury or property damage; 3. Unlawfully causing inhabited structures or property to burn; 4. Unlawfully causing a fire of a structure or forest land; 5. Other than his own, unless there is injury to others.
Unlawful Sexual Intercourse **261.5 PC** *Felony (Wobbler)*	1. Act of sexual intercourse; 2. Female not wife of perpetrator; 3. Female under 18.
Unlawful Taking ("Joy-riding") **499b PC** *Misdemeanor*	1. Without permission of owner; 2. Takes any bicycle, motorcycle, vessel, or boat; 3. For purpose of temporary use.

APPENDIX B

PENAL CODE INDEX

(In Alphabetical Order by Offense or Subject)

APPENDIX C

PENAL CODE—KEY SECTIONS

(With Test)

The following are important or frequently used sections of the Penal Code. Students should know the following and be prepared for a test as directed by the instructor.

SECTION	OFFENSE
148	Resisting arrest
148.5	False crime report
182	Conspiracy
187	Murder
192	Manslaughter
203	Mayhem
207	Kidnapping
211	Robbery
217.1	Assault on judge
220	Assault to rape
240	Simple assault
242	Battery
245	ADW
261	Rape
272	Contributing
273a	Cruelty to child
273d	Child beating
273.5	Spouse/Cohabitant injury
278	Child stealing
286	Sodomy
288	Crimes against children
288a	Oral Copulation
290	Sex crime registration
311	Obscene matter
314	Indecent exposure
374c	Shooting from highway

SECTION	OFFENSE
404	Riot
407	Unlawful assembly
415	Disturbing peace
417	Brandishing firearm
451	Arson of dwelling
459	Burglary
466	Burglary tools
470	Forgery
484	Theft
485	Theft lost property
496	Receiving stolen property
503	Embezzlement
518	Extortion
532	False pretense fraud
537	Defrauding motel
556	Unlawful sign posting
594	Malicious mischief
597	Cruelty to animals
602	Trespass
603	Unlawful forcible entry
647	Disorderly conduct
647.6	Molesting child (under 18)
647(b)	Prostitution
647(g)	Prowler
647(h)	Window peeking

PENAL CODE—KEY SECTIONS QUIZ 1 (MATCHING TEST)

Match each definition with its code section by placing the number preceding the code section in the parentheses on each of the following.

1. 374c	[ ] Resisting arrest
2. 290	[ ] False crime report
3. 288	[ ] Conspiracy
4. 274	[ ] Murder
5. 245	[ ] Manslaughter
6. 240	[ ] Mayhem
7. 217.1	[ ] Kidnapping
8. 207	[ ] Robbery
9. 192	[ ] Assault on judge
10. 182	[ ] Shooting from highway
11. 148	[ ] Sex crime registration
12. 148.5	[ ] Simple assault
13. 187	[ ] ADW
14. 203	[ ] Child molesting (under 14)
15. 211	[ ] Contributing to minorís delinquency
16. 278	[ ] Child stealing
17. 242	
18. 272	

PENAL CODE—KEY SECTIONS QUIZ 2 (MATCHING TEST)

Match each definition with its code section by placing the number preceding the code section in the parentheses on each of the following.

1. 314	[ ] Felony child beating
2. 288a	[ ] Possession burglary tools
3. 286	[ ] Burglary
4. 273a-d	[ ] Rape
5. 261	[ ] Arson of structure
6. 242	[ ] Indecent exposure
7. 220	[ ] Brandishing firearm
8. 404	[ ] Battery
9. 407	[ ] Sodomy
10. 415	[ ] Riot
11. 417	[ ] Assault to rape
12. 451	[ ] Oral copulation
13. 459	[ ] Disturbing peace
14. 466	[ ] Unlawful assembly
15. 470	[ ] Obscene matter
16. 311	[ ] Prostitution
17. 647	
18. 647(b)	

PENAL CODE—KEY SECTIONS QUIZ 3 (MATCHING TEST)

Match each definition with its code section by placing the number preceding the code section in the parentheses on each of the following.

1. 647.6	[ ] Disorderly conduct (a-h)
2. 647(g)	[ ] Extortion
3. 647	[ ] Receiving stolen property
4. 603	[ ] Prowler
5. 602	[ ] Fraud
6. 597	[ ] Defrauding innkeeper
7. 594	[ ] Molesting children (under 18)
8. 556	[ ] Theft of lost property
9. 537	[ ] Trespass
10. 540	[ ] Forcible entry (residence)
11. 470	[ ] Theft
12. 494	[ ] Unlawful sign posting
13. 496	[ ] Embezzlement
14. 485	[ ] Cruelty to animals
15. 484	[ ] Malicious mischief
16. 532	[ ] Forgery
17. 518	
18. 503	

PENAL CODE EXAMINATION

Choose the one best answer in each of the following multiple choice questions.

1. Resisting arrest
   a. 148 d. 240
   b. 148.5 e. 242
   c. 217

2. Murder
   a. 182 d. 203
   b. 197 e. 207
   c. 192

3. Kidnapping
   a. 88 d. 203
   b. 273 e. 207
   c. 278

4. Robbery
   a. 209 d. 411
   b. 207 e. 484
   c. 211

5. Assault with intent to murder
   a. 182 d. 217
   b. 187 e. 245
   c. 192

6. Assault with intent to rape
   a. 187 d. 245
   b. 220 e. 278
   c. 242

7. Simple assault
   a. 217 d. 242
   b. 220 e. 245
   c. 240

8. Battery
   a. 217 d. 242
   b. 220 e. 245
   c. 240

9. Assault with deadly weapon (ADW)
   a. 187 d. 240
   b. 217 e. 245
   c. 220

10. Rape
   a. 217 d. 278
   b. 220 e. 287
   c. 261

11. Contributing to delinquency of a minor
   a. 272 d. 314
   b. 273d e. 288
   c. 647

12. Felony child beating
   a. 240d d. 273d
   b. 242 e. 278
   c. 245

13. Child stealing
   a. 207 d. 278
   b. 217 e. 647.6
   c. 273d

14. Molesting child under 14 years
   a. 278 d. 288a
   b. 286 e. 311
   c. 288

15. Indecent exposure
   a. 314 d. 272
   b. 311 e. 261
   c. 288a

16. Shooting from a highway
   a. 602 d. 347
   b. 603 e. 374c
   c. 647(c)

17. Disturbing the peace
   a. 404 d. 417
   b. 407 e. 447a
   c. 415

18. Brandishing firearm in threatening manner
   a. 415 d. 470
   b. 417 e. 217
   c. 447

19. Burglary
   a. 484 d. 470
   b. 459 e. 603
   c. 466

20. Possession of burglary tools
   a. 484 d. 470
   b. 459 e. 503
   c. 466

21. Theft defined
   a. 484 d. 594
   b. 485 e. 603
   c. 496

22. Malicious mischief
   a. 404 d. 647a
   b. 415 e. 594
   c. 647

23. Trespass
   a. 556 d. 602
   b. 597 e. 603
   c. 601

24. Disorderly conduct
   a. 148 d. 642(a-h)
   b. 242 e. 647
   c. 415

25. Prowler
   a. 642 g d. 647(g)
   b. 647(a) e. 647(h)
   c. 647(b)

APPENDIX D

BASIC LEGAL RESEARCH—CASE LAW AND HOW TO FIND IT

Introduction. The purpose of this section is to explain the techniques of doing basic legal research. In other words, how to find case law. This ability is important for at least three key reasons:

1. Courts, by their decisions in criminal cases, frequently define the meanings of words, phrases, and terms found in the Penal Code and other codes describing criminal offenses.
2. The courts interpret the intent of the legislature relative to criminal law; i.e., a court decision will frequently explain and define the specific act that the legislature intended to make a crime.
3. The courts also rule on the constitutionality of particular penal statutes; i.e., whether or not all or any part of a specific Penal Code section is in conflict with the Constitution (U.S. or state).

One must frequently find and read case law (court decisions) in order to fully understand the meaning and scope of a Penal Code section. One also needs to have some knowledge of case law to determine whether or not a specific act is, in fact, a violation of a certain Penal Code section. For example, *PC 459*, which defines burglary, reads in part: "Any person who enters . . . any building . . . with intent to commit grand or petit larceny or any felony is guilty of burglary." Let us now assume that someone is caught stealing money from the coin slot in a phone booth. The question may be: did the suspect commit burglary if he or she entered the phone booth with intent to commit theft? In other words, is the phone booth a "building" within the meaning of *PC 459*?

Case Use: An Example. The only way to answer the above question is to research case law pertaining to burglary. We find our answer in *People v. Nunez (1970) 86 Cal Rptr. 707, 7 C.A. 3d 655*. In this case, the court held that a telephone booth with three walls, a door, roof, and floor was a "building" within the meaning of *PC 459*. We now have our answer. A phone booth may indeed be burglarized, and one who enters same with intent to steal (even if there is no forced entry) can be found guilty of burglary.

The Law Library. When a student is given his or her first assignment to research a case, he or she generally does so with some apprehension. Students may imagine a law library as a confusing collection of large and difficult to understand volumes. Fortunately, this is a gross misconception. Law libraries are well designed, easily understood, and surprisingly simple to use. And the computerization of most resources has drastically reduced research time. Such services as LEXIS and WESTLAW can quickly locate the law, and the availability of most published reports on CD-Rom has brought the entire law library to the desktop PC.

THE CALIFORNIA COURT SYSTEM

For case law to have any great effect in modifying criminal statutes (written laws), it must come from either a California court, a federal appellate court, or a Supreme Court. A brief look at the structure and jurisdiction of California and federal courts will give a better understanding of how cases are reported.

Superior Courts. Each of the 58 counties in California has one superior court, some with many divisions. The superior court has original jurisdiction in all criminal offenses, including juvenile offenses.

District Courts of Appeal. In California, there are six district courts of appeal. With the exception of the fifth district court, each has two or more divisions. Each division has at least three judges. The agreement of two is needed for a judgment. These courts are not trial courts; rather, they hear appeals from decisions arrived at in superior courts of original jurisdiction.

California Supreme Court. The California Supreme Court is empowered to hear appeals from all California inferior courts. The Supreme Court meets in San Francisco and consists of a chief justice and six associate justices who may sit in two departments or as a single group (called "sitting in bank"). The chief justice presides when the court sits in bank or may sit with either department during its deliberations.

THE FEDERAL COURT SYSTEM

Federal District Courts. In criminal cases, the federal district courts are principal trial courts for the federal judicial system. A person accused of a federal crime would have his or her case adjudicated in a federal district court. Federal district courts are *not* appellate courts.

Federal Courts of Appeal (Circuit Courts). The federal circuit courts are the federal courts of appeal. When a criminal case originates as an action in a federal district court, the circuit court would ordinarily be the final court of appeal to review the district court decision.

United States Supreme Court. The Supreme Court's judicial power extends to all cases arising under the United States Constitution, laws, and treaties. The Court's appellate jurisdiction is subject to regulations of Congress. The rules governing review of state court decisions distinguish between those cases in which the court *must* review the state court decision (mandatory review on appeal) and those in which the court *may* review the state court decision (discretionary review upon application for a writ of *certiorari*).

Review by the Supreme Court in criminal cases occurs only after a final decision in the highest court of a state. Review by appeal is mandatory where the state court decided against the validity of a treaty or statute of the United States. Mandatory appeal also applies where a state court rules in favor of a state law being challenged as in conflict with the Constitution, treaties, or laws of the United States. Some criminal cases that go from state courts to the United States Supreme Court may be based upon the right to appeal, where a direct conflict exists between a state law and a federal law. But a large number of criminal cases come to the Supreme Court through the Court's discretionary power to grant *certiorari* (a writ from a superior court to an inferior court directing it to send up for review a certified record of its proceedings in a designated case).

An example of this latter discretionary power is found in the case of *Gideon v. Wainwright*. This was a case where the defendant, Gideon, through a writ of *certiorari*, appealed to the United States Supreme Court for a review of his conviction. Gideon claimed the state of Florida had denied him his constitutional right to an attorney as provided under the Sixth Amendment of the U.S. Constitution, and as required of all states through the due process clause of the Fourteenth Amendment. A denial of due process is frequently defined as the failure to observe that fundamental fairness essential to the very concept of justice.

Armed with this brief summary of the California and federal court structure, the student now has an adequate foundation for gaining more insight into case law, its purpose, intent, and effect on statute law.

FEDERAL CASE LAW: DECISIONS OF THE FEDERAL COURTS

The United States Supreme Court. The official reports of the decisions of the U.S. Supreme Court are published in the *United States Reports*. They are also published in the *Supreme Court Reporter* and the *Lawyers Edition, Supreme Court Reports*. The latter contains selected cases that are fully reported and include briefs (written arguments and points of law) filed by opposing counsel.

Since U.S. Supreme Court cases are published in three separate sources, a complete citation of a U.S. Supreme Court case would include citing all three reporters (source books). Thus if we were citing the Gideon case, referred to earlier, we would find it listed in each reporter as follows:

1. *United States Reports: Gideon* [appellant] *v. Wainwright*, [respondent] *372* [volume number]. U.S. [United States Reports] *335* [page number].
2. *Supreme Court Reporter: Gideon v. Wainwright, 83* [volume number] *S. Ct.* [Supreme Court Reporter] *792* [page number].
3. *Lawyer's Edition of Supreme Court Reports: Gideon v. Wainwright, 9 L. Ed.* [Lawyer's Edition, Supreme Court Reports] *2d* [second series] *799* [page number] *1963* [date].

Discussion. A court decision, as you will note above, is cited by giving: (1) the names of the parties involved, (2) the volume number, (3) the name of the reporting publisher (book) in which the case is reported, (4) the page on which the case begins, and (5) the date of the decision, where appropriate. Thus in the preceding example. *Gideon* is the last name of the appellant (person appealing a decision of a lower court) and *Wainwright*, is the last name of the respondent (person or agency who is required to respond to the issue being appealed).

The Federal Courts of Appeal (Circuit Courts). Decisions of the U.S. courts of appeal are published in the *Federal Reporter.* A typical citation (case reference) includes (1) the name of the case, (2) volume and page number where the case can be found, (3) identification of the circuit in which the case was decided, and (4) the year the decision was made.

Example. *Smayda* [appellant] v. *United States* [respondent] *50F. 2d* [Federal Reporter, second series] 251 [page number] *(9th Cir. 1966)* [name of the court and the date]. When seen as a citation, it would look like this: *Smayda v. United States, 50F. 2d 251 (9th Cir. 1966).*

The Federal District Courts. Even though federal district courts are trial courts and do not hear appeals, many of their decisions are reported in the *Federal Supplement*. They are cited as in the example below.

Example. *Books Inc. v. Leary, 291 F. Supp.* [Federal Supplement] *622 (S.D.N.Y.)* [Southern District of New York] *1968.* When seen as a citation the last example would look like this: *Books Inc. v. Leary, 291 F. Supp. 622 (S.D.N.Y.) 1968.*

Combination Federal and State Reporters. Both federal and state decisions appear in sets of two specialized reporters. They are (1) The *American Law Reports* and (2) the *American Law Reports, 2d. American Law Reports* are annotated and contain the full text of selected decisions under which cases on the same point of law are noted.

American Law Reports, 2d, contain a detailed discussion on a practical point of current law, followed by a report of a representative case from a state or federal court involving the problem annotated (noted). When a case has been annotated in the *American Law Reports,* this information is given as follows: *Mosco v. United States 89 A.L.R. 2d 715.*

This then concludes the essential information needed for researching cases in the *federal* court system. Let us now turn our attention to how cases are reported in the California state court system.

CALIFORNIA CASE LAW: DECISIONS OF APPELLATE COURTS

California Appellate and Supreme Court cases are reported by two different publishers: Bancroft-Whitney and West Publishing Company. Bancroft-Whitney publishes two sets of volumes. One is called *California Reports.* (Series 1, 2, 3 and 4), which carry only California *Supreme Court* cases. The other is *California Appellate Reports* (Series 1, 2, 3 and 4), which carry only California *appellate court* cases, as the title implies. Citations of cases reported in each of the above series of volumes are written almost the same way federal cases are cited.

California Supreme Court Decisions: First let us examine a citation on a case reported in Bancroft-Whitney's *California Reports*. *People* [appellant] *v. Mason*, [respondent] *5 [volume number] C.* [California Reports] *3d* [third series] *759* [page number]. Without the words of explanation that appear in brackets in the example above, the citation would look like this: *People v. Mason, 5 C 3d 759.* Noting that this case was reported in the third (3d) series, indicates that it is relatively recent. Older and very old cases are reported in the first or second series. The *Mason* case was one appealed by the People to the California State Supreme Court following a motion to suppress evidence granted by a San Diego Superior Court under *P.C. 1538.1.* The case was dismissed against the defendant and the People (San Diego County District Attorney's office) are appealing to get the superior court's ruling reversed by the Supreme Court.

District Court of Appeal. Had this case been heard by a California district court of appeal, the decision of that appeal would have been recorded in the *California Appellate Reports* and cited as follows: *People* [plaintiff] *v. Nugent*, [defendant] *18* [volume number] *C.A. 3d* [California Appellate Reports, third series] *911* [page number]. Again, without the words of explanation in the brackets, the actual citation would read: *People v. Nugent, 18 C.A. 3d 911.*

Combined California State Supreme and Appellate Court Reports. As mentioned previously, West Publishing Company also reports the decisions of both the state supreme court and the California district courts of appeal. West's publication is the *West California Reporter,* which carries both California Supreme Court and appellate court cases in the same series of volumes. A typical *West California Reporter* citation would be: *Mozzetti v. Superior Court, 94 Cal. Rptr.* [California Reporter] *412.*

Because of this dual reporting system, both publishers also cross-cite their cases to give the reader the citation for the same case reported in the other publisher's reports. Thus, a typical case would be cited by West as: *People v. Wilson, 94 Cal. Rptr.* [West California Reporter] *923* and cross-cited in West to Bancroft-Whitney as: *17 Cal. App.* [California Appellate Reports] *3d 598.* A case found in Bancroft-Whitney's *California Appellate Reports* third series, would be cited as: *People v. Clay, 18 C.A. 3d 964,* and would be cross-cited to *West California Reporter* as: *Cal. Rptr. 213.* It is most important to note, in order to avoid confusion, that when a case is cross-cited by *West California Reporter* to Bancroft-Whitney's *California Appellate Reports.* West uses the abbreviation, *Cal. App.* Both C.A. (used by Bancroft-Whitney) and Cal. App. mean the same thing and refer to the same source, which is Bancroft-Whitney's *California Appellate Reports.*

Additionally, both publishers publish advance sheets in paperback form until a sufficient number of cases are adjudicated and collected to publish a hardbound volume to add to the series. It is strongly suggested that students go to their college library or the local county law library and practice finding cases until this rather simple procedure becomes routine.

Case Law Reference Source Review. The following will provide the student with a ready reference to those publications that report federal and state cases. The names of the reference books, along with their standard reference abbreviation is given for each of the courts previously discussed.

Supreme Court Reports

1. *United States Reports*, abbreviated: U.S.
2. *Supreme Court Reporter*, abbreviated: S. Ct.
3. Lawyer's Edition, Supreme Court Reports, abbreviated: L. Ed.

Federal Appeals Courts

Federal Reporter abbreviated: F. , F2d or F3d

Federal District Courts (not appeals courts)

Federal Supplement, abbreviated: F. Supp.

Combination Federal—State Reporter

1. *American Law Reports*, abbreviated: A.L.R.
2. *American Law Reports*, (second series), abbreviated: A.L.R. 2d

California Supreme Court Reporters

1. *California Reports*, abbreviated: C.
2. *West California Reporter*, abbreviated: Cal. Rptr.

California District Court of Appeals

1. *California Appellate Reports*, abbreviated: C.A. or Cal. App.
2. *West California Reporter*, abbreviated: Cal. Rptr.

SOURCES OF CASE LAW CITATIONS

A most appropriate question at this point might be: where does one find sources for case citations? The answer: in annotated penal codes, legal encyclopedias, legal digests, and in *Shepard's Citator*. All are in either the college library or the local county law library, and most are also available on CD-Rom or other computer resources. Each of these will be discussed briefly, below.

Annotated Codes. An annotated California Penal Code consists generally of several volumes, published either by West Publishing Company as *West's California Codes, Annotated*, or Bancroft-Whitney Company as *Deering's California Codes, Annotated.*

These annotated codes are structured similarly to an unannotated penal code except following each statute you will find excerpts from case decisions that interpret, explain, and clarify the penal statute in terms of its separate components or elements. As an example, take *P.C. 220, Assault with Intent to Commit Mayhem:* "Every person who assaults another with intent to commit mayhem, is punishable by imprisonment for two, four, or six years."

This statute states what the law is categorically. However, to find out whether a specific act meets the requirements of this law, we need to know how courts in the past have interpreted this statute. The annotations will give some help in this regard. Following the statute will be several excerpts from previously decided cases (*stare decisis*) arranged conceptually, e.g., (1) in general, (2) intent, (3) evidence, (4) instructions, (5) methods or means, and (6) defenses. Each contains excerpts from selected cases bearing on that particular element or aspect of the offense, with the appropriate citation to refer the reader to the case in the respective reporter. Thus, under methods or means, one will find: "An assault to commit mayhem is a crime irrespective of the mode or means by which the assault is committed. *People v. Owens (1906) 3 CA 750, 86.*"

Legal Encyclopedias. There are several works recognized as standards in the field of criminal law, two of the best being *Perkins on Criminal Law,* Foundation Press, second edition, and *California Crimes,* Bender-Moss Company, B.E. Witkin, two volumes plus supplement. Both offer quite detailed and thorough information on common crimes and both profusely cite cases for amplification of points made.

A student who wants more information concerning a specific crime should go to the library, find the crime in the table of contents and read the material. Should the student then need to brief a case, he or she can use any of the cases cited by the author on that point of law or criminal statute.

Legal Digests. Every law library subscribes to numerous legal digests, which are structured according to subject matter and deal extensively with legal concepts such as diminished capacity, former jeopardy, defenses, and so on, and stress new or changing philosophies, procedures, and interpretations of the law. They also list numerous case citations on which the student can follow up.

Shepard's California Citations, Statute Edition. This citator is invaluable to the law student. In this volume the student will find all of the codes for the state of California, including the Penal Code. The student who is interested in finding case citations as assignments, can go to the citator, find the Penal Code section, and locate the section number he or she is interested in, and find scores of case citations regarding that particular penal statute. Additionally, by referring to the abbreviation key, the student can determine if any particular case had been criticized (c), overruled (o), or reversed (r) to determine if the case is still valid.

REPORTING IN "BRIEF" FORM

Now that you have learned how to find case law, we will proceed to the next logical step—how to read and report case law in a logical and meaningful manner.

Basically, an appealed lawsuit is initiated because one of the parties involved (the appellant) wishes to dispute or contest the adverse ruling of an inferior court. To justify the appeal, the appellant, through an attorney, takes issue either on, for example, a point of law, a constitutional infringement, insufficiency of evidence, or a procedural defect in the trial court proceedings.

We will now look at the standard form that most appeal cases take.

The first item after the citation in a case is a brief statement of the kind of controversy involved. That is, whether it was a criminal prosecution, a tort, or a civil recovery lawsuit. This is followed by a brief accounting of how the case got to this particular court. Such statements may say, for example, "This is an appeal by defendant from an adverse judgment," or "from an order of the lower court denying his motion for a new trial."

Next in order is a short statement of the facts that resulted in the case being brought to trial; who the parties are, what they did or did not do, what happened to them, who brought the action, and what outcome is wanted.

Next comes a statement of the question or questions the court is called upon to decide, i.e., the various issues (either of law or fact) that must be settled before a decision on the controversy can be reached. An issue can best be understood as a statement of some aspect of a general question of law, such as whether a particular act alleged constitutes the crime charged.

After the issues have been stated, the pro (for) and con (against) arguments by the appellant and respondent are given and discussed by the court. This is where logic comes into play. There are two main kinds of logical reasoning—inductive and deductive. Inductive reasoning involves the formulation of general propositions from a consideration of specific problems or observations. Conversely, deductive reasoning involves the application of a general proposition already formulated to some specific situation or problem so that a conclusion can be drawn from it.

Finally, after the argument on all the issues, the court states the general conclusion to be drawn therefrom; ending with a statement of the court's decision, such as "judgment affirmed"; "judgment reversed"; or "case remanded, new trial ordered."

Some Rules to Follow When Writing Briefs:

1. Read the case through at least once before beginning to brief it. Be certain that you have the facts, issues, conclusions, and findings in your mind before beginning to write.
2. Write the brief in your own words—don't just copy from the case. However, make sure your statements are accurate and pertinent.
3. Organize your brief. Put the essential matters in a logical order, but be as concise as possible. Do not equate a long, rambling brief with a good brief. Use this format:
   a. Facts: what happened to whom, and what was the result. This should be a short resume of the occurrences that precipitated a lawsuit. Generally, this can be adequately done in a paragraph or two.
   b. The facts are followed by a statement of the issues to be resolved by the court.
   c. Next is a restatement of the conclusion that the court has drawn from the facts and issues.
   d. Finally the finding or decision of the court is stated.

The following is an example of the format to follow:

CASE CITATION

People v. King Kong
1 C. 5th. 69.

Facts: Defendant was convicted of kidnapping [*P.C. 207*], and forcible rape [*P.C. 261(2)*], and is appealing his conviction. Defendant seized one Fay Wray, on the evening of July 4, 1936, from a restraining pedestal outside of the wall surrounding Megetum City, County of Ohwow. From there, he carried her to his cave on Lookout Mountain where he forcibly raped her. Later, she was able to escape and was found by her boyfriend, one Bruce Cabot, wandering aimlessly in the forest.

Issues:

1. The evidence at the trial proceedings was insufficient to prove that the taking was done without the consent of the victim and, therefore, was not kidnapping under *PC 207*.
2. Defendant's sentence of terms prescribed by law on both *PC 207* and *PC 261(2)*, to run concurrently, violates *PC 654* prohibiting double punishment in that kidnapping and subsequent rape were one continuous act—the kidnapping merely being necessary to the act of rape.

Conclusions: As to appellant's claim of insufficient evidence to convict under PC 207, we find the record does support the jury's finding of guilty insofar as there was evidence sufficient to show a taking, without consent of the victim, by considerable force (considering the relative size and strength of the appellant Kong).

As to appellant's claim under *PC 654,* we find that the evidence amply supports his contention that the kidnapping was incidental to his intent to rape and should apply. (Cases cited).

Findings:

1. Judgment affirmed as to conviction of PC 261(2).
2. Judgment reversed as to concurrent sentencing under PC 207.

Shepards: Not cited.

This admittedly facetious example contains the four areas needed in an adequate brief and hopefully deals with each. Thus, a brief should consist of:

1. **Name** and citation of case,
2. **Facts** or summary of occurrence,
3. **Issues** to be resolved,
4. **Conclusions** drawn from those issues,
5. **Findings** of the court relative to the issues and the court's **conclusions.**

This brief narrative, the author hopes, will provide the student with the understanding and skill necessary to meaningfully research case law.

APPENDIX E

INDEX OF CODE SECTIONS

Included in *California Criminal Law Concepts* (In Numerical Order)

PENAL CODE NO.	SUBJECT	TEXT SECTION	PAGE NO.
148.9	Giving False Identification	7.12	101
149	Excessive force by officer	7.11	100
150	Posse comitatus	7.16	109
152	Concealing accidental death	6.10	79
152.3	Mandatory reporting	13.4	202
153	Compounding crime	6.5	74
160	Soliciting inmate bail business	18.17	272
171c	Firearms in State capital	9.8	144
171.5	Prohibited weapons at airports	9.8	144
182	Conspiracy	6.11	79
184	Overt act in conspiracy	6.12	80
186.26	Soliciting gang members	6.4	73
186.33	Gang liability	5.4	63
187	Murder, statute of limitations	1.7	8
187	Murder, defined	11.2	164
188	Malice defined	11.2	164
189	Degrees of murder	11.3	165
190	Murder, penalty	11.4	167
190	Murder, 1st degree	11.4	167
190.5	No death penalty under age 18	11.4	169
192	Manslaughter, statute of limitation	1.7	8
192	Manslaughter defined	11.6	170
193	Manslaughter, penalty	11.9	173
194	Time of death after injury	11.1	163
195	Excusable homicide	11.10	173
196	Justifiable homicide, police	11.11	174
197	Justifiable homicide, others	11.12	175
203	Mayhem	10.11	157
207	Kidnapping defined	12.3	183
209(a)	Kidnapping for ransom	12.4	184
209(b)	Kidnapping for robbery	12.4	184
210	Posing as kidnapper for ransom	12.5	185
211	Robbery defined	15.1	225
212.5	Degrees of robbery	15.2	227
213	Robbery, penalty	15.5	228
218	Train wrecking	10.10	157
219.1	Throwing object at common carriers	10.7	155
219.2	Shooting at common carrier	10.7	155
222	Administering stupefying drugs	10.9	156
220	Assault to commit certain felonies	10.8	156
236	False imprisonment	12.1	181
240	Assault defined	10.1	149
241	Assault, penalty	10.1	149
242	Battery defined	10.2	151
243(c)	Battery, police, firefighter	10.2	152
243(f)(5)	Injury in battery defined	10.2	152
244	Assault with caustic chemicals	10.5	155
245	Assault with deadly weapon (ADW)	10.4	154
245.6	Hazing	10.4	155

PENAL CODE NO.	SUBJECT	TEXT SECTION	PAGE NO.
347	Poisoning food, medicine, water	10.6	155
347b	Poisoning alcoholic beverages	10.6	155
370	Public Urination	13.1	199
402b	Abandoned appliances	18.9	269
403	Disturbing public meetings	8.7	122
404	Riot defined	8.4	121
404.6	Inciting riot	8.5	122
405a	Lynching	8.6	122
406	Rout defined	8.4	121
407	Unlawful assembly	8.2	119
409	Refusal to disperse	8.3	120
415	Disturbing the peace	8.1	117
415.5	Disturbing peace, schools	8.1	117
415.5	School disturbance	8.10	126
416	Assembly to disturb peace	8.3	120
417	Exhibiting firearm	10.3	153
417.4	Imitation firearms	10.3	153
417.25	Laser pointers	10.3	154
418	Forcible entry, detainer	8.9	125
422.6	Hate crime	8.7	123
450	Arson, subject of	18.5	267
451	Arson, penalty	18.5	268
452	Unlawfully causing fire	18.6	268
453	Possession of flammables	18.7	269
455	Attempt to burn	18.5	268
459	Burglary defined	14.1	213
460	Degrees of Burglary	14.5	217
461	Burglary, penalty	14.6	217
464	Burglary with explosives	14.7	218
466	Possession, burglary tools	14.8	218
466.5	Illegal car master key	14.8	218
466.7	Illegal possession, car key	14.8	219
467	Possession of deadly weapon	10.3	154
470	Forgery defined	18.1	265
473	Forgery, penalty	18.4	267
474	False phone messages	18.17	271
475a	Possession fraudulent check	18.3	266
476	Fictitious check defined	18.3	266
476a	Check, insufficient funds	18.3	266
484	Theft defined	16.1	235
484	Theft, false pretenses	16.6	238
484	Theft, trick or device	16.7	239
488	Petty theft defined	16.11	244
484(b)	Theft, labor or materials	16.1	236
484e	Theft of access card	16.9	241
484f	Forgery, access card	16.9	241
484f	Altered access card	18.3	266
484i	Access card forgery	16.9	242
485	Theft, lost property	16.10	242

PENAL CODE NO.	SUBJECT	TEXT SECTION	PAGE NO.
603	Unlawful forced entry	14.9	219
605	Landmarks, signs, destroying	18.12	269
622	Monuments, artworks, destroying	18.13	270
625b	Tampering with aircraft	18.14	270
626.2	School, unlawfully remaining at	8.10	126
626.7	Unauthorized reentry on school grounds	8.10	126
629.7	Obtaining false DMV documents	6.10	79
631	Wiretapping	18.16	270
632	Eavesdropping	18.16	270
632.5	Intercepting cell phone	18.16	270
633	Law enforcement recording	18.16	270
633.5	Evidentiary recording	18.16	271
636.5	Intercepting safety communication	18.16	270
637.7	Electronic tracking	18.16	270
646.9	Stalking or threatening violence	12.2	183
647	Disorderly conduct	8.11	128
647.6	Child molesting	13.8	206
647c	Obstructing sidewalk	8.8	125
647(a)	Lewd conduct	8.11	128
647(b)	Soliciting prostitution	8.11	128
647(c)	Begging	8.11	128
647(d)	Loitering, public toilets	8.11	128
647(e)	Lodging without permission	8.11	128
647(f)	Drunk in public	8.11	128
647(h)	Prowling	8.11	128
647(i)	Window peeping	8.11	128
653f	Soliciting commission of crime	6.4	72
653b	Loitering near schools	13.9	206
653k	Switch-blade knife	9.1	137
653m	Obscene phone calls	8.1	118
653y	Misusing 911 telephone line	6.10	78
653aa	Internet piracy	16.16	248
653w	Possession or Sale of Pirated Recordings	16.16	248
660	Threatening letter	15.11	230
664	Attempt defined	6.1	71
666	Petty theft with prior	2.10	27
666	Prior convictions, theft	16.13	245
668	Foreign convictions	16.13	245
679.05	Domestic violence victim rights	10.14	158
680	Victims' DNA Rights	12.9	191
692	Lawful resistance to crime	10.2	153
701	Threatened crimes	7.17	110
789	Stolen property, other states	16.15	247
799	Statute of limitations, no limits	1.7	8
800(a)	Statute of limitations, 3 years	1.7	8
801	Statute of limitations, misdemeanors	1.7	7
802	Statute of limitations, out-of-state	1.7	8
802.5	Statute of limitations, general	1.7	7
803	Indictment "found" defined	1.7	7

PENAL CODE NO.	SUBJECT	TEXT SECTION	PAGE NO.
CODE NO.	**BUSINESS AND PROFESSION CODE**		
4149	Possession, needles and syringes	17.9	260
4145	Possession of hypodermic needles	17.9	189
4211	Dangerous drugs defined	17.2	255
CODE NO.	**FISH AND GAME CODE**		
2006	Loaded rifle in vehicle	9.8	143
CODE NO.	**GOVERNMENT CODE**		
6254.21	Posting officials' addresses on internet	7.12	101
8594	Amber alert activation	12.3	183
CODE NO.	**HARBORS AND NAVIGATION CODE**		
21	Vessel defined	14.4	216
CODE NO.	**HEALTH AND SAFETY CODE**		
7052	Penetration of a cadaver	12.7	
11014	Drug defined	17.2	255
11014.5	Drug paraphernalia defined	17.9	260
11018	Marijuana defined	17.2	255
11054	Schedule I, controlled substance	17.3	256
11055	Schedule II, controlled substance	17.3	256
11056	Schedule III, controlled substance	17.3	256
11057	Schedule IV, controlled substance	17.3	256
11058	Schedule V, controlled substance	17.3	256
11350	Controlled substance possession	17.4	256
11351	Controlled substance, possession for sale	17.7	258
11351	Drugs, possessing for sale	17.7	258
11352	Controlled substance, transportation	17.7	258
11352	Heroin, selling	17.7	258
11353	Minors, using in drug activity	17.7	259
11355	Fake drugs	17.8	259
11357	Marijuana, possession	17.4	257
11353.5	Drugs on school grounds	17.7	259
11358	Marijuana, planting, cultivation	17.4	257
11359	Marijuana, possession for sale	17.4	257
11362.5	Marijuana, medical use	17.4	257
11364	Paraphernalia, drug	17.9	260
11365	Presence where drugs used	17.10	260
11377	Drugs, possession of	17.5	257
11379	Drugs, manufacturing	17.7	259
11383.5	Unlawful Possession of Precursors	17.7	259
11550	Under influence of drugs defined	17.6	258
11590	Drug offender registration	17.11	260
120291	Exposing another to HIV	10.4	155

APPENDIX F

LIST OF LANDMARK COURT DECISIONS

(Indicating Key Holding)

1. *People v.* ***Aranda*** (1965) 63 Cal. 2d 518. The statement of one defendant cannot be admitted at a joint trial to implicate a codefendant.
2. ***Brady*** *v. Maryland* (1963) 373 US 83. The government must promptly disclose to the defense any exculpatory (tending to show innocence) evidence or witnesses.
3. *Illinois v.* ***Gates*** (1983) 462 US 416. Probable cause for a search or arrest requires only a "fair probability" of criminality.
4. *In re* ***Gault*** (1967) 387 US 1. Fundamental due process, including the right to counsel, applies to juvenile court proceedings.
5. ***Gideon*** *v. Wainwright* (1963) 372 US 335. The Sixth Amendment guarantee of the right to counsel applies to state prosecutions.
6. *In re* ***Gladys R.*** (1970) 1 Cal. 3d 855. A minor under the age of 14 must be shown beyond a reasonable doubt to have been aware of the wrongfulness of his or her act.
7. ***Katz*** *v. US* (1967) 389 US 347. Warrantless searches and seizures are presumed unreasonable, subject to specific exceptions.
8. *In re* ***Lance W.*** (1985) 37 Cal. 3d 873. Proposition 8 mandates application of federal exclusionary principles, abolishing "state grounds" expansions.
9. *US v.* ***Leon*** (1984) 468 US 897. Evidence seized under an invalid warrant need not be suppressed if executing officers reasonably relied on it in good faith.
10. ***Mapp*** *v. Ohio* (1961) 367 US 643. The Fourth Amendment exclusionary rule applies to state prosecutions.
11. ***Massiah*** *v. US* (1964) 377 US 201. Statements elicited from a represented suspect, after indictment or arraignment, and without counsel present, cannot be used to prove guilt in that case.
12. *People v.* ***May*** (1988) 44 Cal. 3d 309. Due to Proposition 8, California courts must apply federal rulings on Miranda and right to counsel issues.
13. *Riverside County v.* ***McLaughlin*** (1991) 114 L Ed 2d 49. Warrantless arrests must be judicially reviewed for probable cause within 48 hours, or the suspect must be released.
14. ***Mincey*** *v. Arizona* (1978) 437 US 385. There is no "homicide scene exception" to the search warrant requirement.
15. ***Miranda*** *v. Arizona* (1966) 384 US 436. Advising a suspect of his or her rights against self-incrimination neutralizes the compulsion presumed to result from custodial police interrogation.
16. ***Pitchess*** *v. Superior Court* (1974) 11 Cal. 3d 531. Information from an officer's personnel file may have to be disclosed to a defendant who claims the officer used excessive force.
17. *People v.* ***Ramey*** (1976) 16 Cal. 3d 263. Entry into the home to search or arrest is unreasonable unless supported by warrant, consent or exigent (urgent) circumstances.
18. ***Steagald*** *v. US* (1981) 451 US 204. Entry into a third party's residence to arrest another requires a search warrant for the third party's premises, in the absence of consent or exigency.
19. ***Terry*** *v. Ohio* (1968) 392 US 1. Police must have reasonable suspicion to justify a detention or a weapons frisk.
20. ***Wong Sun*** *v. US* (1963) 371 US 471. Evidence derived from unreasonable search or seizure may be suppressed as "fruit of the poisonous tree.

SUBJECT INDEX